W9-AFZ-643

Easy Grammar: Grade 4

Wanda C. Phillips

Easy Grammar Systems
P. O. Box 25970
Scottsdale, Arizona 85255

Printed in the United States
www.easygrammar.com

© 2006

<u>Easy Grammar: Grade 4</u> may be reproduced by the purchaser for student, noncommercial use only. Permission is not granted for district-wide, school-wide, or system-wide use. Reproduction for any commercial use is strictly forbidden. Copyrighted material. All rights reserved. No part of this book may be reproduced, stored in any retrieval system, or transmitted in any form or by any means electronic, mechanical, digital, recording, or otherwise.

DEDICATION

To the professors at George Fox University—
where faith and learning are integrated

TABLE OF CONTENTS

NOUNS   153

TYPES of SENTENCES   211

A student workbook entitled **Easy Grammar Grade 4 Student Workbook** is available. This workbook does not include an answer key or strategies for effective teaching. In addition, tests are not included.

Easy Grammar Grade 4 Student Test Booklet is now available; this contains a pre-assessment test, all unit tests and cumulative tests, and a post-assessment test.

Correlation pages for **Easy Grammar: Grade 4** and **Easy Grammar Grade 4 Student Workbook** have been placed throughout this textbook. Also, a correlation of teacher edition pages and workbook pages has been placed at the back of this text.

Dear Educator,

Thank you for considering this text. ***Easy Grammar: Grade 4*** will provide wonderful learning for your students. As the name implies, the process is easy. I have kept the vocabulary simple and, in most cases, the sentences rather short. My goal is for all students to **understand** and **enjoy** English.

I have put "my teaching experience" into this text. I have spent extra time providing you with additional strategies and tips that have helped my former students to learn. Although some may criticize my use of the first person perspective in the notes provided throughout this text, I feel that, in sharing my experience, you and your students will benefit.

Although capitalization, punctuation, and friendly letter units are located near the end of the book, you may teach them when you choose. However, allow me to share how I incorporate these units. Again, this isn't the "perfect" way; it simply worked for me during many years as an educator.

I recommend that you begin with students **memorizing** the list of prepositions and continue through the preposition unit and the pages of direct objects. Then, teach the capitalization unit. This unit is set up so that only a few rules are introduced at a time; capitalization, however, can be challenging. Teach it slowly and thoroughly. After completing the capitalization unit, I suggest that you return to the verb unit.

Before the noun unit, you may want to teach the punctuation unit. In teaching capitalization and punctuation at the beginning of the year, one can also use ***Daily Grams: Guided Review Aiding Mastery Skills – Grade 4***. Students review concepts on a daily basis. I have placed the first ten lessons of this review text on pages 562-573 of this text for you to try with your students. In using these, you can discern the value of ***Daily Grams***. You can go to www.easygrammar.com on the Internet for more sample pages.

Also, I suggest that you model friendly letters during the first week of school. Have students write a friendly letter at least every other week during the first semester and at least once a month throughout the second semester. Mastery comes with practice!

My major request is that you teach grammar concepts in order. This text is set up with **unit reviews**, **unit tests**, **cumulative reviews**, and **cumulative tests**. If grammar is taught sequentially, continuity occurs and mastery is enhanced.

Please relax. This text is very, very, very easy to teach. If I have done my job, students will be learning to use grammar as a tool for speaking and writing properly.

Sincerely,
Wanda C. Phillips

NOTE TO TEACHER: *This is a very important page; please read it carefully.*

The ***Note to Teacher*** pages are very important. Please read the entire note. I have provided you with suggestions and additional strategies that have helped students learn.

As in all good teaching, **glean** what you will and use what is appropriate for your students' needs and your style of teaching.

Please read the **answer key** page before assigning each worksheet. I have occasionally placed advice there.

I recommend that students use a **highlighter** to mark rules. Be sure to tell students exactly what you want them to highlight. Otherwise, they may mark too much. Also, be sure that students stay with you in the marking process. Some may tend to jump ahead in their delight with highlighting.

Easy Grammar Grade 4 Student Workbooks are available for student use. They include rules and worksheets contained within this text. They do not include strategies for effective teaching or answers.

Please be enthusiastic in your teaching of English. We want students to become interested and excited about learning their language!

Why should I use <u>Easy Grammar: Grade 4</u>?

Easy Grammar: Grade 4 uses a unique approach. Students memorize and learn prepositions first. Many "fun" pages that will help students to learn and to identify prepositions are included at the beginning of this book. Reading the remainder of this introduction will help you to understand how the approach works. You may encounter concepts on this page (and the next) that may make you doubtful about your own knowledge. Let me assure you that *Easy Grammar* is as the name implies---*EASY*!

1. In a step-by-step manner, students learn to identify prepositional phrases and to delete them from the sentence.

2. After a prepositional phrase is crossed out, the student no longer needs to be concerned with it. **The subject and verb won't be in a prepositional phrase.*** This makes it very easy to determine subject and verb of a sentence.

3. **Example:** In the following sentence, students who do not use this approach may respond that the subject is *beard, carriage,* or *driver.* For a verb, student response may include *smiling.*

   One man with a long gray beard spoke to a smiling carriage driver.

   The prepositional approach eliminates the guessing. Prepositional phrases are crossed out. Therefore, the subject and verb of a sentence are readily determined.

   One <u>man</u> ~~with a long gray beard~~ <u>spoke</u> ~~to a smiling carriage driver.~~

4. In using this process, students are actively engaged in learning. They love the "hands-on" process, and using it helps them to be successful.

*most of the time

i

5. This approach is used periodically throughout the text in order for students to understand other concepts such as direct objects, subject/verb agreement, etc.

❀ ❀ ❀

Another important difference of *Easy Grammar* texts is that concepts are **introduced and reviewed throughout the school year**. For example, you will be introduced to direct objects after a preposition unit. In the verb unit, you will use direct objects with the irregular verbs, sit/set, rise/raise, and lie/lay. You will encounter them again in the pronoun unit. In addition, **reviews and cumulative reviews** are provided along the way to help insure mastery learning.

❀ ❀ ❀

IMPORTANT QUESTIONS:

How may prepositions are introduced in *Easy Grammar: Grade 4*?

❀ *Easy Grammar: Grade 4* includes only **40** prepositions for students to learn. Games have been included, and concepts are presented in a way that fourth graders will easily understand.

Should I use *Daily Grams: Guided Review Aiding Mastery Skills – Grade 4* along with this text?

❀ Yes! In fact, you will find the first 10 pages of *Daily Grams: Grade 4* on pages 563-573 for you to introduce to your students. Copy each *Daily Grams* page (day) for your students to do at the beginning of each class. It should take only about 10 minutes for students to complete it *and* for you to discuss it with them. *Daily Grams: Grade 4* is especially effective for reinforcing capitulation and punctuation usage, grammar usage, sentence combining for improved writing skills, and various other concepts.

Does this text have a writing section?

❀ Yes! A section regarding writing sentences begins on page 522. Students will learn to write sentences containing items in a series and appositives.

TO THE TEACHER: Information Regarding Student Test Booklet

The student test booklet begins with a pre-assessment and ends with an identical post-assessment. The pre-assessment is found on pages 1 – 6; the post-assessment appears on pages 43 – 48.

The test booklet has been designed with teachers in mind. Tests are arranged so that students can remove each test without affecting other tests in the booklet. Obviously, the test booklet can be used in a multitude of ways. Use it in the manner that works best for you and your students.

Test Booklet Pages Correlated with Teacher Edition Answer Key Pages:

	BOOKLET PAGES	TEACHER ED. PAGES
Grade 4 **PRE-ASSESSMENT**	1-6	574-580
Preposition Test	7	58
Verb Test	9-10	138, 140
Cumulative Test (End of Verb Unit)	11-12	148, 150
Noun Test	13-14	188, 190
Cumulative Test (End of Noun Unit)	15-17	204, 206, 208
Adjective Test	19	248
Cumulative Test (End of Adjective Unit)	21-24	262, 264, 266, 268
Adverb Test	25	328
Cumulative Test (End of Adverb Unit)	27-30	346, 348, 350, 352
Pronoun Test	31	402
Cumulative Test (End of Pronoun Unit)	33-37	422, 424, 426, 428, 430
Capitalization Test	39	482
Punctuation Test	41	520
Grade 4 **Post-ASSESSMENT**	43-48	574-580

TO THE TEACHER: <u>**Assessment Information**</u>

EXTREMELY IMPORTANT

An assessment is provided on the next eight pages.
(Answers are on pages 574-578).

1. Please allow students to take this test before beginning any lessons. Although the assessment is eight pages in length, it should not take students long to complete. For the pretest, you may want to tell students to leave an answer blank if they don't know it. (This usually places students in a more relaxed mode.)

2. Score the test and review it for information regarding the level of each student's understanding.

(I recommend that you do not share the pretest results with students. If the score is low, a child may feel deflated before he begins this approach to grammar and usage. Students' scores on last year's standardized tests may be reviewed to determine areas of strengths and weaknesses, also.)

3. After scoring the test, please store it somewhere to be retrieved **after** the student takes it as a posttest. After you have scored the posttest, share both the pretest and posttest results with students so that they can see their increase in understanding. This is positive in that students can see the product of their work and can **internalize success**. (Consider *individual conferences* to discuss the pre and post tests' results.)

<u>**SCORING**</u>: I have provided one method of scoring in the answer key that follows this test. You will note that I place more points in usage than I do on such items as identification of nouns. You may disagree. Please feel free to determine which areas you consider most important and to create your own scoring rubric. However, be sure that you use the same method of scoring for **both** the pretest and the posttest. The assessment has been designed mainly as a tool to help students visualize their academic growth.

<u>*Note:*</u> Deletion of prepositional phrases has only been suggested (not graded) on the assessment. I suggest that you use this process all year so that it becomes an automatic tool.

Name_____   **Assessment**

Date_____   **Pre-Post**

A. Sentence Types:
   Directions: Write the sentence type on the line.

1. _____   Go slowly.

2. _____   Is that your cat?

3. _____   My balloon popped!

4. _____   She makes dolls.

B. Capitalization:
   Directions: Write a capital letter above any word that should be capitalized.

1. did governor ruiz read <u>indian in the cupboard</u> to your class at aztec school?

2. the visitor from spain spoke to the rotary club about the mexican war.

3. has mom bought berryland* iced tea and african daisies at caremart company

    on cole avenue in taneytown?

4. one student asked, "is the erie canal in new york?"

5. dear pam,

        my dad and i will attend prescott pioneers day in june.

                        your friend,

                        paco

C. Common and Proper Nouns:
   Directions: Place a ✓ if the noun is common.

1. ____   TURTLE   3. ____   BEAGLE   5. ____   SUPERMAN

2. ____   ATLANTA   4. ____   CANADA   6. ____   BRICKLAYER

D. Concrete and Abstract Nouns:
  Directions: Place a ☒ if the noun is abstract.

1. ____ fear   2. ____ faith   3. ____ fig   4. ____ forest

E. Singular and Plural Nouns:
  Directions: Write the correct spelling of each plural noun.

1. berry - _____   5. replay - _____

2. tax - _____   6. sofa - _____

3. mouse - _____   7. gas - _____

4. deer - _____   8. patch - _____

F. Possessive Nouns:
  Directions: Write the possessive.

1. room belonging to his sister - _____

2. an office used by more than one woman - _____

3. wading pool shared by two toddlers - _____

G. Identifying Nouns:
  Directions: Circle any nouns.

1. Three movies about birds of the desert were shown at our library yesterday.

H. Punctuation:
  Directions: Insert needed punctuation.

1. No we wont be moving to Purdy Washington

2. Kama asked Was Emma born on Thursday May 20 1982

3. They hope to sell forty two tickets for our teams carnival by 4 30 today

4. By the way wash your ears face and neck with this suds free soap

5. His new address is 22 Brook Avenue Nyles MI   49102

I. Subjects and Verbs:
   Directions: Underline the subject once and the verb or verb phrase twice.
   Note: Crossing out prepositional phrases will help you.

1.   A package from Emily arrived before dinner on Friday.

2.   A nurse and an aide helped the patient into bed.

3.   Four of the girls looked at the stars during the outdoor party.

4.   Come inside the house through the front door.

J. Contractions:
   Directions: Write the contraction.

1.   were not - _____   3. I have - _____   5. would not - _____

2.   they will - _____   4. will not - _____   6. what is - _____

K. You're/Your, It's/Its, and They're/Their/There:
   Directions: Circle the correct word.

1.   Take (there, their, they're) picture.

2.   I think that (you're, your) upset.

3.   Let me know when (it's, its) time to leave.

L. Subject-Verb Agreement:
   Directions: Underline the subject once. Underline the verb that agrees twice.

1.   Your idea (sound, sounds) interesting.

2.   The woman with the huge green glasses (take, takes) orders.

3.   His brother and she (hikes, hike) everywhere.

M. Irregular Verbs:
   Directions: Underline the subject once and the correct verb phrase twice.

1.   The dog was (lying, laying) on the porch.

2. Parker had (rode, ridden) her horse fast.

3. She has (ate, eaten) lunch.

4. I could have (run, ran) more than fifty yards.

5. We were (given, gave) large red markers.

6. My pencil is (broke, broken).

7. Have you (did, done) your homework?

8. We should have (set, sat) our lunches in the ice chest.

9. The bell may have already (rang, rung).

10. Kama's balloon had (busted, burst).

N. Tenses:
   Directions: Underline the subject once and the verb or verb phrase twice. Write the tense in the blank.

1. _____ The child colored a picture.

2. _____ You will turn left at the next street.

3. _____ Their dad is a beekeeper.

O. Usage and Knowledge:

1. Circle any infinitive that is a regular verb: to flash   to fly   to flip

2. Circle the interjection: **Wow! This soup is hot and spicy.**

3. Circle the possessive pronoun: **The girls are enjoying their new puppy.**

4. Write the antecedent of the possessive pronoun in sentence 3:   _____

5. Circle the conjunction: **Yikes! Mo or Bo has fallen in the stream.**

6. Circle the correct answer: We haven't received (no, any) money.

7. Circle the correct answer: My brother acts (strange, strangely) sometimes.

8.   Circle the correct answer: I didn't play very (good, well) in the first game.

9.   Circle the correct answer: Are you feeling (good, well)?

P.   Identifying Adjectives:
     Directions: Circle any adjective.

1. One elderly lady wore silver sandals with many stones and a low heel.

Q.   Degrees of Adjectives:
     Directions: Circle the correct answer.

1.   The fifth storm was (more violent, most violent).

2.   This is the (uglier, ugliest) mask of the two.

3.   You are (more creative, most creative) than I.

R.   Adverbs:
     Directions: Circle any adverbs.

1.   My friend talks too loudly sometimes.

2.   They never go anywhere early.

S.   Degrees of Adverbs:
     Directions: Circle the correct answer.

1.   Paco runs (faster, fastest) in his high school.

2.   Kit answers the phone (more politely , mostly politely) than his brother.

3.   When we travel, Aunt Jo stops (more often, most often) than Uncle Bo.

T.   Pronouns:
     Directions: Circle the correct answer.

1.   (Me and Lana, Lana and I, Lana and me) made a clay pot.

2.   Don't hit Jacob and (I, me)!

3. The scouts must take (his, their) canteens.

4. (They, Them) attend a rodeo every year.

5. Our grandparents and (we, us) are going to Idaho.

6. The baker fried the doughnuts (hisself, himself).

7. Matt left with Sarah and (she, her).

U. Nouns Used as Subjects, Direct Objects, and Objects of the Preposition:
   Directions: Look at the boldfaced word. Write **S.** for subject, **D.O.** for direct object, and **O.P.** for object of the preposition.

1. ____ During the **winter**, Tara skis.

2. ____ Give the **rattle** to the baby.

3. ____ After the parade, our **family** went to a café for lunch.

TO THE TEACHER:

The **list of prepositions** on page 1 must be **memorized** and **learned**. <u>This is an absolute requirement for student success</u>. (During a summer school session, I made a huge error in not requiring mastery; students did not do nearly as well!) Pages 2-11 contain fun activities for helping children to gain mastery of the list. You may also wish to divide the list into learning and writing the <u>a's</u>, then the <u>b's</u>, and so on. You may choose to divide the list of forty prepositions into sets of five or ten. Do whatever is comfortable for you as long as the end result is that students have mastered the list. Mastery of the list should precede page 12.

The **bingo game** is quite fun. Reproduce a blank game for each student. Instruct students to randomly fill in the card as has been done on page 6. Before the game, duplicate the list, cut out the words, and paste each word on a two inch square piece of paper. (Yes, you can simply write the prepositions on small squares.) Place these into a small box or envelope. At game time, pull out a square and read the preposition. I recommend that you say the preposition and then use it in a prepositional phrase. You may wish to use the prepositional phrase in a sentence. No, students haven't been introduced to prepositional phrases at this point, but it's a great way to make them aware of how prepositions are used in our language.

Examples: **after** ---------------- **after** the game
After the game, we went out for pizza.

🍓🍓🍓🍓🍓🍓🍓🍓🍓🍓🍓🍓🍓🍓🍓🍓🍓🍓🍓🍓

to ------------------- **to** me
Please give that **to** me.

Continue in this manner until someone has bingo. The question always arises if students should be given a reward for winning. I have found over the years that children are delighted with some token reward whether it be a small sticker, extra points, or food. (Use your discretion and do whatever is applicable to your teaching philosophy.)

The question arises if you have to teach this book in sequence. You may teach capitalization, punctuation, sentence types, and friendly letter when you choose. However, <u>grammar concepts should be taught</u> sequentially.

A definition of prepositions has been provided on the following page.
Because the definition can be confusing, you may choose to modify or skip it.

DEFINITION

A preposition is "a relation or function word...that connects a lexical word, usually a noun or pronoun, or a syntactic construction to another element of the sentence, as to a verb, to a noun, or to an adjective..."

-Webster's New World Dictionary

PREPOSITIONS

about	in
above	inside
across	into
after	near
against	of
along	off
around	on
at	out
before	outside
behind	over
below	past
beneath	through
beside	throughout
between	to
by	toward
down	under
during	until
except	up
for	with
from	without

Name_____

WORKBOOK PAGE 2

Date_____

A.   Directions: Write the preposition with the opposite meaning.

1. up - ___down_____

2. in - ___out_____

3. above - ___below or beneath___

4. over - ___under_____

5. inside - ___outside_____

6. with - ___without_____

7. before - ___after_____

8. on - ___off_____

9. to - ___from_____

B.   Directions: Unscramble the following prepositions.

1. nulit - ___until_____

2. otaub - ___about_____

3. enar - ___near_____

4. gloan - ___along_____

5. weeetbn - ___between_____

6. drungi - ___during_____

7. hendbi - ___behind_____

8. saitgan - ___against_____

9. rossac - ___across_____

2

Date_____

A. Directions: Write the preposition with the opposite meaning.

1. up - _____

2. in - _____

3. above - _____

4. over - _____

5. inside - _____

6. with - _____

7. before - _____

8. on - _____

9. to - _____

B. Directions: Unscramble the following prepositions.

1. nulit - _____

2. otaub - _____

3. enar - _____

4. gloan - _____

5. weeetbn - _____

6. drungi - _____

7. hendbi - _____

8. saitgan - _____

9. rossac - _____

A.   Directions: Write the prepositions that begin with **a**:

1. about   4. after   7. around

2. above   5. against   8. at

3. across   6. along

B.   Directions: Write the prepositions that begin with **b**:

1. before   4. beneath   7. by

2. behind   5. beside

3. below   6. between

C.   Directions: Write the prepositions that begin with **d**:

1. down   2. during

D.   Directions: Write the prepositions that begin with **o**:

1. of   3. on   5. outside

2. off   4. out   6. over

E.   Directions: Write the prepositions that begin with **t**:

1. through   3. to

2. throughout   4. toward

F.   Directions: Write the prepositions that begin with **u**:

1. under   2. until   3. up

4

Name_____   **PREPOSITIONS**

Date_____

A. Directions: Write the prepositions that begin with **a**:

1. _ b _ _ _ _   4. _ _ t _ _   7. _ r _ _ _ _ _

2. _ _ _ v _   5. _ g _ _ _ _ t   8. _ t

3. _ c _ _ s _   6. _ l _ _ _

B. Directions: Write the prepositions that begin with **b**:

1. _ _ f _ _ _   4. _ e _ e _ _ _   7. _ y

2. _ _ h _ _ _   5. _ _ s _ _ e

3. _ _ l _ _   6. _ _ t _ _ _ n

C. Directions: Write the prepositions that begin with **d**:

1. _ _ w _   2. _ _ _ _ _ g

D. Directions: Write the prepositions that begin with **o**:

1. _ f   3. _ n   5. _ _ _ s _ _ _

2. _ _ f   4. _ _ t   6. _ _ _ r

E. Directions: Write the prepositions that begin with **t**:

1. _ h _ _ _ _ h   3. _ _

2. _ _ r _ _ _ _ _ u _   4. _ _ _ _ r _

F. Directions: Write the prepositions that begin with **u**:

1. _ _ _ _ _ r   2. _ _ _ i _   3. _ p

5

with	during	above	past	between
by	down	along	before	near
toward	out	FREE	to	under
across	from	beside	behind	on
below	around	into	until	through

		FREE		

A.   Directions: Write the prepositions that have only two letters:

1. __at__   3. __in__   5. __on__   7. __up__

2. __by__   4. __of__   6. __to__

B.   Directions: Write the prepositions that have three letters:

1. __for__   2. __off__   3. __out__

C.   Directions: Write the prepositions that have four letters:

1. __down__   3. __into__   5. __over__   7. __with__

2. __from__   4. __near__   6. __past__

D.   Directions: Write the prepositions that have five letters:

1. __about__   3. __after__   5. __below__   7. __until__

2. __above__   4. __along__   6. __under__

E.   Directions: Write the prepositions that have six letters:

1. __across__   4. __behind__   7. __except__

2. __around__   5. __beside__   8. __inside__

3. __before__   6. __during__   9. __toward__

F.   Directions: Write the prepositions that have seven letters:

1. __against__   3. __between__   5. __through__

2. __beneath__   4. __outside__   6. __without__

8

Name_____ **PREPOSITIONS**

Date_____

A. Directions: Write the prepositions that have only two letters:

1. _____   3. _____   5. _____   7. _____

2. _____   4. _____   6. _____

B. Directions: Write the prepositions that have three letters:

1. _____   2. _____   3. _____

C. Directions: Write the prepositions that have four letters:

1. _____   3. _____   5. _____   7. _____

2. _____   4. _____   6. _____

D. Directions: Write the prepositions that have five letters:

1. _____   3. _____   5. _____   7. _____

2. _____   4. _____   6. _____

E. Directions: Write the prepositions that have six letters:

1. _____   4. _____   7. _____

2. _____   5. _____   8. _____

3. _____   6. _____   9. _____

F. Directions: Write the prepositions that have seven letters:

1. _____   3. _____   5. _____

2. _____   4. _____   6. _____

You may want to do this worksheet orally.

A. Directions: Prepositions add meaning to a sentence. Draw a desk. On the lines
       at the bottom of this page, write sentences explaining how a desk can
       be used. Be sure to use a preposition in each sentence.

PICTURE OF A DESK

Examples: You can put something **into** a desk.

A calculator may be **inside** a desk.

Answers may vary.   Representative answers:

1.   You can slide something **across** a desk._____

2.   You can lean **against** a desk._____

3.   You can sit **beneath** a desk._____

4.   You can look **at** a desk._____

5.   You can take something **from** a desk._____

6.   You might crawl **under** a desk._____

7.   A paper may be **on** the desk._____

8.   A desk may have drawers **with** handles._____

9.   A desk can be made **of** wood._____

Name_____

Date_____

A. Directions: Prepositions add meaning to a sentence. Draw a desk. On the lines at the bottom of this page, write sentences explaining how a desk can be used. Be sure to use a preposition in each sentence.

Examples: You can put something **into** a desk.

A calculator may be **inside** a desk.

1. _____

2. _____

3. _____

4. _____

5. _____

6. _____

7. _____

8. _____

9. _____

WORKBOOK PAGE 7
Date_____
Answers are in boldfaced print.
A. Directions: Circle any preposition(s) in the following sentences.

1. A gray kitten drank milk **from** a small dish.

2. This package is **for** Mrs. Smith.

3. Don't leave **without** me.

4. That puppy **with** short ears is cute.

5. The next game starts **at** ten o'clock.

6. Put the ice cream **into** the freezer, please.

7. The soup **of** the day was potato.

8. Come and sit **by** me.

9. We walked **around** the park.

10. A sign hangs **over** their door.

11. I'll be ready **in** a minute.

12. They sat **under** an oak tree **for** a picnic.

13. Let's go **to** the store **after** breakfast.

14. A child ran **down** the steps and **through** the hallway.

15. She jumped **off** the swing and fell **on** the ground.

16. All desserts **except** peach pie had been sold.

17. **During** the summer months, the Jones family may go **to** Canada.

18. His favorite spot **in** the winter is **outside** his bedroom window.

19. Mayor Dalton leaves **for** his office **before** dawn.

20. Birds visit their feeder **throughout** the fall.

Name_____   **PREPOSITIONS**

Date_____

A. Directions: Circle any preposition(s) in the following sentences.

1. A gray kitten drank milk from a small dish.

2. This package is for Mrs. Smith.

3. Don't leave without me.

4. That puppy with short ears is cute.

5. The next game starts at ten o'clock.

6. Put the ice cream into the freezer, please.

7. The soup of the day was potato.

8. Come and sit by me.

9. We walked around the park.

10. A sign hangs over their door.

11. I'll be ready in a minute.

12. They sat under an oak tree for a picnic.

13. Let's go to the store after breakfast.

14. A child ran down the steps and through the hallway.

15. She jumped off the swing and fell on the ground.

16. All desserts except peach pie had been sold.

17. During the summer months, the Jones family may go to Canada.

18. His favorite spot in the winter is outside his bedroom window.

19. Mayor Dalton leaves for his office before dawn.

20. Birds visit their feeder throughout the fall.

Name_____   **PREPOSITIONS**

WORKBOOK PAGE 8

Date_____

Answers are in boldfaced print.

A.   Directions: Circle any preposition(s) in the following sentences.

1.   A book **about** snakes is **beside** the lizard one.

2.   Several dishes **inside** the old cupboard were covered **with** dust.

3.   Marco lives **in** the country **near** a wide brook.

4.   A shovel is leaning **against** the barn **below** the hayloft window.

5.   We walked **beneath** many poplar trees **along** the narrow lane.

6.   Place your bicycle **between** the two houses **until** this evening.

7.   The group rode horses **up** a long trail **past** an old mine.

8.   The lady **across** the street keeps a broom **behind** her front door.

9.   **Toward** the end **of** the day, six boys played basketball **at** the park.

10.   A fisherman rushed **out** the door and threw his line **into** the stream.

11.   **During** the hurricane, everyone went **inside** the large building **for** shelter.

12.   **Throughout** the race, the car drivers had stayed **on** course.

13.   Mrs. Sung traveled **to** Orlando **without** her luggage.

14.   **Before** the show, we walked **around** the theater.

15.   Everyone **except** Paco jumped **off** the diving board.

16.   Several elderly people sat **by** the street light **near** a pond.

17.   We waited **beside** the road **after** the parade.

18.   **Before** Christmas, gifts were placed **beneath** a large pine tree.

19.   Lina and Kana walked **through** the courthouse door and turned **to** the left.

20.   The sun sinks **behind** those mountains **at** the end **of** each day.

14

Name_____ **PREPOSITIONS**

Date_____

A. Directions: Circle any preposition(s) in the following sentences.

1.   A book about snakes is beside the lizard one.

2.   Several dishes inside the old cupboard were covered with dust.

3.   Marco lives in the country near a wide brook.

4.   A shovel is leaning against the barn below the hayloft window.

5.   We walked beneath many poplar trees along the narrow lane.

6.   Place your bicycle between the two houses until this evening.

7.   The group rode horses up a long trail past an old mine.

8.   The lady across the street keeps a broom behind her front door.

9.   Toward the end of the day, six boys played basketball at the park.

10.   A fisherman rushed out the door and threw his line into the stream.

11.   During the hurricane, everyone went inside the large building for shelter.

12.   Throughout the race, the car drivers had stayed on course.

13.   Mrs. Sung traveled to Orlando without her luggage.

14.   Before the show, we walked around the theater.

15.   Everyone except Paco jumped off the diving board.

16.   Several elderly people sat by the street light near a pond.

17.   We waited beside the road after the parade.

18.   Before Christmas, gifts were placed beneath a large pine tree.

19.   Lina and Kana walked through the courthouse door and turned to the left.

20.   The sun sinks behind those mountains at the end of each day.   15

TO THE TEACHER: Please read carefully.

Up to this point, students have only been asked to identify prepositions. The following pages will introduce them to the concepts of a prepositional phrase, deleting prepositional phrases, object of the preposition, and determining subject and verb of a sentence.

Please read the lesson before teaching the following page(s):

Students need to be introduced to the meaning of a phrase. **A phrase is simply a group of words**. Your job is to introduce the lesson showing a phrase may be two words (turning sharply) or more than two words (near the library). **A phrase doesn't express a complete thought.**

Students need to understand that a prepositional phrase begins with a preposition and ends with a noun or pronoun. At this point, students have not been introduced to nouns. Although a prepositional phrase may end with an <u>abstract noun</u> (with much *happiness*), most end with a <u>concrete noun</u> (with my mother). **Therefore, teach students that most prepositional phrases end with something you can see.** Of course, prepositional phrases may end with a <u>pronoun</u>. Rather than teaching that concept at this point, the words *me, him, her, us,* and *them* have been included to serve as a guide (with *me*). Students need to know that the word that ends a prepositional phrase is called an <u>object of the preposition</u>.

    Example: with my mother   mother = object of the preposition

Teach students to delete each prepositional phrase: ~~with me~~. I recommend giving a student an index card so that a straight line can be drawn. If the child makes wavy lines, he may not cross out the entire phrase. This causes mistakes when determining the subject and verb of a sentence. (Do not allow the students to scribble out the entire phrase. Later, under adverbs, the students will be checking for certain adverbs within a prepositional phrase.*) You will find that this active, "hands on" approach is enjoyable, serves a definite purpose, and keeps students from becoming distracted.

Teach students that if two prepositional phrases are side by side, they need to mark two separate lines: ~~with my aunt to the store~~.

↑

🍓🍓🍓🍓🍓🍓🍓🍓🍓🍓🍓🍓🍓🍓🍓🍓🍓🍓🍓🍓🍓🍓🍓🍓🍓🍓🍓🍓🍓🍓🍓🍓🍓🍓🍓🍓🍓🍓🍓

Page 19, Part A, requires students to finish prepositional phrases. Part B requires identification of simple prepositional phrases. The student will need to draw one straight line through the prepositional phrase. Be sure to model this and ascertain that each student is doing this procedure correctly. Be sure to monitor student work.

Page 21 requires the student to delete prepositional phrases from sentences. Again, insist on straight lines. Modeling expectations and monitoring student work are very important in the teaching process.

Page 23 requires students to delete prepositional phrases. Students are also instructed to label the object of the preposition - O.P.

*Level 1 includes this.

A **prepositional phrase** is a **group of words** that **begins with a preposition**. A prepositional phrase ends with a noun (usually something you can see) or a pronoun (such as *him*, *her*, *them*, *us*, or *me*).

      Example: down the steps

                 with a huge umbrella

                 after lunch

                 between us

When you see a prepositional phrase in a sentence, cross it out like this: ~~between us~~ If two are side by side, lift your pencil and mark two separate lines: ~~with me~~ ~~for lunch~~

🍓🍓🍓🍓🍓🍓🍓🍓🍓🍓🍓🍓🍓🍓🍓🍓🍓🍓🍓🍓🍓🍓🍓🍓🍓🍓🍓🍓🍓🍓🍓🍓🍓🍓🍓🍓

A. Directions: Add a word or words to each preposition to form a prepositional phrase:

Answers may vary. Representative answers:

1. <u>under the bed, under the car, under a pillow</u>

2. <u>inside the box, inside a house, inside the refrigerator</u>

3. <u>for a moment, for you, for my mother, for a very long time</u>

4. <u>across the ocean, across the room, across a divided highway, across the street</u>

5. <u>in a race, in a hurry, in a parade, in her purse</u>

6. <u>during the storm, during the game, during the movie, during the service</u>

B. Directions: Cross out any prepositional phrase(s) in the following sentences.

1. The mop is ~~in the closet~~.

2. I went ~~to the store~~.

3. Sit ~~by me~~.

Name_____   **PREPOSITIONS**

Date_____

A **prepositional phrase** is a **group of words** that **begins with a preposition**.
A prepositional phrase ends with a noun (usually something you can see) or a
pronoun (such as *him, her, them, us,* or *me*).

     Example: down the steps

                 with a huge umbrella

                 after lunch

                 between us

When you see a prepositional phrase in a sentence, cross it out like this: ~~between us~~
If two are side by side, lift your pencil and mark two separate lines: ~~with me~~ ~~for lunch~~

A. Directions: Add a word or words to each preposition to form a prepositional
                    phrase:

1. <u>under</u> _____

2. <u>inside</u> _____

3. <u>for</u> _____

4. <u>across</u> _____

5. <u>in</u> _____

6. <u>during</u> _____

B. Directions: Cross out any prepositional phrase(s) in the following sentences.

1. The mop is in the closet.

2. I went to the store.

3. Sit by me.

Name_____   **PREPOSITIONS**

WORKBOOK PAGE 10

Date_____

Answers are in boldfaced print.

A. Directions: Cross out any prepositional phrase(s) in the following sentences.

Remember: **A prepositional phrase begins with a preposition and ends with a noun (usually something you can see) or a pronoun (such as *me, him, her, us,* or *them*).**

1.   We bought hot dogs ~~for the picnic~~.

2.   Their uncle lives ~~in Oregon~~.

3.   Our car is parked ~~past that alley~~.

4.   A tourist walked ~~over the old bridge~~.

5.   The coach walked quickly ~~toward us~~.

6.   Mrs. Martin always runs ~~before breakfast~~.

7.   Their cat sleeps ~~under an old chair~~.

8.   The father put bread ~~into a toaster~~.

9.   Several ladies picked berries ~~along the road~~.

10.   Sue's favorite doll has a white hat ~~with blue ribbons~~.

11.   Several balloons were hung ~~near the front door~~.

12.   We cannot leave ~~without our swimming suits~~.

13.   ~~Outside the city~~, Bill's family has a small cottage.

14.   The workers leaned their shovels ~~against the wall~~.

15.   The letter ~~from James~~ is ~~on the counter~~.

16.   A fountain is located ~~in the middle of the park~~.

17.   This shirt was given ~~to me~~ ~~by my aunt~~.

18.   The children raced ~~down several steps~~ and rushed ~~into the yard~~.

20

A. Directions: Cross out any prepositional phrase(s) in the following sentences.

Remember: **A prepositional phrase begins with a preposition and ends with a noun (usually something you can see) or a pronoun (such as *me, him, her, us,* or *them*).**

1. We bought hot dogs for the picnic.

2. Their uncle lives in Oregon.

3. Our car is parked past that alley.

4. A tourist walked over the old bridge.

5. The coach walked quickly toward us.

6. Mrs. Martin always runs before breakfast.

7. Their cat sleeps under an old chair.

8. The father put bread into a toaster.

9. Several ladies picked berries along the road.

10. Sue's favorite doll has a white hat with blue ribbons.

11. Several balloons were hung near the front door.

12. We cannot leave without our swimming suits.

13. Outside the city, Bill's family has a small cottage.

14. The workers leaned their shovels against the wall.

15. The letter from James is on the counter.

16. A fountain is located in the middle of the park.

17. This shirt was given to me by my aunt.

18. The children raced down several steps and rushed into the yard.

The word (noun or pronoun) that ends a prepositional phrase is called the object of the preposition.

                                                    O.P.
          Example: Put the groceries ~~into the cupboard~~.

🍓🍓🍓🍓🍓🍓🍓🍓🍓🍓🍓🍓🍓🍓🍓🍓🍓🍓🍓🍓🍓🍓🍓🍓🍓🍓🍓🍓🍓🍓🍓🍓🍓🍓🍓

Directions: Cross out the prepositional phrase in each sentence.   Label the object of the preposition - **O.P.**

                         O.P.
1. He rode ~~around the block~~.
                     O.P.
2. Sit ~~by the door~~.
                         O.P.
3. A robin flew ~~into its nest~~.
                         O.P.
4. Len fell ~~over his bike~~.
                     O.P.
5. Come ~~with me~~.
                             O.P.
6. The host talked ~~to the audience~~.
                                 O.P.
7. A worker threw garbage ~~into the truck~~.
                             O.P.
8. Their aunt plays tennis ~~at a club~~.
                                 O.P.
9. The cherry pickers ate lunch ~~under a tree~~.
                         O.P.
10. A corsage ~~of pink roses~~ was delivered.
                                 O.P.
11. Wilma made a salad ~~with frozen grapes~~.
                         O.P.
12. A taxi driver ran ~~over a curb~~.
                             O.P.
13. This television show is ~~about Hawaii~~.
                         O.P.
14. A gymnast climbed ~~up a rope~~.
                         O.P.
15. His sandals are made ~~of leather~~.
22

The word (noun or pronoun) that ends a prepositional phrase is called the object of the preposition.

                                        O.P.
        Example: Put the groceries ~~into the cupboard~~.

Directions: Cross out the prepositional phrase in each sentence.   Label the object of
              the preposition - **O.P.**

   1.   He rode around the block.

   2.   Sit by the door.

   3.   A robin flew into its nest.

   4.   Len fell over his bike.

   5.   Come with me.

   6.   The host talked to the audience.

   7.   A worker threw garbage into the truck.

   8.   Their aunt plays tennis at a club.

   9.   The cherry pickers ate lunch under a tree.

  10.   A corsage of pink roses was delivered.

  11.   Wilma made a salad with frozen grapes.

  12.   A taxi driver ran over a curb.

  13.   This television show is about Hawaii.

  14.   A gymnast climbed up a rope.

  15.   His sandals are made of leather.

TO THE TEACHER: **Please read carefully.**
Segments of this page are placed on the following page for student use.

A prepositional phrase will not be the subject or verb of a sentence.*

HOW TO TEACH SUBJECTS:
Teach students to cross out prepositional phrases.   Then, teach them to read the remaining words.   When you are introducing this concept, you may want to suggest that your students read the remaining words orally and in unison.   This prepares students for reading them silently later.

> In the pond, several fish swam near the surface.
> ~~In the pond~~, several fish swam ~~near the surface~~.

> Oral reading: several fish swam

Be sure that students understand that <u>pond</u> can't possibly be the subject.   Why?   After we have deleted a word, it won't serve as the subject.*

To find the subject, simply teach students to ask themselves **who** or **what** the sentence is about.   (This is an oversimplification, but it works.)   Again, be sure that students understand that *pond* or *surface* cannot be the subject because they have been omitted.

> **Recommendation**:   If you are using a chalkboard or overhead projector, visually erase any prepositional phrases.   This helps children "see" that those words won't, at this point, serve a purpose.

After reading "several fish swam," ask students about **who** or **what** we are talking. They will readily determine that *fish* is the subject.   (If anyone says *several*, guide him to understand that *several* modifies (or goes over to) *fish*: several fish.   *Fish* is the subject. Teach students to place one line under the subject: several <u>fish</u> swam.

HOW TO TEACH VERBS:
After students have determined the subject, instruct them to decide **what happened** (or **is happening**) or **what "is"** in the sentence.   **The verb will never be in a prepositional phrase.**

> Oral reading: several fish swam

Guide students to use the subject, *fish*, and ask what happened. What did the fish do? The fish swam.   *Swam* is the verb and requires double underlining: several <u>fish</u> <u>swam</u>.

24   * This holds true 99% of the time   ***PAGE 25 = WORKBOOK PAGE 12***

A prepositional phrase will not be the subject or verb of a sentence.*

SUBJECTS:

Crossing out prepositional phrases will help you to find the subject of a sentence.

Example: In the pond, several fish swam near the surface.

~~In the pond~~, several fish swam ~~near the surface~~.

Pond can't be the subject.   Why?   *Pond* is in a prepositional phrase.

Remember: The subject will not be found in a prepositional phrase.   When you cross out the prepositional phrase, it's like pretending that those words have disappeared from the page.

To find the subject, look at the remaining words.   Read them.   Then, ask yourself **who** or **what** the sentence is about.

Example: several fish swam

We are talking about fish; *fish* is the subject.   Place one straight line under fish.

Example: several <u>fish</u> swam

VERBS:

To find the verb, decide **what happened** (or **is happening**) or **what "is"** in the sentence. **The verb will never be in a prepositional phrase.**

Oral reading: several fish swam

Repeat your subject, *fish*, and ask yourself, " What did the fish do?" The fish *swam*. Swam is the verb.   Place double underlining under the verb: several <u>fish</u> <u>swam</u>.

* This holds true 99% of the time.

Directions: Cross out the prepositional phrase in each sentence.   Underline the
subject once and the verb twice.

Example: His <u>dad</u> <u><u>lives</u></u> ~~near Mt. St. Helens~~.

1.   <u>I</u> <u><u>left</u></u> ~~without money~~.

2.   The <u>soap</u> <u><u>is</u></u> ~~below the sink~~.

3.   A <u>bug</u> <u><u>flew</u></u> ~~up his sleeve~~.

4.   Many <u>horses</u> <u><u>trotted</u></u> ~~along the wide path~~.

5.   Her <u>cousin</u> <u><u>lives</u></u> ~~near a waterfall~~.

6.   ~~Inside the box~~ <u><u>was</u></u> a small <u>quilt</u>.

7.   The <u>van</u> ~~beside the blue car~~ <u><u>is</u></u> mine.

8.   <u>Everyone</u> ~~except Sandy~~ <u><u>left</u></u> early.

9.   A <u>toddler</u> <u><u>crawled</u></u> ~~over his friend~~.

10.   A <u>rabbit</u> <u><u>nibbled</u></u> ~~beneath a bush~~.

11.   <u>We</u> <u><u>peeked</u></u> ~~under the bed~~.

12.   <u>Shawn</u> <u><u>looked</u></u> ~~toward his laughing friends~~.

13.   The <u>runner</u> <u><u>jumped</u></u> ~~over the hurdle~~.

14.   A <u>ring</u> <u><u>fell</u></u> ~~to the floor~~.

15.   This <u>letter</u> <u><u>is</u></u> ~~from their senator~~.

16.   My <u>grandmother</u> <u><u>golfs</u></u> ~~with her friend~~.

17.   <u>Chad</u> <u><u>shopped</u></u> ~~without his mother~~.

18.   <u>She</u> <u><u>placed</u></u> her towel ~~between several sunbathers~~.

26

Directions: Cross out the prepositional phrase in each sentence.   Underline the
subject once and the verb twice.

Example: His <u>dad</u> <u><u>lives</u></u> ~~near Mt. St. Helens~~.

1. I left without money.

2. The soap is below the sink.

3. A bug flew up his sleeve.

4. Many horses trotted along the wide path.

5. Her cousin lives near a waterfall.

6. Inside the box was a small quilt.

7. The van beside the blue car is mine.

8. Everyone except Sandy left early.

9. A toddler crawled over his friend.

10. A rabbit nibbled beneath a bush.

11. We peeked under the bed.

12. Shawn looked toward his laughing friends.

13. The runner jumped over the hurdle.

14. A ring fell to the floor.

15. This letter is from their senator.

16. My grandmother golfs with her friend.

17. Chad shopped without his mother.

18. She placed her towel between several sunbathers.

WORKBOOK PAGE 14

Date_____

Directions: Cross out any prepositional phrase(s).   Underline the subject once and the verb twice.

Example: His <u>sunglasses</u> <u><u>are</u></u> ~~beneath the sofa in the living room~~.

1.   Several <u>hens</u> <u><u>gathered</u></u> ~~by the shed~~.

2.   <u>Daisies</u> <u><u>grow</u></u> ~~outside their fence~~.

3.   A <u>seal</u> <u><u>swam</u></u> ~~toward the shore~~.

4.   <u>Marty</u> <u><u>fell</u></u> ~~off the bottom of the slide~~.

5.   A <u>dog</u> ~~without a leash~~ <u><u>trotted</u></u> ~~by them~~.

6.   Nightly, the <u>woman</u> <u><u>looks</u></u> ~~through her telescope~~.

7.   <u>They</u> <u><u>rushed</u></u> ~~across the yard after a rubber ball~~.

8.   <u>Mr. Carlson</u> <u><u>read</u></u> a book ~~about tigers to his son~~.

9.   <u>She</u> <u><u>rode</u></u> ~~around the corral on her favorite pinto~~.

10.   The <u>teenagers</u> <u><u>walked</u></u> ~~down the beach past the pier~~.

11.   A <u>dog</u> <u><u>darted</u></u> ~~across the street by the firehouse~~.

12.   <u>We</u> <u><u>walked</u></u> ~~between the aisles at the supermarket~~.

13.   The <u>drummer</u> <u><u>waited</u></u> ~~beside the road after the parade~~.

14.   The <u>sun</u> <u><u>sinks</u></u> ~~behind the mountains toward the end of the day~~.

15.   <u>They</u> <u><u>played</u></u> ~~against a team with blue and white jerseys~~.

28

Date_____

Directions: Cross out any prepositional phrase(s).   Underline the subject once and
the verb twice.

Example: His <u>sunglasses</u> <u>are</u> ~~beneath the sofa in the living room~~.

1.   Several hens gathered by the shed.

2.   Daisies grow outside their fence.

3.   A seal swam toward the shore.

4.   Marty fell off the bottom of the slide.

5.   A dog without a leash trotted by them.

6.   Nightly, the woman looks through her telescope.

7.   They rushed across the yard after a rubber ball.

8.   Mr. Carlson read a book about tigers to his son.

9.   She rode around the corral on her favorite pinto.

10.   The teenagers walked down the beach past the pier.

11.   A dog darted across the street by the firehouse.

12.   We walked between the aisles at the supermarket.

13.   The drummer waited beside the road after the parade.

14.   The sun sinks behind the mountains toward the end of the day.

15.   They played against a team with blue and white jerseys.

TO THE TEACHER: <u>Please read each lesson contained on these pages</u>. Students will be given instruction of the individual concept at the top of each worksheet. However, ideally, you will teach the concept before proceeding to each worksheet discussion.

Page 33: **Concept: Some sentences will contain a compound subject.** Teach students the meaning of compound. Because teaching is more effective when combining auditory and visual learning, I draw pictures when appropriate. With my students, I draw a picture of an arm bone, and we talk about a compound bone fracture. We discuss and dramatically depict how the bone is broken **and** punctures the skin (Ouch!). Frequently, at least one student has had a compound fracture and is willing to show us the places the bone had been broken and had protruded. <u>Your goal at this point is to be sure that students understand that **compound means more than one**</u>.

Compound subject simply means that we will be talking about more than one "who" or "what" in the sentence. Compounds are usually joined with the conjunctions, *and* or *or*.

Examples: <u>Marge</u> and <u>Tommy</u> play basketball together.
My <u>neighbor</u> or his <u>son</u> purchased a new car.

Page 35: **Concept: In an imperative sentence, one that gives a command, the subject is often not said.** The person to whom the speaker is talking automatically knows he or she is being addressed. In English, we call this "You understood." It is written: (<u>You</u>)!

To explain this concept, I share with students that my sons usually know by my use of *you* if they are in trouble. If I am very concerned (or upset), I say, "You come here, please." In this sentence, *you* appears and is, of course, the subject of the sentence. However, in most cases, I simply say, "Come here, please." In this sentence, *you* is understood.

30

Example: (You) Come here, please.

You may want to allow students to give each other commands (appropriate to the classroom, of course). You may get such commands as "Stand up." or "Stick out your tongue." Write these on the board and model how to write (You) and determine the verb.

Examples: (You) Stand up.

(You) Stick out your tongue.

Note: As a veteran teacher, I am hesitant to allow students to act out the commands. Whereas the command to stand up is innocuous enough, one involving hitting someone can present problems.   In addition, I am very careful; a command relating to something such as standing on one's head may cause injury. Yes, we want to have active learning and for the students to have fun. However, be wise in your judgments.

Page 37:   **Concept:**   **Sometimes, a prepositional phrase will contain more than one object. This a called a compound object.**

Review the meaning of compound. This concept is taught best by example. However, a helpful trick is to always look at the word after an object of the preposition. If that word is a conjunction, check to see if the ensuing word(s) may be part of the prepositional phrase.

Example: I went ~~with my mom and dad~~ to San Diego.

Page 39:   **Concept:**   **Some sentences will contain a compound verb.**

Review the meaning of compound. Then, explain that the subject often "does" or "is" more than one item.

Example: The bowler always throws the ball and yells.

In order to determine verb, first find the subject of the sentence. In this case, bowler is *who* of the sentence. What does the bowler do? He does two things: *throws* and *yells*.

Compound Subjects:

Sometimes a sentence will contain a compound subject.

Compound subject simply means that there will be **more than one** "who" or "what" in the sentence.   Compounds are usually joined with the conjunctions, *and* or *or*.

> Examples: His <u>father</u> and <u>mother</u> have arrived.
>
> <u>Janis</u>, <u>Kelly</u>, or <u>I</u> will be going, also.

Crossing out prepositional phrases will make it easier to find a compound subject.

> Example: The <u>lady</u> ~~with the red hat~~ and her <u>mother</u> are opera singers.

🍓🍓🍓🍓🍓🍓🍓🍓🍓🍓🍓🍓🍓🍓🍓🍓🍓🍓🍓🍓🍓🍓🍓🍓🍓🍓🍓🍓🍓🍓🍓🍓🍓🍓🍓

Directions: Cross out any prepositional phrase(s).   Underline the subject once and the verb twice.

1. His <u>dog</u> and <u>cat</u> <u>play</u> ~~in his backyard~~.

2. Your <u>aunt</u> and <u>uncle</u> ~~from Texas~~ <u>are</u> here.

3. A <u>pear</u> or <u>peach</u> <u>is</u> ~~in the refrigerator~~.

4. The <u>mayor</u> and her <u>husband</u> <u>arrived</u> ~~at the dinner~~.

5. <u>Dr. Shank</u> and his <u>nurse</u> <u>talked</u> ~~to the young patient~~.

6. <u>Paper</u> and <u>pencils</u> <u>are</u> ~~inside the desk~~.

7. <u>Mark</u>, <u>Kim</u>, or <u>Denise</u> <u>left</u> ~~for the park~~.

8. A <u>candle</u>, three flower <u>pots</u>, a <u>vase</u>, and a red <u>box</u> <u>are</u> ~~on the shelf~~ ~~above the sink~~.

9. A <u>bag</u> ~~of corn~~ and a <u>carton</u> ~~of fruit~~ <u>were</u> ~~under a wooden bench~~.

Compound Subjects:

Sometimes a sentence will contain a compound subject.

Compound subject simply means that there will be **more than one** "who" or "what" in the sentence.   Compounds are usually joined with the conjunctions, *and* or *or*.

> Examples: His <u>father</u> and <u>mother</u> have arrived.
>
> <u>Janis</u>, <u>Kelly</u>, or <u>I</u> will be going, also.

Crossing out prepositional phrases will make it easier to find a compound subject.

> Example: The <u>lady</u> ~~with the red hat~~ and her <u>mother</u> are opera singers.

Directions: Cross out any prepositional phrase(s).   Underline the subject once and the verb twice.

1.   His dog and cat play in his backyard.

2.   Your aunt and uncle from Texas are here.

3.   A pear or peach is in the refrigerator.

4.   The mayor and her husband arrived at the dinner.

5.   Dr. Shank and his nurse talked to the young patient.

6.   Paper and pencils are inside the desk.

7.   Mark, Kim, or Denise left for the park.

8.   A candle, three flower pots, a vase, and a red box are on the shelf above the sink.

9.   A bag of corn and a carton of fruit were under a wooden bench.

An imperative sentence gives a command.   Usually, the subject is not written.   The person knows that the message is intended for him.

Example: Pass the butter, please.

Notice that the sentence doesn't say, "You pass the butter, please."   The *you* has been omitted because it's understood for whom the message was intended.   The subject is written: (You) and said: "You understood."

Example: Follow this road.

(You) Follow this road.

Crossing out prepositional phrases will help:

Example: Sit by me for a few minutes.

(You) sit ~~by me for a few minutes~~.

🍓🍓🍓🍓🍓🍓🍓🍓🍓🍓🍓🍓🍓🍓🍓🍓🍓🍓🍓🍓🍓🍓🍓🍓🍓🍓🍓🍓🍓🍓🍓🍓🍓🍓

Directions: Cross out any prepositional phrase(s).   Underline the subject once and the verb twice.

(You)
1. <u>Give</u> this ~~to your brother~~.

(You)
2. Please <u>look</u> ~~into the camera~~.

(You)
3. <u>Drive</u> ~~by my friend's house~~.

(You)
4. <u>Take</u> the saw ~~to the tree trimmer~~.

(You)
5. <u>Go</u> ~~after lunch~~ ~~without me~~.

(You)
6. <u>Sign</u> ~~on the dotted line~~.

(You)
7. Please <u>search</u> ~~under the table for the lost keys~~.

34

An imperative sentence gives a command. Usually, the subject is not written. The person knows that the message is intended for him.

Example: Pass the butter, please.

Notice that the sentence doesn't say, "You pass the butter, please." The *you* has been omitted because it's understood for whom the message was intended. The subject is written: (You) and said: "You understood."

Example: Follow this road.

(You) Follow this road.

Crossing out prepositional phrases will help:

Example: Sit by me for a few minutes.

(You) sit ~~by me for a few minutes~~.

🍓🍓🍓🍓🍓🍓🍓🍓🍓🍓🍓🍓🍓🍓🍓🍓🍓🍓🍓🍓🍓🍓🍓🍓🍓🍓🍓🍓🍓🍓🍓🍓🍓🍓🍓🍓🍓

Directions: Cross out any prepositional phrase(s). Underline the subject once and the verb twice.

1. Give this to your brother.

2. Please look into the camera.

3. Drive by my friend's house.

4. Take the saw to the tree trimmer.

5. Go after lunch without me.

6. Sign on the dotted line.

7. Please search under the table for the lost keys.

Name_____

WORKBOOK PAGE 17

Date_____

PREPOSITIONS
Compound Objects
of the Preposition

Compound Objects of the Preposition:

Sometimes, a prepositional phrase will contain more than one object. This a called a compound object.

O.P.   O.P.

Example: for Carol and me   Carol = object of the preposition

me = object of the preposition

Note: Look at the word after an object of the preposition. If *and* or *or* follows the noun or pronoun, check to see if there may be another noun or pronoun ending the prepositional phrase.

O.P.   O.P.

Example: He <u>walked</u> ~~without his shoes or socks~~.

🍓🍓🍓🍓🍓🍓🍓🍓🍓🍓🍓🍓🍓🍓🍓🍓🍓🍓🍓🍓🍓🍓🍓🍓🍓🍓🍓🍓

Directions: Cross out any prepositional phrase(s). Underline the subject once and the verb twice.

1. The <u>shirt</u> ~~with dots and stripes~~ <u>is</u> unusual.
    (You)
2. <u>Go</u> ~~with your cousin or David~~.

3. The <u>gift</u> ~~from Sam and Dora~~ <u>was</u> large.

4. <u>She</u> <u>eats</u> her sandwiches ~~without tomato or lettuce~~.

5. Their family <u>reunion</u> <u>is</u> ~~in July or August~~.
    (You)
6. <u>Take</u> this ~~with you for your lunch or dinner~~.

7. The <u>road</u> ~~to Payson and Alpine~~ <u>has</u> many bumps.

8. Your gardening <u>tool</u> <u>is</u> ~~in the shed on the table or chair~~.

9. ~~Throughout the fall and winter~~, <u>we</u> <u>watch</u> birds ~~at that feeder~~.

36

Compound Objects of the Preposition:

Sometimes, a prepositional phrase will contain more than one object. This a called a compound object.

O.P.   O.P.

Example: for Carol and me   Carol = object of the preposition

me = object of the preposition

Note: Look at the word after an object of the preposition. If *and* or *or* follows the noun or pronoun, check to see if there may be another noun or pronoun ending the prepositional phrase.

O.P.   O.P.

Example: He walked without his shoes or socks.

🍓🍓🍓🍓🍓🍓🍓🍓🍓🍓🍓🍓🍓🍓🍓🍓🍓🍓🍓🍓🍓🍓🍓🍓🍓🍓🍓🍓🍓🍓🍓🍓🍓🍓🍓

Directions: Cross out any prepositional phrase(s). Underline the subject once and the verb twice.

1. The shirt with dots and stripes is unusual.

2. Go with your cousin or David.

3. The gift from Sam and Dora was large.

4. She eats her sandwiches without tomato or lettuce.

5. Their family reunion is in July or August.

6. Take this with you for your lunch or dinner.

7. The road to Payson and Alpine has many bumps.

8. Your gardening tool is in the shed on the table or chair.

9. Throughout the fall and winter, we watch birds at that feeder.

Compound Verbs:

Sometimes a sentence contains more than one verb. This is called a compound verb. This means that the subject often "does" more than one item.

In order to determine a verb, first cross out any prepositional phrases. Then, find the subject of the sentence. Next, decide what the subject *is* (*was*) or *does* (*did*).

Examples: A <u>sparrow</u> <u>sits</u> ~~on the fence~~ and <u>chirps</u>.

What does the sparrow do? Two things: sits and chirps

The nurse <u>took</u> a bandage, <u>opened</u> it, and <u>placed</u> it ~~on the man's arm~~.

What did the nurse do? Three things: took, opened, and placed

🍓🍓🍓🍓🍓🍓🍓🍓🍓🍓🍓🍓🍓🍓🍓🍓🍓🍓🍓🍓🍓🍓🍓🍓🍓🍓🍓🍓🍓🍓🍓🍓🍓🍓🍓

Directions: Cross out any prepositional phrase(s).   Underline the subject once and the verb twice.

1.   A pretty <u>receptionist</u> <u>smiled</u> and <u>handed</u> a paper ~~to a businesswoman~~.

2.   ~~After breakfast~~, <u>Joe</u> <u>washed</u>, <u>rinsed</u>, and <u>dried</u> the dirty dishes.

3.   <u>Harriet</u> <u>waved</u> her hat, <u>yelled</u>, and <u>stomped</u> her foot ~~in excitement~~.

4.   The <u>winner</u> ~~of the race~~ <u>dashed</u> ~~across the finish line~~ and <u>fell</u>.

5.   <u>One</u> ~~of the boys~~ <u>clapped</u> his hands and <u>cheered</u> happily.

6.   <u>Mr. Adams</u> <u>drives</u> ~~to a bus stop~~ and <u>travels</u> ~~by bus to his office~~.

7.   A <u>tiger</u> <u>has</u> stripes, <u>eats</u> meat, and <u>lives</u> ~~in Asia~~.

8.   The delivery <u>person</u> <u>knocked</u>, <u>waited</u> ~~for a few minutes~~, and <u>left</u> the package ~~beside the door~~.

9.   A <u>deer</u> ~~with a fawn~~ <u>stepped</u> ~~into the meadow~~ and <u>stared</u> ~~toward us~~.

38

Name_____

Date_____

Compound Verbs:

    Sometimes a sentence contains more than one verb. This is called a compound verb. This means that the subject often "does" more than one item.

In order to determine a verb, first cross out any prepositional phrases. Then, find the subject of the sentence. Next, decide what the subject *is* (*was*) or *does* (*did*).

  Examples: A sparrow sits ~~on the fence~~ and chirps.

          What does the sparrow do? Two things: sits and chirps

          The nurse took a bandage, opened it, and placed it ~~on the man's arm~~.

          What did the nurse do? Three things: took, opened, and placed

Directions: Cross out any prepositional phrase(s). Underline the subject once and the verb twice.

1. A pretty receptionist smiled and handed a paper to a businesswoman.

2. After breakfast, Joe washed, rinsed, and dried the dirty dishes.

3. Harriet waved her hat, yelled, and stomped her foot in excitement.

4. The winner of the race dashed across the finish line and fell.

5. One of the boys clapped his hands and cheered happily.

6. Mr. Adams drives to a bus stop and travels by bus to his office.

7. A tiger has stripes, eats meat, and lives in Asia.

8. The delivery person knocked, waited for a few minutes, and left the package beside the door.

9. A deer with a fawn stepped into the meadow and stared toward us.

39

TO THE TEACHER: <u>Please read each lesson contained on these pages.</u>   Students will be given a discussion of the individual concept at the top of each worksheet. However, ideally, you will teach the concept before proceeding to each worksheet discussion.

Page 43:   **Concept:** *To* plus a verb is called an **infinitive**.

> Examples: to run   to want
>
> to laugh   to begin

Do not delete infinitives. Place each infinitive in parenthesis ( ).

> Examples: <u>I like</u> (to swim).
>
> <u>Sherry wants</u> (to go) ~~on a hayride~~.

To plus a noun or pronoun makes up a prepositional phrase.   Cross out any prepositional phrase.

> Example: <u>Miss Simmons loves</u> (to travel) ~~to other countries~~.

Note: Technically, an infinitive phrase is composed of an infinitive + word(s). For example, I want to go swimming. *To go swimming* is an infinitive phrase serving as a noun (direct object). Although this is "nice to know," teaching this additional information only confuses students. The question may arise concerning the word, *swimming* , in the sentence. If it does, you can choose to answer it. However, be sure to add that, at this point, knowing this additional information is not important.

Page 45:   **Concept:**   **A verb phrase is composed of one or more helping verbs plus a main verb.** There are twenty-three helping verbs. (These are also referred to as auxiliary verbs.) Later, students will be required to memorize the list. However, at this point, the students will be given the list to use in identification. (You may want to make a list to post in the classroom.)

do, does, did   has, have, had   may, might, must
can, shall, will   could, should, would
is, am, are, was, were, be, being, been

verb phrase	**=**	**helping verb(s)**	**+**	**main verb**
Examples: may leave	=	may	+	leave
should have decided	=	should have	+	decided

Students need to comprehend that verbs from the above list can serve as the main verb.

Examples: The <u>fireman</u> <u>was</u> very brave.   (main verb)

The <u>girl</u> <u>was fishing</u> ~~in the stream~~.   (helping verb)

I would suggest that you do this lesson orally. It's important for students to "hear" verb phrases. The next lesson will include finding verb phrases. At that time, you may wish for students to work on their own.

Page 47: **Concept:** ***Not* is never part of a verb phrase.** *Not* is an adverb. Teach students to box *not* immediately. This prevents underlining it as part of the verb phrase. This lesson will also reinforce determining verb phrases.

Page 49: **Concept:** **To determine the subject of an interrogative sentence, one that asks a question, first change the sentence into a statement (declarative sentence).**

Examples: interrogative: Are you going with me?
        declarative: <u>You</u> <u>are going</u> ~~with me~~.

        interrogative: Did Mike take his sleeping bag with him?
        declarative: <u>Mike</u> <u>did take</u> his sleeping bag ~~with him~~.

I realize that this sometimes sounds awkward; however, there is value in teaching students to follow the practice. Also, remind students that usually a helping verb is located at the beginning of an interrogative sentence.   41

To plus a verb is called an infinitive.

Examples: to go   to cry   to clean   to sing

Do not cross out infinitives. Place each infinitive in parenthesis (to sing). This will help you to remember not to mark it as a prepositional phrase.

Example: The librarian wants **(to read)** us a book.

Important note: *To* plus a noun or pronoun makes up a prepositional phrase. Cross out any prepositional phrase.

to the store = prepositional phrase   to + store (noun)

to go = infinitive   to + go (verb)

In a sentence, cross out the prepositional phrase. Place parenthesis around the infinitive.

Example: Kyle wants **(**to go**)** ~~to the store~~.

Directions: Cross out any prepositional phrase(s).   Place parenthesis ( ) around each infinitive. Underline the subject once and the verb twice.

1. Jacob loves (to read) ~~about reptiles~~.

2. Heidi wanted (to be) an airplane pilot.

3. ~~In the winter~~, Grandma loves (to ski).

4. They promised (to write) soon.

5. Some tourists decided (to drive) ~~by a marina~~.

6. Karen needs (to take) her backpack ~~with her~~.

7. Several ~~of the actors~~ tried (to add) lines ~~without the permission of the director~~.

42

To **plus a verb is called an infinitive.**

Examples: to go   to cry   to clean   to sing

Do not cross out infinitives. Place each infinitive in parenthesis **(** to sing **)**. This will help you to remember not to mark it as a prepositional phrase.

Example: The librarian wants **(to read)** us a book.

Important note: *To* plus a noun or pronoun makes up a prepositional phrase. Cross out any prepositional phrase.

to the store = prepositional phrase   to + store (noun)
to go = infinitive   to + go   (verb)

In a sentence, cross out the prepositional phrase. Place parenthesis around the infinitive.

Example: <u>Kyle</u> <u>wants</u> **(to go)** ~~to the store~~.

🍓🍓🍓🍓🍓🍓🍓🍓🍓🍓🍓🍓🍓🍓🍓🍓🍓🍓🍓🍓🍓🍓🍓🍓🍓🍓🍓🍓🍓🍓🍓

Directions: Cross out any prepositional phrase(s).   Place parenthesis ( ) around each infinitive. Underline the subject once and the verb twice.

1.   Jacob loves to read about reptiles.

2.   Heidi wanted to be an airplane pilot.

3.   In the winter, Grandma loves to ski.

4.   They promised to write soon.

5.   Some tourists decided to drive by a marina.

6.   Karen needs to take her backpack with her.

7.   Several of the actors tried to add lines without the permission of the director.

A verb phrase is composed of one or more helping verbs plus a main verb. There are twenty-three helping verbs. These are also called auxiliary verbs.

do	has	may	can	could	is	were
does	have	might	shall	should	am	be
did	had	must	will	would	are	being
					was	been

The main verb is the last part of a verb phrase.

verb phrase	=	**helping verb(s)**	+	**main verb**
will learn	=	will	+	learn
could have brought	=	could have	+	brought

🍓🍓🍓🍓🍓🍓🍓🍓🍓🍓🍓🍓🍓🍓🍓🍓🍓🍓🍓🍓🍓🍓🍓🍓🍓🍓🍓🍓🍓🍓🍓🍓

Directions: Cross out any prepositional phrase(s). Underline the subject once and the verb phrase twice.

1. I do love (to bake) ~~during the afternoon~~.

2. A bug has bitten you ~~on the arm~~.

3. You may come ~~with us~~.

4. Isaac might have crawled ~~under the table~~.

5. Mrs. Park should clean ~~above her oven~~.

6. They are going ~~through the tunnel~~.

7. I shall eat ~~before the play~~.

8. The waitress must serve drinks ~~before the food~~.

9. Everyone ~~except Annie~~ will be leaving ~~by bus~~.

10. The bread had been broken ~~into three chunks~~.

A verb phrase is composed of one or more helping verbs plus a main verb. There are twenty-three helping verbs. These are also called auxiliary verbs.

do	has	may	can	could	is	were
does	have	might	shall	should	am	be
did	had	must	will	would	are	being
					was	been

The main verb is the last part of a verb phrase.

verb phrase	=	**helping verb(s)**	+	**main verb**
will learn	=	will	+	learn
could have brought	=	could have	+	brought

Directions: Cross out any prepositional phrase(s). Underline the subject once and the verb phrase twice.

1. I do love to bake during the afternoon.

2. A bug has bitten you on the arm.

3. You may come with us.

4. Isaac might have crawled under the table.

5. Mrs. Park should clean above her oven.

6. They are going through the tunnel.

7. I shall eat before the play.

8. The waitress must serve drinks before the food.

9. Everyone except Annie will be leaving by bus.

10. The bread had been broken into three chunks.

Not (or **n't**) **is never part of a verb phrase.**   Not is an adverb.   Box not

immediately.   This keeps you from underlining not as part of a verb phrase.

Example: Her <u>father</u> <u>will</u> **not** <u>be going</u> ~~with them~~.

Remember: A verb phrase is composed of one or more helping verbs plus a main

verb. The main verb is the last part of a verb phrase.

do	**has**	**may**	**can**	**could**	**is**	**were**
does	**have**	**might**	**shall**	**should**	**am**	**be**
did	**had**	**must**	**will**	**would**	**are**	**being**
					was	**been**

🍓🍓🍓🍓🍓🍓🍓🍓🍓🍓🍓🍓🍓🍓🍓🍓🍓🍓🍓🍓🍓🍓🍓🍓🍓🍓🍓🍓

Directions: Cross out any prepositional phrase(s).   Box not. Underline the subject
            once and the verb phrase twice.
***Not* has been boldfaced (rather than boxed) throughout this text.**

1. <u>You</u> <u>must</u> **not** <u>go</u> ~~until Friday~~.

2. The small <u>boy</u> <u>would</u>**n't** <u>play</u> ~~with his friends~~.

3. <u>She</u> <u>must</u> **not** <u>have stayed</u> ~~inside the hotel~~.

4. That tall <u>girl</u> <u>can</u>**not** <u>play</u> ~~against the new team~~.

5. A few <u>hikers</u> <u>could</u> **not** <u>reach</u> the top ~~of the hill~~.

6. <u>One</u> ~~of the clerks~~ <u>would</u> **not** <u>leave</u> ~~after his shift~~.

7. <u>John</u> <u>does</u> **not** <u>fish</u> ~~beside other people~~.

8. <u>I</u> <u>shall</u> **not** <u>change</u> my mind ~~about the pool cover~~.

9. <u>Hannah</u> <u>has</u>**n't** <u>typed</u> ~~on a computer~~ yet.

10. <u>He</u> <u>may</u> **not** <u>have stopped</u> ~~at the store~~.

46

Name_____

Date_____

Not (or n't) is never part of a verb phrase. <u>Not</u> is an adverb. Box <u>not</u> immediately. This keeps you from underlining <u>not</u> as part of a verb phrase.

       Example: Her <u>father</u> <u>will</u> [not] <u>be going</u> ~~with them~~.

Remember: A verb phrase is composed of one or more helping verbs plus a main verb. The main verb is the last part of a verb phrase.

do	**has**	**may**	**can**	**could**	**is**	**were**
does	**have**	**might**	**shall**	**should**	**am**	**be**
did	**had**	**must**	**will**	**would**	**are**	**being**
					was	**been**

Directions: Cross out any prepositional phrase(s). Box <u>not</u>. Underline the subject once and the verb phrase twice.

1. You must not go until Friday.

2. The small boy wouldn't play with his friends.

3. She must not have stayed inside the hotel.

4. That tall girl cannot play against the new team.

5. A few hikers could not reach the top of the hill.

6. One of the clerks would not leave after his shift.

7. John does not fish beside other people.

8. I shall not change my mind about the pool cover.

9. Hannah hasn't typed on a computer yet.

10. He may not have stopped at the store.

An interrogative sentence asks a question. To determine the subject and verb of an interrogative sentence, first change the sentence into a statement (declarative sentence).

Example: Is your mother here?
            Your <u>mother</u> <u>is</u> here.

Follow these steps:
1. Delete any prepositional phrase(s).
2. Find the subject (*who* or *what* the sentence is about).
3. Determine the verb: what *is* [*was*] or *happens* [*happened*].
   Often, an interrogative sentence contains a verb phrase.

   verb phrase = helping verb(s) + main verb

Example: interrogative: Has George been to Maine?
             declarative: <u>George</u> <u>has been</u> ~~to Maine~~.

This list of helping verbs will help you to identify a verb phrase.

do	has	may	can	could	is	were
does	have	might	shall	should	am	be
did	had	must	will	would	are	being
					was	been

Directions: Rewrite the sentence, changing it into a statement. Then, cross out any prepositional phrase(s). Underline the subject once and the verb or verb phrase twice.

1. Are we in the last row?

   _____ <u>We</u> <u>are</u> ~~in the last row~~._____

2. May I sit near the door?

   _____ <u>I</u> <u>may sit</u> ~~near the door~~._____

3. Will Toby go to camp?

   _____ <u>Toby</u> <u>will go</u> ~~to camp~~._____

48

Name_____   **PREPOSITIONS**

Date_____

An interrogative sentence asks a question. To determine the subject and verb of an interrogative sentence, first change the sentence into a statement (declarative sentence).

> Example: Is your mother here?
> Your <u>mother</u> <u>is</u> here.

Follow these steps:
1. Delete any prepositional phrase(s).
2. Find the subject (*who* or *what* the sentence is about).
3. Determine the verb: what *is* [*was*] or *happens* [*happened*].
   Often, an interrogative sentence contains a verb phrase.

   verb phrase = helping verb(s) + main verb

> Example: interrogative: Has George been to Maine?
> declarative: <u>George</u> <u>has been</u> ~~to Maine~~.

This list of helping verbs will help you to identify a verb phrase.

do	has	may	can	could	is	were
does	have	might	shall	should	am	be
did	had	must	will	would	are	being
					was	been

🍓🍓🍓🍓🍓🍓🍓🍓🍓🍓🍓🍓🍓🍓🍓🍓🍓🍓🍓🍓🍓🍓🍓🍓🍓🍓🍓🍓🍓🍓🍓🍓🍓🍓

Directions: Rewrite the sentence, changing it into a statement. Then, cross out any prepositional phrase(s). Underline the subject once and the verb or verb phrase twice.

1. Are we in the last row?

   _____

2. May I sit near the door?

   _____

3. Will Toby go to camp?

   _____

49

Name_____

WORKBOOK PAGE 23

Date_____

A. **Preposition List:**
   Directions: List the forty prepositions:

1. about	16. down	31. past
2. above	17. during	32. through
3. across	18. except	33. throughout
4. after	19. for	34. to
5. against	20. from	35. toward
6. along	21. in	36. under
7. around	22. inside	37. until
8. at	23. into	38. up
9. before	24. near	39. with
10. behind	25. of	40. without
11. below	26. off	
12. beneath	27. on	
13. beside	28. out	
14. between	29. outside	
15. by	30. over	

B. **Object of the Preposition:**
   Directions: Cross out any prepositional phrase(s). Label the object of the
                     preposition - O.P.

                         O.P.   O.P.
1. ~~During the winter~~, rabbits nibble grass ~~above the snow~~.

                                   O.P.   O.P.   O.P.
2. Peggy fished ~~across the stream~~ and sat ~~on a small rock for the entire day~~.

50

Name_____   **Preposition Review**

Date_____

A. **Preposition List:**

Directions: List the forty prepositions:

1. _____   16. _____   31. _____

2. _____   17. _____   32. _____

3. _____   18. _____   33. _____

4. _____   19. _____   34. _____

5. _____   20. _____   35. _____

6. _____   21. _____   36. _____

7. _____   22. _____   37. _____

8. _____   23. _____   38. _____

9. _____   24. _____   39. _____

10. _____   25. _____   40. _____

11. _____   26. _____

12. _____   27. _____

13. _____   28. _____

14. _____   29. _____

15. _____   30. _____

B. **Object of the Preposition:**

Directions: Cross out any prepositional phrase(s). Label the object of the
preposition - O.P.

1. During the winter, rabbits nibble grass above the snow.

2. Peggy fished across the stream and sat on a small rock for the entire day.   51

C. **Subject/Verb:**
   Directions: Cross out any prepositional phrase(s).   Underline the subject once
   and the verb twice.

1. A <u>ladybug</u> <u>crawled</u> ~~up his arm~~.

2. <u>They</u> <u>talked</u> ~~about their summer jobs~~.

3. A green <u>vine</u> <u>grows</u> ~~above her window~~.

4. <u>We</u> <u>leaned</u> ~~over the side of the bridge~~.

5. A <u>guide</u> <u>pointed</u> ~~toward a round building~~.

D. **Compound Subjects:**
   Directions: Cross out any prepositional phrase(s).   Underline the subject once
   and the verb twice.

1. <u>Lori</u> and <u>Jeff</u> <u>live</u> ~~by a river~~.

2. <u>Salt</u> and <u>pepper</u> <u>are</u> ~~behind the sugar bowl~~.

3. <u>Peter</u> and his <u>friend</u> <u>rode</u> ~~around the block~~.

4. A <u>guard</u> and a <u>customer</u> <u>chatted</u> ~~outside the jewelry shop~~.

5. The <u>cow</u> and her <u>calf</u> <u>stood</u> ~~beneath a shade tree~~.

E. **Imperative Sentences:**
   Directions: Cross out any prepositional phrase(s).   Underline the subject once
   and the verb twice.
   <u>(You)</u>
1. Please <u>put</u> this ~~into the oven~~.
   <u>(You)</u>
2. <u>Stay</u> ~~off the grass~~.
   <u>(You)</u>
3. <u>Nail</u> this shelf ~~above the mirror~~.
   <u>(You)</u>
4. ~~After dinner~~, please <u>rinse</u> the plates.
   <u>(You)</u>
5. <u>Look</u> ~~in the garage for a tire pump~~.

52

Name_____   **Preposition Review**

Date_____

C. **Subject/Verb:**
    Directions: Cross out any prepositional phrase(s).   Underline the subject once
                and the verb twice.

1. A ladybug crawled up his arm.

2. They talked about their summer jobs.

3. A green vine grows above her window.

4. We leaned over the side of the bridge.

5. A guide pointed toward a round building.

D. **Compound Subjects:**
    Directions: Cross out any prepositional phrase(s).   Underline the subject once
                and the verb twice.

1. Lori and Jeff live by a river.

2. Salt and pepper are behind the sugar bowl.

3. Peter and his friend rode around the block.

4. A guard and a customer chatted outside the jewelry shop.

5. The cow and her calf stood beneath a shade tree.

E. **Imperative Sentences:**
    Directions: Cross out any prepositional phrase(s).   Underline the subject once
                and the verb twice.

1. Please put this into the oven.

2. Stay off the grass.

3. Nail this shelf above the mirror.

4. After dinner, please rinse the plates.

5. Look in the garage for a tire pump.

F. **Compound Objects of the Prepositions:**
    Directions: Cross out any prepositional phrase(s).   Underline the subject once
    and the verb twice.

1. <u>Warren</u> <u>has</u> a snack ~~of cookies and milk~~ each afternoon.

2. <u>We</u> <u>went</u> ~~to the amusement park with Frances, Susan, and Katie.~~

3. A birthday <u>card</u> ~~from her aunt and uncle~~ <u>was</u> ~~on the kitchen counter.~~

4. That <u>flower</u> <u>blooms</u> only ~~in the morning and evening.~~

5. A new <u>deli</u> <u>serves</u> cream cheese ~~on bagels or rye toast.~~

G. **Compound Verbs:**
    Directions: Cross out any prepositional phrase(s).   Underline the subject once
    and the verb twice.

1. A <u>shopper</u> <u>rushed</u> ~~toward the door~~ but suddenly <u>stopped</u>.

2. All <u>desserts</u> ~~except the pie~~ <u>are</u> sugarless and <u>taste</u> wonderful.

3. <u>Children</u> <u>played</u> volleyball and <u>ran</u> ~~around the playground during recess.~~

4. Her <u>aunt</u> <u>lives</u> ~~near me~~ and <u>jogs</u> ~~by my house~~ daily.

5. <u>They</u> <u>went</u> ~~outside the roller-skating rink~~ and <u>talked</u> ~~for an hour.~~

H. **Verb Phrases:**
    Directions: Cross out any prepositional phrase(s).   Underline the subject once
    and the verb phrase twice.

1. <u>I</u> <u>might have discovered</u> a new path ~~to the cave~~.

2. <u>We</u> <u>had waited</u> ~~for the bus~~ ~~over an hour.~~

3. The <u>coach</u> <u>had given</u> her tips ~~about sliding~~.

4. <u>Senator Link</u> <u>is walking</u> ~~down the aisle with his daughter.~~

5. ~~By sundown~~, <u>we</u> <u>will be packing</u> the car ~~for our trip.~~

54

F. **Compound Objects of the Prepositions:**
   Directions: Cross out any prepositional phrase(s).   Underline the subject once
   and the verb twice.

1. Warren has a snack of cookies and milk each afternoon.

2. We went to the amusement park with Frances, Susan, and Katie.

3. A birthday card from her aunt and uncle was on the kitchen counter.

4. That flower blooms only in the morning and evening.

5. A new deli serves cream cheese on bagels or rye toast.

G. **Compound Verbs:**
   Directions: Cross out any prepositional phrase(s).   Underline the subject once
   and the verb twice.

1. A shopper rushed toward the door but suddenly stopped.

2. All desserts except the pie are sugarless and taste wonderful.

3. Children played volleyball and ran around the playground during recess.

4. Her aunt lives near me and jogs by my house daily.

5. They went outside the roller-skating rink and talked for an hour.

H. **Verb Phrases:**
   Directions: Cross out any prepositional phrase(s).   Underline the subject once
   and the verb phrase twice.

1. I might have discovered a new path to the cave.

2. We had waited for the bus over an hour.

3. The coach had given her tips about sliding.

4. Senator Link is walking down the aisle with his daughter.

5. By sundown, we will be packing the car for our trip.   55

I. **Verb Phrases and <u>Not</u>:**

   Directions: Cross out any prepositional phrase(s).   Underline the subject once
   and the verb phrase twice.   Be sure to box *not*.

1. <u>I</u> shall **not** <u>speak</u> ~~with you about your behavior~~ again.

2. <u>He</u> <u>has</u>**n't** <u>applied</u> ~~for a college scholarship~~.

3. The <u>postman</u> <u>can</u>**not** <u>deliver</u> mail ~~in the evening~~.

4. <u>Cynthia</u> <u>would</u> **not** <u>have forgotten</u> (to brush) her teeth.

5. <u>They</u> <u>couldn</u>**'t** <u>travel</u> ~~through Wales on their tour of Great Britain~~.

J. **Interrogative Sentences:**

   Directions: Cross out any prepositional phrase(s).   Underline the subject once
   and the verb phrase twice.

1. <u>Will</u> <u>you</u> <u>walk</u> ~~along the road with us~~?

2. <u>Do</u> the <u>Andersons</u> <u>go</u> ~~to church~~ every Sunday?

3. <u>Are</u> <u>you</u> <u>using</u> the computer ~~from noon until two o'clock~~?

4. <u>Did</u> <u>Tina</u> <u>date</u> ~~during her sophomore year of college~~?

5. <u>Has</u> the <u>janitor</u> <u>fixed</u> the door ~~in the women's bathroom~~?

K. **Prepositions:**

   Directions: Cross out any prepositional phrase(s).   Underline the subject once
   and the verb phrase twice.

1. <u>One</u> ~~of the gorillas~~ <u>held</u> her baby ~~under her arm~~.

2. <u>Jody</u> <u>has</u>**n't** <u>been hired</u> ~~by the water company~~ yet.

3. ~~At the meeting~~, the <u>women</u> <u>spoke</u> ~~about their projects~~ and <u>planned</u> a fashion show.

4. ~~During June, July, or August~~, <u>they</u> <u>go</u> ~~to the shore~~ (to relax).

5. <u>Do</u> Janet's <u>dad</u> and her <u>grandfather</u> <u>fish</u> ~~in a trout stream near Caledonia Park~~?

56

Date_____

I. **Verb Phrases and <u>Not</u>:**
    Directions: Cross out any prepositional phrase(s).   Underline the subject once
                and the verb phrase twice. Be sure to box *not*.

1. I shall not speak with you about your behavior again.

2. He hasn't applied for a college scholarship.

3. The postman cannot deliver mail in the evening.

4. Cynthia would not have forgotten to brush her teeth.

5. They couldn't travel through Wales on their tour of Great Britain.

J. **Interrogative Sentences:**
    Directions: Cross out any prepositional phrase(s).   Underline the subject once
                and the verb/verb phrase twice.

1. Will you walk along the road with us?

2. Do the Andersons go to church every Sunday?

3. Are you using the computer from noon until two o'clock?

4. Did Tina date during her sophomore year of college?

5. Has the janitor fixed the door in the women's bathroom?

K. **Prepositions:**
    Directions: Cross out any prepositional phrase(s).   Underline the subject once
                and the verb/verb phrase twice.

1. One of the gorillas held her baby under her arm.

2. Jody hasn't been hired by the water company yet.

3. At the meeting, the women spoke about their projects and planned a fashion show.

4. During June, July, or August, they go to the shore to relax.

5. Do Janet's dad and her grandfather fish in a trout stream near Caledonia Park?

Name_____   **Preposition Test**

Date_____

Total points = 53! This number was determined by counting subject as one point, verb as one point, and each prepositional phrase as one point. If students delete an infinitive as a prepositional phrase, subtract one point. If, in a command, students do not give (You) as a subject, take away a point. However, do not count another point off if they underline another word as the subject.

Directions: Cross out any prepositional phrase(s).   Underline the subject once and the verb twice.

1.   The temperature is ~~below zero~~.

2.   An ice cube rolled ~~across the floor~~.

3.   A gray squirrel scurried ~~up a tree~~.

4.   His glasses are ~~under the sofa~~.

5.   ~~After the baseball game~~, the team ate ~~at a pizza parlor~~.

6.   ~~During the storm~~, rain beat ~~against our windows~~.

7.   A policeman and detective searched ~~for a clue~~.

8.   A duck ~~with her little ducklings~~ swam ~~past the swimmers~~.

9.   The student wrote his name ~~on his book and notebook~~.

10.   Two plumbers went ~~into the cellar~~ (to fix) some pipes.

11.   They washed clothes ~~in the morning~~ and ironed ~~before dinner~~.

12.   Everyone ~~except Clark~~ sledded ~~without boots~~.

13.   ~~Throughout April and May~~, many people sit ~~by the old fountain~~.

14.   (You) Plant these flowers ~~along the sidewalk~~ ~~inside the back gate~~.

15.   A book ~~about hamsters~~ was a gift ~~from Jack and his brother~~.

58

Directions: Cross out any prepositional phrase(s).   Underline the subject once and
the verb twice.

1.   The temperature is below zero.

2.   An ice cube rolled across the floor.

3.   A gray squirrel scurried up a tree.

4.   His glasses are under the sofa.

5.   After the baseball game, the team ate at a pizza parlor.

6.   During the storm, rain beat against our windows.

7.   A policeman and detective searched for a clue.

8.   A duck with her little ducklings swam past the swimmers.

9.   The student wrote his name on his book and notebook.

10.   Two plumbers went into the cellar to fix some pipes.

11.   They washed clothes in the morning and ironed before dinner.

12.   Everyone except Clark sledded without boots.

13.   Throughout April and May, many people sit by the old fountain.

14.   Plant these flowers along the sidewalk inside the back gate.

15.   A book about hamsters was a gift from Jack and his brother.

TO THE TEACHER:

<u>**Easy Grammar: Grades 4 and 5**</u> does not include the teaching of a word serving in some cases as a preposition and in other cases as an adverb. (Students are given a cursory introduction to this concept in the adverb unit.)

Example: The child fell **down**.

Here, *down* is an adverb.

The child fell **down** two steps.

Here, *down* is a preposition starting the prepositional phrase, *down two steps*.

At fourth grade level, I do not feel that mastery of this concept is necessary. Therefore, the basic idea is introduced. A more complete understanding of the concept is included in <u>Easy Grammar: Level 1</u>, <u>Easy Grammar</u>,* and <u>Easy Grammar *Plus*</u>.

Please peruse the **scope and seqence** on the back of this text.

*****Easy Grammar Plus** is identical to *Easy Grammar* except the plus version has added reviews, cumulative reviews, tests, and cumulative tests.**

60

TO THE TEACHER: <u>Please read each lesson contained on this page</u>. Students will be given a discussion of the individual concept at the top of each worksheet. However, ideally, you will teach the concept before proceeding to the worksheet discussion.

Page 63: **Concept:** **Some sentences will contain a direct object.**

This concept is actually being introduced here. Although students will be reintroduced to it in the verb unit, it has been placed here to give students even more success. (We truly want them to say, "English is easy; I can do this!")

When teaching this lesson, I recommend that you actually "do" an action and have students walk through the process. For example, drop a quarter on the floor. Say, "I dropped a quarter." What is the object that I dropped? Students will respond--quarter. Explain that's called a direct object. It receives the action of the verb. Quarter is the object I dropped. Therefore, quarter is called a direct object.

Then, perform another action. For example, you may wish to fly a paper airplane. You may say, "I am flying a paper airplane." What's the object that I am flying? Students will respond that the object or direct object is airplane.

Note: You may wish to have students perform actions that include direct objects. However, keep in mind that this activity can easily produce chaos or may include hitting ("I hit Jim."). Use discretion!

Date_____

Direct Objects: **Direct objects receive the action of the verb.**

Example: Kerry hit a ball.

What is the **object** Kerry hit?   Answer: ball
Ball is the direct object.

Sometimes, there will be a compound direct object.

Example: The clerk sold shoes and sandals.

What are the **objects** the clerk sold?   Answer: shoes and sandals

To find a direct object:

1.   Determine the subject of the sentence.

2.   Find the verb. Ask what the subject is doing or did. **You will always have a verb that shows action in a sentence containing a direct object.**

3.   Determine what object is being affected by the verb. Label the direct object- D.O.

🍓🍓🍓🍓🍓🍓🍓🍓🍓🍓🍓🍓🍓🍓🍓🍓🍓🍓🍓🍓🍓🍓🍓🍓🍓🍓🍓🍓🍓🍓🍓🍓🍓🍓🍓🍓🍓

Directions: Cross out any prepositional phrase(s).   Underline the subject once and
            the verb/verb phrase twice.   Label the direct object - D.O.

　　　　　　　　　　　　　D.O.
1.   A <u>maid</u> ~~at the hotel~~ <u>shook</u> the rug.

　　　　　　　　　　D.O.
2.   <u>Gordon</u> <u>placed</u> a mat ~~under the dog~~.

　　　　　　　　　　　D.O.
3.   <u>They</u> <u>read</u> a book ~~during the afternoon~~.

　　　　　　　　　　D.O.
4.   <u>Harry</u> <u>flies</u> kites ~~on windy days~~.

　　　　　　　　　　　D.O.
5.   Our <u>brother</u> <u>cooked</u> dinner ~~for everyone~~.

　　　　　　　　　　D.O.
6.   A <u>bellman</u> <u>carried</u> our suitcases ~~to our room~~.

　　　　　　　　　D.O.　　　D.O.
7.   <u>Jill</u> <u>feeds</u> her dog and cat ~~before breakfast~~.

　　　　　　　　　　D.O.　　　　　　　　D.O.
8.   <u>I</u> <u>bought</u> a straw hat and a flowered dress today.

Direct Objects: **Direct objects receive the action of the verb.**

Example: Kerry hit a ball.

What is the **object** Kerry hit?   Answer: ball
Ball is the direct object.

Sometimes, there will be a compound direct object.

Example: The clerk sold shoes and sandals.

What are the **objects** the clerk sold?   Answer: shoes and sandals

To find a direct object:

1.   Determine the subject of the sentence.

2.   Find the verb. Ask what the subject is doing or did. **You will always have a verb that shows action in a sentence containing a direct object.**

3.   Determine what object is being affected by the verb. Label the direct object- D.O.

Directions: Cross out any prepositional phrase(s).   Underline the subject once and the verb/verb phrase twice.   Label the direct object - D.O.

1.   A maid at the hotel shook the rug.

2.   Gordon placed a mat under the dog.

3.   They read a book during the afternoon.

4.   Harry flies kites on windy days.

5.   Our brother cooked dinner for everyone.

6.   A bellman carried our suitcases to our room.

7.   Jill feeds her dog and cat before breakfast.

8.   I bought a straw hat and a flowered dress today.   63

A. Directions: Cross out any prepositional phrase(s).   Underline the subject once
                 and the verb/verb phrase twice.   Label any direct object - D.O.

               D.O.
1. We ate candy.

                        D.O.
2. Aunt Freda threw the ball ~~to me~~.

                           D.O.
3. Jason and Penny had caught three fish ~~at the lake~~.

                        D.O.
4. ~~For Christmas~~, Kent received two shirts.

                    D.O.
5. ~~At the beach~~, she wrote her name ~~in the sand~~.

    (You)   **D.O.**
6. Give this vase ~~of flowers to your mother~~.

                         D.O.
7. ~~During the rodeo~~, a cowboy roped a steer.

                  D.O.
8. A monkey grabbed the banana ~~from his friend~~.

                D.O.
9. I answered the telephone ~~on the first ring~~.

B. Directions: Cross out any prepositional phrase(s).   Underline the subject once
                 and the verb/verb phrase twice.   Label any direct object(s) - D.O.

Remember: There may be two direct objects in a sentence.
                   D.O.   **D.O.**
      I ate an ice cream cone and drank juice.

This is called a compound direct object.
                   D.O.   **D.O.**
      The mechanic fixed the tire and the fender.

             D.O.   **D.O.**
1. His neighbor has made a quilt and a pillow ~~for her grandson~~.

             D.O.   **D.O.**
2. The lady served coffee and cake ~~to her guests~~.

             D.O.   **D.O.**
3. She skinned her knees and her left hand.

             D.O.   **D.O.**
4. The elderly man carried an umbrella and several packages.

             D.O.   **D.O.**
5. We visited a historic house and a museum ~~in Salem~~.

64

Name_____

Date_____

A. **Directions:** Cross out any prepositional phrase(s).   Underline the subject once and the verb/verb phrase twice.   Label any direct object - D.O.

1. We ate candy.

2. Aunt Freda threw the ball to me.

3. Jason and Penny had caught three fish at the lake.

4. For Christmas, Kent received two shirts.

5. At the beach, she wrote her name in the sand.

6. Give this vase of flowers to your mother.

7. During the rodeo, a cowboy roped a steer.

8. A monkey grabbed the banana from his friend.

9. I answered the telephone on the first ring.

B. **Directions:** Cross out any prepositional phrase(s).   Underline the subject once and the verb/verb phrase twice.   Label any direct object(s) - D.O.

Remember: There may be two direct objects in a sentence.
                                 D.O.   **D.O.**
I ate an ice cream cone and drank juice.
                This is called a compound direct object.
                                 D.O.   **D.O**.
The mechanic fixed the tire and the fender.

1. His neighbor has made a quilt and a pillow for her grandson.

2. The lady served coffee and cake to her guests.

3. She skinned her knees and her left hand.

4. The elderly man carried an umbrella and several packages.

5. We visited a historic house and a museum in Salem.   65

TO THE TEACHER:

I shall try to offer helpful hints throughout this text. Having taught many years, I have been influenced by other teachers and have developed techniques and strategies of my own. When I offer suggestions or recommendations, I am not coming from an authoritarian perspective. I am simply sharing ideas that have worked for me. Glean what is applicable to your style of teaching and your students' needs. Try some of the ideas. Don't be discouraged if during the first try, your students don't respond well. Even if the idea flops, you may wish to try the strategy the ensuing school year. I've had ideas work beautifully one year, only to have them fail the following school year. I've also had the reverse hold true. It seems that each class has a definitive personality and responds differently.

I give very little grammar homework. I want my students to complete worksheets in class so that I can answer questions and offer help!!!

AN IDEA FOR COMPLETING WORKSHEETS:

After students have completed a worksheet individually, I ask them to **stand**. As other students who are finished stand, I pair them. Their task is to compare answers and discuss if they disagree. Their first point of reference is information provided in the text. If they still disagree, they may discuss it with me. After everyone has paired, we discuss answers orally.

a. I try to pair students who are strong in concepts with those who are weak. However, sometimes I allow them to choose their own partner.

b. My classroom becomes somewhat noisy. However, my students are trained to use a "quiet" voice for such activities.

c. Some students will finish earlier than others. This is where training students to always have a free-reading book is of extreme importance. Students read until others are finished. (This may sound rather utopian, but I've done this successfully every year. Students can meet your expectations and be happy students!)

d. Students do need to be trained how to participate in this activity. However, they love to do it. It's another strategy for fun, active learning.

66

VERBS

TO THE TEACHER: Read this information before teaching the ensuing pages.

Teach the entire verb unit slowly and thoroughly.

Pages 69:   **Concept:**   **Verbs can show action or state a fact.**

Page 69 states this concept and shows the conjugation of *to be*. Ascertain that students comprehend how *to be* is used in our language.

Page 71 wants students to determine if the verb shows action. Don't confuse them with too much information now. We simply want students to decide if the verb shows action.

Page 73:   **Concept:**   **Determining if some words are part of the verb.**

This page explains how to determine if a word such as *happy* is part of the verb. Teach students to make such a word an infinitive (*to happy*)and say it with *today*, *yesterday*, and *tomorrow*. Today I happy. Yesterday I happied. Tomorrow I shall happy. You are not only informally introducing students to tenses, but also you are showing them that *happy* is not a verb and, thus, will not be part of a verb phrase.

Also, teach students that words ending in ly are usually adverbs. Occasionally, they are adjectives. Do not include a word ending in ly as part of a verb phrase.

Example: That <u>dog is</u> friendly.
                    Friendly is not part of the verb.

PAGE 69 = WORKBOOK PAGE 29

Verbs

The verb of a sentence expresses an action or simply states a fact.

Examples:	Jenny <u>jumped</u> onto a rubber raft.	(action)
	A worker <u>dug</u> a hole for the post.	(action)
	Their father <u>is</u> in the army.	(fact)
	The winners <u>were</u> Cindy and Rick.	(fact)

Verbs that simply state a fact are often called **state of being verbs.**

You need to memorize and learn the conjugation of *to be*:

is, am, are, was, were, be, being, been

<u>Present Tense:</u>
Singular*:	is	(A sailor <u>is</u> the winner.)
	am	(<u>I am</u> sleepy.)
Plural**:	are	(Several cows <u>are</u> near a stream.)

<u>Past Tense:</u>
Singular:	was	(A <u>sailor was</u> the winner.)
Plural:	were	(Several <u>cows were</u> near a stream.)

*Singular means one. **Plural means more than one.

Directions: In the space provided, write <u>Yes</u> if the boldfaced verb shows action. Write
<u>No</u> if the boldfaced verb does not show action.

Example: ____No____   He **<u>appears</u>** to be very happy.

1. ____Yes____   Pam **<u>hit</u>** the ball hard.

2. ____Yes____   A waiter **<u>carried</u>** a large tray on his shoulder.

3. ____Yes____   Marcy's dog **<u>licks</u>** my hand.

4. ____No____   James **<u>is</u>** a good athlete.

5. ____Yes____   Before breakfast, Peter **<u>wipes</u>** all of the counter tops.

6. ____No____   Mr. Potter **<u>became</u>** a dentist.

7. ____Yes____   Their gerbil constantly **<u>runs</u>** around in its cage.

8. ____No____   The girl **<u>seems</u>** sad and lonely.

9. ____Yes____   After Pioneer Days, the mayor **<u>shaved</u>** his beard.

10. ____Yes____   The policewoman **<u>motioned</u>** for us to stop.

11. ____No____   Her friend **<u>was</u>** a contestant in a beauty contest.

12. ____Yes____   A jackrabbit **<u>jumped</u>** beside the road.

13. ____Yes____   He **<u>sings</u>** in the shower.

14. ____No____   I **<u>am</u>** rather puzzled by your remark.

15. ____Yes____   I **<u>shook</u>** hands with Governor Jacobs.

Name_____

Date_____

Directions: In the space provided, write <u>Yes</u> if the boldfaced verb shows action. Write <u>No</u> if the boldfaced verb does not show action.

Example: ____No____ He **appears** to be very happy.

1. _____ Pam **hit** the ball hard.

2. _____ A waiter **carried** a large tray on his shoulder.

3. _____ Marcy's dog **licks** my hand.

4. _____ James **is** a good athlete.

5. _____ Before breakfast, Peter **wipes** all of the counter tops.

6. _____ Mr. Potter **became** a dentist.

7. _____ Their gerbil constantly **runs** around in its cage.

8. _____ The girl **seems** sad and lonely.

9. _____ After Pioneer Days, the mayor **shaved** his beard.

10. _____ The policewoman **motioned** for us to stop.

11. _____ Her friend **was** a contestant in a beauty contest.

12. _____ A jackrabbit **jumped** beside the road.

13. _____ He **sings** in the shower.

14. _____ I **am** rather puzzled by your remark.

15. _____ I **shook** hands with Governor Jacobs.

WORKBOOK PAGE 31
Sometimes, it is hard to decide if a word is part of a verb (verb phrase).

Example: Bud is glad to be an actor.

In this sentence, is *glad* part of the verb?

If you are unsure, try placing *to* before the word: <u>to glad</u>.   This makes it an infinitive.   Then, use the word in three short sentences:

<u>Today, I</u> glad.
<u>Yesterday, I</u> gladded.
<u>Tomorrow, I shall</u> glad.

This doesn't make sense. You can't use *glad* as a verb.   Therefore, you will not underline *glad* as part of the verb.

Example: <u>Bud is</u> glad (to be) an actor.

Words ending in <u>ly</u> are usually adverbs.   Occasionally, they are adjectives.   Do not include a word ending in <u>ly</u> as part of a verb.

Example: She sleeps soundly throughout the night.

Soundly is not part of the verb.

<u>She sleeps</u> soundly ~~throughout the night~~.

Directions: Cross out any prepositional phrases.   Underline the subject once and the verb/verb phrase twice.

1. <u>Kelly is</u> good ~~for her babysitter~~.

2. The <u>builder talked</u> quietly ~~with the owner~~.

3. <u>Mrs. Thomas became</u> upset ~~about her phone bill~~.

4. ~~For a beginner~~, <u>you play</u> tennis very well.

5. ~~During the afternoon~~, the <u>children played</u> happily ~~in the sandbox~~.

72

Sometimes, it is hard to decide if a word is part of a verb (verb phrase).

Example: Bud is glad to be an actor.

In this sentence, is *glad* part of the verb?

If you are unsure, try placing *to* before the word: <u>to glad</u>.   This makes it an infinitive.   Then, use the word in three short sentences:

<u>Today, I</u> glad.
<u>Yesterday, I</u> gladded.
<u>Tomorrow, I shall</u> glad.

This doesn't make sense. You can't use *glad* as a verb.   Therefore, you will not underline *glad* as part of the verb.

Example: <u>Bud is</u> glad (to be) an actor.

🍓 🍓

Words ending in <u>ly</u> are usually adverbs.   Occasionally, they are adjectives.   Do not include a word ending in <u>ly</u> as part of a verb.

Example: She sleeps soundly throughout the night.

Soundly is not part of the verb.

<u>She sleeps</u> soundly ~~throughout the night~~.

🍓🍓🍓🍓🍓🍓🍓🍓🍓🍓🍓🍓🍓🍓🍓🍓🍓🍓🍓🍓🍓🍓🍓🍓🍓🍓🍓🍓🍓🍓🍓🍓🍓

Directions: Cross out any prepositional phrases.   Underline the subject once and the verb/verb phrase twice.

1.   Kelly is good for her babysitter.

2.   The builder talked quietly with the owner.

3.   Mrs. Thomas became upset about her phone bill.

4.   For a beginner, you play tennis very well.

5.   During the afternoon, the children played happily in the sandbox.   73

TO THE TEACHER: <u>Please read each lesson contained on these pages</u>. Students will be given a discussion of the individual concept at the top of each worksheet. However, ideally, you will teach the concept before proceeding to each worksheet discussion.

Page 77: **Concept:** **Contractions:** Students need to understand that *to contract* means to get smaller. A contraction in grammar usually refers to the combining of two words and omitting a letter or letters. Page 79 deals with contractions that are formed by combining a pronoun and a verb.

Be sure that students understand that the apostrophe needs to be placed exactly where a letter or letters have been omitted. I also advise that you require students to break the word when inserting an apostrophe.

Page 81: **Concept:** **Contractions:** This page teaches contractions that are formed by combining a verb + *not* or by shortening *cannot*.

Page 83: **Concept:** **Contractions and Homonyms:** This page explains the use of *you're/your, it's/its*, and *they're/their/there*.

Teach students that *you're* is a contraction meaning *you are*. *Your* is a possessive; it will own something: (your bike). If students want a quick way to check their choice, have them say the "you're" form as <u>you are</u> in the sentence.

Examples: I want to know if you're going.
I want to know if **you are** going.   (correct)

74

Is your tire flat?

(Many students can answer <u>your what</u> and connect it to tire: your tire.   However, use this check:

Is **you are** tire flat?   Students readily "hear" that this is incorrect and will use the possessive pronoun, *your*.

Teach <u>it's</u> and <u>its</u> in the same manner. <u>It's</u> is a contraction meaning it is. <u>Its</u> is a possessive pronoun.

Examples: It's raining.
It is raining.   (correct)

The bird builds its nest of twigs.
The bird builds **it is** nest of twigs.   (incorrect)

Teaching *they're, their,* and *there* is more difficult.   Teach <u>they're</u> and <u>their</u> in the same way.   <u>They're</u> is a contraction for **they are**.   <u>Their</u> is a possessive pronoun.

Examples: They're fun to know.
They are fun to know.   (correct)

Their dad is funny.
They are dad is funny.   (incorrect)

However, teach students that <u>there</u> is an adverb (technically telling *where*).

Examples: I want to go there.   (Where? there)

There are five puppies in the litter.

Take this sentence apart; first, delete the prepositional phrase, find the subject, and determine the verb.

There <u>are</u> five <u>puppies</u> ~~in the litter~~.   (*There* won't be a subject.)

If we turn the sentence around, it will read: Five puppies are there.   Where? Now, we can answer: there.

75

CONTRACTIONS

"To contract" means to draw together or make smaller.   In forming contractions, we draw together two words to make a shorter word.   We insert an **apostrophe** where we have left out a letter or letters.

Suggestions:

1. Make sure that your apostrophe (**'**) is curved.   Otherwise, it may look like a chicken scratch.

2. Place an apostrophe **exactly** where the letter or letters are missing.

CONTRACTION	=	WORD	+	VERB	CONTRACTION	=	VERB	+	WORD
I'm	=	I	+	am	don't	=	do	+	not
I've	=	I	+	have	doesn't	=	does	+	not
I'd	=	I	+	would	didn't	=	did	+	not
I'll	=	I	+	shall (will)*	hasn't	=	has	+	not
you'll	=	you	+	will	hadn't	=	had	+	not
they'll	=	they	+	will	haven't	=	have	+	not
we'll	=	we	+	will	isn't	=	is	+	not
he's	=	he	+	is	aren't	=	are	+	not
he'd	=	he	+	would	wasn't	=	was	+	not
she's	=	she	+	is	weren't	=	were	+	not
that's	=	that	+	is	mustn't	=	must	+	not
they've	=	they	+	have	mightn't	=	might	+	not
it's	=	it	+	is	shouldn't	=	should	+	not
who's	=	who	+	is	couldn't	=	could	+	not
what's	=	what	+	is	wouldn't	=	would	+	not
where's	=	where	+	is	won't	=	will	+	not
here's	=	here	+	is	can't	=	can	+	not
there's	=	there	+	is	(Can + not is written *cannot*.)				

*Technically, *I shall* is correct.

Directions: Write the contraction in the space provided.

1. ___we're_____   Ask if **we are** allowed to water-ski with you.

2. ___I'd_____   **I would** rather stay here.

3. ___he's_____   I wonder if **he is** the first contestant.

4. ___I'm_____   He said, "**I am** very happy to meet you."

5. ___They're_____   **They are** headed for the Grand Canyon.

6. ___she's_____   If **she is** ready, let's go.

7. ___You're_____   **You are** standing on my foot.

8. ___I'll_____   **I shall** answer his letter soon.

9. ___What's_____   Jane asked, "**What is** your new address?"

10. ___That's_____   **That is** amazing!

11. ___They've_____   **They have** no idea that he plans to visit them.

12. ___you'll_____   I think that **you will** enjoy this show.

13. ___who's_____   Do you know **who is** pitching?

14. ___Here's_____   **Here is** the magazine that you wanted, Melody.

15. ___it's_____   Are you aware that **it is** midnight?

Name_____

Date_____

Directions: Write the contraction in the space provided.

1. _____ Ask if **we are** allowed to water-ski with you.

2. _____ **I would** rather stay here.

3. _____ I wonder if **he is** the first contestant.

4. _____ He said, "**I am** very happy to meet you."

5. _____ **They are** headed for the Grand Canyon.

6. _____ If **she is** ready, let's go.

7. _____ **You are** standing on my foot.

8. _____ **I shall** answer his letter soon.

9. _____ Jane asked, "**What is** your new address?"

10. _____ **That is** amazing!

11. _____ **They have** no idea that he plans to visit them.

12. _____ I think that **you will** enjoy this show.

13. _____ Do you know **who is** pitching?

14. _____ **Here is** the magazine that you wanted, Melody.

15. _____ Are you aware that **it is** midnight?

Directions: Write the contraction in the space provided.

1. _____hadn't_____   Lemon **had not** been added to the iced tea.

2. _____isn't_____   This silverware **is not** clean.

3. _____wouldn't_____   The porter **would not** take a tip.

4. _____haven't_____   Those golfers **have not** played well lately.

5. _____Don't_____   **Do not** send money in the mail.

6. _____weren't_____   The minister and his wife **were not** there.

7. _____didn't_____   General Grant **did not** serve at the Battle of Gettysburg.

8. _____won't_____   His grandmother **will not** fly on an airplane.

9. _____can't_____   I **cannot** read that signature.

10. _____aren't_____   You **are not** supposed to take your brother's toys.

11. _____couldn't_____   The teacher **could not** tell the twins apart.

12. _____hasn't_____   He **has not** studied about the first permanent English colony in America.

13. _____mustn't_____   You **must not** talk during the symphony.

14. _____shouldn't_____   We **should not** leave before noon.

15. _____wasn't_____   Mark Twain **was not** the writer's real name.

Directions: Write the contraction in the space provided.

1. _____ Lemon **had not** been added to the iced tea.

2. _____ This silverware **is not** clean.

3. _____ The porter **would not** take a tip.

4. _____ Those golfers **have not** played well lately.

5. _____ **Do not** send money in the mail.

6. _____ The minister and his wife **were not** there.

7. _____ General Grant **did not** serve at the Battle of Gettysburg.

8. _____ His grandmother **will not** fly on an airplane.

9. _____ I **cannot** read that signature.

10. _____ You **are not** supposed to take your brother's toys.

11. _____ The teacher **could not** tell the twins apart.

12. _____ He **has not** studied about the first permanent English colony in America.

13. _____ You **must not** talk during the symphony.

14. _____ We **should not** leave before noon.

15. _____ Mark Twain **was not** the writer's real name.

PAGE 83 = WORKBOOK PAGE 35

You're/Your
It's/Its
They're/Their/There

A. **You're** is a contraction meaning *you are*. **Your** is a possessive pronoun; it will answer: your (what?).   A quick way to check your choice is to say <u>you are</u> in the sentence.

    Examples: You're nice.
                     You are nice.   (correct)

                       Your room is messy.
                       Your what?   your room
                       You are room is messy.   (Incorrect)

B. **It's** is a contraction meaning it is.   **Its** is a possessive pronoun; it will answer : your (what?).

    Examples: It's time to go.
                     It is time to go.   (correct)

                       The dog chased **its** tail.
                       Its what?   its tail
                       The dog chased it is tail.   (incorrect)

C. **They're** is a contraction meaning they are. **Their** is a possessive pronoun; it will answer their (what?).

    Examples: They're picking cherries.
                     They are picking cherries   (correct)

                       Their old car is rusty.
                       Their what?   old car
                       They are old car is rusty.   (incorrect)

There is an adverb (technically telling *where*).

    Examples: I want to go there.   (Where? there)

                     There are five girls in that class.
                     There <u>are</u> five <u>girls</u> ~~in that class~~.
                     Five <u>girls</u> <u>are</u> there.   (Where?   there)   83

Name_____
WORKBOOK PAGE 36
Date_____

VERBS
You're/Your
It's/Its
They're/Their/There

Directions: Circle the correct answer.
Answers are in boldfaced print.

1. (**Your**, You're) button is open.

2. (They're, **Their**, There) uncle is a cook.

3. (**You're**, Your) funny!

4. A bird flapped (it's, **its**) wings and flew off.

5. (They're, Their, **There**) are many trout in that stream.

6. Do you know that (**it's**, its) raining?

7. (**They're**, Their, There) in a hurry.

8. (You're, **Your**) opinion about the crime may be correct.

9. The club received an award for (it's, **its**) help in the community.

10. The snake raised (it's, **its**) head and slithered away.

11. (**You're**, Your) the first person to ask that question.

12. Please ask Mrs. Dunn if she thinks (**it's**, its) going to rain.

13. (They're, **Their**, There) ideas were not based on fact.

14. (They're, Their, **There**) are many former Easterners living in Arizona.

15. Several children threw (they're, **their**, there) candy wrappers on the table.

16. The team won (it's, **its**) first game.

17. If (**you're**, your) finished with (you're, **your**) chores, we can play chess.

18. The United States is known for (it's, **its**) kindness toward other nations.

19. The Johnsons want (they're, **their**, there) daughter to go to college.

20. (**They're**, Their, There) moving to another state.

Name_____

Date_____

Directions: Circle the correct answer.

1.   (Your, You're) button is open.

2.   (They're, Their, There) uncle is a cook.

3.   (You're, Your) funny!

4.   A bird flapped (it's, its) wings and flew off.

5.   (They're, Their, There) are many trout in that stream.

6.   Do you know that (it's, its) raining?

7.   (They're, Their, There) in a hurry.

8.   (You're, Your) opinion about the crime may be correct.

9.   The club received an award for (it's, its) help in the community.

10.   The snake raised (it's, its) head and slithered away.

11.   (You're, Your) the first person to ask that question.

12.   Please ask Mrs. Dunn if she thinks (it's, its) going to rain.

13.   (They're, Their, There) ideas were not based on fact.

14.   (They're, Their, There) are many former Easterners living in Arizona.

15.   Several children threw (they're, their, there) candy wrappers on the table.

16.   The team won (it's, its) first game.

17.   If (you're, your) finished with (you're, your) chores, we can play chess.

18.   The United States is known for (it's, its) kindness toward other nations.

19.   The Johnsons want (they're, their, there) daughter to go to college.

20.   (They're, Their, There) moving to another state.

<u>Verbs</u>

The student must **memorize** these twenty-three helping verbs and list them.   I have placed them in groups for ease of learning.   We say them aloud together.   When we arrive at the "could" column, I say, "Can" and motion for the response of *could*; I continue with *shall* and show that it relates to *should*.   Students quickly perceive that *will* relates to *would*.   This is just one more <u>mnemonic</u> device for learning the list.

Be sure that students have complete mastery of these auxiliary (helping) verbs.   We practice saying the list and have a "study with a buddy" time.   Remember that <u>mastery is our goal</u>.   Use methods with which you are comfortable to insure the learning of this list. (This list has been placed on the next page for student use.)

do	has	may	can	could	is	were
does	have	might	shall	should	am	be
did	had	must	will	would	are	being
					was	been

Students have already been introduced to the concept of *verb phrase*.   Now, we need to ascertain that students gain mastery of this concept.   This information has been duplicated on the next page so that students have a handy reference.

A verb phrase is composed of one or more helping verbs plus a main verb. The main verb is the last part of a verb phrase.

> Examples: <u>I must erase</u> my error.
> The <u>clerk should have given</u> me a larger bag.

<u>verb phrase</u>	=	<u>helping verb(s)</u>	+	<u>main verb</u>
must erase	=	must	+	erase
should have given	=	should have	+	given

86

Helping (Auxiliary) Verbs:

do	has	may	can	could	is	were
does	have	might	shall	should	am	be
did	had	must	will	would	are	being
					was	been

♓♓♓♓♓♓♓♓♓♓♓♓♓♓♓♓♓♓♓♓♓♓♓♓♓♓♓♓♓♓♓♓♓♓♓♓

Verb Phrase:

A verb phrase is composed of one or more helping verbs plus a main verb. The main verb is the last part of a verb phrase.

Examples: I <u>must erase</u> my error.
The <u>clerk</u> <u>should have given</u> me a larger bag.

<u>verb phrase</u>	=	<u>helping verb(s)</u>	+	<u>main verb</u>
must erase	=	must	+	erase
should have given	=	should have	+	given

Remember: *Not* is an adverb.   Box *not*; don't underline *not* as part of a verb phrase.

Changing an **interrogative sentence** to a declarative sentence may help you to find the subject and verb phrase.

Example: Is your friend playing soccer?

Your <u>friend</u> <u>is playing</u> soccer.

🍓🍓🍓🍓🍓🍓🍓🍓🍓🍓🍓🍓🍓🍓🍓🍓🍓🍓🍓🍓🍓🍓🍓🍓🍓🍓🍓🍓🍓🍓🍓🍓🍓🍓🍓🍓🍓🍓🍓

Directions: Cross out any prepositional phrases. Underline the subject once and the verb phrase twice. Place the helping verb(s) and the main verb on the line indicated.

Example: <u>She</u> <u>has visited</u> ~~for three days~~.   ___has___   ___visited___

	HELPING VERB(S)	MAIN VERB
1. <u>He</u> <u>has seen</u> that movie twice.	has	seen
2. <u>You</u> <u>are listed</u> ~~in this phone book~~.	are	listed
3. The <u>train</u> <u>had</u> **not** <u>arrived</u> early.	had	arrived
4. <u>Dad</u> <u>must talk</u> ~~with the principal~~.	must	talk
5. ~~In October~~, <u>we</u> <u>may go</u> ~~to the fair~~.	may	go
6. Her <u>project</u> <u>was chosen</u> ~~by the judges~~.	was	chosen
7. Mike's <u>mother</u> <u>might shop</u> today.	might	shop
8. <u>They</u> <u>must sell</u> their house ~~before June~~.	must	sell
9. His older <u>brother</u> <u>is wearing</u> his shirt.	is	wearing
10. <u>Can</u> Miss <u>Harmon</u> <u>play</u> the drums?	Can	play

88

Name_____

Date_____

Remember: *Not* is an adverb. Box *not*; don't underline *not* as part of a verb phrase.

Changing an **interrogative sentence** to a declarative sentence may help you to find the subject and verb phrase.

Example: Is your friend playing soccer?
Your <u>friend is playing</u> soccer.

🍓🍓🍓🍓🍓🍓🍓🍓🍓🍓🍓🍓🍓🍓🍓🍓🍓🍓🍓🍓🍓🍓🍓🍓🍓🍓🍓🍓🍓🍓🍓

Directions: Cross out any prepositional phrases. Underline the subject once and the verb phrase twice. Place the helping verb(s) and the main verb on the line indicated.

Example: <u>She has visited</u> ~~for three days~~. _____has_____ _____visited_____

	HELPING VERB(S)	**MAIN VERB**

1. He has seen that movie twice. _____ _____

2. You are listed in this phone book. _____ _____

3. The train had not arrived early. _____ _____

4. Dad must talk with the principal. _____ _____

5. In October, we may go to the fair. _____ _____

6. Her project was chosen by the judges. _____ _____

7. Mike's mother might shop today. _____ _____

8. They must sell their house before June. _____ _____

9. His older brother is wearing his shirt. _____ _____

10. Can Miss Harmon play the drums? _____ _____

89

Directions: Cross out any prepositional phrases. Underline the subject once and the verb phrase twice. Place the helping verb(s) and the main verb on the line indicated.

	HELPING VERB(S)	MAIN VERB
1. The <u>butcher</u> <u>had wrapped</u> several pork chops ~~in white paper~~.	had	wrapped
2. <u>Oranges</u> <u>are grown</u> ~~in Florida~~.	are	grown
3. <u>You</u> <u>should have seen</u> that parade.	should have	seen
4. <u>May</u> <u>I</u> <u>ask</u> you a question?	May	ask
5. <u>Amy</u> <u>will</u> **not** <u>be diving</u> ~~from the high diving board~~.	will be	diving
6. That <u>house</u> <u>has been painted</u> several times.	has been	painted
7. <u>Would</u> <u>you</u> <u>help</u> Kenny ~~with his shoes~~?	Would	help
8. Many <u>trees</u> <u>had been planted</u> ~~in the forest~~.	had been	planted
9. <u>Charlotte</u> <u>might be going</u> ~~to Dallas~~ soon.	might be	going
10. <u>Will</u> <u>you</u> <u>hand</u> these books ~~to the librarian~~?	Will	hand

Name_____

Date_____

Directions: Cross out any prepositional phrases. Underline the subject once and the verb phrase twice. Place the helping verb(s) and the main verb on the line indicated.

	HELPING VERB(S)	**MAIN VERB**

1.   The butcher had wrapped several pork chops in white paper.   _____ _____

2.   Oranges are grown in Florida.   _____ _____

3.   You should have seen that parade.   _____ _____

4.   May I ask you a question?   _____ _____

5.   Amy will not be diving from the high diving board.   _____ _____

6.   That house has been painted several times.   _____ _____

7.   Would you help Kenny with his shoes?   _____ _____

8.   Many trees had been planted in the forest.   _____ _____

9.   Charlotte might be going to Dallas soon.   _____ _____

10.   Will you hand these books to the librarian?   _____ _____

Page 93:   **Concept:**   **Regular and Irregular Verbs**

Be sure that students understand the concept of regular and irregular verbs. You will briefly introduce tenses in the form of the past tense. You will also introduce the past participle which is a form of the verb but **not** a tense.

Past tense is easy. Refer to it as something that has occurred. Teach students that they will place *has*, *have*, or *had* before a past participle form. (Actually, other helping verbs such as *was* or *were* could be used, but let's keep it simple.)

Past tense is formed in regular verbs by adding <u>ed</u> to the verb for both the past and past participle.

Examples: to jump   past: jump**ed**   past participle: (had) jump**ed**

           to clean   past: clean**ed**   past participle: (had) clean**ed**

Ed is not added to either the past tense or the past participle form of an irregular verb.

Examples: to leave   past: left   past participle: (had) left

           to chose   past: chose   past participle: (had) chosen

On page 95, students will simply determine if the verb is regular or irregular. However, throughout the school year, occasionally ask if a verb in a sentence is regular or irregular.

VERBS
Regular and Irregular

Verbs may be regular or irregular. This refers to how they form the past tense and past participle form.

A. **Regular Verbs:**

Past tense means time that has already happened. In regular verbs, <u>ed</u> is added to form the past tense.

The past participle is **not** a tense. It is simply a form of the verb. Place *has, have,* or *had* before the past participle form.

Examples:

INFINITIVE	PRESENT	PAST	PAST PARTICIPLE
to yell	yell(s)	yell**ed**	(has, have, or had) yell**ed**
to crawl	crawl(s)	crawl**ed**	(has, have, or had) crawl**ed**
to laugh	laugh(s)	laugh**ed**	(has, have, or had) laugh**ed**

B. **Irregular Verbs:**

In an irregular verb, <u>ed</u> is not added to the past tense or to the past participle.

Examples:

INFINITIVE	PRESENT	PAST	PAST PARTICIPLE
to sing	sings(s)	sang	(has, have, or had) sung
to ride	ride(s)	rode	(has, have, or had) ridden
to bring	bring(s)	brought	(has, have, or had) brought

Name_____

WORKBOOK PAGE 41

Date_____

VERBS
Regular or
Irregular?

Directions: In the space provided, write <u>RV</u> If the verb is a regular verb. Write <u>IV</u> if the
verb is an irregular verb.

1. ___RV___   Joyce <u>sanded</u> an antique chest.

2. ___IV___   An egg <u>broke</u> in his hand.

3. ___RV___   The umpire <u>called</u> to the batter.

4. ___IV___   A fish <u>swam</u> around in the pool.

5. ___RV___   The nurse <u>helped</u> a patient out of bed.

6. ___IV___   The accountant <u>sent</u> a bill to his client.

7. ___IV___   The bell <u>rang</u> before school.

8. ___RV___   Marianne <u>scooped</u> out several helpings of beans.

9. ___RV___   The butler <u>answered</u> the door.

10. ___IV___   Several bubbles <u>burst</u> in the air.

11. ___RV___   We <u>climbed</u> a large oak tree.

12. ___IV___   Someone <u>drank</u> all the milk.

13. ___RV___   A telephone operator <u>remained</u> on the line.

14. ___RV___   The girls <u>sneaked</u> behind their dad's chair.

15. ___IV___   The runner <u>stole</u> second base.

16. ___IV___   He <u>laid</u> a towel by his beach blanket.

17. ___IV___   The museum guide <u>spoke</u> about modern art.

18. ___IV___   They <u>swam</u> all afternoon.

19. ___RV___   The carpenter <u>sawed</u> a piece of lumber.

20. ___IV___   Mom <u>saw</u> Dr. Blevins at the supermarket.

Directions: In the space provided, write <u>RV</u> If the verb is a regular verb. Write <u>IV</u> if the
verb is an irregular verb.

1. _____   Joyce <u>sanded</u> an antique chest.

2. _____   An egg <u>broke</u> in his hand.

3. _____   The umpire <u>called</u> to the batter.

4. _____   A fish <u>swam</u> around in the pool.

5. _____   The nurse <u>helped</u> a patient out of bed.

6. _____   The accountant <u>sent</u> a bill to his client.

7. _____   The bell <u>rang</u> before school.

8. _____   Marianne <u>scooped</u> out several helpings of beans.

9. _____   The butler <u>answered</u> the door.

10. _____   Several bubbles <u>burst</u> in the air.

11. _____   We <u>climbed</u> a large oak tree.

12. _____   Someone <u>drank</u> all the milk.

13. _____   A telephone operator <u>remained</u> on the line.

14. _____   The girls <u>sneaked</u> behind their dad's chair.

15. _____   The runner <u>stole</u> second base.

16. _____   He <u>laid</u> a towel by his beach blanket.

17. _____   The museum guide <u>spoke</u> about modern art.

18. _____   They <u>swam</u> all afternoon.

19. _____   The carpenter <u>sawed</u> a piece of lumber.

20. _____   Mom <u>saw</u> Dr. Blevins at the supermarket.

TO THE TEACHER: The information on these two pages is **extremely important**. Please, please, please read it. Your students will benefit!

Pages 98 and 99: **Concept: Irregular Verbs**

Students are introduced to a list of irregular verbs. These should be mastered. **Before students see this list**, give them a "quiz." (Don't count it, please.) Give the quiz in this manner: Have students clear their work area of all materials but paper and pencil. Open your book to pages 98-99. Carefully explain that you will say the infinitive, the present, the past, and *has, have,* or *had*. Students will write *had** plus the past participle form. At this point, some will be confused. Model an example on the board. Say to students, " I shall say the infinitive; in this case, *to begin*. Next, I shall say the present tense: *Today, I begin*. Then, I shall say the past tense: *Yesterday, I began*. I shall next say: *had*, followed by a pause. On your paper, write *had* and the word (past participle form) that fits. In this case, you would write *had begun* on your paper. Begin, began, had begun!" You may need to model several irregular verbs.

Give the entire list. I recommend that you do the list **in order** for ease in correcting. However, be aware that the first infinitive, *to be*, will be the most difficult. Tell students that *to be* is one of the hardest and that you will say it again later.

The suggestion to give these in order has rationale. It's simply easier to correct. In correcting, you may want to collect student papers and correct them yourself. I don't recommend it. I, personally, prefer having students exchange papers and correcting a classmate's quiz. First, it allows students to hear the past participle form being given orally, and it saves time. However, do stress with students the importance of correcting very carefully; we are, in fact, helping that student to learn. Remind students that no grade will be given. This is serious business. **If students misuse a past participle, they are probably using it improperly in both speaking and writing.** The entire purpose of this "quiz" is to help students find out which irregular verbs they are using incorrectly. We, then, will be doing some activities that will help students learn the correct form of those irregular verbs. Be sure that you give this "pep talk" **prior to correcting the quiz.**

My recommendation is that you give answers for the entire list as you presented it on the quiz. "To be: Today: I *am*, you *are*, or he *is*. Yesterday: I *was* or we *were*.

PAGE 98 = WORKBOOK PAGE 42

We had _____." This is tricky. If you give all of the answers, students may become bored. Therefore, walk around the class and look over student's shoulder. Call on a student for an answer **only** when you have discerned that the student, in fact, has the correct answer. In other words, you do not want students to hear an incorrect answer.

The corrected paper should be returned to the student. He should open his workbook or you need to give him a list of irregular verbs. Using a highlighter or a pencil, each student will mark only the past participle forms that he missed. This becomes his personal study list. (I collect the "quiz" papers so that when actual quiz time does eventually occur, students only have to take the ones originally missed. I team them with partners. Using the highlighted list, the partner gives the infinitive. I use the original "quiz" only to ascertain that students include all originally incorrect.)

Now, let the fun begin! English doesn't have to be boring nor do we have to stay in our seats all of the time. The following pneumonic device will be remembered by your fourth graders. You will need room for students to be active. It may be wise to take the class to the playground when it's not being used. Find a shady place for students to sit. I recommend that you assign students to read independently. (They'll be distracted, but, in this instance, don't worry about it.) **All students will need the list of irregular verbs that they have highlighted.** Tell students that you will call out each infinitive. If they missed that particular past participle, they need to join you (without books or papers). Go a distance from those reading independently.

The students who join you will be saying *had* + the past participle form <u>twenty-one times</u> **and** performing an action with it. (Yes, this does help students to learn!) These actions may be rigorous such as 21 jumping jacks as they say "had begun," or it may be something as simple as punching the air (not each other) as they say "had run." **Suggestion:** Don't get too rigorous. Also, if you are doing jumping jacks or something that requires more energy, tell students that they may stop, but just do the clap and say the past participle form. I try to do mostly moderate (such as a slow skip) to light (such as a hula step) as **we** say the past participle form 21 times. This activity will take a great deal of time; you may want to break it into several short time periods. However, my students love it, and they seem to **master** the verb form more easily.

*You may choose for students to use has, have, or had.

PAGE 99 = WORKBOOK PAGE 43

IRREGULAR VERBS

Infinitive	Present	Past	Present Participle	Past Participle*
To be	is, am, are	was, were	being	been
To beat	beat(s)	beat	beating	beaten
To begin	begin(s)	began	beginning	begun
To blow	blow(s)	blew	blowing	blown
To break	break(s)	broke	breaking	broken
To bring	bring(s)	brought	bringing	brought
To burst	burst(s)	burst	bursting	burst
To buy	buy(s)	bought	buying	bought
To choose	choose(s)	chose	choosing	chosen
To come	come(s)	came	coming	come
To do	do, does	did	doing	done
To drink	drink(s)	drank	drinking	drunk
To drive	drive(s)	drove	driving	driven
To eat	eat(s)	ate	eating	eaten
To fall	fall(s)	fell	falling	fallen
To fly	fly, flies	flew	flying	flown
To freeze	freeze(s)	froze	freezing	frozen
To give	give(s)	gave	giving	given
To go	go, goes	went	going	gone
To grow	grow(s)	grew	growing	grown
To have	have, has	had	having	had
To hang	hang(s)	hanged, hung**	hanging	hanged, hung**
To know	know(s)	knew	knowing	known
To lay	lay(s)	laid	laying	laid
To leave	leave(s)	left	leaving	left

---

*Uses a helping verb such as <u>has</u>, <u>have</u>, or <u>had</u>.

**Use *hung* when referring to objects.

IRREGULAR VERBS

Infinitive	Present	Past	Present Participle	Past Participle*
To lie	lie(s)	lay	lying	lain
To ride	ride(s)	rode	riding	ridden
To ring	ring(s)	rang	ringing	rung
To rise	rises(s)	rose	rising	risen
To run	run(s)	ran	running	run
To see	see(s)	saw	seeing	seen
To set	set(s)	set	setting	set
To shake	shake(s)	shook	shaking	shaken
To sing	sing(s)	sang	singing	sung
To sink	sink(s)	sank	sinking	sunk
To sit	sit(s)	sat	sitting	sat
To speak	speak(s)	spoke	speaking	spoken
To spring	spring(s)	sprang	springing	sprung
To steal	steal(s)	stole	stealing	stolen
To swim	swim(s)	swam	swimming	swum
To swear	swear(s)	swore	swearing	sworn
To take	take(s)	took	taking	taken
To teach	teach(s)	taught	teaching	taught
To throw	throw(s)	threw	throwing	thrown
To wear	wear(s)	wore	wearing	worn
To write	write(s)	wrote	writing	written

---

*Uses a helping verb such as <u>has</u>, <u>have</u>, <u>had</u>. These may also use other helping verbs such as <u>was</u> or <u>were</u>.

Directions: Cross out any prepositional phrases.   Underline the subject once and the verb phrase twice.

1.   Josh had (rode, ridden) his dirt bike to Corey's house.

2.   I have (drunk, drank) too much water.

3.   Corn is (grew, grown) in Iowa.

4.   Jim had (bought, buyed) a fishing pole.

5.   Jill has (went, gone) to church.

6.   They had (ran, run) a mile.

7.   The President of the United States was (swore, sworn) into office.

8.   Those girls have (swum, swam) for an hour.

9.   The pitcher had (threw, thrown) two strikes.

10.   During the night, snow had (fell, fallen).

11.   His pants have (shrunk, shrank) in the dryer.

12.   That grass was (ate, eaten) by two goats.

13.   A pirate ship had (sank, sunk) off the coast of Florida.

14.   I have (saw, seen) the ship, Queen Mary.

15.   Several speeches were (gave, given) before the election.

Name_____   **VERBS**
                                        Irregular Verbs
Date_____

Directions: Cross out any prepositional phrases.   Underline the subject once and the
              verb phrase twice.

1.   Josh had (rode, ridden) his dirt bike to Corey's house.

2.   I have (drunk, drank) too much water.

3.   Corn is (grew, grown) in Iowa.

4.   Jim had (bought, buyed) a fishing pole.

5.   Jill has (went, gone) to church.

6.   They had (ran, run) a mile.

7.   The President of the United States was (swore, sworn) into office.

8.   Those girls have (swum, swam) for an hour.

9.   The pitcher had (threw, thrown) two strikes.

10.   During the night, snow had (fell, fallen).

11.   His pants have (shrunk, shrank) in the dryer.

12.   That grass was (ate, eaten) by two goats.

13.   A pirate ship had (sank, sunk) off the coast of Florida.

14.   I have (saw, seen) the ship, Queen Mary.

15.   Several speeches were (gave, given) before the election.

Name_____

VERBS

Date_____

Irregular Verbs

Remember: 1. *Not* is never a verb. Box *not*.

2. To determine the verb phrase of a question (interrogative), change it
   to a statement (declarative). You may want to do this mentally.

Directions: Cross out any prepositional phrases. Underline the subject once and the
verb phrase twice.

1. The wind had (blew, blown) throughout the night.

2. Roses were (chose, chosen) for the bridal bouquet.

3. You have (taught, teached) us so much.

4. Several flags were (flown, flew) on Memorial Day.

5. The carnival had (began, begun) at four o'clock.

6. She has **not** (worn, wore) a short gown to the prom.

7. Egg whites were beaten for the pudding.

8. Her balloons have **not** (burst, busted).

9. At Christmas, stockings are (hanged, hung) above the fireplace.

10. The Richards family has (drove, driven) from Denver to New York City.

11. Were ice cubes (froze, frozen) into animal shapes?

12. At the restaurant, their cellular phone had (rung, rang).

13. A leak has (sprang, sprung) in the pipes.

14. Our former neighbors have (came, come) with their children.

15. Has he (brung, brought) a sack lunch and a drink?

102

Name_____

VERBS
Irregular Verbs

Date_____

Remember: 1. *Not* is never a verb. Box *not.*

2. To determine the verb phrase of a question (interrogative), change it to a statement (declarative). You may want to do this mentally.

Directions: Cross out any prepositional phrases. Underline the subject once and the verb phrase twice.

1. The wind had (blew, blown) throughout the night.

2. Roses were (chose, chosen) for the bridal bouquet.

3. You have (taught, teached) us so much.

4. Several flags were (flown, flew) on Memorial Day.

5. The carnival had (began, begun) at four o'clock.

6. She has not (worn, wore) a short gown to the prom.

7. Egg whites were beaten for the pudding.

8. Her balloons have not (burst, busted).

9. At Christmas, stockings are (hanged, hung) above the fireplace.

10. The Richards family has (drove, driven) from Denver to New York City.

11. Were ice cubes (froze, frozen) into animal shapes?

12. At the restaurant, their cellular phone had (rung, rang).

13. A leak has (sprang, sprung) in the pipes.

14. Our former neighbors have (came, come) with their children.

15. Has he (brung, brought) a sack lunch and a drink?

103

Remember: 1. *Not* is never a verb. Box *not.*

2. To determine the verb phrase of a question (interrogative), change it to a statement (declarative). You may want to do this mentally.

Directions: Cross out any prepositional phrases. Underline the subject once and the verb phrase twice.

1. The <u>rollerbladers</u> <u>had</u> (fell, <u>fallen</u>) three times.

2. <u>You</u> <u>must have</u> (knew, <u>known</u>) him ~~for a long time~~.

3. A <u>thief</u> <u>may have</u> (stole, <u>stolen</u>) her car.

4. The <u>choir</u> <u>should have</u> (<u>sung</u>, sang) longer.

5. <u>I</u> <u>could</u> **not** <u>have</u> (threw, <u>thrown</u>) the ball again.

6. <u>We</u> <u>have</u> (hanged, <u>hung</u>) a picture ~~of our great grandmother on the wall~~.

7. <u>They</u> <u>must have</u> (saw, <u>seen</u>) my sister ~~at the mall~~.

8. ~~After this piece of pie~~, <u>I</u> <u>shall have</u> (ate, <u>eaten</u>) four slices.

9. Pearl <u>necklaces</u> <u>had been</u> (gave, <u>given</u>) ~~by the bride to her attendants~~.

10. Many <u>pictures</u> ~~of that model~~ <u>will have been</u> (took, <u>taken</u>) ~~by the end of the session~~.

Name_____

Date_____

Remember: 1. *Not* is never a verb. Box *not.*

2. To determine the verb phrase of a question (interrogative), change it to a statement (declarative). You may want to do this mentally.

🍓🍓🍓🍓🍓🍓🍓🍓🍓🍓🍓🍓🍓🍓🍓🍓🍓🍓🍓🍓🍓🍓🍓🍓🍓🍓🍓🍓🍓🍓🍓🍓🍓🍓

Directions: Cross out any prepositional phrases. Underline the subject once and the verb phrase twice.

1. The rollerbladers had (fell, fallen) three times.

2. You must have (knew, known) him for a long time.

3. A thief may have (stole, stolen) her car.

4. The choir should have (sung, sang) longer.

5. I could not have (threw, thrown) the ball again.

6. We have (hanged, hung) a picture of our great grandmother on the wall.

7. They must have (saw, seen) my sister at the mall.

8. After this piece of pie, I shall have (ate, eaten) four slices.

9. Pearl necklaces had been (gave, given) by the bride to her attendants.

10. Many pictures of that model will have been (took, taken) by the end of the session.

TO THE TEACHER:

One purpose of teaching direct objects is to learn proper grammar usage. There's no glory just in identifying a direct object in the sentence. A purpose becomes quite clear when teaching *sit/set*, *rise/raise*, and *lie/lay*.

Remind students that a prepositional phrase will not be the subject, verb, <u>direct object</u>, or anything important in the sentence*.

For your information:
At this level, we are dealing with the active voice. In the passive voice, a direct object may not be used with *to set*. **For our purposes, active voice will be used.**

        Active Voice: I set the silver bank on the table.
        Passive Voice: The silver bank had been set on the table.

Page 107:   **Concept:**   **Sit/Set**
Part A of this page reviews direct objects. **Do part A orally.** Then, in Part B, students are introduced to the concept that ***to set* requires a direct object. Do this part orally.**

A conjugation of both *to set* and *to sit* are given on page 107. (Students have not been introduced formally to tenses, so take this part slowly.) <u>Be sure to discuss the forms with your students</u>. Explain that *to sit* does not require an object; it's something you can do alone. You can sit on a chair. You can do that without help. *Set* requires a direct object. *Set* means to place. In order *to place*, there must be a "thing" to place. (Exceptions: The sun sets. Hens set.)

Recommendation: Have students stand up. Have them sit as they say, "I sit." Then, have them pick up something and place it as they say, "I set_____ on my desk." Solicit answers (direct objects) from students. Active participation helps students to master concepts.

Page 109:   **Concept:**   **Rise/Raise**
Part A is another review of direct objects.
Part B presents the conjugation of *to rise*, an irregular verb, and *to raise*, a regular verb. Show students that some "things" can go up without help: smoke, the sun, a person. I point out that students usually rise in the morning. No one pulls them out of bed. They rise on their own volition.
To teach *to raise*, tell students that if they use *raise* in a sentence, they must have a direct object. Ask students to

*99% of the time

name "objects" that are raised. Possible responses include hand, flag, chicken, and money.

Recommendation: Have students stand up. As they do so, guide them to say, "I rise." Have them sit. Then, have them pick up something and say, "I raise (or am raising) ___." Solicit answers (direct objects) from students.

Page 111: **Concept: Lie/Lay** (*To lie* in this text refers to a prone position, not to fibbing.)

At this grade level, we will do our best to introduce this concept in a very easy manner. First, spend time discussing these two irregular verbs. I always tell my students that I would like to "cream" those who made the past of *to lie* the same word as the present of *to lay*.   Life is unfair! However, stress that *to lie* means to rest.   (I have students lie on the floor. They, then, say, "I lie on the floor." Next, they stand. I guide them to say, "A minute ago I lay on the floor. I was lying on the floor. I had lain there for a few seconds." (You may wish to do this over a period of a few days. They need to use the correct words.

Make sure that students understand that t*o lay* means to place. Therefore, they must have something placed (direct object). <u>The words **lays, laid** and **laying** will always have a direct object</u>. If *lay* means to place, it will have a direct object.

Students will use their knowledge of prepositional phrases.

Example: A baby (lies, lays) in her crib.
A <u>baby</u> (<u>lies</u>, lays) ~~in her crib~~. (*Lays* requires a direct object. Students already know that this sentence can't possibly have a direct object because *in her crib* has been deleted. Hence, a baby lies; also, make sure that students can see that the baby rests in her crib.

Example: Carla (lay, laid) the garden hose in the shed.
D.O.
<u>Carla</u> (lay, <u>laid</u>) the garden hose ~~in the shed~~.

Note: This is a very difficult concept. Don't be discouraged if some of your students are confused. In <u>Easy Grammar: Level 1</u> and in <u>Easy Grammar Plus</u>, they will be reintroduced to the concept. Sometimes, students simply need more maturity or a second "look" at a concept in order to understand it.   107

🍓 Part A: **Direct Objects**
Directions: Cross out any prepositional phrases. Underline the subject once and the
            verb/verb phrase twice. Label any direct object - <u>D.O.</u>

                        D.O.
1. We <u>barbecued</u> chicken ~~for our picnic~~.

                        D.O.
2. The <u>teenagers</u> <u>ate</u> popcorn ~~during the movie~~.

                        D.O.
3. The <u>children</u> <u>placed</u> money ~~in the offering plate~~.

🍓🍓🍓🍓🍓🍓🍓🍓🍓🍓🍓🍓🍓🍓🍓🍓🍓🍓🍓🍓🍓🍓🍓🍓🍓🍓🍓🍓🍓🍓🍓🍓🍓🍓🍓🍓🍓🍓🍓

🍓 Part B: *SIT/SET*
To sit means to rest.
To set means to place or put.

Infinitive	Present	Past	Present Participle	Past Participle
to sit	sit(s)	sat	sitting	(had) sat
to set	set(s)	set	setting	(had) set

To set **requires a direct object.**

Examples: I (sit, set) in the first row.
              I (<u>sit</u>, set) ~~in the first row~~. (There is no direct object. Also, I "rest" in the first row.)

              I have (sat, set) my lunch there.
                        D.O.
              <u>I</u> <u>have</u> (sat, <u>set</u>) my lunch there. (When you use *set*, you must label the direct
                                                                  object. What is the object I set? Answer: lunch)

Directions: Cross out any prepositional phrases. Underline the subject once.
            Underline the verb or verb phrase twice. Label any direct object - <u>D.O.</u>

1. <u>They</u> (<u>sat</u>, set) ~~with me.~~

                        D.O.
2. <u>She</u> (sits, <u>sets</u>) her alarm clock ~~at night.~~

3. <u>I</u> <u>have</u> (<u>sat</u>, set) here ~~for a long time~~.

4. <u>Dad</u> <u>is</u> (<u>sitting</u>, setting) ~~behind my sister~~.

                        D.O.
5. The <u>hostess</u> <u>has</u> (sat, <u>set</u>) glasses ~~of lemonade~~ ~~on the table~~.

    <u>(You)</u>   D.O.
6. (Sit, <u>Set</u>) that box ~~under the bench~~.

108

Date_____

🍓 Part A: **Direct Objects**
Directions: Cross out any prepositional phrases. Underline the subject once and the
verb/verb phrase twice. Label any direct object - <u>D.O.</u>

1.   We barbecued chicken for our picnic.

2.   The teenagers ate popcorn during the movie.

3.   The children placed money in the offering plate.

🍓🍓

🍓 Part B: *SIT/SET*
To sit means to rest.
To set means to place or put.

Infinitive	Present	Past	Present Participle	Past Participle
to sit	sit(s)	sat	sitting	(had) sat
to set	set(s)	set	setting	(had) set

***To set* requires a direct object.**

Examples: I (sit, set) in the first row.
I (<u>sit</u>, set) ~~in the first row~~. (There is no direct object. Also, I "rest" in the first row.)

I have (sat, set) my lunch there.
D.O.
<u>I have</u> (sat, <u>set</u>) my lunch there. (When you use *set*, you must label the direct
object. What is the object I set? Answer: lunch)

Directions: Cross out any prepositional phrases. Underline the subject once.
Underline the verb or verb phrase twice. Label any direct object - <u>D.O.</u>

1.   They (sat, set) with me.

2.   She (sits, sets) her alarm clock at night.

3.   I have (sat, set) here for a long time.

4.   Dad is (sitting, setting) behind my sister.

5.   The hostess has (sat, set) glasses of lemonade on the table.

6.   (Sit, Set) that box under the bench.   109

WORKBOOK PAGE 48   Rise/Raise
Date_____

🍓 Part A: **Direct Objects**
Directions: Cross out any prepositional phrases. Underline the subject once and the
                       verb/verb phrase twice.   Label any direct object - D.O.

                 D.O.
1. I put my cafeteria tray on the table.

                       D.O.
2. The postman handed the package to the lady.

                D.O.
3. Vicki bought shoes at the department store.

🍓🍓🍓🍓🍓🍓🍓🍓🍓🍓🍓🍓🍓🍓🍓🍓🍓🍓🍓🍓🍓🍓🍓🍓🍓🍓🍓🍓🍓🍓🍓🍓

🍓 Part B: ***RISE/RAISE***
To rise means to go up without help.
To raise means to lift or go up (with help).

Infinitive	Present	Past	Present Participle	Past Participle
to rise	rise(s)	rose	rising	(had) risen
to raise	raise(s)	raised	raising	(had) raised

To raise **requires a direct object.**

Examples: Smoke (rises, raises) in the air.
                      Smoke (rises, raises) in the air.   Smoke goes up on its own. Also, with *raises*,

                                                                           there must be a direct object. Because in the air
                                                                           has been crossed out, the sentence can't have a
                                                                           direct object.

                      Mr. Clay (rose, raised) his hand.
                                                  D.O.
                      Mr. Clay (rose, raised) his hand. With *to raise*, a direct object is required. What
                                                                           did Mr. Clay raise? Answer: hand

Directions: Cross out any prepositional phrases.   Underline the subject once and the
                       verb or verb phrase twice. Label any direct object - D.O.

                  D.O.
1. Laura (rose, raised) her glass to her lips.

2. We (rose, raised) to our feet for the prayer.

3. The sun has (risen, raised) already.

110

Date_____

🍓 Part A: **Direct Objects**
Directions: Cross out any prepositional phrases. Underline the subject once and the
            verb/verb phrase twice. Label any direct object - <u>D.O.</u>

1. I put my cafeteria tray on the table.

2. The postman handed the package to the lady.

3. Vicki bought shoes at the department store.

🍓🍓🍓🍓🍓🍓🍓🍓🍓🍓🍓🍓🍓🍓🍓🍓🍓🍓🍓🍓🍓🍓🍓🍓🍓🍓🍓🍓🍓🍓🍓🍓

🍓 Part B: ***RISE/RAISE***
To rise means to go up without help.
To raise means to lift or go up (with help).

<u>Infinitive</u>	<u>Present</u>	<u>Past</u>	<u>Present Participle</u>	<u>Past Participle</u>
to rise	rise(s)	rose	rising	(had) risen
to raise	raise(s)	raised	raising	(had) raised

To raise **requires a direct object.**

Examples: Smoke (rises, raises) in the air.
          <u>Smoke</u> (<u>rises</u>, raises) ~~in the air~~. Smoke goes up on its own. Also, with *raises*,
                                                there must be a direct object. Because <u>in the air</u>
                                                has been crossed out, the sentence can't have a
                                                direct object.

          Mr. Clay (rose, raised) his hand.
                                D.O.
          <u>Mr. Clay</u> (rose, <u>raised</u>) his hand. With *to raise*, a direct object is required. What
                                                did Mr. Clay raise? Answer: hand

Directions: Cross out any prepositional phrases.   Underline the subject once and the
            verb or verb phrase twice. Label any direct object - <u>D.O.</u>

1. Laura (rose, raised) her glass to her lips.

2. We (rose, raised) to our feet for the prayer.

3. The sun has (risen, raised) already.

🍓 Part A: **Direct Objects**
Directions: Cross out any prepositional phrases. Underline the subject once and the
              verb/verb phrase twice. Label any direct object - <u>D.O.</u>

                        D.O.
1. The <u>dentist</u> <u>gave</u> toothbrushes ~~to her patients~~.

                        D.O.
2. A <u>mechanic</u> <u>lifted</u> the hood ~~of the car~~.

                        D.O.
3. Betty's <u>father</u> <u>placed</u> the child ~~on his shoulders~~.

🍓🍓🍓🍓🍓🍓🍓🍓🍓🍓🍓🍓🍓🍓🍓🍓🍓🍓🍓🍓🍓🍓🍓🍓🍓🍓🍓🍓🍓🍓🍓🍓

🍓 Part B: **LIE/LAY**
To lie means to rest.
To lay means to place.

Infinitive	Present	Past	Present Participle	Past Participle
to lay	lay(s)	laid*	laying*	(had) laid*
to lie	lie(s)	lay	lying	(had) lain

To lie means <u>to rest</u>. Try inserting "rest" when you are using *lie* in a sentence.
Lays, laid, and laying will have a direct object.

Examples:
    Ned (lies, lays) tile for a living.
              D.O.
    <u>Ned</u> (lies, <u>lays</u>) tile ~~for a living~~.   With **lays**, you must have a direct object.

                                           What is the object Ned "places"? Answer: tile

    I had (laid, lain) on the sofa.
    <u>I</u> <u>had</u> (laid, <u>lain</u>) ~~on the sofa~~.   *Lain* refers to resting.   I had rested on the sofa. Also,

                                           *on the sof*a has been crossed out. Therefore, there is
                                           no direct object. To use *laid*, there must be a direct
                                           object in the sentence.

Directions: Cross out any prepositional phrases. Underline the subject once and the
              verb or verb phrase twice. Label any direct object - <u>D.O.</u>

1. Their <u>cat</u> usually (<u>lies</u>, lays) ~~by the front door~~.
                        D.O.
2. <u>Clark</u> (<u>laid</u>, lay) his books ~~on his bed~~.

3. A few <u>cows</u> <u>are</u> (<u>lying</u>, laying) ~~in the field~~.

112

Name_____

Date_____

🍓 Part A: **Direct Objects**
Directions: Cross out any prepositional phrases. Underline the subject once and the
verb/verb phrase twice. Label any direct object - <u>D.O.</u>

1. The dentist gave toothbrushes to her patients.

2. A mechanic lifted the hood of the car.

3. Betty's father placed the child on his shoulders.

🍓🍓🍓🍓🍓🍓🍓🍓🍓🍓🍓🍓🍓🍓🍓🍓🍓🍓🍓🍓🍓🍓🍓🍓🍓🍓🍓🍓🍓🍓🍓🍓🍓🍓🍓🍓🍓

🍓 Part B: *LIE/LAY*
To lie means to rest.
To lay means to place.

Infinitive	Present	Past	Present Participle	Past Participle
to lay	lay(s)	laid*	laying*	(had) laid*
to lie	lie(s)	lay	lying	(had) lain

To lie means <u>to rest</u>. Try inserting "rest" when you are using *lie* in a sentence.
***Lays, laid*, and *laying* will have a direct object.**

Examples:
     Ned (lies, lays) tile for a living.
                    D.O.
     <u>Ned</u> (lies, <u>lays</u>) tile ~~for a living~~.   With *lays*, you must have a direct object.
                                                              What is the object Ned "places"? Answer: tile

     I had (laid, lain) on the sofa.
     <u>I had</u> (laid, <u>lain</u>) ~~on the sofa~~.   *Lain* refers to resting. I had rested on the sofa. Also,
                                                           on the sofa has been crossed out. Therefore, there is
                                                           no direct object. To use *laid,* there must be a direct
                                                           object in the sentence.

Directions: Cross out any prepositional phrases. Underline the subject once and the
verb or verb phrase twice. Label any direct object - <u>D.O.</u>

1. Their cat usually (lies, lays) by the front door.

2. Clark (laid, lay) his books on his bed.

3. A few cows are (lying, laying) in the field.   113

FOR THE TEACHER: Read this page carefully. A student page appears on page 115.

VERB TENSES:

A. <u>**Present Tense**</u>:

     Be sure that students understand that **tense means time.** **Present tense signifies present time.** Although present can mean at this moment, it is easier to use "today" as a point of reference for present tense. It's helpful for students to know that present tense never has a helping verb.*

To form the present tense, remove *to* from the infinitive:

    1. **If the subject is singular (one), add <u>s</u> to the verb.** (**<u>es</u>** to some)
         Examples: **to like**: A squirrel <u>likes</u> acorns.

                     to ride: The girl <u>rides</u> her horse nearly every morning.

    2. **If the subject is <u>you</u>, <u>I</u>, or is plural (more than one), simply remove the *to* from the infinitive.**
         Examples: **to eat**:   You <u>eat</u> slowly.

                         <u>I eat</u> breakfast every day.

                         Those football players <u>eat</u> a great deal.

B. <u>**Past Tense**</u>:

     Past tense indicates that which **has happened.** Although past can mean a second ago, it is easier to use the term, "yesterday." Teach students that past tense never has a helping verb.*

    1. **To form the past tense of a regular verb, add <u>ed</u> to the verb.**
         to scream: scream**ed**   to follow: follow**ed**

    2. **To form the past tense of an irregular verb, change the verb to its appropriate form.**
         to bring: brought   to steal: stole

C. <u>**Future Tense**</u>:

     Future tense indicates time yet to happen. There are two helping verbs that indicate future tense: ***shall* and *will*.** Although future may be any time yet to occur, using *"tomorrow"* helps students comprehend it. Be sure that students understand that *shall* or *will* must be used with the future tense. (In teaching this, I ask students to share something that they will do soon. This helps to reinforce the concept.)

Note: Although it has become acceptable to use *will* with any subject, encourage students to use *shall* with the pronoun, *I*. *Shall* may also be correctly used with the pronoun, *we*.

    *Helping verbs are used to form tenses; students will learn more complex tenses in <u>Easy Grammar</u> or <u>Easy Grammar Plus</u>.

114   ***PAGE 115 = WORKBOOK PAGE 50***

VERB TENSES:

🍓 Present Tense:

Tense means time. Present tense signifies present time. Although present can mean at this moment, it is easier to use "today" as a point of reference for present tense. Present tense never has a helping verb.

To form the present tense, remove *to* from the infinitive:

1. **If the subject is singular (one), add <u>s</u> to the verb. (<u>es</u> to some)**

   Examples: **to play**: A <u>child plays</u> with his toys. (one child)

   to sing: <u>She sings</u> constantly. (she - one person)

2. **If the subject is <u>you</u>, <u>I</u>, or is plural (more than one), simply remove the *to* from the infinitive.**
   Examples: **to swim**: <u>You swim</u> well.
   <u>I swim</u> daily.
   Those <u>adults</u> seldom <u>swim</u>.

🍓 Past Tense:

Past tense indicates that which has happened. Although past can mean a second ago, it is easier to use the term, "yesterday." Past tense never has a helping verb.

1. **To form the past tense of a regular verb, add <u>ed</u> to the verb.**
   to knock: knock**ed**   He <u>knocked</u> on the door.
   to scrub: scrubb**ed**   We <u>scrubbed</u> the floor with brushes.

2. **To form the past tense of an irregular verb, change the verb to its appropriate form.**
   to fall: **fell**   The <u>skater fell</u> down.
   to drive: **drove**   They <u>drove</u> a motor home.

🍓 Future Tense:

Future tense indicates time yet to happen. There are two helping verbs that indicate future tense: *shall* **and** *will*. Future may be any time yet to occur; however, to make it easier, we shall use "tomorrow" as a guide.

1. *Will* is most frequently used in forming the future tense.
2. *Shall* **is used with the pronoun,** *I*. (<u>I shall see</u> you tomorrow.)
   Shall may be used with *we*.

115

Directions: Read each sentence. The verb or verb phrase has been underlined for you. Write the tense of the verb on each line.

Remember: The verb tenses are *present*, *past*, and *future*.

Example: _____present_____ She <u>wants</u> a sled for Christmas.

1. _____past_____ Her sister <u>pretended</u> to be angry.

2. _____future_____ I <u>shall frost</u> this cake.

3. _____present_____ Stephanie <u>studies</u> for tests.

4. _____past_____ The game <u>ended</u> early.

5. _____present_____ Large weeds <u>grow</u> in the vacant lot.

6. _____future_____ That store <u>will open</u> at nine tomorrow.

7. _____past_____ Micah <u>rolled</u> his sleeping bag.

8. _____present_____ Larry often <u>makes</u> a pie for dinner.

9. _____future_____ I <u>shall leave</u> before breakfast.

10. _____past_____ Jenny <u>stirred</u> the pasta salad.

11. _____present_____ Alice and I <u>love</u> board games.

12. _____present_____ You <u>are</u> correct.

13. _____past_____ Jason <u>hid</u> his brother's jacket.

14. _____future_____ <u>Will</u> you please <u>help</u> me?

116

Name_____ **VERBS**
Tenses
Date_____

Directions: Read each sentence. The verb or verb phrase has been underlined for
you. Write the tense of the verb on each line.

Remember: The verb tenses are *present*, *past*, and *future*.

Example: _____present_____ She <u>wants</u> a sled for Christmas.

1. _____ Her sister <u>pretended</u> to be angry.

2. _____ I <u>shall frost</u> this cake.

3. _____ Stephanie <u>studies</u> for tests.

4. _____ The game <u>ended</u> early.

5. _____ Large weeds <u>grow</u> in the vacant lot.

6. _____ That store <u>will open</u> at nine tomorrow.

7. _____ Micah <u>rolled</u> his sleeping bag.

8. _____ Larry often <u>makes</u> a pie for dinner.

9. _____ I <u>shall leave</u> before breakfast.

10. _____ Jenny <u>stirred</u> the pasta salad.

11. _____ Alice and I <u>love</u> board games.

12. _____ You <u>are</u> correct.

13. _____ Jason <u>hid</u> his brother's jacket.

14. _____ <u>Will</u> you please <u>help</u> me?

Directions: Read each sentence.   The subject and verb/verb phrase have been underlined for you. Write the tense of the verb on each line.

Remember: The verb tenses are *present, past,* and *future.*

Example: _____past_____   The <u>canoe glided</u> across the water.

1.   _____present_____   <u>Nancy attends</u> college.

2.   _____future_____   <u>Nancy will attend</u> college in the fall.

3.   _____past_____   <u>Nancy attended</u> college in Hawaii.

1.   _____present_____   Her <u>parents send</u> her brownies at Easter.

2.   _____past_____   Her <u>parents sent</u> her brownies.

3.   _____future_____   Her <u>parents will send</u> her brownies soon.

1.   _____past_____   <u>Firefighters fought</u> the blaze.

2.   _____future_____   <u>Firefighters will fight</u> the blaze.

3.   _____present_____   <u>Firefighters fight</u> blazes each summer.

1.   _____future_____   <u>I shall feed</u> the horses.

2.   _____past_____   <u>I fed</u> the horses at Uncle Ted's farm.

3.   _____present_____   <u>Uncle Ted</u> and <u>I</u> usually <u>feed</u> the horses early.

Name_____

Date_____

VERBS
Tenses

Directions: Read each sentence. The subject and verb/verb phrase have been
underlined for you. Write the tense of the verb on each line.

Remember: The verb tenses are *present*, *past*, and *future*.

Example: _____past_____ The <u>canoe glided</u> across the water.

1. _____ <u>Nancy attends</u> college.

2. _____ <u>Nancy will attend</u> college in the fall.

3. _____ <u>Nancy attended</u> college in Hawaii.

1. _____ Her <u>parents send</u> her brownies at Easter.

2. _____ Her <u>parents sent</u> her brownies.

3. _____ Her <u>parents will send</u> her brownies soon.

1. _____ <u>Firefighters fought</u> the blaze.

2. _____ <u>Firefighters will fight</u> the blaze.

3. _____ <u>Firefighters fight</u> blazes each summer.

1. _____ <u>I shall feed</u> the horses.

2. _____ <u>I fed</u> the horses at Uncle Ted's farm.

3. _____ <u>Uncle Ted</u> and <u>I</u> usually <u>feed</u> the horses early.

Directions: Cross out any prepositional phrases. Underline the subject once and the
verb/verb phrase twice. On the line provided, write the tense: *present,*
past, or *future.*

to walk:

1. ____past_____   He <u>walked</u> ~~to the bus~~.

2. ____present_____   The <u>lady</u> <u>walks</u> ~~with her friend~~.

3. ____future_____   <u>I</u> <u>shall walk</u> my dog.

to play:

1. ____present_____   <u>Cody</u> and <u>Charlene</u> <u>play</u> ~~on the swings~~.

2. ____past_____   A young <u>boy</u> <u>played</u> the piano.

3. ____future_____   The <u>Suns</u> <u>will play</u> ~~at that arena~~.

to take:

1. ____future_____   <u>You</u> <u>will take</u> a test ~~on Thursday~~.

2. ____past_____   <u>They</u> <u>took</u> their cat ~~to the animal hospital~~.

3. ____present_____   <u>Kim</u> <u>takes</u> golfing lessons.

to drink:

1. ____present_____   <u>I</u> <u>drink</u> milk.

2. ____past_____   A <u>baby</u> <u>drank</u> juice.

3. ____future_____   The <u>kitten</u> <u>will drink</u> ~~from that bowl~~.

120

Name_____   **VERBS**
                                         Tenses

Date_____

Directions: Cross out any prepositional phrases. Underline the subject once and the
              verb/verb phrase twice. On the line provided, write the tense: *present*,
              past, or *future*.

to walk:

1. _____   He walked to the bus.

2. _____   The lady walks with her friend.

3. _____   I shall walk my dog.

to play:

1. _____   Cody and Charlene play on the swings.

2. _____   A young boy played the piano.

3. _____   The Suns will play at that arena.

to take:

1. _____   You will take a test on Thursday.

2. _____   They took their cat to the animal hospital.

3. _____   Kim takes golfing lessons.

to drink:

1. _____   I drink milk.

2. _____   A baby drank juice.

3. _____   The kitten will drink from that bowl.

FOR THE TEACHER: Please read this page.   A student page follows.

PAGE 123 = WORKBOOK PAGE 54

SUBJECT VERB AGREEMENT (Present Tense):

1. Review present tense: Present tense means present time. "Today" is a good point of reference.
2. Students will need to understand the terms, *singular* and *plural*. **Singular means one; plural means more than one.**

🍓🍓

A.   **If the subject is singular (one), add s to the verb:**

> Example: One <s>of the horses</s> limps. (Continue to teach students to delete

prepositional phrases to help find the subject. This is extremely important in making subject and verb agree.)

🍓**EXCEPTIONS:**

1.   **Some irregular verbs completely change form for the present tense.**

> Examples: to have: One <u>student has</u> a watch with a second hand.
>
> to be: Each <u>person is</u> responsible for his own actions.

2.   **The pronoun, *I*, is singular; however, the verb does not add s.**

> Example: I <u>love</u> spaghetti.

B.   **If the subject is plural (more than one), do not add s to the verb.**

> Examples: Two <u>friends eat</u> lunch together.
>
> Those <u>clowns make</u> balloon animals.

Sometimes, the subject will be compound (two or more);   do not add s if the subjects are joined by *and*.

> Example: His <u>grandmother</u> and <u>grandfather live</u> with his family.

In most irregular verbs, do not add s to the verb if the subject is plural.

> Example: A few <u>ladies hike</u> that trail often.

🍓**EXCEPTION:**   **Some irregular verbs completely change form for the present tense.**

> Example: Those <u>cabins are</u> near a highway.

🍓🍓

This next concept is very difficult and is introduced formally in <u>Easy Grammar: Level 1.</u>   I haven't provided any sentences that will help students to master this concept.

If a compound subject (two or more) is joined by *or*, follow these rules:

> A. **If the subject closer to the verb is singular, add s to the verb.**

> Example: Their <u>teachers</u> or **principal** <u>presents</u> awards.

> B. **If the subject closer to the verb is plural, don't add s to the verb.**

122   Example: Their <u>principal</u> or **teachers** <u>present</u> awards.

SUBJECT VERB AGREEMENT:

The subject and verb need to agree in number in the present tense. There are several ways to do this:

A. **If the subject is singular (one), add s to the verb:**

        Examples: A <u>bee</u> <u>stings</u>.

                      Her <u>friend</u> <u>leaves</u> for the Army soon.

        Some verbs add es.

            Example: The <u>juggler</u> <u>does</u> a great job.

EXCEPTIONS:

   1. **Some irregular verbs completely change form for the present tense.**

        Example: A <u>nurse</u> <u>is</u> here to help.

   2. **The pronoun, I, is singular; however, the verb does not add s.**

        Example: <u>I</u> <u>like</u> your new picture.

B. **If the subject is plural (more than one), do not add s to the verb.**

        Examples: Two <u>friends</u> <u>eat</u> lunch together.

                      Those <u>clowns</u> <u>make</u> balloon animals.

  Sometimes, the subject will be compound (two or more); do not add s if the subjects are joined by *and*.

        Example: His <u>grandmother</u> and <u>grandfather</u> <u>live</u> with his family.

  In most irregular verbs, do not add s to the verb if the subject is plural.

        Example: A few <u>ladies</u> <u>hike</u> that trail often.

EXCEPTION: **Some irregular verbs completely change form for the present tense.**

        Example: Those <u>cabins</u> <u>are</u> near a highway.

Directions: Read each sentence.   The subject has been underlined.   Circle the verb
that agrees with the subject.
Answers are in boldfaced print.

1.   A snail (crawl, **crawls**) slowly.

2.   Ostriches (**run**, runs) fast.

3.   Mandy (**has**, have) a cocker spaniel puppy.

4.   Camels (**spit**, spits).

5.   Finches (**make**, makes) great pets.

6.   Each of those girls (own, **owns**) a dog.

7.   Joel and Suzanne (**help**, helps) at a local hospital.

8.   One (need, **needs**) to listen carefully.

9.   Butterflies (**leave**, leaves) a cocoon.

10.   We (is, **are**) here.

11.   Rattlesnakes (**shed**, sheds) their skin.

12.   They (**surf**, surfs) every summer.

13.   A police officer (watch, **watches**) our neighborhood carefully.

14.   Date palms (**grow**, grows) in Arizona.

15.   Everyone of the students (**is**, are) on the honor roll.

Name_____   **VERBS**
                                         Subject/Verb Agreement
Date_____

Directions: Read each sentence.   The subject has been underlined.   Circle the verb
             that agrees with the subject.

1. A <u>snail</u> (crawl, crawls) slowly.

2. <u>Ostriches</u> (run, runs) fast.

3. <u>Mandy</u> (has, have) a cocker spaniel puppy.

4. <u>Camels</u> (spit, spits).

5. <u>Finches</u> (make, makes) great pets.

6. <u>Each</u> of those girls (own, owns) a dog.

7. <u>Joel</u> and <u>Suzanne</u> (help, helps) at a local hospital.

8. <u>One</u> (need, needs) to listen carefully.

9. <u>Butterflies</u> (leave, leaves) a cocoon.

10. <u>We</u> (is, are) here.

11. <u>Rattlesnakes</u> (shed, sheds) their skin.

12. <u>They</u> (surf, surfs) every summer.

13. A police <u>officer</u> (watch, watches) our neighborhood carefully.

14. Date <u>palms</u> (grow, grows) in Arizona.

15. <u>Everyone</u> of the students (is, are) on the honor roll.

Answers are in boldfaced print.
Directions: Read each sentence.   Underline the subject once; circle the verb that
             agrees with the subject.
Remember: You may want to cross out prepositional phrases. This helps to find the
             subject.
Although directions don't require it, prepositional phrases have been deleted.

1. Several <u>mops</u> (**have,** has) old handles.

2. Those <u>spiders</u> (**spin,** spins) a large web.

3. A <u>yellowhammer</u> (peck, **pecks**) trees.

4. <u>One</u> ~~of the boats~~ (anchor, **anchors**) ~~in Boston~~.

5. His <u>competitors</u> (lifts, **lift**) heavier weights.

6. A <u>porbeagle</u> (**is,** are) a shark ~~with a pointed nose~~.

7. The <u>child</u> (push, **pushes**) a small cart ~~in the grocery store~~.

8. <u>Everyone</u> ~~of the girls~~ (**is,** are) ~~on the team~~.

9. <u>Blennies</u> (**swim,** swims) ~~in a sea~~.

10. Several <u>oxen</u> (**pull,** pulls) the heavy cart.

11. The <u>tail</u> ~~of a racerunner~~ (**is,** are) nine inches.

12. <u>She</u> (look, **looks**) ~~through a telescope~~.

13. <u>Each</u> ~~of the children~~ (take, **takes**) a nap.

14. <u>Maria</u> (cook, **cooks**) ~~for her entire family~~.

15. Many <u>types</u> ~~of beans~~ (**grow,** grows) ~~in their garden~~.

126

Directions: Read each sentence. Underline the subject once; circle the verb that agrees with the subject.

Remember: You may want to cross out prepositional phrases. This helps to find the subject.

1. Several mops (have, has) old handles.

2. Those spiders (spin, spins) a large web.

3. A yellowhammer (peck, pecks) trees.

4. One of the boats (anchor, anchors) in Boston.

5. His competitors (lifts, lift) heavier weights.

6. A porbeagle (is, are) a shark with a pointed nose.

7. The child (push, pushes) a small cart in the grocery store.

8. Everyone of the girls (is, are) on the team.

9. Blennies (swim, swims) in a sea.

10. Several oxen (pull, pulls) the heavy cart.

11. The tail of a racerunner (is, are) nine inches.

12. She (look, looks) through a telescope.

13. Each of the children (take, takes) a nap.

14. Maria (cook, cooks) for her entire family.

15. Many types of beans (grow, grows) in their garden.   127

WORKBOOK PAGE 57

🍓🍓🍓**This review is lengthy. You may want to complete it over a period of a few days.**

A. **Contractions:**

Answers are in boldfaced print.

Directions: Write the contraction in the space provided.

1. we are - **we're**   6. I am - **I'm**

2. must not - **mustn't**   7. could not - **couldn't**

3. she is - **she's**   8. cannot - **can't**

4. have not - **haven't**   9. they have - **they've**

5. they are - **they're**   10. will not - **won't**

B. **Helping (Auxiliary) Verbs:**

Directions: List the twenty-three helping verbs.

do, does, did   has, have, had

may, must, might   shall, will, can   could, would, should

is, am, are, was, were, be, being, been

C. **Action?:**

Directions: Write <u>Yes</u> if the boldfaced verb shows action; write <u>No</u> if the boldfaced verb does not show action.

1. **Yes**   She **picked** flowers by the road.

2. **Yes**   Two deer **nibble** grass in the meadow each evening.

3. **Yes**   He **swung** the bat.

4. **No**   I **need** a new toothbrush.

5. **Yes**   She **reads** the newspaper after dinner.

6. **No**   This milk **seems** sour.

128

Name_____   **Verb Review**

Date_____

A. **Contractions:**

Directions: Write the contraction in the space provided.

1. we are - _____

2. must not - _____

3. she is - _____

4. have not - _____

5. they are - _____

6. I am -_____

7. could not - _____

8. cannot - _____

9. they have - _____

10. will not - _____

B. **Helping (Auxiliary) Verbs:**

Directions: List the twenty-three helping verbs.

_____

_____

_____

C. **Action?:**

Directions: Write <u>Yes</u> if the boldfaced verb shows action; write <u>No</u> if the boldfaced verb does not show action.

1. _____   She **picked** flowers by the road.

2. _____   Two deer **nibble** grass in the meadow each evening.

3. _____   He **swung** the bat.

4. _____   I **need** a new toothbrush.

5. _____   She **reads** the newspaper after dinner.

6. _____   This milk **seems** sour.

WORKBOOK PAGE 58

D. **Regular or Irregular:**

Directions: Write <u>RV</u> if the verb is regular. Write <u>IV</u> if the verb is irregular.

Remember: Regular verbs add <u>ed</u> to the past and past participle.

1. <u> RV </u> to work   4. <u> IV </u> to fly   7. <u> IV </u> to write

2. <u> RV </u> to land   5. <u> RV </u> to help   8. <u> IV </u> to be

3. <u> IV </u> to slide   6. <u> RV </u> to promise   9. <u> RV </u> to want

E. **Subject/Verb:**

Directions: Cross out any prepositional phrases.   Underline the subject once
and the verb/verb phrase twice.

1. Tigers live ~~in India~~.

2. A trolley came ~~toward us~~.

3. We placed a saddle ~~on the horse~~.

4. That lamp shade is broken.

5. We cleared trash ~~along the road~~.

6. Michael and Becky swim ~~after work~~.

7. The lobby ~~of that hotel~~ is beautiful.

8. A large rattlesnake crawled ~~across the desert~~.

9. Many ~~of the guests~~ had **not** eaten lunch.

10. His best outfit was ruined ~~in the wash~~.

130

D. **Regular or Irregular:**

   Directions: Write <u>RV</u> if the verb is regular. Write <u>IV</u> if the verb is irregular.

Remember: Regular verbs add <u>ed</u> to the past and past participle.

1. _____ to work   4. _____ to fly   7. _____ to write

2. _____ to land   5. _____ to help   8. _____ to be

3. _____ to slide   6. _____ to promise 9. _____ to want

E. **Subject/Verb:**

   Directions: Cross out any prepositional phrases.   Underline the subject once
            and the verb/verb phrase twice.

1. Tigers live in India.

2. A trolley came toward us.

3. We placed a saddle on the horse.

4. That lamp shade is broken.

5. We cleared trash along the road.

6. Michael and Becky swim after work.

7. The lobby of that hotel is beautiful.

8. A large rattlesnake crawled across the desert.

9. Many of the guests had not eaten lunch.

10. His best outfit was ruined in the wash.

Name_____   **Verb Review**

Date_____

🍓🍓🍓**IMPORTANT: Before assigning the next page, decide if you want students to follow the directions or to cross out prepositional phrases, underline the subject once and the verb phrase twice. Both modes of response have been given.**

F.   **Irregular Verbs:**

Directions: Circle the correct verb.

1.   A <u>brush has</u> (fell, **fallen**) ~~behind the sink~~.

2.   One <u>piece</u> ~~of the blueberry pie~~ <u>has been</u> (ate, **eaten**).

3.   <u>He has</u> (brung, **brought**) a new toy.

4.   My <u>father has</u> (**flown**, flew) ~~to Virginia~~.

5.   A <u>waitress was</u> (gave, **given**) a large tip.

6.   His <u>camera has</u> (laid, **lain**) ~~on the grass~~ all day.

7.   <u>Have you</u> (did, **done**) your errands?

8.   <u>You must have</u> (**left,** leaved) your wallet ~~in the car~~.

9.   <u>Has</u> the <u>runner</u> (stole, **stolen**) third base?

10.   The <u>inside</u> ~~of the muffin~~ <u>has</u> (**sunk**, sank).

11.   A strong <u>wind has</u> (**blown**, blew) ~~throughout the day~~.

12.   <u>We had</u> (saw, **seen**) a picture ~~of an old castle~~.

13.   The <u>gift was</u> (boughten, **bought**) ~~for ten dollars~~.

14.   <u>He could have</u> (swam, **swum**) two more laps.

15.   <u>Someone had</u> (<u>driven</u>, drove) ~~over the curb~~.

16.   The child's <u>condition had</u> (began, **begun**) (to improve).

17.   <u>Has he</u> (drank, **drunk**) his milk?

18. <u>He has</u> *not* (rode, **ridden**) a jet ski.

19.   <u>I shall have</u> (**run**, ran) ten miles ~~by Friday~~.

132

Date_____

F. **Irregular Verbs:**

Directions: Circle the correct verb.

1. A brush has (fell, fallen) behind the sink.

2. One piece of the blueberry pie has been (ate, eaten).

3. He has (brung, brought) a new toy.

4. My father has (flown, flew) to Virginia.

5. A waitress was (gave, given) a large tip.

6. His camera has (laid, lain) on the grass all day.

7. Have you (did, done) your errands?

8. You must have (left, leaved) your wallet in the car.

9. Has the runner (stole, stolen) third base?

10. The inside of the muffin has (sunk, sank).

11. A strong wind has (blown, blew) throughout the day.

12. We had (saw, seen) a picture of an old castle.

13. The gift was (boughten, bought) for ten dollars.

14. He could have (swam, swum) two more laps.

15. Someone had (driven, drove) over the curb.

16. The child's condition had (began, begun) to improve.

17. Has he (drank, drunk) his milk?

18. He has not (rode, ridden) a jet ski.

19. I shall have (run, ran) ten miles by Friday.

G. **Sit/Set, Rise/Raise, and Lie/Lay:**

   Directions: Cross out any prepositional phrases. Underline the subject once
                 and the verb/verb phrase twice.   Label any direct object - <u>D.O.</u>

Remember: **With *to set*, *to raise*, and *to lay*, you must have a direct object.**
              ***Lays*, *laid*, and *laying* must have a direct object.**

                              D.O.

1. <u>I</u> (<u>raised</u>, rose) my hand.

2. A <u>cord</u> <u>is</u> (<u>lying</u>, laying) ~~on the floor~~.

3. The <u>bread</u> <u>has</u> (raised, <u>risen</u>) ~~in a warm spot~~.

                            D.O.

4. <u>Mom</u> <u>had</u> (<u>laid</u>, lain) the photographs ~~on the desk~~.

5. The <u>house</u> (<u>sits</u>, sets) ~~on a cliff~~.

                                  D.O.

6. Her <u>secretary</u> (lies, <u>lays</u>) the office mail ~~on a file cabinet~~.

                            D.O.

7. <u>Grandpa</u> always (sits, <u>sets</u>) firewood ~~by the fireplace~~.

H. **Tenses:**

   Directions: Cross out any prepositional phrases. Underline the subject once
                 and the verb/verb phrase twice. Write the tense on the line.

Remember: The tenses that we have learned are ***present*, *past*, and *future*.**

1. _____past_____   A <u>jackrabbit</u> <u>hopped</u> ~~in the road~~.

2. _____present_____   Our nation's <u>capital</u> <u>is</u> Washington, D.C.

3. _____future_____   My <u>cousin</u> <u>will</u> <u>cook</u> hot dogs ~~for us~~.

4. _____present_____   Our <u>dog</u> <u>lies</u> ~~on her stomach~~.

5. _____past_____   <u>Kent</u> <u>watched</u> the parade.

6. _____future_____   The <u>potter</u> <u>will</u> <u>use</u> his wheel.

7. _____past_____   <u>Jacob</u> <u>came</u> ~~for a visit~~.

8. _____future_____   <u>I</u> <u>shall</u> <u>read</u> ~~to you~~.

134

G.   **Sit/Set, Rise/Raise, and Lie/Lay:**

>   Directions: Cross out any prepositional phrases. Underline the subject once
>   and the verb/verb phrase twice.   Label any direct object - <u>D.O.</u>

Remember: **With *to set*, *to raise*, and *to lay*, you must have a direct object.**
Lays, _laid_, and _laying_ must have a direct object.

1.   I (raised, rose) my hand.

2.   The cord is (lying, laying) on the floor.

3.   The bread has (raised, risen) in a warm spot.

4.   Mom had (laid, lain) the photographs on the desk.

5.   The house (sits, sets) on a cliff.

6.   Her secretary (lies, lays) the office mail on a file cabinet.

7.   Grandpa always (sits, sets) firewood by the fireplace.

H.   **Tenses:**

>   Directions: Cross out any prepositional phrases. Underline the subject once
>   and the verb/verb phrase twice. Write the tense on the line.

Remember: The tenses that we have learned are ***present***, ***past***, and ***future***.

1.   _____   A jackrabbit hopped in the road.

2.   _____   Our nation's capital is Washington, D.C.

3.   _____   My cousin will cook hot dogs for us.

4.   _____   Our dog lies on her stomach.

5.   _____   Kent watched the parade.

6.   _____   The potter will use his wheel.

7.   _____   Jacob came for a visit.

8.   _____   I shall read to you.

WORKBOOK PAGE 61

Date_____

🍓🍓🍓**Important Note:** **In part K, directions do not indicate to cross out prepositional phrases and underline the subject once. However, you may wish for students to do so in order to determine subject/verb agreement more readily.**

I. **Helping Verb(s) + Main Verb:**

    Directions: Cross out any prepositional phrases. Underline the subject once and the verb/verb phrase twice. Write the helping verb(s) and the main verb on the lines.

		Helping Verb(s)	Main Verb
1.	We <u>must leave</u> soon.	must	leave
2.	A <u>coyote</u> <u>has run</u> ~~across the road~~.	has	run
3.	A window <u>washer</u> <u>was finished</u>.	was	finished
4.	<u>I</u> <u>should have gone</u> ~~with you~~.	should have	gone
5.	<u>Did</u> <u>you</u> <u>receive</u> a trophy?	Did	receive

J. **You're/Your, It's/Its, and They're/Their/There:**

    Directions: Circle the correct word.

1. Does (you're, **your**) bird have water?

2. If (**you're**, your) going, please hurry.

3. A cow lifted (it's, **its**) head and mooed.

4. Janice said that (**it's**, its) difficult to use the balance beam.

5. (They're, **Their**, There) brother lives in Idaho.

6. (They're, Their, **There**) are several dirty dishes in the sink.

7. Let's ask when (**they're**, their, there) boarding the airplane.

Although directions do not indicate, prepositional phrases have been deleted, and the subject has been underlined.

K. **Subject/Verb Agreement:**

    Directions: Select the correct verb.

1. A <u>penguin</u> (waddle, **waddles**) ~~over the snow~~.

2. <u>They</u> (**pick**, picks) peaches ~~at an orchard~~.

3. Fresh <u>marshmallows</u> (is, **are**) ~~in the cupboard~~.

4. <u>One</u> ~~of the boys~~ (need, **needs**) a hair cut.

5. <u>Geysers</u> (spurts, **spurt**) water ~~at that national park~~.

136 6. My <u>friend</u> (go, **goes**) ~~to the Ozark Mountains~~ each summer.

Name_____

Date_____

I. **Helping Verb(s) + Main Verb:**
   Directions: Cross out any prepositional phrases. Underline the subject once
   and the verb/verb phrase twice.   Write the helping verb(s) and the
   main verb on the lines.

	Helping Verb(s)	**Main Verb**

1. We must leave soon.   _____ _____

2. A coyote has run across the road.   _____ _____

3. A window washer was finished.   _____ _____

4. I should have gone with you.   _____ _____

5. Did you receive a trophy?   _____ _____

J. **You're/Your, It's/Its, and They're/Their/There:**
   Directions: Circle the correct word.

1. Does (you're, your) bird have water?
2. If (you're, your) going, please hurry.
3. A cow lifted (it's, its) head and mooed.
4. Janice said that (it's, its) difficult to use the balance beam.
5. (They're, Their, There) brother lives in Idaho.
6. (They're, Their, There) are several dirty dishes in the sink.
7. Let's ask when (they're, their, there) boarding the airplane.

K. **Subject/Verb Agreement:**
   Directions: Select the correct verb.

1. A penguin (waddle, waddles) over the snow.
2. They (pick, picks) peaches at an orchard.
3. Fresh marshmallows (is, are) in the cupboard.
4. One of the boys (need, needs) a hair cut.
5. Geysers (spurts, spurt) water at that national park.
6. My friend (go, goes) to the Ozark Mountains each summer.   137

Name_____ **Verb Test**

Date_____

🍓🍓🍓**Please note that in most sentences, students have ɴᴏᴛ been instructed to delete prepositional phrases or to underline the subject once and verb/verb phrase twice. Because students have practiced doing this in the lessons and it helps to insure correct response, you may choose to have students follow this process. However, if you feel that your students can do well without this process, by all means, follow the instructions provided. Both modes of response have been included.**

A. Directions: Write the contraction.

1. they are - __they're__   4. I am - __I'm__   7. you are - __you're__

2. cannot - __can't__   5. he is - __he's__   8. I shall - __I'll__

3. they have - __they've__   6. did not - __didn't__   9. will not - __won't__

B. Directions: Write <u>Yes</u> if the boldfaced verb shows action; write <u>No</u> if the boldfaced verb does not show action.

1. __Yes__ The priest **kneels** at the altar.

2. __No__ She **became** a firefighter.

3. __Yes__ His mother **whistles** often.

4. __Yes__ Roy and Frances **skydive**.

5. __No__ Mr. Collins **is** nice.

C. Directions: Write <u>RV</u> if the verb is a regular verb; write <u>IV</u> if the verb is irregular.

1. __IV__ to say   3. __RV__ to shop   5. __IV__ to see

2. __RV__ to live   4. __IV__ to stand   6. __RV__ to hope

D. Directions: Circle the correct verb.

1. The track <u>star had</u> (<u>run</u>, ran) a great race.

2. <u>Brett has</u> (did, <u>done</u>) his guitar lesson.

3. <u>Have you</u> (saw, <u>seen</u>) a hummingbird?

4. <u>Pioneers had</u> (rode, <u>ridden</u>) ~~across the desert in covered wagons~~.

5. <u>Has</u> your <u>brother</u> ever (<u>drunk</u>, drank) flavored iced tea?

6. Several <u>branches</u> <u>must have</u> (<u>fallen</u>, fell) ~~during the storm~~.

7. <u>You</u> <u>should</u> *not* <u>have</u> (swam, <u>swum</u>) ~~by yourself~~.

8. The accident <u>victims</u> <u>were</u> (<u>flown</u>, flew) ~~to a nearby hospital~~.

9. Our <u>cat has</u> (laid, <u>lain</u>) ~~on the sofa~~ all afternoon.

10. He has (sat, <u>set</u>) the video ~~on the front seat of his car~~.

138 11. The <u>lawyer</u> (lay, <u>laid</u>) her pen ~~by a note pad~~.

Name_____   **Verb Test**

Date_____

A. Directions: Write the contraction.

1. they are - _____   4. I am - _____   7. you are - _____

2. cannot - _____   5. he is - _____   8. I shall - _____

3. they have - _____   6. did not - _____   9. will not - _____

B. Directions: Write <u>Yes</u> if the boldfaced verb shows action; write <u>No</u> if the
            boldfaced verb does not show action.

1. _____   The priest **kneels** at the altar.

2. _____   She **became** a firefighter.

3. _____   His mother **whistles** often.

4. _____   Roy and Frances **skydive**.

5. _____   Mr. Collins **is** nice.

C. Directions: Write <u>RV</u> if the verb is a regular verb; write <u>IV</u> if the verb is irregular.

1. _____ to say   3. _____ to shop   5. _____ to see

2. _____ to live   4. _____ to stand   6. _____ to hope

D. Directions: Circle the correct verb.

1.   The track star had (run, ran) a great race.

2. Brett has (did, done) his guitar lesson.

3. Have you (saw, seen) a hummingbird?

4. Pioneers had (rode, ridden) across the desert in covered wagons.

5. Has your brother ever (drunk, drank) flavored iced tea?

6. Several branches must have (fallen, fell) during the storm.

7. You should not have (swam, swum) by yourself.

8. The accident victims were (flown, flew) to a nearby hospital.

9. Our cat has (laid, lain) on the sofa all afternoon.

10. He has (sat, set) the video on the front seat of his car.

11. The lawyer (lay, laid) her pen by a note pad.   139

12. Have <u>you</u> (ate, <u>eaten</u>) yet?

13. Their <u>friend has</u> (came, <u>come</u>) ~~by train~~.

14. (<u>You</u>) Please (<u>raise</u>, rise) the flag.

15. <u>We</u> (brang, <u>brought</u>) our sleeping bags.

E.   Directions: Write the tense of the boldfaced verb or verb phrase.

1.   <u>present</u>   He **studies** every day.

2.   <u>past</u>   John and Eric **studied** for an hour.

3.   <u>future</u>   I **shall study** this map.

4.   <u>past</u>   Carla **washed** her car with hot, soapy water.

5.   <u>present</u>   Diana **sponges** spots from her carpeting.

F.   Directions: Circle the correct word.

1.   Are you aware that (**it's**, its) time to leave?

2.   Does (you're, **your**) play open tonight?

3.   (**They're**, Their, There) very happy.

4.   Several girls refused to give (they're, **their**, there) apples away.

5.   The cat licked (it's, **its**) sore paw.

G.   Directions: Circle the verb that agrees with the subject.   Additional information has been given.

1.   Many cast iron <u>kettles</u> (<u>hang</u>, hangs) ~~in front of the antique shop~~.

2.   A <u>rhinoceros</u> (<u>has</u>, have) one or two horns ~~on his snout~~.

3.   That <u>chef</u> (stir, <u>stirs</u>) fried green onion ~~into the stew~~.

4.   <u>One</u> ~~of the boys~~ usually (hit, <u>hits</u>) the ball ~~to left field~~.

5.   Those <u>ladies</u> (is, <u>are</u>) ~~on a bus tour~~.

H.   Directions: Cross out any prepositional phrases. Underline the subject once and
                              the verb/verb phrase twice.

1.   A <u>woman</u> <u>waded</u> ~~in the lake~~.

2.   The <u>family</u> <u>will eat</u> ~~at a cafe~~.

3.   The <u>road</u> <u>leads</u> ~~to an old barn~~.

4.   <u>She</u> <u>washed</u> her hair and <u>dried</u> it.

5.   ~~Before the meeting~~, <u>they</u> <u>must have talked</u> ~~about their decision~~.

140

12. Have you (ate, eaten) yet?

13. Their friend has (came, come) by train.

14. Please (raise, rise) the flag.

15. We (brang, brought) our sleeping bags.

E. Directions: Write the tense of the boldfaced verb or verb phrase.

1. _____ He **studies** every day.

2. _____ John and Eric **studied** for an hour.

3. _____ I **shall study** this map.

4. _____ Carla **washed** her car with hot, soapy water.

5. _____ Diana **sponges** spots from her carpeting.

F. Directions: Circle the correct word.

1. Are you aware that (it's, its) time to leave?

2. Does (you're, your) play open tonight?

3. (They're, Their, There) very happy.

4. Several girls refused to give (they're, their, there) apples away.

5. The cat licked (it's, its) sore paw.

G. Directions: Circle the verb that agrees with the subject.

1. Many cast iron kettles (hang, hangs) in front of the antique shop.

2. A rhinoceros (has, have) one or two horns on his snout.

3. That chef (stir, stirs) fried green onion into the stew.

4. One of the boys usually (hit, hits) the ball to left field.

5. Those ladies (is, are) on a bus tour.

H. Directions: Cross out any prepositional phrases. Underline the subject once and the verb/verb phrase twice.

1. A woman waded in the lake.

2. The family will eat at a cafe.

3. The road leads to an old barn.

4. She washed her hair and dried it.

5. Before the meeting, they must have talked about their decision.

Name_____   **Cumulative Review**
WORKBOOK PAGE 62   **Verb Unit**
Date_____

🍓🍓🍓**You may wish to do this review over several days.**

A. **Preposition List:**

Directions: List the forty prepositions that you have learned.

1. about	16. down	31. past
2. above	17. during	32. through
3. across	18. except	33. throughout
4. after	19. for	34. to
5. against	20. from	35. toward
6. along	21. in	36. under
7. around	22. inside	37. until
8. at	23. into	38. up
9. before	24. near	39. with
10. behind	25. of	40. without
11. below	26. off	
12. beneath	27. on	
13. beside	28. out	
14. between	29. outside	
15. by	30. over	

B. **Object of the Preposition:**
Directions: Cross out any prepositional phrases. Label the object of the
preposition - O.P.

O.P.
1. The tree trimmer climbed ~~on a ladder~~.

O.P.
2. His house is ~~near a creek~~.

O.P.
3. A bee buzzed ~~around my head~~.

142

A. **Preposition List:**
    Directions: List the forty prepositions that you have learned.

1. _____   16. _____   31. _____

2. _____   17. _____   32. _____

3. _____   18. _____   33. _____

4. _____   19. _____   34. _____

5. _____   20. _____   35. _____

6. _____   21. _____   36. _____

7. _____   22. _____   37. _____

8. _____   23. _____   38. _____

9. _____   24. _____   39. _____

10. _____   25. _____   40. _____

11. _____   26. _____

12. _____   27. _____

13. _____   28. _____

14. _____   29. _____

15. _____   30. _____

B. **Object of the Preposition:**
    Directions: Cross out any prepositional phrases. Label the object of the
                 preposition - O.P.

1. The tree trimmer climbed on a ladder.

2. His house is near a creek.

3. A bee buzzed around my head.   143

C. **Compound Subjects:**

Directions: Cross out any prepositional phrases. Underline the subject once and the verb/verb phrase twice.

Remember: Compound means more than one.

1. Miss Putnam or Mrs. Poe lives ~~in Rhode Island~~.

2. Opossums and monkeys hang ~~by their tails~~.

3. His socks, jersey, and shorts are ~~in the washing machine~~.

D. **Imperative Sentences:**

Directions: Cross out any prepositional phrases. Underline the subject once and the verb/verb phrase twice.

Remember: An imperative sentence gives a command.
(You)
1. Stay ~~with me~~.
    (You)
2. Pass the bread, please.
    (You)
3. Write ~~in black ink~~.

E. **Compound Objects of the Preposition:**

Directions: Cross out any prepositional phrases. Underline the subject once and the verb/verb phrase twice.

Remember: Compound means more than one.

1. We drew pictures ~~with crayons and colored pencils~~.

2. That package is ~~for Jim and Jan~~.

3. A volunteer handed booklets ~~to Dawn and me~~.

144

C. **Compound Subjects:**

Directions: Cross out any prepositional phrases. Underline the subject once and the verb/verb phrase twice.

Remember: **Compound means more than one.**

1. Miss Putnam or Mrs. Poe lives in Rhode Island.

2. Opossums and monkeys hang by their tails.

3. His socks, jersey, and shorts are in the washing machine.

D. **Imperative Sentences:**

Directions: Cross out any prepositional phrases. Underline the subject once and the verb/verb phrase twice.

Remember: **An imperative sentence gives a command.**

1. Stay with me.

2. Pass the bread, please.

3. Write in black ink.

E. **Compound Objects of the Preposition:**

Directions: Cross out any prepositional phrases. Underline the subject once and the verb/verb phrase twice.

Remember: **Compound means more than one.**

1. We drew pictures with crayons and colored pencils.

2. That package is for Jim and Jan.

3. A volunteer handed booklets to Dawn and me.

F. **Compound Verbs:**

Directions: Cross out any prepositional phrases. Underline the subject once and the verb/verb phrase twice.

Remember: Compound means more than one.

1. A <u>seal</u> <u>yelps</u> and <u>claps</u>.

2. A <u>spectator</u> <u>waved</u> her hands and <u>cheered</u>.

3. A <u>teenager</u> <u>stomped</u> his foot and <u>muttered</u>.

G. **Infinitives:**

Directions: Cross out any prepositional phrases. Underline the subject once and the verb twice. Place an infinitive in parenthesis ( ).

Remember: To + a verb = infinitive. Do not cross out any infinitives.

Examples: to run
to taste

1. <u>You</u> <u>seem</u> (to be) angry.

2. <u>We</u> <u>like</u> (to feed) ducks ~~at the park~~.

3. Their <u>sister</u> <u>started</u> (to drive).

H. **Prepositions:**

Directions: Cross out any prepositional phrases. Underline the subject once and the verb/verb phrase twice. Label any direct object - <u>D.O.</u>

                      D.O.
1. <u>Allen</u> <u>writes</u> letters ~~to his friends~~.

                      D.O.
2. <u>I</u> <u>set</u> the broom ~~beside the back door~~.

                      D.O.
146 3. <u>Mr. Scott</u> <u>took</u> a trip ~~with a friend~~.

F. **Compound Verbs:**

    Directions: Cross out any prepositional phrases. Underline the subject once and the verb/verb phrase twice.

Remember: Compound means more than one.

1. A seal yelps and claps.

2. A spectator waved her hands and cheered.

3. A teenager stomped his foot and muttered.

G. **Infinitives:**

    Directions: Cross out any prepositional phrases. Underline the subject once and the verb twice. Place an infinitive in parenthesis (   ).

Remember: To + a verb = infinitive. Do not cross out any infinitives.

    Examples: to run
                 to taste

1. You seem to be angry.

2. We like to feed ducks at the park.

3. Their sister started to drive.

H. **Prepositions:**

    Directions: Cross out any prepositional phrases. Underline the subject once and the verb/verb phrase twice. Label any direct object - <u>D.O.</u>

1. Allen writes letters to his friends.

2. I set the broom beside the back door.

3. Mr. Scott took a trip with a friend.   147

A. Preposition List:

Directions: List forty prepositions.

1. about	16. down	31. past
2. above	17. during	32. through
3. across	18. except	33. throughout
4. after	19. for	34. to
5. against	20. from	35. toward
6. along	21. in	36. under
7. around	22. inside	37. until
8. at	23. into	38. up
9. before	24. near	39. with
10. behind	25. of	40. without
11. below	26. off	
12. beneath	27. on	
13. beside	28. out	
14. between	29. outside	
15. by	30. over	

B. Object of the Preposition:

Directions: Cross out any prepositional phrases. Label the object of the
preposition - O.P.

                  O.P.

1.   Your <u>coat</u> <u>is</u> ~~on the floor~~.

                      O.P.

2.   <u>Janell</u> <u>looks</u> ~~for baseball cards~~.

A. **Preposition List:**
   Directions: List forty prepositions.

1. _____   16. _____   31. _____

2. _____   17. _____   32. _____

3. _____   18. _____   33. _____

4. _____   19. _____   34. _____

5. _____   20. _____   35. _____

6. _____   21. _____   36. _____

7. _____   22. _____   37. _____

8. _____   23. _____   38. _____

9. _____   24. _____   39. _____

10. _____   25. _____   40. _____

11. _____   26. _____

12. _____   27. _____

13. _____   28. _____

14. _____   29. _____

15. _____   30. _____

B. **Object of the Preposition:**
   Directions: Cross out any prepositional phrases. Label the object of the
                 preposition - O.P.

1. Your coat is on the floor.

2. Janell looks for baseball cards.

C. **Compound Subjects:**

    Directions: Cross out any prepositional phrases. Underline the subject once and the verb/verb phrase twice.

1. His <u>bat</u> and <u>ball</u> <u>are</u> ~~in the garage~~.

2. <u>Phoenix</u> and <u>Sacramento</u> <u>are</u> capital cities.

🍓🍓🍓

D. **Imperative Sentences:**

    Directions: Cross out any prepositional phrases. Underline the subject once and the verb/verb phrase twice.

1. <u>(You)</u> <u>Go</u> ~~to the store~~, please.

2. <u>(You)</u> ~~After lunch~~, <u>mail</u> this envelope.

🍓🍓🍓

E. **Compound Objects of the Preposition:**

    Directions: Cross out any prepositional phrases. Underline the subject once and the verb/verb phrase twice.

1. <u>He</u> <u>left</u> ~~without a jacket or sweater~~.

2. <u>Flowers</u> <u>are growing</u> ~~by the shed and barn~~.

🍓🍓🍓

F. **Compound Verbs:**

    Directions: Cross out any prepositional phrases. Underline the subject once and the verb/verb phrase twice.

1. <u>I</u> <u>moved</u> furniture and <u>cleaned</u>.

2. <u>Matt</u> <u>writes</u> stories and <u>sends</u> them ~~to his grandpa~~.

🍓🍓🍓

G. **Infinitives:**

    Directions: Cross out any prepositional phrases. Underline the subject once and the verb twice. Place an infinitive in parenthesis ( ).

1. <u>I</u> <u>like</u> (to talk).

2. <u>Wolves</u> <u>need</u> (to wander)

🍓🍓🍓

H. **Direct Objects:**

    Directions: Cross out any prepositional phrases. Underline the subject once and the verb/verb phrase twice. Label any direct object-<u>D.O.</u>

                                         D.O.

   1. <u>Jake</u> <u>milks</u> cows ~~in the morning~~.

                                         D.O.

150   2. The college <u>student</u> <u>purchased</u> towels ~~for his new apartment~~.

C. **Compound Subjects:**
   Directions: Cross out any prepositional phrases. Underline the subject once and the verb/verb phrase twice.

1. His bat and ball are in the garage.

2. Phoenix and Sacramento are capital cities.

D. **Imperative Sentences:**
   Directions: Cross out any prepositional phrases. Underline the subject once and the verb/verb phrase twice.

1. Go to the store, please.

2. After lunch, mail this envelope

E. **Compound Objects of the Preposition:**
   Directions: Cross out any prepositional phrases. Underline the subject once and the verb/verb phrase twice.

1. He left without a jacket or sweater.

2. Flowers are growing by the shed and barn.

F. **Compound Verbs:**
   Directions: Cross out any prepositional phrases. Underline the subject once and the verb/verb phrase twice.

1. I moved furniture and cleaned.

2. Matt writes stories and sends them to his grandpa.

G. **Infinitives:**
   Directions: Cross out any prepositional phrases. Underline the subject once and the verb twice. Place an infinitive in parenthesis ( ).

1. I like to talk.

2. Wolves need to wander.

H. **Direct Objects:**
   Directions: Cross out any prepositional phrases. Underline the subject once and the verb/verb phrase twice. Label any direct object-D.O.

1. Jake milks cows in the morning.

2. The college student purchased towels for his new apartment.

151

TO THE TEACHER: Please read carefully.

You may have noted that linking verbs were not taught. These are introduced in *Easy Grammar: Grade 5*.

The noun unit begins on the next page.   A definition of nouns is given. Beware! Students often can recite the definition without truly understanding noun identification or usage.

The concepts covered at this level are easy to divide. Teach each concept thoroughly before proceeding.

Students are not introduced to appositives, indirect objects, or predicate nominatives. These concepts are introduced at other levels.

NOUNS

TO THE TEACHER: Please read carefully.

PAGE 155 = WORKBOOK PAGE 65

Page 155: Concept: Noun Definition and Concrete/Abstract Nouns:

A. Definition: The definition is provided on page 155. Be sure to break nouns into "mini" concepts. Talk about *people* first. Discuss those which may be included, i.e. Dinah, cousin, Abraham Lincoln, etc. Then, discuss *places*, i. e. zoo, park, town, Canada, etc. Next, discuss *things*. I recommend that you point to objects in the room and ask, "Is this a "thing" (noun)?" Ask students to hold up a noun. I ask students to say, "I am holding a(n) _____; a(n) _____ is a noun." The last part of the discussion focuses on *ideas*. I am, at this point, sketchy about *ideas* because I explain this more thoroughly when teaching concrete and abstract nouns.

<u>Game</u>: This simple game helps students to understand nouns. Divide the class into groups of three to five. Tell students that the class will take a walk around the school. No talking will be allowed, and no one will carry paper or pencil. The purpose of the walk will be to observe and remember as many nouns as possible. Upon returning, each group will sit together; a leader for writing the list will be selected. Give the students two to five minutes to write as many nouns as they can remember; time it. Expect some noise, and watch the enthusiasm. At the end of the time period, have each group record its total number. I recommend that you allow students to exchange group answers and check if a noun may have been listed twice. This accomplishes two goals; first, students are reinforcing what nouns are, and it saves time. I usually award a prize (sticker, bookmark, candy, etc.) to each person in the winning group.

B. Concrete and Abstract Nouns:

When introducing concrete and abstract nouns, I ask students to pretend they are holding a piece of concrete. We discuss the size, the color, how much it weighs, etc. I even ask them to pretend to juggle it. Using the idea of a piece of concrete, we then discuss that a concrete noun is one that you can see. (We do discuss air and smoke as being concrete. Although air can't be "seen," one can "see" its atoms under a high-powered microscope.)

Abstract nouns may be too "abstract" for some of your fourth grade students. Of course, you will want to explain that a word such as *love* is an abstract noun. It can't be seen, but it expresses an idea. *Love* is a type of noun called an abstract noun. However, don't be surprised if you have to teach this concept circuitously. If a student is having difficulty determining if a noun is concrete or abstract, have him first determine if he can "see" it. If he can't, the noun is probably abstract.

154

NOUNS

A. **Definition:** **A noun names a person, place, thing, or idea.**

Examples:

  person: Judy, aunt, teacher, dentist, George Washington

  place: park, beach, zoo, Washington, D.C.

  thing: knife, rose, mustard

  idea: happiness, love, knowledge

B. **Concrete and Abstract Nouns:**

1. **Concrete nouns can be seen: book, camera, tree.**

   Some concrete nouns cannot "technically" be seen unless they are examined in very small parts called atoms.   Examples of this are *air* and *wind*.

2. **Abstract nouns are those that cannot be seen.** They usually represent an idea. Examples of abstract nouns are *love* and *kindness*.

Name_____

Date_____

NOUNS
Abstract or Concrete?

Directions: Each set contains a concrete noun and an abstract noun. In the space
provided, write <u>C</u> if the noun is concrete and <u>A</u> if the noun is abstract.

A.
1. __C__   drum

2. __A__   love

B.
1. __A__   happiness

2. __C__   plant

C.
1. __A__   fun

2. __C__   bread

D.
1. __A__   time

2. __C__   basket

E.
1. __C__   sand

2. __A__   joy

F.
1. __C__   tongue

2. __A__   freedom

G.
1. __A__   hope

2. __C__   fan

H.
1. __C__   bear

2. __A__   fear

I.
1. __A__   courage

2. __C__   cream

J.
1. __C__   applesauce

2. __A__   kindness

K.
1. __C__   air

2. __A__   faith

L.
1. __A__   friendship

2. __C__   raft

156

Name_____   **NOUNS**
                                                 Concrete or Abstract?

Date_____

Directions: Each set contains a concrete noun and an abstract noun. In the space
              provided, write <u>C</u> if the noun is concrete and <u>A</u> if the noun is abstract.

A.   G.
1. _____   drum   1. _____   hope

2. _____   love   2. _____   fan

B.   H.
1. _____   happiness   1. _____   bear

2. _____   plant   2. _____   fear

C.   I.
1. _____   fun   1. _____   courage

2. _____   bread   2. _____   cream

D.   J.
1. _____   time   1. _____   applesauce

2. _____   basket   2. _____   kindness

E.   K.
1. _____   sand   1. _____   air

2. _____   joy   2. _____   faith

F.   L.
1. _____   tongue   1. _____   friendship

2. _____   freedom   2. _____   raft

157

TO THE TEACHER:

Common and Proper Nouns

The ensuing page teaches common and proper nouns. Usually, students readily understand this concept. It is ideal to solicit answers from your students. I recommend that you do a "mini" group activity. Form small groups (2-5 people per group). Each student needs his own paper. Instruct students to fold their papers in the middle vertically. At the top of the first column, write *common noun*. At the top of the second column, write *type of common noun*. Provide a few examples so that students understand this activity.

Examples: building   bank
             bird   canary

Then, allow students enough time to discuss and write their group's answers. (Having each student write his own list helps to reinforce the fact that types aren't capitalized.) Be sure to give students ample time to share answers.

Important note: You may run into the problem of a type of something that is an exception to the capitalization rule.

Examples: <u>common noun</u>   <u>type (common noun)</u>
             horse   Arabian* horse
             cheese   Swiss cheese

*You will need to explain that there are some exceptions. A proper noun is based on a particular place. For example, *Arabian* comes from a place, *Arabia*. Therefore, you capitalize *Arabian* horse (but not <u>horse</u>). You would not capitalize the type of horse called a *pinto*; it does not refer to a particular place.

A **proper noun** names a specific person, place, or thing. In teaching this, it is fun to use a map and ask for volunteers to find a specific place that you name. Another way to proceed is for you to say a place such as a lake, ask for a volunteer to give the name of a lake and for that person to call on another volunteer to locate that lake on the map. I ask the last volunteer to point to the lake and say its name again. Then, I reinforce by asking if the lake named by the student is a proper noun because it is a specific one.

Although proper nouns are easily taught, it is sometimes better understood by students when they are required to determine if a noun is common or proper. Page 161 provides an avenue for that practice.

PAGE 159 = WORKBOOK PAGE 67

158

COMMON AND PROPER NOUNS

A common noun does not name a specific person, place, or thing. Most nouns are common. Do not capitalize common nouns.

       Examples: person: boy, girl, cousin, nurse, mayor

                    place: park, zoo, ceiling

                    thing: egg, rope, train

Types of common nouns are still common and are not capitalized.

       Examples:

common noun	type (common noun)
flower	daisy
dog	terrier
horse	palomino
building	tower

A proper noun names a specific person, place, or thing. Capitalize a proper noun.

common noun	proper noun
boy	**Gary**
girl	**Sarah**
cat	**Whiskers**
doctor	**Dr. Jones**
park	**Green Park**
zoo	**San Diego Zoo**
train	**Oriental Express**

Name_____

NOUNS
Common and Proper

Date_____

ANSWERS WILL VARY. REPRESENTATIVE ANSWERS HAVE BEEN GIVEN.

Directions: Write a proper noun for each common noun.

A.
1. common noun: state

2. proper noun: Utah, Vermont

B.
1. common noun: country

2. proper noun: United States, Spain

C.
1. common noun: lake

2. proper noun: Lake Tahoe, Bartlett Lake

D.
1. common noun: mountain

2. proper noun: Mt. Rushmore, Pike's Peak

E.
1. common noun: day

2. proper noun: Sunday, Monday

F.
1. common noun: month

2. proper noun: January, April, May

G.
1. common noun: town

2. proper noun: Cashtown, Eloy

H.
1. common noun: street

2. proper noun: Adams Street, Briar Lane

I.
1. common noun: holiday

2. proper noun: Christmas, Memorial Day

J.
1. common noun: river

2. proper noun: Mississippi River, Po River

K.
1. common noun: school

2. proper noun: Loma School, Horizon High

L.
1. common noun: hospital

2. proper noun: Grove Hospital, Mayo Clinic

M.
1. common noun: store

2. proper noun: Pleasantries, Jo's Deli

N.
1. common noun: church

2. proper noun: Scottsdale Bible Church

Name_____   **NOUNS**
                                          Common and Proper
Date_____

Directions: Write a proper noun for each common noun.

A.   H.
1. common noun: state   1. common noun: street

2. proper noun: _____   2. proper noun: _____

B.   I.
1. common noun: country   1. common noun: holiday

2. proper noun: _____   2. proper noun: _____

C.   J.
1. common noun: lake   1. common noun: river

2. proper noun: _____   2. proper noun: _____

D.   K.
1. common noun: mountain   1. common noun: school

2. proper noun: _____   2. proper noun: _____

E.   L.
1. common noun: day   1. common noun: hospital

2. proper noun: _____   2. proper noun: _____

F.   M.
1. common noun: month   1. common noun: store

2. proper noun: _____   2. proper noun: _____

G.   N.
1. common noun: town   1. common noun: church

2. proper noun: _____   2. proper noun: _____

TO THE TEACHER: This is a difficult concept. Teach it slowly and thoroughly. I recommend that you teach it in one lesson and stop. On the second day, **reteach** the lesson using your own examples, and then do p. 165. **Review** the following day and do p. 167 orally.

NOUN DETERMINERS

Page 163: Concept: Classification of Noun Determiners

You will teach students to use noun "determiners" to locate many nouns in a sentence. Although some nouns will not have determiners as signals, many do. Therefore, it does help students to know that <u>when a determiner appears in a sentence, they need to look for an ensuing noun.</u>

Determiners are actually adjectives. However, in this unit, it's easier to refer to them as determiners. (In the adjective unit, they will be called determining adjectives.) Since determiners signal that a noun (or pronoun) may follow, teach students to closely examine the sentence and decide if a noun is following a determiner. <u>Questions and activities that may help you to teach noun determiners:</u>

1. **articles: a, an, the**

    What are the three articles that are determiners? (It is here that I teach my "now famous" **hula** dance. I ask students to stand. We "hula" to the left, singing "A, an, the," and hula to the right singing, "are articles." We do the hula every day while we are learning determiners and periodically throughout the year. Although students may roll their eyes and giggle, they are getting up from their seats and moving. It's fun, and they remember the articles.)

2. **demonstratives: this, that, those, these**

    What are the four words called demonstratives that are determiners? I stress that these four begin with **th**. (We also discuss that *this* and *these* are used when items are close whereas *that* and *those* are mostly used for items in a distance.)

3. **numbers:**

    Give an example of a number preceding a noun; be sure to make clear that these are signals to look for an ensuing noun.

    Example: I'll take five. Here, *five* doesn't signal a noun. We don't know *five what*.
    I'll take five minutes to finish. Here *five* signals the noun, *minutes*.

4. **possessive pronouns: my, his, her, your, its, our, their, whose**

    I ask students to fill in this space (without using a person's name) to show ownership: _____ bike. If they are having a difficult time, I place *my* in the space. Students readily understand.

5. **Possessive nouns (used as adjectives):**

    I return to _____ bike; however, this time, I ask for a person's name. I also ask students to write their own name with *'s* and add a possession. We discuss that the possession is a noun.

6. **Indefinites: some, many, few, several, no, any, etc.**

    "How many dollars do you have in your pocket?" I ask students how they might respond if they really don't want me to know the exact number. Their responses: *some* dollars, *few* dollars, *many* dollars, *several* dollars. I stress that they don't want to give a definite number; they want to be indefinite. (Some will try *a lot of* ; this is more than one word. Also, *no money* sounds rather definite, but *no* is an indefinite.)

    Example: Do you want a few? Here *few* is <u>not</u> a determiner. A noun does not follow it.
    Do you want a few grapes. Here *few* is a determiner; few precedes the noun, *grapes*.

Pages 165 and 167: Concept: Using Determiners to Identify Nouns

The process I use sounds laborious; however, it goes quite quickly and seems to work well. We read the sentence orally. "My aunt lives near a zoo." I proceed through each of the classifications. For example, is *a, an*, or *the* in the sentence? Yes, *a*. We circle *a*. *A what?* The word that answers *what* is a noun: *zoo*. We underline *zoo* as a noun. Then, we go through *this, that, those*, and *these*. No. Next, I ask if there are numbers in the sentence. No. I proceed by asking if a possessive pronoun is in the sentence. (I allow my *students to look at their chart.*) Yes, *my* is a possessive pronoun. We circle *my*. *My what? My aunt.* We underline *aunt* as a noun. (Although I know that no other determiners are in the sentence, I continue.) Is there a possessive noun such as *Annie's*? No. Last, are there any indefinites? No. With each sentence, we follow this line of questioning, but we do so rather quickly and with enthusiasm. We then look one more time to determine if any nouns without determiners are in the sentence.

PAGE 163 = WORKBOOK PAGE 69

NOUN DETERMINERS

Determiners are words that signal that a noun may follow. They simply help you to identify nouns in a sentence. Determiners are stop signs. When you see a determiner, stop and check if a noun follows it.

🍓🍓🍓🍓🍓🍓🍓🍓🍓🍓🍓🍓🍓🍓🍓🍓🍓🍓🍓🍓🍓🍓🍓🍓🍓🍓🍓🍓🍓🍓🍓

Classification of Determiners:

1. **Articles: a, an, the**

   Example: **The** tire is flat.

2. **Demonstratives: this, that, those, these**

   Example: Do you like **this** gum?

3. **Numbers**

   Example: **Two** boys laughed and cheered.

4. **Possessive pronouns: my, his, her, your, its, our, their, whose**

   Example: **My** cousin is **your** neighbor.

5. **Possessive nouns:**

   Example: Has the **dog's** leash been found?

   Note: Both the word that owns (*dog's*) and the noun that it owns (*leash*) are considered nouns. Underline both as nouns.

6. **Indefinites: some, few, many, several, no, any**

   Example: **Several** guests arrived.

🍓🍓🍓🍓🍓🍓🍓🍓🍓🍓🍓🍓🍓🍓🍓🍓🍓🍓🍓🍓🍓🍓🍓🍓🍓🍓🍓🍓🍓🍓🍓

IMPORTANT: There may be two determiners before a noun.

Her first tooth came in.

IMPORTANT: There may be determiner + descriptive word or words before the noun.

A *large white* cake had been made.

IMPORTANT: There may be nouns without determiners in a sentence. Always look for any word that states a person, place, thing, or idea.

Dad and **his** friend went to Seattle.

NOUNS
Determiners

Classification of Determiners:
1. Articles: **a, an, the**
2. Demonstratives: **this, that, those, these**
3. Numbers: Example: **fifty** people
4. Possessive pronouns: **my, his, her, your, its, our, their, whose**
5. Possessive nouns: Example: **Joyce's** car
6. Indefinites: **some, few, many, several, no, any**

Directions: A determiner appears in boldfaced print. Find the noun that it determines.
              Write both the determiner and the noun on the line.

Example: Is **your** toe broken? _____your toe_____

1. **Kim's** tricycle is red.   _____Kim's tricycle_____

2. **Her** aunt arrived today.   _____Her aunt_____

3. Where is **the** fan?   _____the fan_____

4. **Five** puppies were born.   _____Five puppies_____

5. **Many** tourists come here.   _____Many tourists_____

6. He bought **an** umbrella.   _____an umbrella_____

7. Please hand me **that** knife.   _____that knife_____

8. **This** day has been fun.   _____This day_____

9. **Grandpa's** back hurts.   _____Grandpa's back_____

10. I took **my** temperature.   _____my temperature_____

11. **Several** hikers rested.   _____Several hikers_____

12. We ate **three** pies.   _____three pies_____

13. Is **your** watch new?   _____your watch_____

14. **These** stones are smooth.   _____These stones_____

164

Name_____

Date_____

Classification of Determiners:
1. Articles: **a, an, the**
2. Demonstratives: **this, that, those, these**
3. Numbers: Example: **fifty** people
4. Possessive pronouns: **my, his, her, your, its, our, their, whose**
5. Possessive nouns: Example: **Joyce's** car
6. Indefinites: **some, few, many, several, no, any**

Directions: A determiner appears in boldfaced print. Find the noun that it determines. Write both the determiner and the noun on the line.

Example: Is **your** toe broken? _____your toe_____

1. **Kim's** tricycle is red. _____

2. **Her** aunt arrived today. _____

3. Where is **the** fan? _____

4. **Five** puppies were born. _____

5. **Many** tourists come here. _____

6. He bought **an** umbrella. _____

7. Please hand me **that** knife. _____

8. **This** day has been fun. _____

9. **Grandpa's** back hurts. _____

10. I took **my** temperature. _____

11. **Several** hikers rested. _____

12. We ate **three** pies. _____

13. Is **your** watch new? _____

14. **These** stones are smooth. _____

165

Determiners are in boldfaced print; nouns are underlined.
Classification of Determiners:
1. Articles: **a, an, the**
2. Demonstratives: **this, that, those, these**
3. Numbers: Example: **fifty** people
4. Possessive pronouns: **my, his, her, your, its, our, their, whose**
5. Possessive nouns: Example: **Joyce's** car
6. Indefinites: **some, few, many, several, no, any**

Directions: Circle each determiner. Underline the noun that follows each determiner.

        Example: **The** cat licked **its** paw.

1.   **The** tree is beside **a** stream.

2.   **This** machine gives **no** change.

3.   Does **your** grandmother live on **an** island?

4.   **Some** people hunt in **those** woods.

5.   **Their** friend lives **five** houses away.

6.   **Several** ducklings waddled after **their** mother.

7.   **Susan's** hair is below **her** waist.

8.   **Whose** cap was left on **the** porch?

9.   **Marilyn's** son washes **his** car in **a n** hour.

10.   **Few** cheerleaders stayed for **a** meeting.

11.   Place **these** bananas in **Ted's** sack.

12.   **That** baby has **her first** tooth.

13.   **Many** campers prefer **a** shady spot.

14.   Is **Laura's** gerbil in **its** cage?

15.   **A** cobbler repaired **four** shoes.
166

Date_____

Classification of Determiners:
1. Articles: **a, an, the**
2. Demonstratives: **this, that, those, these**
3. Numbers: Example: **fifty** people
4. Possessive pronouns: **my, his, her, your, its, our, their, whose**
5. Possessive nouns: Example: **Joyce's** car
6. Indefinites: **some, few, many, several, no, any**

Directions: Circle each determiner. Underline the noun that follows each determiner.

Example: The cat licked its paw.

1. The tree is beside a stream.

2. This machine gives no change.

3. Does your grandmother live on an island?

4. Some people hunt in those woods.

5. Their friend lives five houses away.

6. Several ducklings waddled after their mother.

7. Susan's hair is below her waist.

8. Whose cap was left on the porch?

9. Marilyn's son washes his car in an hour.

10. Few cheerleaders stayed for a meeting.

11. Place these bananas in Ted's sack.

12. That baby has her first tooth.

13. Many campers prefer a shady spot.

14. Is Laura's gerbil in its cage?

15. A cobbler repaired four shoes.

TO THE TEACHER: The concept of singular and plural is not quite as difficult as determiners. However, please read the lesson carefully.

SINGULAR AND PLURAL NOUNS

Be sure that students understand the terms, singular and plural. Some tend to confuse plural and possessive.

Although all rules have been included, I recommend that you place emphasis on rules 1 - 6. The rules are important. In fact, I require students to memorize rule 2. In doing so, we say it orally *many* times.

Please teach students to use a dictionary to determine the plural. "If in doubt, look it up!" (I allow my students to use a dictionary on tests. Yes, tests! I feel very strongly that this is one of the best "skills" you can teach children.) Be sure that students understand that if no plural is given in the dictionary, simply add <u>s</u> (or <u>es</u> as explained in rule 2) to form the plural.

In teaching plurals, I suggest that you give each student a dictionary. Spend time looking up words. Explain that <u>pl</u> means plural, more than one. Let them see how the dictionary lists the plural spelling. You will want to share that if two plural forms are given, the first one is preferred. (My students are required to use the first form.)

Here is a list of words that may prove helpful in using a dictionary to find plural spellings:

Rule 1:	mongoose	(You may choose to discuss this. Will it become mongeese or mongooses?)
Rule 2:	doss or thatch	
Rule 3:	cay	
Rule 4:	dory	
Rule 5:	louse	
Rule 6:	doe	
Rule 7:	elf	
Rule 8:	spoof	
Rule 9:	zero	
Rule 10:	father-in-law	

Formation of plural nouns is very important. It's a concept that students will use throughout their lives. Ascertain that students can apply these rules to words on spelling lists, etc. When students make spelling errors in their own writing, make sure that they comprehend the application of the rules. In the revision and editing stage of their writing, students should be encouraged to use dictionaries. (I personally allow them to use dictionaries when doing the "rough" draft if they choose. Some teachers, believing this to stifle creativity, prefer that students wait until all thoughts are on paper.)

PAGE 169 = WORKBOOK PAGE 72

  PAGE 170 = WORKBOOK PAGE 73   PAGE 171 = WORKBOOK PAGE 74

SINGULAR AND PLURAL NOUNS

Singular means one.

Plural means more than one.

Rule 1:   The **plural of most nouns** is made by adding **s** to the singular form.

comb	kite
combs	kites

Rule 2:   When a singular noun ends in **s**, **sh**, **ch**, **x**, or **z**, add **es** to form the plural.

bu**s**	fla**sh**	pat**ch**	si**x**	fuz**z**
buses	flashes	patches	sixes	fuzzes

Rule 3:   When a singular noun ends in a **vowel + y** (**ay**, **ey**, **iy**, **oy**, or **uy**), add **s** to form the plural.

d**ay**	donk**ey**	to**y**	gu**y**
days	donkeys	toys	guys

Rule 4:   When a singular noun ends in a **consonant + y**, change the **y to i** and add **es**.

la**dy**	ber**ry**	ba**by**
ladies	berries	babies

Rule 5:   Some nouns totally change in the plural form.

man	child	goose
men	children	geese

🍓🍓 **Use a dictionary to determine the plural form of nouns.**

In a dictionary, **pl** or **pl.** = plural

If the word changes to form the plural, the dictionary will spell out the plural.

Example: chĭld (child) n., *pl.* **children**   1. baby or infant

If two spellings are given, the first is preferred.

Example: cac tus (kak´tus) n., *pl.* **cacti, cactuses**
The dictionary may also give the endings as: *pl.* **ti** or **tuses**.

Rule 6:   Some nouns are the same in singular and plural forms.

deer   moose
deer   moose

Use a dictionary to determine the plural form of nouns.

In a dictionary, *pl* or *pl.* = plural

If two spellings are given, the first is preferred.

Example: doe (dō) n., *pl.* **doe or does**

Rule 7:   Some nouns ending in **f**, change the **f** to **v** and add **es** to form the plural.

loaf   calf
loaves   calves

Use a dictionary to determine the plural form.

If a noun changes from **f** to **v** in the plural, the dictionary will show it.

Example: loaf (lōf) n., *pl.* loaves   1. a shaped mass of bread

When two spellings are given for the plural, the first is preferred.

Example: hoof (hōōf) n., *pl.* **hoofs** or **hooves**

170

Rule 8:   Some nouns ending in **f** do not change. They simply add **s**.

      roof   proof
      roofs   proofs

 <u>Use a dictionary to determine the plural form of nouns.</u>

Rule 9:   Some nouns ending in **o**, add **s** to form the plural.

      yo-yo   piano
      yo-yos   pianos

Some nouns ending in **o** add **es** to form the plural.

    tomato   potato

    tomatoes   potatoes

Some nouns ending in **o** add **s** or **es** to form the plural.

    hobo   zero
    hoboes or hobos   zeros or zeroes

When two spellings are provided, the first is preferred.

> **Note:**   Notice that the preferred spelling for hobo adds **es** where the preferred spelling of the plural form of zero simply adds **s**. **Always use a dictionary.**

Rule 10:   Some hyphenated nouns add **s** to the first part when forming the plural.

        father-in-law
        father<u>s</u>-in-law

Some non-hyphenated words that serve as a singular noun add **s** to the first part when forming the plural.

        editor in chief
        editor<u>s</u> in chief

 <u>Use a dictionary to determine the plural form of nouns.</u>   171

Name_____   **NOUNS**
WORKBOOK PAGE 75   **Plurals**
Date_____

Sometimes, dictionaries provide various answers. If a child has a different answer, ask him to show you the entry.
Directions: Write the plural form in the space provided.

Remember: A.   You may use the rules found on pages 169-171.

   B.   You may use a dictionary.

1. bill - ___bills_____

2. yo-yo - ___yo-yos_____

3. mouse - ___mice_____

4. horse - ___horses_____

5. key - ___keys_____

6. ruby - ___rubies_____

7. paw - ___paws_____

8. tooth - ___teeth_____

9. wife - ___wives_____

10. child - ___children_____

11. blueberry - ___blueberries_____

12. wish - ___wishes_____

13. man - ___men_____

14. pinch - ___pinches_____

15. class - ___classes_____
172

Name_____

Date_____

Directions: Write the plural form in the space provided.

Remember: A.   You may use the rules found on pages 169-171.

B.   You may use a dictionary.

1.   bill - _____

2.   yo-yo - _____

3.   mouse - _____

4.   horse - _____

5.   key - _____

6.   ruby - _____

7.   paw - _____

8.   tooth - _____

9.   wife - _____

10.   child - _____

11.   blueberry - _____

12.   wish - _____

13.   man - _____

14.   pinch - _____

15.   class - _____

Directions: Write the plural form in the space provided.

Remember: A.   You may use the rules found on pages 169-171.

B.   You may use a dictionary.

1.   day -   ___days_____

2.   fly -   ___flies_____

3.   reef -   ___reefs_____

4.   fez -   ___fezes___   (a type of hat)_____

5.   foot -   ___feet_____

6.   monkey -   ___monkeys_____

7.   sheep -   ___sheep_____

8.   dish -   ___dishes_____

9.   sister-in law -   ___sisters-in-law_____

10.   scratch -   ___scratches_____

11.   tree -   ___trees_____

12.   half -   ___halves_____

13.   mix -   ___mixes_____

14.   cartoon -   ___cartoons_____

15.   tomato -   ___tomatoes_____

Name_____ **NOUNS**
Plurals

Date_____

Directions: Write the plural form in the space provided.

Remember: A. You may use the rules found on pages 169-171.

B. You may use a dictionary.

1. day - _____

2. fly - _____

3. reef - _____

4. fez - _____

5. foot - _____

6. monkey - _____

7. sheep - _____

8. dish - _____

9. sister-in law - _____

10. scratch - _____

11. tree - _____

12. half - _____

13. mix - _____

14. cartoon - _____

15. tomato - _____

TO THE TEACHER: You will need to make some decisions as to how you want to represent rules. There are some discrepancies about singular nouns.

PAGE 177 = WORKBOOK PAGE 77

POSSESSIVE NOUNS

Many years ago, there were four rules for forming possessives. Then, a major change occurred, and only three rules appeared. I have continued to use the three-rule approach. For your information, the rule that was dropped states that if a singular noun ends in <u>s</u>, add only an apostrophe to the word.

     Example: Chris' book

You will find this approach in most journalistic writing. I have seen, however, both ways used in major books. I, personally, have enjoyed the 3-rule approach because it is so much easier for students to comprehend. Answers in this text do not reflect the fourth rule.

Students will first need to understand what possessive signifies. Usually, we say ownership. However, I have included a few other specific reasons for their use: 1. Possessive nouns can show that something belongs to an item: (a shoe's laces). 2. Possessive nouns can show that something is shared: (horses' corral) 3. Possessive nouns can show that an item contain's something: (tray's paints) 4. Possessive nouns can show that someone is using something: (Mark's chess board)

IMPORTANT: Teach students that it doesn't matter how many items are owned. This has nothing to do with how the possessive is formed.   Example: gardener's tool
**   gardener's tools**

Rule 1: To form the possessive of a **singular** noun, **add 's**.

I recommend that you teach this concept on the board or overhead and give many examples before reading the rules on the next page.   Pick up a pen and remove its cap. Ask students how you would write the possessive. Stress that it's one pen (pen's cap). Take off your shoe, hold it up, and ask how you would write the heel of that shoe (shoe's heel).   Travel about. Find something that belongs to a student. Ask how you would write the person's name showing possession. Continue with other students and items they own.   Write these on the board. <u>Stress that it's simple</u>; just add **'s**. (It's ideal if you have a student whose name ends in <u>s</u>; show the class how he would write his name as a possessive).
*You may have some students who find it difficult to determine if a word such as *family* or *class* is singular or plural. Ask the child if he would use *is* or *are* in a sentence with the word as a subject. If the word is singular, *is* will be used. If the word is plural, *are* will be used. This helps students immensely.
IMPORTANT: AT ONE TIME, A 4th RULE WAS USED. IT STATED THAT SINGULAR NOUNS ENDING IN <u>S</u> ONLY ADD AN APOSTROPHE (Chris' hat). Although I have provided answers that reflect the updated rule, you may wish to teach that concept both ways.

Rule 2: To form the possessive of a **plural** noun **ending in <u>s</u>, add ' after the <u>s</u>**.
    boys' bathroom   fourth graders' playground

Rule 3: To form the possessive of a **plural** noun **not ending in <u>s</u>**, add **'s**.

Students seem to understand *child* and *children* easily. Lead them to determine items which children may own or share: children's playground, etc. *Man-men* and *woman-women* are other examples that are rather easy for students to use in comprehending this concept.

Important note: There are rules that won't be introduced until later.
                  Mary and Todd**'s** house: both own the same house

176   Peter**'s** and Micah**'s** basketballs: each owns his own basketball

POSSESSIVE NOUNS

To possess means to own.
    Example: Tansy's house

Possessive nouns can show that something belongs to an item.
    Example: the chair's back

Possessive nouns can show that something is shared.
    Example: the joggers' path

Possessive nouns can show that an item contains something.
    Example: the well's water

Possessive nouns can show that someone is using something.
    Example: an artist's canvas

There are three simple rules for forming the possessive:

Rule 1: To form the possessive of a **singular** noun, **add 's**.

        Examples: a truck belonging to Rana: Rana**'s** truck

                        lid on a jar: a jar**'s** lid

                        shoes belonging to Elias: Elias**'s** shoes

Important: It does not matter with what letter the word ends. A singular noun adds **'s** to form the possessive.

Rule 2: To form the possessive of a **plural** noun **ending in s, add ' after the s**.

        Examples: a barn belonging to several horses: horse**s'** barn

                        dishes shared by two cats: cat**s'** dishes

Rule 3: To form the possessive of a **plural** noun **not ending in s**, add **'s**.

        Examples: a dessert shared by two children: children's dessert

                        a bathroom used by many women: women's bathroom

Directions: Write the possessive noun and the item in the space provided.

Example: a baton belonging to a twirler: _____twirler's baton_____

Remember:

1.   If a noun is singular (one), add **'s**.

2.   If a noun is plural (more than one) and ends in **s**, add **'**.

3.   If a noun is plural and does **not** end in **s**, add **'s**.

1.   a robe than belongs to a man

   _____a man's robe_____

2.   a sweater belonging to her sister

   _____her sister's sweater or sister's sweater_____

3.   shoes that belong to Philip

   _____Philip's shoes_____

4.   a book that is shared by several teachers

   _____several teachers' book or teachers' book_____

5.   diamonds that are in a ring

   _____a ring's diamonds_____

6.   a bicycle belonging to James

   _____James's bicycle_____

7.   a sailboat belonging to more than one woman

   _____women's sailboat_____

Name_____

NOUNS
Possessives

Date_____

Directions: Write the possessive noun and the item in the space provided.

Example: a baton belonging to a twirler: _____twirler's baton_____

Remember:
1. If a noun is singular (one), add **'s**.

2. If a noun is plural (more than one) and ends in **s**, add **'**.

3. If a noun is plural and does **not** end in **s**, add **'s**.

🍓🍓🍓🍓🍓🍓🍓🍓🍓🍓🍓🍓🍓🍓🍓🍓🍓🍓🍓🍓🍓🍓🍓🍓🍓🍓🍓🍓🍓🍓🍓🍓

1. a robe than belongs to a man

_____

2. a sweater belonging to her sister

_____

3. shoes that belong to Philip

_____

4. a book that is shared by several teachers

_____

5. diamonds that are in a ring

_____

6. a bicycle belonging to James

_____

7. a sailboat belonging to more than one woman

_____

Directions: Write the possessive noun and the item in the space provided.

Example: a baton belonging to a twirler: _____twirler's baton_____

Remember:

1.   If a noun is singular (one), add **'s**.

2.   If a noun is plural (more than one) and ends in **s**, add **'**.

3.   If a noun is plural and does **not** end in **s**, add **'s**.

🍓🍓🍓🍓🍓🍓🍓🍓🍓🍓🍓🍓🍓🍓🍓🍓🍓🍓🍓🍓🍓🍓🍓🍓🍓🍓🍓🍓🍓🍓🍓🍓🍓🍓

1.   a conference attended by attorneys

   ____attorneys' conference_____

2.   a cast belonging to Peter

   ____Peter's cast_____

3.   a path shared by runners

   ____runners' path_____

4.   hamsters belonging to Frances

   ____Frances's hamsters_____

5.   a lunch shared by two boys

   ____two boys' lunch_____

6.   a play for children

   ____a children's play_____

7.   holes in a shirt

   ____a shirt's holes_____

180

Name_____   **NOUNS**
                                        Possessives

Date_____

Directions: Write the possessive noun and the item in the space provided.

          Example: a baton belonging to a twirler: _____twirler's baton_____

Remember:
1.   If a noun is singular (one), add **'s**.

2.   If a noun is plural (more than one) and ends in **s**, add **'**.

3.   If a noun is plural and does **not** end in **s**, add **'s**.

🍓🍓🍓🍓🍓🍓🍓🍓🍓🍓🍓🍓🍓🍓🍓🍓🍓🍓🍓🍓🍓🍓🍓🍓🍓🍓🍓🍓🍓🍓🍓🍓🍓🍓

1.   a conference attended by attorneys

_____

2.   a cast belonging to Peter

_____

3.   a path shared by runners

_____

4.   hamsters belonging to Frances

_____

5.   a lunch shared by two boys

_____

6.   a play for children

_____

7.   holes in a shirt

_____

Name_____   **Noun Review**

Date_____

A. **Definition:**

Directions: Fill in the blanks.

A noun names a __person__, __place__, __thing__, or

__idea__.

B. **Concrete and Abstract Nouns:**

Directions: Write <u>C</u> if the noun is concrete; write <u>A</u> if the noun is abstract.

1. __C__ parrot   5. __C__ gravy   9. __C__ air

2. __A__ honesty   6. __C__ salt   10. __C__ tile

3. __A__ truth   7. __A__ love   11. __A__ joy

4. __C__ tar   8. __A__ happiness   12. __C__ log

C. **Common and Proper Nouns:**

Directions: Write <u>C</u> if the noun is common; write <u>P</u> is the noun is proper.

1. __P__ BRIAN   5. __C__ OCEAN   9. __C__ SOAP

2. __C__ COMPUTER   6. __C__ MOTEL   10. __P__ UTAH

3. __P__ ATLANTA   7. __P__ MEXICO   11. __C__ COW

4. __P__ SKUNK CREEK   8. __P__ BARTLETT LAKE 12. __C__ BIRD

Name_____   **Noun Review**

Date_____

A. **Definition:**

   Directions: Fill in the blanks.

   A noun names a _____, _____, _____, or

   _____.

B. **Concrete and Abstract Nouns:**

   Directions: Write <u>C</u> if the noun is concrete;   write <u>A</u> if the noun is abstract.

   1. _____ parrot   5. _____ gravy   9. _____ air

   2. _____ honesty   6. _____ salt   10. _____ tile

   3. _____ truth   7. _____ love   11. _____ joy

   4. _____ tar   8. _____ happiness   12. _____ log

C. **Common and Proper Nouns:**

   Directions: Write <u>C</u> if the noun is common; write <u>P</u> is the noun is proper.

   1. _____ BRIAN   5. _____ OCEAN   9. _____ SOAP

   2. _____ COMPUTER   6. _____ MOTEL   10. _____ UTAH

   3. _____ ATLANTA   7. _____ MEXICO   11. _____ COW

   4. _____ SKUNK CREEK   8. _____ BARTLETT LAKE 12. _____ BIRD

WORKBOOK PAGE 81
Date_____

D. **Noun Determiners:**

    Directions: Fill in the blank.

1. The three articles that are noun determiners are ___a___, ___an___, and ___the___.

2. The four demonstrative determiners are ___this___, ___that___, ___these___, and ___those___.

3. Write an example of a number used as a determiner.
    Answers Will Vary/Representative Answers: six reindeer, seventy dollars

4. The possessive pronouns that can serve as determiners are ___my___, ___his___,

    ___her___, ___your___, ___its___, ___our___, ___their___, and ___whose___.

5. Write an example of a possessive noun used as a determiner.

    Answers Will Vary/Representative Answers: John's artwork, car's engine

6. Write three examples of indefinites that can serve as determiners: ___no___,
    Answers Will Vary/Representative Answers: few, many, several,
    ___any___, and ___some___,

E. **Noun Identification:**
Determiners are in boldfaced print; nouns are underlined.
    Directions: Underline any nouns in each sentence.

Remember: You may wish to circle determiners to help you find most nouns.

1. **His** <u>company</u> is in **an** <u>air</u> <u>park</u>.

2. **Gary's** <u>sister</u> has **two** <u>puppies</u>.

3. **Several** <u>trees</u> line **that** <u>street</u>.

4. Does **their** <u>niece</u> go to **a** <u>university</u>?

5. **Your** hot <u>dog</u> is burned in **the** <u>middle</u>.

6. **These** <u>pants</u> were **three** <u>dollars</u> at **a** yard <u>sale</u>.

7. **Many** <u>fashions</u> were shown during **the** <u>show</u> in <u>Dallas</u>.

184

D. **Noun Determiners:**

    Directions: Fill in the blank.

1. The three articles that are noun determiners are _____, _____, and _____.

2. The four demonstrative determiners are _____, _____, _____, and _____.

3. Write an example of a number used as a determiner.

    _____

4. The possessive pronouns that can serve as determiners are _____, _____, _____, _____, _____, _____, _____, and _____.

5.   Write an example of a possessive noun used as a determiner.

    _____

6. Write three examples of indefinites that can serve as determiners: _____, _____, and _____.

E. **Noun Identification:**

    Directions: Underline any nouns in each sentence.

Remember: You may wish to circle determiners to help you find most nouns.

1. His company is in an air park.

2. Gary's sister has two puppies.

3. Several trees line that street.

4. Does their niece go to a university?

5. Your hot dog is burned in the middle.

6. These pants were three dollars at a yard sale.

7. Many fashions were shown during the show in Dallas.

F. **Singular and Plural Nouns:**   Encourage students to use the dictionary,
     Directions: Write the plural.   especially for *die*.

1. pony - ____ponies____   7. blade - ____blades____

2. roll - ____rolls____   8. die - ____dice____

3. watch - ____watches____   9. country - ____countries____

4. leaf - ____leaves____   10. puff - ____puffs____

5. potato - ____potatoes____   11. man - ____men____

6. cactus - ____cacti____   12. piano - ____pianos____

G. **Possessive Nouns**
     Directions: Write the possessive form.

1. slippers that belong to their mother

        ____their mother's slippers or mother's slippers____

2. house that belongs to Harvey

        ____Harvey's house____

3. vacation taken by three girls

        ____three girls' vacation or girls' vacation____

4. a party given by more than one lady

        ____ladies' party____

5. a notebook belonging to Chris

        ____Chris's notebook____

6. organization belonging to more than one man

        ____men's organization____

Name_____   **Noun Review**

Date_____

F. **Singular and Plural Nouns:**
   Directions: Write the plural.

1. pony - _____   7. blade - _____

2. roll - _____   8. die - _____

3. watch - _____   9. country - _____

4. leaf - _____   10. puff - _____

5. potato - _____   11. man - _____

6. cactus - _____   12. piano - _____

G. **Possessive Nouns**
   Directions: Write the possessive form.

1. slippers that belong to their mother

   _____

2. house that belongs to Harvey

   _____

3. vacation taken by three girls

   _____

4. a party given by more than one lady

   _____

5. a notebook belonging to Chris

   _____

6. organization belonging to more than one man

   _____

Name_____ **Noun Test**

Date_____
Because determiners are used to identify nouns, no section for listing them is included.

A. Concrete and Abstract Nouns:

Directions: Write <u>C</u> if the noun is concrete; write <u>A</u> if the noun is abstract.

1. __A__   love   3. __C__   applesauce   5. __A__   faith

2. __C__   air   4. __A__   kindness   6. __C__   boat

B. Common and Proper Nouns:

Directions: Write <u>CN</u> if the noun is common; write <u>PN</u> if the noun is proper.

1. __PN__   HUDSON BAY   4. __PN__   COLORADO   7. __CN__   JUNK

2. __CN__   FIREPLACE   5. __PN__   VERDE RIVER   8. __PN__   MARY

3. __PN__   CANADA   6. __CN__   FRUIT BAR   9. __CN__   LAKE

C. Noun Identification:
Determiners are in boldfaced print.   Nouns are underlined.

Directions: Underline any nouns in each sentence.

Remember: You may wish to circle determiners to help you find most nouns.

1. **Josh's** <u>dad</u> is **a** <u>fireman</u> in <u>Washington</u>.

2. Has **your** <u>brother</u> gone with **his** <u>friends</u>?

3. **An** <u>elephant</u> was used in **that** <u>movie</u>.

4. **Whose** <u>coats</u> are lying on **these two** <u>chairs</u>?

5. **Some** lively <u>children</u> are swinging in **those** magnolia <u>trees</u>.

6. In <u>June</u>, **our** <u>family</u> will take **many** short <u>trips</u> to **the** <u>beach</u>.

188

Name_____   **Noun Test**

Date_____

A. Concrete and Abstract Nouns:

Directions: Write C if the noun is concrete; write A if the noun is abstract.

1. _____ love   3. _____ applesauce   5. _____ faith

2. _____ air   4. _____ kindness   6. _____ boat

B. Common and Proper Nouns:

Directions: Write CN if the noun is common; write PN if the noun is proper.

1. _____ HUDSON BAY   4. _____ COLORADO   7. _____ JUNK

2. _____ FIREPLACE   5. _____ VERDE RIVER   8. _____ MARY

3. _____ CANADA   6. _____ FRUIT BAR   9. _____ LAKE

C. Noun Identification:

Directions: Underline any nouns in each sentence.

Remember: You may wish to circle determiners to help you find most nouns.

1. Josh's dad is a fireman in Washington.

2. Has your brother gone with his friends?

3. An elephant was used in that movie.

4. Whose coats are lying on these two chairs?

5. Some lively children are swinging in those magnolia trees.

6. In June, our family will take many short trips to the beach.

7. **No** <u>fruit</u> was served at **Judy's** <u>breakfast</u> on <u>Saturday</u>.

D. **Singular and Plural Nouns:**

Directions: Write the plural.

1. bulb - <u>   bulbs   </u>

2. penny - <u>   pennies   </u>

3. tooth - <u>   teeth   </u>

4. wish - <u>   wishes   </u>

5. calf - <u>   calves   </u>

6. mouse - <u> mice </u>

7. carp - <u> carp (carps = second listing)</u>

8. bay - <u>   bays   </u>

9. bus - <u>   buses   </u>

10. roof - <u>   roofs   </u>

11. tomato - <u> tomatoes </u>

12. fez - <u>   fezes   </u>

E **Possessive Nouns**

Directions: Write the possessive form.

1. a package that belongs to Andy

<u>   Andy's package   </u>

2. a path for horses

<u>   horses' path   </u>

3. a club belonging to more than one woman

<u>   women's club   </u>

4. skates belonging to Frances

<u>   Frances's skates   </u>

5. a playground belonging to more than one child

<u>   children's playground   </u>

7. No fruit was served at Judy's breakfast on Saturday.

D. **Singular and Plural Nouns:**

Directions: Write the plural.

1. bulb - _____

2. penny - _____

3. tooth - _____

4. wish - _____

5. calf - _____

6. mouse - _____

7. carp - _____

8. bay - _____

9. bus - _____

10. roof - _____

11. tomato - _____

12. fez - _____

E. **Possessive Nouns**

Directions: Write the possessive form.

1. a package that belongs to Andy

_____

2. a path for horses

_____

3. a club belonging to more than one woman

_____

4. skates belonging to Frances

_____

5. a playground belonging to more than one child

_____

A. **Preposition List:**

Directions: List forty prepositions.

1.	about	16.	down	31.	past
2.	above	17.	during	32.	through
3.	across	18.	except	33.	throughout
4.	after	19.	for	34.	to
5.	against	20.	from	35.	toward
6.	along	21.	in	36.	under
7.	around	22.	inside	37.	until
8.	at	23.	into	38.	up
9.	before	24.	near	39.	with
10.	behind	25.	of	40.	without
11.	below	26.	off		
12.	beneath	27.	on		
13.	beside	28.	out		
14.	between	29.	outside		
15.	by	30.	over		

B. **Object of the Preposition:**
Directions: Cross out any prepositional phrases. Label the object of the preposition - O.P.

O.P.

1. A ground hog emerged ~~from his hole~~.

O.P.

2. My tether ball is tied ~~with a rope~~.

192

A. **Preposition List:**

Directions: List forty prepositions.

1. _____   16. _____   31. _____

2. _____   17. _____   32. _____

3. _____   18. _____   33. _____

4. _____   19. _____   34. _____

5. _____   20. _____   35. _____

6. _____   21. _____   36. _____

7. _____   22. _____   37. _____

8. _____   23. _____   38. _____

9. _____   24. _____   39. _____

10. _____   25. _____   40. _____

11. _____   26. _____

12. _____   27. _____

13. _____   28. _____

14. _____   29. _____

15. _____   30. _____

B. **Object of the Preposition:**
   Directions: Cross out any prepositional phrases. Label the object of the
               preposition - O.P.

1. A ground hog emerged from his hole.

2. My tether ball is tied with a rope.   193

C. **Compound Subject:**

Directions: Cross out any prepositional phrases. Underline the subject once and the verb/verb phrase twice.

Remember: **Compound means more than one.**

1. <u>Martha</u> and her <u>mother</u> <u>shop</u> ~~at a nearby supermarket~~.

2. ~~During the spring~~, <u>tulips</u> and <u>irises</u> <u>bloom</u> ~~in their garden~~.

3. A <u>mare</u> and her <u>colt</u> <u>stood</u> quietly ~~beside a rippling stream~~.

🍓🍓🍓🍓🍓🍓🍓🍓🍓🍓🍓🍓🍓🍓🍓🍓🍓🍓🍓🍓🍓🍓🍓🍓🍓🍓🍓🍓🍓🍓🍓🍓🍓

D. **Imperative Sentences:**

Directions: Cross out any prepositional phrases. Underline the subject once and the verb/verb phrase twice.

Remember: **An imperative sentence gives a command.**

1. <u>(You)</u> <u>Smile</u>.

2. <u>(You)</u> <u>Mail</u> our letters ~~at the post office~~, please.

🍓🍓🍓🍓🍓🍓🍓🍓🍓🍓🍓🍓🍓🍓🍓🍓🍓🍓🍓🍓🍓🍓🍓🍓🍓🍓🍓🍓🍓🍓🍓🍓🍓

E. **Compound Objects of the Preposition:**

Directions: Cross out any prepositional phrases. Underline the subject once and the verb/verb phrase twice.

Remember: **Compound means more than one.**

1. <u>(You)</u> <u>place</u> the boxes ~~against that wall and this door~~.

2. A <u>package</u> <u>arrived</u> ~~from Don and Joy~~.

3. <u>Flies</u> <u>swarmed</u> ~~around Brian, Terry, and me~~.

194

C. **Compound Subject:**

Directions: Cross out any prepositional phrases. Underline the subject once
and the verb/verb phrase twice.

Remember: Compound means more than one.

1.   Martha and her mother shop at a nearby supermarket.

2.   During the spring, tulips and irises bloom in their garden.

3.   A mare and her colt stood quietly beside a rippling stream.

D.   **Imperative Sentences:**

Directions: Cross out any prepositional phrases. Underline the subject once
and the verb/verb phrase twice.

Remember: An imperative sentence gives a command.

1.   Smile.

2.   Mail our letters at the post office, please.

E.   **Compound Objects of the Preposition:**

Directions: Cross out any prepositional phrases. Underline the subject once
and the verb/verb phrase twice.

Remember: Compound means more than one.

1.   Place the boxes against that wall and this door.

2.   A package arrived from Don and Joy.

3.   Flies swarmed around Brian, Terry, and me.

F. **Compound Verbs:**

   Directions: Cross out any prepositional phrases. Underline the subject once
                and the verb/verb phrase twice.

Remember: Compound means more than one.

1. ~~Before a meal~~, we wash our hands and dry them.

2. The doctor looked ~~at the chart~~ and smiled ~~at his patient~~.

🍓🍓🍓🍓🍓🍓🍓🍓🍓🍓🍓🍓🍓🍓🍓🍓🍓🍓🍓🍓🍓🍓🍓🍓🍓🍓🍓🍓🍓🍓🍓🍓🍓🍓🍓🍓🍓

G. **Infinitives:**

   Directions: Cross out any prepositional phrases. Underline the subject once
                and the verb twice. Place an infinitive in parentheses (   ).

Remember: To + a verb = infinitive.   Do not cross out any infinitives.

1. His sister wants (to be) an actress.

2. Jenny forgot (to go) ~~to the dentist~~.

🍓🍓🍓🍓🍓🍓🍓🍓🍓🍓🍓🍓🍓🍓🍓🍓🍓🍓🍓🍓🍓🍓🍓🍓🍓🍓🍓🍓🍓🍓🍓🍓🍓🍓🍓🍓🍓

H. **Prepositions:**

   Directions: Cross out any prepositional phrases. Underline the subject once
                and the verb/verb phrase twice. Label any direct object - D.O.

                                          D.O.
1. ~~After the birthday party~~, Mother washed the table.

                          D.O.
2. The orthodontist put braces ~~on Jill's teeth~~.

                           D.O.
3. A detective searched the office ~~for clues about the recent theft~~.

                        D.O.
4. Many ~~of the players~~ tossed footballs ~~before the game~~.

                      D.O.   D.O.
5. Her guest brought her candy and flowers.

196

F. **Compound Verbs:**

Directions: Cross out any prepositional phrases. Underline the subject once and the verb/verb phrase twice.

Remember: Compound means more than one.

1. Before a meal, we wash our hands and dry them.

2. The doctor looked at the chart and smiled at his patient.

G. **Infinitives:**

Directions: Cross out any prepositional phrases. Underline the subject once and the verb twice. Place an infinitive in parenthesis ( ).

Remember: To + a verb = infinitive.   Do not cross out any infinitives.

1. His sister wants to be an actress.

2. Jenny forgot to go to the dentist.

H. **Prepositions:**

Directions: Cross out any prepositional phrases. Underline the subject once and the verb/verb phrase twice. Label any direct object - <u>D.O.</u>

1. After the birthday party, Mother washed the table.

2. The orthodontist put braces on Jill's teeth.

3. A detective searched the office for clues about the recent theft.

4. Many of the players tossed footballs before the game.

5. Her guest brought her candy and flowers.

Name_____

WORKBOOK PAGE 86

Date_____

I. **Contractions:**

Directions: Write the contraction in the space provided.

1. should not - ___shouldn't___   6. you are - ___you're___

2. I shall - ___I'll___   7. who is - ___who's___

3. is not - ___isn't___   8. will not - ___won't___

4. we are - ___we're___   9. they have - ___they've___

5. they will - ___they'll___   10. it is - ___it's___

🍓🍓🍓🍓🍓🍓🍓🍓🍓🍓🍓🍓🍓🍓🍓🍓🍓🍓🍓🍓🍓🍓🍓🍓🍓🍓🍓🍓🍓

J. **Helping (Auxiliary) Verbs:**

Directions: List the twenty-three helping verbs.

do	has	may	can	could	is	were
does	have	might	shall	should	am	be
did	had	must	will	would	are	being
					was	been

🍓🍓🍓🍓🍓🍓🍓🍓🍓🍓🍓🍓🍓🍓🍓🍓🍓🍓🍓🍓🍓🍓🍓🍓🍓🍓🍓🍓🍓

K. **Action?:**

Directions: Write <u>Yes</u> if the boldfaced verb shows action; write <u>No</u> if the boldfaced verb does not show action.

1. ___Yes___   The comic **laughed** at his own jokes.

2. ___No___   That clerk **appears** to be confused.

3. ___Yes___   A customer **tasted** several types of cheese.

4. ___No___   Those fishing nets **have** too many rips.

198

I. **Contractions:**

Directions: Write the contraction in the space provided.

1. should not - _____   6. you are - _____

2. I shall - _____   7. who is - _____

3. is not - _____   8. will not - _____

4. we are - _____   9. they have - _____

5. they will - _____   10. it is - _____

J. **Helping (Auxiliary) Verbs:**

Directions: List the twenty-three helping verbs.

_____

_____

_____

K. **Action?:**

Directions: Write <u>Yes</u> if the boldfaced verb shows action; write <u>No</u> if the boldfaced verb does not show action.

1. _____   The comic **laughed** at his own jokes.

2. _____   That clerk **appears** to be confused.

3. _____   A customer **tasted** several types of cheese.

4. _____   Those fishing nets **have** too many rips.

L. **Regular or Irregular:**

Directions: Write <u>RV</u> if the verb is regular. Write <u>IV</u> if the verb is irregular.

Remember: Regular verbs add <u>ed</u> to the past and past participle.

1. <u>IV</u>   to drive   3. <u>IV</u>   to say   5. <u>RV</u>   to stir

2. <u>RV</u>   to paste   4. <u>RV</u>   to float   6. <u>IV</u>   to freeze

🍓🍓🍓🍓🍓🍓🍓🍓🍓🍓🍓🍓🍓🍓🍓🍓🍓🍓🍓🍓🍓🍓🍓🍓🍓🍓🍓🍓🍓

M. **Subject/Verb:**

Directions: Cross out any prepositional phrases.   Underline the subject once and the verb/verb phrase twice.

1. Her <u>speech</u> <u>is</u> ~~about the dangers of smoking~~.

2. A cordless <u>telephone</u> <u>is</u> ~~under the bed~~.

3. The <u>temperature</u> <u>has fallen</u> ~~below zero~~.

🍓🍓🍓🍓🍓🍓🍓🍓🍓🍓🍓🍓🍓🍓🍓🍓🍓🍓🍓🍓🍓🍓🍓🍓🍓🍓🍓🍓🍓

N. **Tenses:**

Directions: Cross out any prepositional phrases. Underline the subject once and the verb/verb phrase twice. Write the tense on the line.

Remember: The tenses that we have learned are ***present***, ***past***, and ***future***.

1. ___present___   <u>Cadets</u> <u>march</u> ~~in several parades~~ each year.

2. ___past___   <u>We</u> <u>mopped</u> the floor ~~with several old cloths~~.

3. ___present___   <u>Mt. Fuji</u> <u>is</u> ~~in Japan~~.

4. ___future___   <u>Jamie</u> <u>will go</u> ~~to Montana~~ tomorrow.

200

L. **Regular or Irregular:**

Directions: Write <u>RV</u> if the verb is regular. Write <u>IV</u> if the verb is irregular.

Remember: Regular verbs add <u>ed</u> to the past and past participle.

1. _____ to drive   3. _____ to say   5. _____ to stir

2. _____ to paste   4. _____ to float   6. _____ to freeze

M. **Subject/Verb:**

Directions: Cross out any prepositional phrases.   Underline the subject once
and the verb/verb phrase twice.

1. Her speech is about the dangers of smoking.

2. A cordless telephone is under the bed.

3. The temperature has fallen below zero.

N. **Tenses:**

Directions: Cross out any prepositional phrases. Underline the subject once
and the verb/verb phrase twice. Write the tense on the line.

Remember: The tenses that we have learned are *present*, *past*, and *future*.

1. _____ Cadets march in several parades each year.

2. _____ We mopped the floor with several old cloths.

3. _____ Mt. Fuji is in Japan.

4. _____ Jamie will go to Montana tomorrow.

WORKBOOK PAGE 88

You may want to have students delete prepositional phrases, underline the subject once and the verb phrase twice.

O. **Irregular Verbs:**

   Directions: Select the correct verb.

1. The <u>dog</u> <u>had</u> (shook, <u>shaken</u>) itself.

2. Our <u>bus</u> <u>has</u> (came, <u>come</u>) early.

3. <u>We</u> <u>were</u> (gave, <u>given</u>) another chance.

4. <u>He</u> <u>had</u> already (did, <u>done</u>) his assignment.

5. A <u>car</u> <u>had been</u> (<u>stolen</u>, stole) ~~during the night~~

6. <u>They</u> <u>were</u> (chose, <u>chosen</u>) (to be) leaders.

🍓🍓🍓🍓🍓🍓🍓🍓🍓🍓🍓🍓🍓🍓🍓🍓🍓🍓🍓🍓🍓🍓🍓🍓🍓🍓🍓🍓🍓🍓🍓🍓🍓🍓

P. **Sit/Set, Rise/Raise, and Lie/Lay:**

   Directions: Cross out any prepositional phrases. Underline the subject once and the verb/verb phrase twice.   Label any direct object - <u>D.O.</u>

   Remember: With *to set, to raise,* and *to lay,* you must have a direct object. *Lays, laid,* and *laying* must have a direct object.

1. The <u>principal</u> (<u>sits</u>, sets) ~~on stage during graduation ceremonies~~.

2. <u>She</u> (<u>rises</u>, raises) early ~~in the morning~~.

                              D.O.
3. The <u>florist</u> (lay, <u>laid</u>) several roses ~~on the counter~~.

🍓🍓🍓🍓🍓🍓🍓🍓🍓🍓🍓🍓🍓🍓🍓🍓🍓🍓🍓🍓🍓🍓🍓🍓🍓🍓🍓🍓🍓🍓🍓🍓🍓🍓

Q. **Subject-Verb Agreement:**

   Directions: Circle the verb that agrees with the subject.

1. Zek (like, <u>likes</u>) to blow bubbles.

2. Mr. Hobbs and his wife (<u>play</u>, plays) tennis daily.

3. Peaches (<u>grow</u>, grows) in that area of Pennsylvania.

4. <u>One</u> ~~of the boys~~ (swim, <u>swims</u>) on a team.

O. **Irregular Verbs:**

   Directions: Select the correct verb.

1. The dog had (shook, shaken) itself.

2. Our bus has (came, come) early.

3. We were (gave, given) another chance.

4. He had already (did, done) his assignment.

5. A car had been (stolen, stole) during the night.

6. They were (chose, chosen) to be leaders.

P. **Sit/Set, Rise/Raise, and Lie/Lay:**

   Directions: Cross out any prepositional phrases. Underline the subject once
               and the verb/verb phrase twice.   Label any direct object - D.O.

   Remember: **With *to set*, *to raise*, and *to lay*, you must have a direct object.
                Lays, *laid*, and *laying* must have a direct object.**

1. The principal (sits, sets) on stage during graduation ceremonies.

2. She (rises, raises) early in the morning.

3. The florist (lay, laid) several roses on the counter.

Q. **Subject-Verb Agreement:**
   Directions: Circle the verb that agrees with the subject.

1. Zek (like, likes) to blow bubbles.

2. Mr. Hobbs and his wife (play, plays) tennis daily.

3. Peaches (grow, grows) in that area of Pennsylvania.

4. One of the boys (swim, swims) on a team.   203

A. **Prepositional Phrases:**

Directions: Cross out any prepositional phrases. Underline the subject once and the verb/verb phrase twice. Label any direct object - D.O.

         D.O.
1. Jack eats lunch ~~at a cafe~~.

2. The fence ~~behind the barn~~ is broken.

3. Kirk lives ~~in West Virginia~~.

4. Chimes resounded ~~through the church~~.

5. Paula left ~~without her lunch bag~~.

6. ~~In the middle of the afternoon~~, his grandmother always naps.

         D.O.
7. (You) Hide this ~~under the bed~~ ~~until the party~~.

                    D.O.
8. Has the weaver woven another rug?

9. Everyone ~~except the hostess~~ gathered ~~around the table~~.

10. The temperature ~~in Phoenix~~ rises ~~above one hundred degrees~~ ~~during the summer~~.

B. **Compounds:**

Directions: Cross out any prepositional phrases. Underline the subject once and the verb/verb phrase twice.

1. A telegram arrived ~~for Annette and Mario~~.

2. He signed a card and placed it ~~inside an envelope~~.

3. The bank's manager and a teller met ~~with the couple~~.

4. Mrs. Sands loves (to cook) and often invites friends ~~for dinner~~.

5. Either Jane or her sister attends a technical school.

6. A teacher read an article ~~about drugs and alcohol~~ ~~to his class~~.

A. **Prepositional Phrases:**

>   Directions: Cross out any prepositional phrases. Underline the subject once
>   and the verb/verb phrase twice. Label any direct object - D.O.

1. Jack eats lunch at a cafe.

2. The fence behind the barn is broken.

3. Kirk lives in West Virginia.

4. Chimes resounded through the church.

5. Paula left without her lunch bag.

6. In the middle of the afternoon, his grandmother always naps.

7. Hide this under the bed until the party.

8. Has the weaver woven another rug?

9. Everyone except the hostess gathered around the table.

10. The temperature in Phoenix rises above one hundred degrees during the
     summer.

B. **Compounds:**

>   Directions: Cross out any prepositional phrases. Underline the subject once
>   and the verb/verb phrase twice.

1. A telegram arrived for Annette and Mario.

2. He signed a card and placed it inside an envelope.

3. The bank's manager and a teller met with the couple.

4. Mrs. Sands loves to cook and often invites friends for dinner.

5. Either Jane or her sister attends a technical school.

6. A teacher read an article about drugs and alcohol to his class.   205

7. His <u>father</u> and <u>mother</u> <u>own</u> a small house ~~outside the city limits~~.

8. <u>She</u> <u>ordered</u> fries and a hamburger ~~without pickles or onions~~.

C. **Contractions:**

    Directions: Write the contraction.

1. I shall - <u>   I'll   </u>   6. they have - <u> they've   </u>

2. does not - <u> doesn't   </u>   7. is not - <u>   isn't   </u>

3. you will - <u>   you'll   </u>   8. what is - <u>   what's   </u>

4. she is - <u>   she's   </u>   9. could not - <u> couldn't   </u>

5. must not - <u> mustn't   </u>   10. I am- <u>   I'm   </u>

D. **Action?:**

    Directions: Write <u>Yes</u> if the boldfaced verb shows action; write <u>No</u> if the boldfaced verb does not show action.

1. <u> No </u>   Cream-filled doughnuts **are** delicious.

2. <u> Yes </u>   Jeff **threw** a baseball.

3. <u> Yes </u>   The pastry chef **tasted** his dessert.

E. **Regular or Irregular:**

    Directions: Write <u>RV</u> if the verb is regular. Write <u>IV</u> if the verb is irregular.

1. <u> IV </u>   to choose   3. <u> RV </u>   to growl   5. <u> IV </u>   to make

2. <u> RV </u>   to frown   4. <u> IV </u>   to ring   6. <u> RV </u>   to chew

F. **Subject-Verb Agreement:**

    Directions: Circle the verb that agrees with the subject.
Answers are in boldfaced print.
1. Several airplanes (dusts, **dust**) crops in that area.

206

7. His father and mother own a small house outside the city limits.

8. She ordered fries and a hamburger without pickles or onions.

C. **Contractions:**

Directions: Write the contraction.

1. I shall - _____   6. they have - _____

2. does not - _____   7. is not - _____

3. you will - _____   8. what is - _____

4. she is - _____   9. could not - _____

5. must not - _____   10. I am- _____

D. **Action?:**

Directions: Write <u>Yes</u> if the boldfaced verb shows action; write <u>No</u> if the boldfaced verb does not show action.

1. _____   Cream-filled doughnuts **are** delicious.

2. _____   Jeff **threw** a baseball.

3. _____   The pastry chef **tasted** his dessert.

E. **Regular or Irregular:**

Directions: Write <u>RV</u> if the verb is regular. Write <u>IV</u> if the verb is irregular.

1. _____ to choose   3. _____ to growl   5. _____ to make

2. _____ to frown   4. _____ to ring   6. _____ to chew

F. **Subject-Verb Agreement:**

Directions: Circle the verb that agrees with the subject.

1. Several airplanes (dusts, dust) crops in that area.

2. <u>One</u> ~~of their friends~~ (**works**, work) ~~in an ice cream shop~~.

3. <u>Megan</u> and her <u>mother</u> (shops, **shop**) often.

4. The <u>man</u> ~~in line with his three children~~ (paint, **paints**) houses ~~for a living~~.

G. **Tenses:**

   Directions: Write the tense (present, past, or future) on the line provided.

Note: You may want to cross out prepositional phrases, underline subject once, and verb/verb phrase twice to help determine the tense.

1. _____present_____ <u>Joel</u> and <u>she</u> <u>are</u> good friends.

2. _____future_____ A <u>queen</u> <u>will attend</u> that celebration.

3. _____past_____ <u>Mozart</u> <u>was</u> a famous composer.

4. _____past_____ <u>Joanna</u> <u>planned</u> her own wedding.

5. _____present_____ His <u>father</u> <u>explores</u> caves ~~on weekends~~.

H. **Irregular Verbs:**

   Directions: Circle the correct verb.

Although directions do not indicate, prepositional phrases have been deleted, subject underlined once, and verb/verb phrase boldfaced.

1. His <u>brothers</u> **have** (drank, **drunk**) all ~~of the soda~~.

2. Where **has** the <u>team</u> (went, **gone**)?

3. A <u>ring</u> **had been** (stole, **stolen**) ~~from the jewelry store~~.

4. Many party <u>favors</u> **had been** (**bought**, boughten) ~~for the party~~.

5. <u>Andy</u> **was** (**chosen**, chose) (to video) the event.

6. The <u>newspaper</u> **is** (laying, **lying**) ~~in the driveway~~.

7. A small <u>tree</u> **has** (grew, **grown**) ~~by the road~~.

8. The <u>patient</u> (**lay**, laid) ~~on his back during surgery~~.

9. **Has** <u>she</u> (shook, **shaken**) the rug ~~in her room~~?

10. <u>He</u> **may have** (came, **come**) ~~to the airport in his own car~~.

208

2. One of their friends (**works**, work) in an ice cream shop.

3. Megan and her mother (shops, **shop**) often.

4. The man in line with his three children (paint, **paints**) houses for a living.

G. **Tenses:**
Directions: Write the tense (present, past, or future) on the line provided.

Note: You may want to cross out prepositional phrases, underline subject once, and verb/verb phrase twice to help determine the tense.

1. _____ Joel and she are good friends.

2. _____ A queen will attend that celebration.

3. _____ Mozart was a famous composer.

4. _____ Joanna planned her own wedding.

5. _____ His father explores caves on weekends.

H. **Irregular Verbs:**
Directions: Circle the correct verb.

1. His brothers have (drank, **drunk**) all of the soda.

2. Where has the team (went, **gone**)?

3. A ring had been (stole, **stolen**) from the jewelry store.

4. Many party favors had been (**bought**, boughten) for the party.

5. Andy was (**chosen**, chose) to video the event.

6. The newspaper is (laying, **lying**) in the driveway.

7. A small tree has (grew, **grown**) by the road.

8. The patient (**lay**, laid) on his back during surgery.

9. Has she (shook, **shaken**) the rug in her room?

10. He may have (came, **come**) to the airport in his own car.

TO THE TEACHER:

PAGE 211 = WORKBOOK PAGE 89

Page 211: **Sentence Types**:

Be sure to teach this concept prior to students reading page 211. Your sentences should be lively. Try to make examples pertain to your students' lives. (For example, if your student, Carla, owns four dogs, your declarative sentence may be,

"*Carla owns four dogs.*")

Most students find sentence types quite easy. However, some may have difficulty understanding that a declarative sentence may imply a question.

Example: Janet asked if we were going.

Page 215: **Conjunctions**:

Coordinating conjunctions are taught at the top of the student worksheet. Although only one page is offered for student practice, this concept will be reviewed at the end of the adjective, adverb, and pronoun units. (Correlative conjunctions are not discussed in this book; they are introduced at a higher level.)

Page 217: **Interjections**:

This concept is taught at the top of the student worksheet. As with conjunctions, just one page is offered for practice. However, review will be offered at the end of ensuing units.

210

SENTENCE TYPES

There are four types of sentences.

1. A **declarative** sentence makes a statement. A declarative sentence ends with a period.

    Examples: John Glenn was one of our first astronauts.

    This caramel apple tastes good.

    Paseo Verde Elementary School is new.

2. An **interrogative** sentence asks a question. An interrogative sentence ends with a question mark.

    Examples: Have you ever been to a fair?

    What's your name?

    Did your friend move to Iowa?

3. An **imperative** sentence gives a command. An imperative sentence ends with a period.

    Examples: Put this in the kitchen, please.

    Write your name on the paper.

    Eat before you leave.

4. An **exclamatory sentence** shows emotion. An exclamatory sentence ends with an exclamation point (mark).

    Examples: The ice cream man is here!

    Stop!

    Slow Down! You're driving too fast!

Directions: Write the sentence type.

Example: _____declarative_____   His neighbor is an engineer.

1. _____interrogative_____   Is Dover in Delaware?

2. _____declarative_____   That table has been sanded well.

3. _____exclamatory_____   We did it!

4. _____imperative_____   Wait for me, please.

5. _____interrogative_____   Must I come along?

6. _____declarative_____   Pilgrims arrived on the ship, Mayflower.

7. _____imperative_____   Place the chicken on the grill.

8. _____interrogative_____   Will the doctor see us today?

9. _____exclamatory_____   I am so surprised!

10. _____exclamatory_____   No! We lost again!

11. _____declarative_____   A torn kite lay by the side of the road.

12. _____declarative_____   Todd asked if we could go with him.

13. _____imperative_____   Don't touch that.

14. _____interrogative_____   Can you snorkel?

15. _____declarative_____   Niagara Falls is on the Canadian border.

212

Name_____

Date_____

Directions: Write the sentence type.

Example: ___declarative___ His neighbor is an engineer.

1. _____ Is Dover in Delaware?

2. _____ That table has been sanded well.

3. _____ We did it!

4. _____ Wait for me, please.

5. _____ Must I come along?

6. _____ Pilgrims arrived on the ship, Mayflower.

7. _____ Place the chicken on the grill.

8. _____ Will the doctor see us today?

9. _____ I am so surprised!

10. _____ No! We lost again!

11. _____ A torn kite lay by the side of the road.

12. _____ Todd asked if we could go with him.

13. _____ Don't touch that.

14. _____ Can you snorkel?

15. _____ Niagara Falls is on the Canadian border.

213

Date_____

Conjunctions are joining words.

The three coordinating conjunctions are **and**, **but**, and **or**.

Examples: Bob **and** Gerald are friends.

You may have ice cream **or** sherbet.

Julie likes Phoenix, **but** it's hot there in the summer.

Directions: Circle any conjunctions.

Answers are in boldfaced print.

1.   Strawberries **and** ice cream were served.

2.   Molly **or** Misty will come with us.

3.   They like to sail, **but** they get seasick.

4.   The sergeant stopped **and** saluted.

5.   Michael likes to read mysteries **or** science fiction.

6.   Marsha **and** her brother seldom visit their grandparents **or** cousins.

7.   The restaurant takes cash **or** credit cards **but** no checks.

8.   Penny **and** her mother laughed **but** looked upset.

9.   Have Tom **and** Cindy decided to marry in December?

10. You may choose to dust **or** to vacuum, **but** you must do one.

Name_____

Date_____

Conjunctions are joining words.

The three coordinating conjunctions are *and*, *but*, and *or*.

      Examples: Bob **and** Gerald are friends.

                   You may have ice cream **or** sherbet.

                   Julie likes Phoenix, **but** it's hot there in the summer.

Directions: Circle any conjunctions.

1. Strawberries and ice cream were served.

2. Molly or Misty will come with us.

3. They like to sail, but they get seasick.

4. The sergeant stopped and saluted.

5. Michael likes to read mysteries or science fiction.

6. Marsha and her brother seldom visit their grandparents or cousins.

7. The restaurant takes cash or credit cards but no checks.

8. Penny and her mother laughed but looked upset.

9. Have Tom and Cindy decided to marry in December.

10. You may choose to dust or to vacuum, but you must do one.

215

An interjection is a word or phrase (more than one word) that shows strong emotion. An interjection ends with an exclamation point (mark).

Examples: Yeah!

Oh rats!

If an expression has both a subject and a verb, it is an **exclamatory sentence**, not an interjection.

Example: Stop!

(You) Stop!

Directions: Circle any interjections.
Answers are in boldfaced print.

1. **Hurrah!** Our team is winning!

2. **Wow!** That car is really neat!

3. **Oh!**   The gas tank is nearly empty!

4.   We won! **Yippee!**

5. **No!** I don't believe it!

6.   This milk is sour!   **Yuck!**

7. **Yeah!** The flight is arriving!

8. **Ouch!** I've burned my finger!

9. **Yikes!** You scared me!

10.   I'd love to go! **Thanks!**

Name_____

Date_____

An interjection is a word or phrase (more than one word) that shows strong emotion. An interjection ends with an exclamation point (mark).

Examples: Yeah!

Oh rats!

If an expression has both a subject and a verb, it is an **exclamatory sentence**, not an interjection.

Example: Stop!

(<u>You</u>) <u>Stop</u>!

🍓🍓🍓🍓🍓🍓🍓🍓🍓🍓🍓🍓🍓🍓🍓🍓🍓🍓🍓🍓🍓🍓🍓🍓🍓🍓🍓🍓🍓🍓🍓🍓🍓
Directions: Circle any interjections.

1. Hurrah! Our team is winning!

2. Wow! That car is really neat!

3. Oh! The gas tank is nearly empty!

4. We won! Yippee!

5. No! I don't believe it!

6. This milk is sour!   Yuck!

7. Yeah!   The flight is arriving!

8. Ouch! I've burned my finger!

9. Yikes! You scared me!

10. I'd love to go! Thanks!

ADJECTIVES

ADJECTIVES

There are two major classifications of adjectives: limiting (or determining) adjectives and descriptive adjectives.

Limiting adjectives should be very easy; students used these in the noun unit. We will refer to them mostly as limiting adjectives. However, you may choose to continue to call them determining adjectives.

In teaching adjectives, be sure to have students check their adjective by drawing an arrow to the word it modifies (goes over to). (**Be sure students understand the term, *modifies*.**) I usually say the adjective and ask "_____ what?"

> Example: That baby is Ida's sister.
> *That* what? *baby*   ***That*** is an adjective that goes over to *baby*.

Limiting (Determining) Adjectives:
1. **Articles: a, an, the**
    Example: **An** apple is **a** fruit.

2. **Demonstratives: this, that, those, these**
    Example: **This** pen is out of ink.

3. **Numbers**
    Example: She has **four** brothers.

4. **Possessive pronouns: my, his, her, your, its, our, their, whose**
    Example: **Their** dog is unusual.

5. **Possessive nouns:**
    Example: **Sharon's** husband is a dock worker.

6. **Indefinites: some, few, many, several, no, any**
    Example: Do you have **any** quarters?

Descriptive adjectives will be presented later.

Page 223: **Limiting (Determining) Adjectives**
Students are merely asked to find the limiting adjective and to draw an arrow to the word it modifies (goes over to).

Page 225: **Limiting Adjective?**
Students are asked to determine if the word serves as an adjective.
(It has not been explained that the word becomes a pronoun if standing alone.) You may wish to have students continue to draw arrows.

ADJECTIVES

There are two major types of adjectives: limiting and descriptive.
You have used limiting adjectives when studying nouns. They were called determiners or determining adjectives.

Limiting Adjectives = Determiners = Determining Adjectives

Limiting (Determining) Adjectives:

1. **Articles: a, an, the**
   Example: **The** bank has closed.

2. **Demonstratives: this, that, those, these**
   Example: Are **those** hangers plastic?

3. **Numbers**
   Example: **Thirteen** students were in the play.

4. **Possessive pronouns: my, his, her, your, its, our, their, whose**
   Example: **Whose** umbrella is missing?

5. **Possessive nouns:**
   Example: **Dan's** friend is a stewardess.

6. **Indefinites: some, few, many, several, no, any**
   Example: I'd like a **few** peanuts, please.

An adjective modifies another word. *Modifies* means *to go over to*. In very simple terms, an adjective answers *what*.

Example: That hat is dirty.

That is an adjective. *That what? That hat. That* is an adjective modifying *hat*.

Sometimes, a word that can be an adjective will appear alone in a sentence. When this happens, the word will not serve as an adjective.

Example: That is unusual.

That what? We don't know. In this sentence, *that* is not an adjective.

221

Limiting (Determining) Adjectives:

1. **Articles: a, an, the**

2. **Demonstratives: this, that, those, these**

3. **Numbers**

4. **Possessive pronouns: my, his, her, your, its, our, their, whose**

5. **Possessive nouns**

6. **Indefinites: some, few, many, several, no, any**

🍓🍓🍓🍓🍓🍓🍓🍓🍓🍓🍓🍓🍓🍓🍓🍓🍓🍓🍓🍓🍓🍓🍓🍓🍓🍓🍓🍓🍓🍓

Limiting adjectives are in boldfaced print; the word modified is underlined.
Directions: Circle any limiting adjective. Draw an arrow from the adjective to the word
                   it modifies (goes over to).

Example: **My** <u>uncle</u> fishes for bass.

1. **That** <u>person</u> is nice.

2. He spent **three** <u>dollars</u>.

3. **No** <u>rain</u> fell.

4. Who ate **our** <u>brownies</u>?

5. **Jim's** <u>brother</u> works with him.

6. Do you want **these** <u>magazines</u>?

7. **The first** <u>batter</u> was Stacy.

8. **His** <u>aunt</u> writes **children's** <u>stories</u>.

9. **Several** <u>pencils</u> are on **the** <u>table</u>.

10. **A** <u>trophy</u> was given to **their** <u>father</u>.

Limiting (Determining) Adjectives:

1. **Articles: a, an, the**
2. **Demonstratives: this, that, those, these**
3. **Numbers**
4. **Possessive pronouns: my, his, her, your, its, our, their, whose**
5. **Possessive nouns**
6. **Indefinites: some, few, many, several, no, any**

Directions: Circle any limiting adjective. Draw an arrow from the adjective to the word
it modifies (goes over to).

Example: (My) uncle fishes for bass.

1. That person is nice.

2. He spent three dollars.

3. No rain fell.

4. Who ate our brownies?

5. Jim's brother works with him.

6. Do you want these magazines?

7. The first batter was Stacy.

8. His aunt writes children's stories.

9. Several pencils are on the table.

10. A trophy was given to their father.

Directions: Write <u>Yes</u> if the boldfaced word serves as a limiting adjective; write
             <u>No</u> if the boldfaced word does not serve as a limiting adjective.

Remember: If a word serves as a limiting adjective, it will modify (go over to)
                another word (noun).

         Example: <u> Yes </u> **This** shoe is made of leather. *This what? This shoe!*

1. <u> Yes </u>   **Many** students are learning Spanish.

2. <u> No </u>   **Many** will attend next week's meeting.

3. <u> Yes </u>   Do you want **these** straws?

4. <u> No </u>   **These** belong to you.

5. <u> Yes </u>   There are **few** lights in the new park.

6. <u> No </u>   **Few** decided to stay.

7. <u> Yes </u>   They own **two** cars.

8. <u> No </u>   Only **two** raised their hands.

9. <u> No </u>   **This** isn't working.

10. <u> Yes </u>   Will you work on **this** project with me?

11. <u> No </u>   **Whose** is this?

12. <u> Yes </u>   **Whose** truck is parked in the driveway?

13. <u> No </u>   I don't have time for **that**.

14. <u> Yes </u>   **That** mountain is very rugged.

Directions: Write <u>Yes</u> if the boldfaced word serves as a limiting adjective; write
<u>No</u> if the boldfaced word does not serve as a limiting adjective.

Remember: If a word serves as a limiting adjective, it will modify (go over to)
another word (noun).

Example: __Yes__ **This** shoe is made of leather. *This what? This shoe!*

1. _____ **Many** students are learning Spanish.

2. _____ **Many** will attend next week's meeting.

3. _____ Do you want **these** straws?

4. _____ **These** belong to you.

5. _____ There are **few** lights in the new park.

6. _____ **Few** decided to stay.

7. _____ They own **two** cars.

8. _____ Only **two** raised their hands.

9. _____ **This** isn't working.

10. _____ Will you work on **this** project with me?

11. _____ **Whose** is this?

12. _____ **Whose** truck is parked in the driveway?

13. _____ I don't have time for **that**.

14. _____ **That** mountain is very rugged.

Descriptive Adjectives

Most adjectives describe. Spend ample time using examples in your classroom to teach this concept:

> globe - **round** globe
>
> hair - **blonde** hair
>
> face - **ugly** face (I make a grotesque face to solicit the word, *ugly*.)
>
> book - **big** book
>
> blouse - **flowered** blouse (I feature students' clothing.)
>
> boy - **happy** boy (Your class clown may like the word, *funny*.)

A very fun way for students to understand that adjectives describe is to divide them into groups of three to five for an activity. Give each group a penny. Give them two minutes (or that which works for you) to work cooperatively and write a list of adjectives that describe the penny (coin). (They will ask you if they can describe items on it like *small lettering*. You will have to determine what is best for your class.) This may prove difficult for some students. However, your goal is for students to understand that adjectives can describe.

> Representative Answers: **shiny** penny
> **thin** coin
> **copper** penny
> **small** coin
> **round** coin

A great assignment (in class or at home) is for students to cut out pictures from magazines, paste the pictures on a paper, and label with an adjective (underlined) and something in the picture. (You may want your students to make a small notebook.)

> Examples: a picture of a baby - <u>sleeping</u> baby
>
> a picture of a room with a sofa - <u>striped</u> sofa

If this is your first time using this technique, I strongly recommend that you make a page or notebook **modeling your expectations**. Students need this! After the first year of doing this "mini" project, ask them if you may keep some of their pages (notebooks) to show future classes. Usually, they love the idea!

Page 229: **Descriptive Adjectives**
This exercise helps students recognize that we use adjectives constantly.

Page 231: **Adjective or Noun?**
This worksheet helps students understand that a word may function differently. If the word describes, it serves as an adjective; if it stands alone, it's a noun.

DESCRIPTIVE ADJECTIVES

Most adjectives describe.

Adjectives modify (go over to) nouns or pronouns.

Most adjectives describe nouns.

Generally, we may say that descriptive adjectives tell **what kind**.

Specifically, they may tell color, type, condition, size, etc.

You know how to identify a noun. Look for any word or words that describe that noun.

Examples: **new** car

New tells *what kind* of car. *New* specifically tells the <u>condition</u> of the car.

yellow car

Yellow tells *what kind* of car. *Yellow* specifically tells the <u>color</u> of the car.

antique car

Antique tells *what kind* of car. *Antique* specifically tells the <u>type</u> of car.

compact car

Compact tells what kind of car. *Compact* specifically tells the <u>size</u> of the car.

🍓Often, more than one adjective will precede a noun (or pronoun).

An **enormous yellow** <u>balloon</u> was hanging from a **tall, steel** <u>post</u>.

(Notice that you do not need a comma between the two descriptive adjectives if one adjective is a color.)

🍓An adjective may occur after the verb and go back to describe the subject.

That <u>baby is</u> **cute**.   *cute* baby

🍓Adjectives may occur after a noun (or pronoun).

Her bathing suit, **sandy** and **wet**, lay on the floor.   227

Name_____   **ADJECTIVES**

WORKBOOK PAGE 97   **Descriptive Adjectives**

Date_____

Answers will vary. Representative answers are given. Answers are in boldfaced print. It may be fun to poll answers and determine which answer was given by most students.

1. **Colors describe.**

Directions: Write a color before each item. Use a color once.

Example: _____**purple**_____ crayon

a. ___**gray, black, white**___ cat   c. ___**yellow, beige, red**___ car

b. ___**gray, black, blue**___ sky   d. ___**white, black, pink**___ house

2. **Words that show size describe.**

Directions: Write a word that shows size before each item. Use a word once.

Example: _____**tiny**_____ flower

a. ___**little, tiny, minute**___ bee   c. ___**thin, wide, large**___ tree

b. ___**enormous, vast, small**___ store   d. ___**huge, skinny, petite**___ dog

3. **Words that show condition describe.**

Directions: Write a word that shows condition before each item. Use a word once.

Example: _____**holey**_____ shirt

a. ___**new, old, shiny**___ shoes   c. ___**damaged, new, clean**___ truck

b. ___**excellent, poor, boring**___ play   d. ___**melted, hard, sticky**___ candy

3. **Words that show "type of" describe.**

Directions: Write a word that shows a "type of" before each item.

Example: _____**credit**_____ card

a. ___**elementary, high, private**___ school   c. ___**jazz, school, dance**___ band

b. ___**green, pinto, chili**___ beans   d. ___**oak, redwood, pine**___ tree

228

Name_____

Date_____

1. **Colors describe.**

    Directions: Write a color before each item. Use a color once.

    Example: _____purple_____ crayon

a. _____ cat   c. _____ car

b. _____ sky   d. _____ house

2. **Words that show size describe.**

    Directions: Write a word that shows size before each item.   Use a word once.

    Example: _____tiny_____ flower

a. _____ bee   c. _____ tree

b. _____ store   d. _____ dog

3. **Words that show condition describe.**

    Directions: Write a word that shows condition before each item. Use a word once.

    Example: _____holey_____ shirt

a. _____ shoes   c. _____ truck

b. _____ play   d. _____ candy

3. **Words that show "type of" describe.**

    Directions: Write a word that shows a "type of" before each item.

    Example: _____credit_____ card

a. _____ school   c. _____ band

b. _____ beans   d. _____ tree

229

Directions: Write <u>Yes</u> if the boldfaced word serves as an adjective; write <u>No</u> if the
boldfaced word does not serve as an adjective.

Remember: If a word serves as an adjective, it will modify (go over to) another word.

Examples: <u>Yes</u> Go out the **back** door. *Back what? Back door!*

<u>No</u> She has a sunburn on her **back**.

1. <u>Yes</u> The **taxi** driver smiled.

2. <u>No</u> We waited for a **taxi**.

3. <u>Yes</u> His mother likes to go to **yard** sales.

4. <u>Yes</u> Their front **yard** is large.

5. <u>No</u> Does he put **salt** on grapefruit?

6. <u>Yes</u> Please pass the **salt** shaker.

7. <u>Yes</u> Most children enjoy a **water** slide.

8. <u>No</u> He added **water** to a vase.

9. <u>No</u> Laura sleeps on her **stomach** most of the time.

10. <u>Yes</u> Do you have a **stomach** ache?

11. <u>No</u> A rabbit nibbled a small **berry**.

12. <u>Yes</u> Bill and Betty made a **berry** pie.

13. <u>No</u> A cook added oil and **garlic** to the frying pan.

14. <u>Yes</u> They love **garlic** bread.

Name_____

ADJECTIVES
Descriptive Adjectives

Date_____

Directions: Write <u>Yes</u> if the boldfaced word serves as an adjective; write <u>No</u> if the
boldfaced word does not serve as an adjective.

Remember: If a word serves as an adjective, it will modify (go over to) another word.

Examples: <u>Yes</u> Go out the **back** door. *Back what? Back door!*
<u>No</u> She has a sunburn on her **back**.

1. _____   The **taxi** driver smiled.

2. _____   We waited for a **taxi**.

3. _____   His mother likes to go to **yard** sales.

4. _____   Their front **yard** is large.

5. _____   Does he put **salt** on grapefruit?

6. _____   Please pass the **salt** shaker.

7. _____   Most children enjoy a **water** slide.

8. _____   He added **water** to a vase.

9. _____   Laura sleeps on her **stomach** most of the time.

10. _____   Do you have a **stomach** ache?

11. _____   A rabbit nibbled a small **berry**.

12. _____   Bill and Betty made a **berry** pie.

13. _____   A cook added oil and **garlic** to the frying pan.

14. _____   They love **garlic** bread.   231

PROPER ADJECTIVES

A proper adjective is derived from a proper noun. Review proper nouns. Students will need to be shown that proper adjectives are formed in a variety of ways:

	Proper Noun	**Proper Adjective**	
<u>Change</u>:	Switzerland	Swiss	village
	China	Chinese	food
	Denmark	Danish	roll
<u>Do not change</u>:	Regency (brand name)	Regency	van
	Idaho	Idaho	potatoes

As stated earlier, **teach a concept before having students read about it.**

Activity: You may wish to divide the class into groups of three to five. Have each student fold a paper into three columns vertically. (I recommend that you model this.) At the top of the paper, have students write Proper Noun as column one's heading, Proper Adjective as column two's heading, and Noun as the heading for column three. Model this on the board. Use the examples given to establish the relationship between proper nouns and proper adjectives. After students understand this, begin group work. Direct each group to brainstorm and list as many proper nouns and proper adjectives as possible in a given amount of time. (For this activity, I have each student write a list because it is a learning situation. As we share answers, I ask pupils to add any new proper nouns and proper adjectives given by their peers. You may wish to add these to your board list.)

Examples:

Proper Noun	Proper Adjective	Noun
Mexico	Mexican	food
New York	New York	subway
England	English	countryside
Arctic	Arctic	storm

Page 235: **Proper Adjectives**
Students will find a proper adjective and the noun it modifies. They will capitalize it and write the proper adjective and noun.

Page 237: **Adjective Identification**
Do most of this page orally with your students. After reading the sentence, ask students to circle any limiting adjectives. I recommend that you state them categorically: *a, an, the* (Give students time to look.), *this, that, those, these,* (When you find one, help students to determine if it modifies or stands alone.) and continue on with each of the classifications. Then, look for descriptive adjectives. Ask, "Is there a word that describes _____?" Guide children to success. (This process may sound tedious, but it goes quickly and serves a purpose.)

232

PROPER ADJECTIVES

Proper adjectives come from proper nouns. A proper noun names a specific person, place, or thing.

Examples:

common noun	proper noun
lake	Lake Elsinore
country	Switzerland

If we want to talk about tourists from Japan, we say **Japanese** tourists. *Japanese* is an adjective modifying (going over to) *tourists*. We do not say *Japan tourists*. We change the proper noun, *Japan*, to the adjective form, *Japanese*. Because the adjective form comes from a proper noun, we capitalize the word and refer to it as a proper adjective.

	Proper Noun	**Proper Adjective**	
Change:	Switzerland	Swiss	village
	China	Chinese	food
	Denmark	Danish	roll

Some proper nouns are the same in the proper adjective form.

Do not change:	Chewytime	Chewytime	gum
	Idaho	Idaho	potatoes

A. Directions: Write the proper adjective form and a noun it can modify.

     Example: Germany - __German forest__

THE NOUN FOLLOWING THE PROPER ADJECTIVE WILL VARY.

1. America - ____American flag____   4. Arabia - ____Arabian horse____

2. Texas - ____Texan or Texas dance____   5. Mooby - ____Mooby milk____

3. Sweden - ____Swedish cookies____   6. Mexico - ____Mexican hat____

B. Directions: Write the proper adjective and the noun it modifies in the space.
              Capitalize the proper adjective in the sentence.

                   C

     Example: We saw a canadian wild goose. ____Canadian (wild) goose____

      F

1. Do you like french bread? _____French bread_____

       U   **S**

2. He raised a united states flag. _____United States flag_____

      S

3. Layla ate a swiss cheese sandwich. ____Swiss cheese_____

        A

4. They fished in an alaskan stream. ____Alaskan stream_____

        D

5. The farmer bought a deerwester tractor. ____Deerwester tractor_____

       A

6. Ira asked about an african tour. _____African tour_____.

        S

7. First graders are learning the spanish language. ____Spanish language____

      P

8. Rafe loves his paterno stereo. ____Paterno stereo_____

       I

9. Salad was served with italian dressing. _____Italian dressing_____

      N

10. She traveled on a nebraska freeway. _____Nebraska freeway_____

      M

11. Do you like mississippi mud pie? ____Mississippi mud pie_____

A. Directions: Write the proper adjective form and a noun it can modify.
       Example: Germany - ___German forest___

1. America - _____   4. Arabia - _____

2. Texas - _____   5. Mooby - _____

3. Sweden - _____   6. Mexico - _____

B. Directions: Write the proper adjective and the noun it modifies in the space.
                 Capitalize the proper adjective in the sentence.
                          C
       Example: We saw a canadian wild goose.   ___Canadian (wild) goose___

1.   Do you like french bread? _____

2.   He raised a united states flag. _____

3.   Layla ate a swiss cheese sandwich. _____

4.   They fished in an alaskan stream. _____

5.   The farmer bought a deerwester tractor. _____

6.   Ira asked about an african tour. _____

7.   First graders are learning the spanish language. _____

8.   Rafe loves his paterno stereo. _____

9.   Salad was served with italian dressing. _____

10.   She traveled on a nebraska freeway. _____

11.   Do you like mississippi mud pie? _____

Answers are in boldfaced print.
Directions: Circle any adjectives.

Suggestion: First, identify any limiting adjectives. Then, reread the sentence and
                     look for descriptive adjectives.

1.   **Palm** trees line **that busy** street.

2.   **Several** ducks waddled down **a** trail.

3.   She bought **red glossy** lipstick.

4.   **Many playful** dolphins swam in **the** ocean.

5.   We drank **an orange** drink with **ice** cubes.

6.   **His** younger sister has **two** mice.

7.   He purchased **a few new wool** sweaters.

8.   Do you want **ice** cream and **a** piece of **peach** pie?

9.   **This chocolate** cake requires **no** eggs.

10.   **A blue suede** jacket was given to **my** friend.

11.   **The** lady, **tall** and **pretty**, was once **a famous** model.

12.   **These potato** chips don't have **any** salt.

13.   **Our favorite vacation** place is near **a hot** spring.

14.   **The laughing** baby rolled **her big brown** eyes.

15.   I bought **a round coffee** table and **some oak** chairs at **garage** sales.

Directions: Circle any adjectives.

Suggestion: First, identify any limiting adjectives. Then, reread the sentence and
look for descriptive adjectives.

1. Palm trees line that busy street.

2. Several ducks waddled down a trail.

3. She bought red glossy lipstick.

4. Many playful dolphins swam in the ocean.

5. We drank an orange drink with ice cubes.

6. His younger sister has two mice.

7. He purchased a few new wool sweaters.

8. Do you want ice cream and a piece of peach pie?

9. This chocolate cake requires no eggs.

10. A blue suede jacket was given to my friend.

11. The lady, tall and pretty, was once a famous model.

12. These potato chips don't have any salt.

13. Our favorite vacation place is near a hot spring.

14. The laughing baby rolled her big brown eyes.

15. I bought a round coffee table and some oak chairs at garage sales.

TO THE TEACHER:

PAGE 239 = WORKBOOK PAGE 102
DEGREES OF ADJECTIVES

At this level, degrees of adjectives will be introduced. Be sure to teach the concept **before** having students read about it. There may be some confusion in that predicate adjectives have not been introduced formally. You will need to share with students that **placement** of adjectives varies.

Examples: John is a **polite** boy. *Polite* precedes the noun, *boy*, in this sentence.
Most adjectives precede the noun they modify.

John, **polite** and helpful, was given a citizenship award.
Polite describes *John* but is placed after the name.

John is **polite**. In this sentence, *polite* comes **after the verb** and describes *John*. This is a special adjective called a predicate adjective. You may choose to merely call it an adjective since predicate adjectives, predicate nominatives, and linking verbs have not been introduced at this level.

After teaching placement of adjectives, it is easier to teach degrees. I ask a rather tall student to stand. I say, "Bill (or whoever) is tall. Is *tall* an adjective that describes Bill?" We agree that it is. Next, I choose a slightly taller pupil and ask that student to stand beside the first student. I say, "We are now going to **compare** these two students. We can say that Bill is tall, but Leslie is ___." Students readily say, " "*Taller.*" I then stress that we **compared two** people. We are discussing **to what degree** *tall* they are. In English, we call this degrees of adjectives. I ask students how many the comparative form compares. With the two students standing in front of them, they readily respond, "*Two.*"

In teaching superlative, I ask an even taller student to join my other two students. "Bill is tall, and Leslie is taller. However, of the three, Ken is ___." Students usually respond, "*Tallest.*" We, then, discuss that this is the **superlative form** and compares **three or more**. (It's a good idea to review this before having the three pupils sit down. "Bill is tall. Leslie is taller. But of the three, Ken is tallest.")

Continue using items in the room. I've used students' shoes with the adjective, *large*. (If you ask students to remove shoes, however, you may get a few comments.) You can use books with the adjective, heavy. Other ideas include a file cabinet, student desk, and your desk with the adjective, wide.
Allow students to share ideas. However, I recommend that you stay away from words such as *smart, fat, ugly,* or *pretty*. You can see that these words used for comparison could be hurtful to students.

There are specific rules taught for forming degrees: one syllable words, two syllable formations, and adjectives of three or more syllables. Adjectives having one syllable and those with three or more syllables are easiest to teach. Two syllable words sometimes add *er/est* as in *prettier/prettiest*. Other two syllable words use *more/most* (or *less/least*): *helpful - more helpful/most helpful*. Some can be used either way: *sincere - sincerer/sincerest* or *more sincere/most sincere*. Again, teach students to use a **dictionary** to determine correct and/or preferred endings.

Note: When making adjective comparisons, the word without *er/est* is sometimes referred to as the positive form. Hence, there are positive, comparative, and superlative forms. At this level, I mention this fact but do not require students to master it.

238

Degrees of Adjectives

Adjectives can make comparisons.
- A. The **comparative form** compares **two**.
- B. The **superlative form** compares **three or more**.

There are several ways to form the comparative and superlative forms:

A. **Comparative**:

1. Add **er** to most one-syllable adjectives:

   dull/duller   bold/bolder

2. Add **er** to some two-syllable adjectives:

   creamy/creamier   dusty/dustier

3. Place **more** (or less) before some two-syllable adjectives:

   faithful/more faithful   likable/more likable

IMPORTANT: Use a dictionary to determine if **er** should be added to a two-syllable adjective.

4. Before adjectives of three or more syllables, add **more** (or less) to make comparisons.

   exciting/more exciting   embarrassed/more embarrassed

5. Some adjectives completely change form.

   good/better   bad/worse

B. **Superlative**:

1. Add **est** to most one-syllable adjectives:

   dull/dullest   bold/boldest

2. Add **est** to some two-syllable adjectives:

   creamy/creamiest   dusty/dustiest

3. Place **most** (or least) before some two-syllable adjectives:

   faithful/most faithful   likable/most likable

Important: Use a dictionary to determine if **est** should be added to a two-syllable adjective.

4. Place **most** (or least) before three-syllable adjectives.

   exciting/most exciting   embarrassed/most embarrassed

5. Some adjectives totally change form.

   good/best   bad/worst

Directions: Write the adjective form in the space provided.

Example: superlative of friendly - _____friendliest_____

1. comparative form of old - _____older_____

2. superlative form of old - _____oldest_____

3. comparative form of happy - _____happier_____

4. superlative form of happy - _____happiest_____

5. comparative form of cheerful - _____more cheerful_____

6. superlative form of cheerful - _____most cheerful_____

7. comparative form of merry - _____merrier_____

8. superlative form of merry - _____merriest_____

9. comparative form of good - _____better_____

10. superlative form of good - _____best_____

11. comparative form of excited - _____more excited_____

12. comparative form of lovable - _____more lovable_____

13. superlative form of cute - _____cutest_____

14. comparative form of lively - _____livelier_____

15. superlative form of dangerous - _____most dangerous_____

Name_____   **ADJECTIVES**
                                               Degrees
Date_____

Directions: Write the adjective form in the space provided.

        Example: superlative of friendly - _____friendliest_____

1. comparative form of old - _____

2. superlative form of old - _____

3. comparative form of happy - _____

4. superlative form of happy - _____

5. comparative form of cheerful - _____

6. superlative form of cheerful - _____

7. comparative form of merry - _____

8. superlative form of merry - _____

9. comparative form of good - _____

10. superlative form of good - _____

11. comparative form of excited - _____

12. comparative form of lovable - _____

13. superlative form of cute - _____

14. comparative form of lively - _____

15. superlative form of dangerous - _____

Answers are in boldfaced print.
Directions: Circle the correct answer.

1. Jody is (**taller**, tallest) than Crissy.

2. My left foot is (**longer**, longest) than my right one.

3. This purse is (**larger**, largest) than that one.

4. Of the three apartments, the first one is (smaller, **smallest**).

5. Marge's dad is the (funnier, **funniest**) one of their family.

6. Shelley is the (**older**, oldest) twin.

7. That is the (more unusual, **most unusual**) painting in the museum.

8. Brittany's was the (faster, **fastest**) car in the race.

9. He is the (more active, **most active**) triplet.

10. Your story sounds (**more believable**, most believable) than his.

11. She is the (louder, **loudest**) cheerleader on the squad.

12. We were (more excited, **most excited**) the third time we rode the roller coaster.

13. The bride was (**more exhausted**, most exhausted) after the rehearsal than after the wedding.

14. Mark's aunt is (**older**, oldest) than his uncle.

15. Of the four trucks, the green one is (shinier, **shiniest**).

242

Directions: Circle the correct answer.

1.   Jody is (taller, tallest) than Crissy.

2.   My left foot is (longer, longest) than my right one.

3.   This purse is (larger, largest) than that one.

4.   Of the three apartments, the first one is (smaller, smallest).

5.   Marge's dad is the (funnier, funniest) one of their family.

6.   Shelley is the (older, oldest) twin.

7.   That is the (more unusual, most unusual) painting in the museum.

8.   Brittany's was the (faster, fastest) car in the race.

9.   He is the (more active, most active) triplet.

10.   Your story sounds (more believable, most believable) than his.

11.   She is the (louder, loudest) cheerleader on the squad.

12.   We were (more excited, most excited) the third time we rode the roller coaster.

13.   The bride was (more exhausted, most exhausted) after the rehearsal than after the wedding.

14.   Mark's aunt is (older, oldest) than his uncle.

15.   Of the four trucks, the green one is (shinier, shiniest).

A. **Limiting Adjectives:**

    Directions: Fill in the blanks.

1. The three articles that serve as limiting adjectives are __a__, __an__, and __the__.

2. The four demonstrative adjectives are __this__, __that__, __those__, and __these__.

3. Write a sentence with a number serving as an adjective: _____
    Answers will vary. Representative answers:
    _____Five candles were on the cake._____

4. The possessive pronouns that can serve as adjectives are __my__, __his__,
    __her__, __your__, __its__, __our__, __their__, and __whose__.

5. Write your name + **'s** and something you own. __Student's name + item__

6. Three indefinites that can serve as adjectives are __some__, __several__,
    and __no__. Other answers include *many*, *few*, and *any*.

B. **Adjective?:**

    Directions: Write <u>Yes</u> if the boldfaced word serves as an adjective. Write <u>No</u> if
    the boldfaced word does not serve as an adjective.

1. __No__   May I have **some**?

2. __Yes__   May I have **some** peas, please.

3. __Yes__   The **gas** tank in their car is quite large.

4. __No__   Must we put **gas** in that lawn mower?

5. __No__   Write your signature on the **line**.

6. __Yes__   Their entire family likes to **line** dance.

244

Date_____

A. **Limiting Adjectives:**

   Directions: Fill in the blanks.

1. The three articles that serve as limiting adjectives are _____, _____, and _____.

2. The four demonstrative adjectives are _____, _____, _____, and

    _____.

3. Write a sentence with a number serving as an adjective: _____

    _____

4. The possessive pronouns that can serve as adjectives are _____, _____,

    _____, _____, _____, _____, _____, and _____.

5. Write your name + **'s** and something you own. _____

6. Three indefinites that can serve as adjectives are _____, _____,

    and _____.

B. **Adjective?:**

   Directions: Write <u>Yes</u> if the boldfaced word serves as an adjective. Write <u>No</u> if
              the boldfaced word does not serve as an adjective.

1. _____   May I have **some**?

2. _____   May I have **some** peas, please.

3. _____   The **gas** tank in their car is quite large.

4. _____   Must we put **gas** in that lawn mower?

5. _____   Write your signature on the **line**.

6. _____   Their entire family likes to **line** dance.

WORKBOOK PAGE 106

Date_____

Answers are in boldfaced print.

C. **Adjective Identification:**

Directions: Circle any adjective.

Suggestion: First, look for limiting adjectives. Then, reread the sentence searching for descriptive adjectives.

1. **One famous** athlete spoke to **a small middle** school.

2. After **the hockey** game, **several** players ate **a large** meal.

3. Does **your** uncle drive **an old black** truck with **shiny chrome** wheels?

4. **No fishing** bait is sold at **that general** store.

5. **His best** friend sends him **unusual baseball** cards.

D. **Proper Adjectives:**

Directions: Capitalize any proper adjective.

    V

1. Dad likes vermont maple syrup on his pancakes.

      I

2. Rod likes to go to indianapolis races.

    A

3. The first american flag may have been made by Betsy Ross.

       S **A**

4. Have your ever seen a south american monkey?

E. **Degrees of Adjectives:**

Directions: Circle the correct answer.

1. Jan is the (happier, **happiest**) student in the class.

2. Mitchell is (**taller**, tallest) than his mother.

3. Of the four kittens, Fluffy is the (more playful, **most playful**).

4. The second play was (gooder, **better**) than the first one.

5. Rattlesnakes are (**more dangerous**, most dangerous) than garter snakes.

246

C. **Adjective Identification:**
   Directions: Circle any adjective.

Suggestion: First, look for limiting adjectives. Then, reread the sentence searching
          for descriptive adjectives.

1. One famous athlete spoke to a small middle school.

2. After the hockey game, several players ate a large meal.

3. Does your uncle drive an old black truck with shiny chrome wheels?

4. No fishing bait is sold at that general store.

5. His best friend sends him unusual baseball cards.

D. **Proper Adjectives:**
   Directions: Capitalize any proper adjective.

1. Dad likes vermont maple syrup on his pancakes.

2. Rod likes to go to indianapolis races.

3. The first american flag may have been made by Betsy Ross.

4. Have your ever seen a south american monkey?

E. **Degrees of Adjectives:**
   Directions: Circle the correct answer.

1. Jan is the (happier, happiest) student in the class.

2. Mitchell is (taller, tallest) than his mother.

3. Of the four kittens, Fluffy is the (more playful, most playful).

4. The second play was (gooder, better) than the first one.

5. Rattlesnakes are (more dangerous, most dangerous) than garter snakes.

Name_____   **Adjective Test**

Date_____
Answers are in boldfaced print.
A. **Adjective Identification:**

    Directions: Circle any adjective.

Suggestion: First, look for limiting adjectives. Then, reread the sentence searching
                for descriptive adjectives.

1.   **Small**, **rusty** nails lay on **the broken** bench.

2.   **These jelly** doughnuts are **good**.

3.   During **our zoo** trip, we saw **many** monkeys.

4.   **The red brick** house was built in **ten** months.

5.   **Their little** turtle now lives near **a marshy** pond.

6.   **An orange tissue** box is on **that** counter.

7.   **The** bride wore **a white silk** gown with **short**, **puffed** sleeves.

B. **Degrees of Adjectives:**
Pungent in #8 is a difficult word. However, it was added so that students could use a
dictionary to determine the correct answer.
    Directions: Circle the correct answer.

1.   Kimberly is the (taller, **tallest**) person in her Sunday school class.

2.   Let's sit in that area; it is (**grassier**, grassiest) than this one.

3.   This rubber band is (more elastic, **most elastic**) of the six that you gave me.

4.   During the fourth performance of the play, we did (goodest, **best**).

5.   This car attendant is (**more agreeable**, most agreeable) than his partner.

6.   A steel plow was (**lighter**, lightest) than the old iron type.

7.   She is the (nimbler, **nimblest**) gymnast in her group.

8.   The garlic odor is (pungenter, **more pungent**) than the onion smell.
248

Name_____   **Adjective Test**

Date_____

A. **Adjective Identification:**

Directions: Circle any adjective.

Suggestion: First, look for limiting adjectives. Then, reread the sentence searching for descriptive adjectives.

1.   Small, rusty nails lay on the broken bench.

2.   These jelly doughnuts are good.

3.   During our zoo trip, we saw many monkeys.

4.   The red brick house was built in ten months.

5.   Their little turtle now lives near a marshy pond.

6.   An orange tissue box is on that counter.

7.   The bride wore a white silk gown with short, puffed sleeves.

B. **Degrees of Adjectives:**

Directions: Circle the correct answer.

1.   Kimberly is the (taller, tallest) person in her Sunday school class.

2.   Let's sit in that area; it is (grassier, grassiest) than this one.

3.   This rubber band is (more elastic, most elastic) of the six that you gave me.

4.   During the fourth performance of the play, we did (goodest, best).

5.   This car attendant is (more agreeable, most agreeable) than his partner.

6.   A steel plow was (lighter, lightest) than the old iron type.

7.   She is the (nimbler, nimblest) gymnast in her group.

8.   The garlic odor is (pungenter, more pungent) than the onion smell.

A. **Object of the Preposition:**

  Directions: Cross out any prepositional phrases. Label the object of the preposition - O.P.

                                    O.P.
1. We dipped chips ~~into a salsa~~.

                                O.P.   O.P.
2. Waves crashed ~~against rocks on the shore~~.

🍓🍓🍓🍓🍓🍓🍓🍓🍓🍓🍓🍓🍓🍓🍓🍓🍓🍓🍓🍓🍓🍓🍓🍓🍓🍓🍓🍓🍓🍓🍓🍓🍓🍓

B. **Prepositions:**

  Directions: Cross out any prepositional phrases. Underline the subject once and the verb/verb phrase twice. Label any direct object - D.O.

1. The <u>class</u> <u>must leave</u> ~~within ten minutes~~.

2. <u>He</u> often <u>sits</u> ~~under a tree during the evening~~.

3. <u>Briana</u> <u>lives</u> ~~about five miles from her grandparents~~.

                            D.O.
4. The <u>family</u> <u>plants</u> corn ~~in their garden~~ each year.

🍓🍓🍓🍓🍓🍓🍓🍓🍓🍓🍓🍓🍓🍓🍓🍓🍓🍓🍓🍓🍓🍓🍓🍓🍓🍓🍓🍓🍓🍓🍓🍓🍓🍓

C. **Compound Subject:**

  Directions: Cross out any prepositional phrases. Underline the subject once and the verb/verb phrase twice.

Remember: Compound means more than one.

1. The <u>coach</u> and <u>players</u> <u>practiced</u> ~~during the evening~~.

2. Her <u>address</u> and telephone <u>number</u> <u>have been changed</u>.

🍓🍓🍓🍓🍓🍓🍓🍓🍓🍓🍓🍓🍓🍓🍓🍓🍓🍓🍓🍓🍓🍓🍓🍓🍓🍓🍓🍓🍓🍓🍓🍓🍓🍓

D. **Imperative Sentences:**

  Directions: Cross out any prepositional phrases. Underline the subject once and the verb/verb phrase twice.

1. <u>(You)</u> <u>Sit</u> ~~in that chair~~, please.

2. <u>(You)</u> <u>Call</u> me ~~after dinner~~.

250

A. **Object of the Preposition:**

Directions: Cross out any prepositional phrases. Label the object of the preposition - <u>O.P.</u>

1. We dipped chips into a salsa.

2. Waves crashed against rocks on the shore.

B. **Prepositions:**

Directions: Cross out any prepositional phrases. Underline the subject once and the verb/verb phrase twice. Label any direct object - <u>D.O.</u>

1. The class must leave within ten minutes.

2. He often sits under a tree during the evening.

3. Briana lives about five miles from her grandparents.

4. The family plants corn in their garden each year.

C. **Compound Subject:**

Directions: Cross out any prepositional phrases. Underline the subject once and the verb/verb phrase twice.

Remember: Compound means more than one.

1. The coach and players practiced during the evening.

2. Her address and telephone number have been changed.

D. **Imperative Sentences:**

Directions: Cross out any prepositional phrases. Underline the subject once and the verb/verb phrase twice.

1. Sit in that chair, please.

2. Call me after dinner.

E.   **Compound Objects of the Preposition:**

Directions: Cross out any prepositional phrases. Underline the subject once and the verb/verb phrase twice.

1. A <u>parachute</u> <u>consists</u> ~~of a canopy and a harness~~.

2. A <u>scientist</u> <u>poured</u> mixtures ~~from a beaker and a test tube~~.

🍓🍓🍓🍓🍓🍓🍓🍓🍓🍓🍓🍓🍓🍓🍓🍓🍓🍓🍓🍓🍓🍓🍓🍓🍓🍓🍓🍓🍓🍓🍓🍓🍓🍓🍓

F.   **Compound Verbs:**

Directions: Cross out any prepositional phrases. Underline the subject once and the verb/verb phrase twice.

1. The <u>minister</u> <u>smiled</u> and <u>told</u> a story ~~about Joseph~~.

2. A <u>bird</u> <u>flutters</u> ~~around the tree~~ and <u>flies</u> ~~through its branches~~.

🍓🍓🍓🍓🍓🍓🍓🍓🍓🍓🍓🍓🍓🍓🍓🍓🍓🍓🍓🍓🍓🍓🍓🍓🍓🍓🍓🍓🍓🍓🍓🍓🍓🍓🍓

G.   **Infinitives:**

Directions: Cross out any prepositional phrases. Underline the subject once and the verb twice. Place an infinitive in parenthesis ( ).

1. His <u>family</u> <u>likes</u> (to ski) ~~in Colorado during January~~.

2. <u>Do</u> <u>you</u> <u>want</u> (to bake) a cake ~~for Tony's birthday~~?

🍓🍓🍓🍓🍓🍓🍓🍓🍓🍓🍓🍓🍓🍓🍓🍓🍓🍓🍓🍓🍓🍓🍓🍓🍓🍓🍓🍓🍓🍓🍓🍓🍓🍓🍓

H.   **Contractions:**

Directions: Write the contraction in the space provided.

1. I have - _____I've_____   5. you will - _____you'll_____

2. where is - _____where's_____   6. I am -_____I'm_____

3. they are - _____they're_____   7. might not - _____mightn't_____

4. could not - _____couldn't_____   8. are not - _____aren't_____

252

E. **Compound Objects of the Preposition:**

   Directions: Cross out any prepositional phrases. Underline the subject once
              and the verb/verb phrase twice.

1. A parachute consists of a canopy and a harness.

2. A scientist poured mixtures from a beaker and a test tube.

🍓🍓🍓🍓🍓🍓🍓🍓🍓🍓🍓🍓🍓🍓🍓🍓🍓🍓🍓🍓🍓🍓🍓🍓🍓🍓🍓🍓🍓🍓🍓🍓🍓🍓

F. **Compound Verbs:**

   Directions: Cross out any prepositional phrases. Underline the subject once
              and the verb/verb phrase twice.

1. The minister smiled and told a story about Joseph.

2. A bird flutters around the tree and flies through its branches.

🍓🍓🍓🍓🍓🍓🍓🍓🍓🍓🍓🍓🍓🍓🍓🍓🍓🍓🍓🍓🍓🍓🍓🍓🍓🍓🍓🍓🍓🍓🍓🍓🍓🍓

G. **Infinitives:**

   Directions: Cross out any prepositional phrases. Underline the subject once
              and the verb twice. Place an infinitive in parentheses ( ).

1. His family likes to ski in Colorado during January.

2. Do you want to bake a cake for Tony's birthday?

🍓🍓🍓🍓🍓🍓🍓🍓🍓🍓🍓🍓🍓🍓🍓🍓🍓🍓🍓🍓🍓🍓🍓🍓🍓🍓🍓🍓🍓🍓🍓🍓🍓🍓

H. **Contractions:**

   Directions: Write the contraction in the space provided.

1. I have - _____   5. you will - _____

2. where is - _____   6. I am - _____

3. they are - _____   7. might not - _____

4. could not - _____   8. are not - _____

253

I. **Action Verb?:**

Directions: Write <u>Yes</u> if the boldfaced verb shows action; write <u>No</u> if the boldfaced verb does not show action.

1. <u>Yes</u>   Brandon **dropped** a quarter into the machine.

2. <u>Yes</u>   The lady **nodded** her head in approval.

3. <u>No</u>   Ms. Dean **seems** frustrated today.

J. **Regular or Irregular:**

Directions: Write <u>RV</u> if the verb is regular. Write <u>IV</u> if the verb is irregular.

Remember: Regular verbs add <u>ed</u> to the past and past participle.

1. <u>IV</u>   to bring   3. <u>IV</u>   to write   5. <u>RV</u>   to wash

2. <u>RV</u>   to follow   4. <u>IV</u>   to do   6. <u>RV</u>   to cook

K. **Tenses:**

Directions: Cross out any prepositional phrases. Underline the subject once and the verb/verb phrase twice. Write the tense on the line.

Remember: The tenses that we have learned are *present*, *past*, and *future*.

1. _____future_____   I shall talk ~~with you~~ later.

2. _____present_____   Most people feed pigeons ~~at that park~~.

3. _____past_____   Two children danced ~~in the talent show~~.

4. _____present_____   Their family camps ~~during the summer~~.

5. _____future_____   Kari will arrive ~~after her soccer game~~.

254

I. **Action Verb?:**

Directions: Write <u>Yes</u> if the boldfaced verb shows action; write <u>No</u> if the boldfaced verb does not show action.

1. _____   Brandon **dropped** a quarter into the machine.

2. _____   The lady **nodded** her head in approval.

3. _____   Ms. Dean **seems** frustrated today.

🍓🍓🍓🍓🍓🍓🍓🍓🍓🍓🍓🍓🍓🍓🍓🍓🍓🍓🍓🍓🍓🍓🍓🍓🍓🍓🍓🍓🍓🍓🍓🍓🍓

J. **Regular or Irregular:**

Directions: Write <u>RV</u> if the verb is regular. Write <u>IV</u> if the verb is irregular.

Remember: Regular verbs add <u>ed</u> to the past and past participle.

1. _____   to bring   3. _____   to write   5. _____   to wash

2. _____   to follow   4. _____   to do   6. _____   to cook

🍓🍓🍓🍓🍓🍓🍓🍓🍓🍓🍓🍓🍓🍓🍓🍓🍓🍓🍓🍓🍓🍓🍓🍓🍓🍓🍓🍓🍓🍓🍓🍓

K. **Tenses:**

Directions: Cross out any prepositional phrases. Underline the subject once and the verb/verb phrase twice. Write the tense on the line.

Remember: The tenses that we have learned are *present*, *past*, and *future*.

1. _____   I shall talk with you later.

2. _____   Most people feed pigeons at that park.

3. _____   Two children danced in the talent show.

4. _____   Their family camps during the summer.

5. _____   Kari will arrive after her soccer game.

Additional information has been provided for sections L and M.

L. **Irregular Verbs:**

   Directions: Circle the correct verb.

   1. Have you (brung, **brought**) money with you?

   2. He may have (took, **taken**) the shuttle to the airport.

   3. I must have (**run**, ran) two miles.

   4. Paul has (drank, **drunk**) several bottles of cola.

   5. He should have (**come**, came) to the game at nine o'clock.

   6. A child (**lay**, laid) on the floor with his dogs.

🍓🍓🍓🍓🍓🍓🍓🍓🍓🍓🍓🍓🍓🍓🍓🍓🍓🍓🍓🍓🍓🍓🍓🍓🍓🍓🍓🍓🍓🍓🍓🍓

M. **Subject-Verb Agreement:**

   Directions: Circle the verb that agrees with the subject.

   1. Kriss Kringle (**is**, are) the British name for Santa Claus.

   2. Several servers (leaves, **leave**) early each day.

   3. One of the ladies (give, **gives**) many items to charity.

   4. Kevin and his sister (travels, **travel**) to Alabama every summer.

🍓🍓🍓🍓🍓🍓🍓🍓🍓🍓🍓🍓🍓🍓🍓🍓🍓🍓🍓🍓🍓🍓🍓🍓🍓🍓🍓🍓🍓🍓🍓🍓

N. **Concrete and Abstract Nouns:**

   Directions: Write C if the noun is concrete; write A if the noun is abstract.

   1. _C_ lizard   3. _C_ mask   5. _C_ smoke
   2. _A_ truth   4. _C_ money   6. _A_ friendship

🍓🍓🍓🍓🍓🍓🍓🍓🍓🍓🍓🍓🍓🍓🍓🍓🍓🍓🍓🍓🍓🍓🍓🍓🍓🍓🍓🍓🍓🍓🍓🍓

O. **Common and Proper Nouns:**

   Directions: Write CN if the noun is common; write PN if the noun is proper.

   1. _CN_ WOMAN   3. _PN_ VERMONT   5. _CN_ KITE
   2. _CN_ APRICOT   4. _PN_ ST. LOUIS   6. _PN_ SPAIN

L. **Irregular Verbs:**

Directions: Circle the correct verb.

1. Have you (brung, brought) money with you?

2. He may have (took, taken) the shuttle to the airport.

3. I must have (run, ran) two miles.

4. Paul has (drank, drunk) several bottles of cola.

5. He should have (come, came) to the game at nine o'clock.

6. A child (lay, laid) on the floor with his dogs.

M. **Subject-Verb Agreement:**

Directions: Circle the verb that agrees with the subject.

1. Kriss Kringle (is, are) the British name for Santa Claus.

2. Several servers (leaves, leave) early each day.

3. One of the ladies (give, gives) many items to charity.

4. Kevin and his sister (travels, travel) to Alabama every summer.

N. **Concrete and Abstract Nouns:**

Directions: Write C if the noun is concrete; write A if the noun is abstract.

1.	_____	lizard	3.	_____	mask	5.	_____	smoke
2.	_____	truth	4.	_____	money	6.	_____	friendship

O. **Common and Proper Nouns:**

Directions: Write CN if the noun is common; write PN if the noun is proper.

1.	_____	WOMAN	3.	_____	VERMONT	5.	_____	KITE
2.	_____	APRICOT	4.	_____	ST. LOUIS	6.	_____	SPAIN

Nouns are boldfaced; determiners are underlined.

P. **Noun Identification:**

Directions: Circle any nouns in each sentence.

Remember: You may wish to underline determiners to help you find most nouns.

1. **Charlie's father** became a **pilot** in the **Navy**.

2. That **can** of sweet **potatoes** is behind two **bags** of **beans**.

3. Those **pictures** of your **trip** to **Oregon** are beautiful.

Q. **Singular and Plural Nouns:**

Directions: Write the plural.

1. key - _____keys_____	5. ox - _____oxen_____
2. glass - _____glasses_____	6. bubble - _____bubbles_____
3. wife - _____wives_____	7. bank - _____banks_____
4. tomato - _____tomatoes_____	8. father-in-law - _____fathers-in-law_____

R. **Possessive Nouns:**

Directions: Write the possessive form.

1. a boat belonging to Melissa

_____Melissa's boat_____

2. a bus shared by many tourists

_____tourists' bus_____

3. a company owned by more than one man

_____men's company_____

4. ferrets belonging to Chris

_____Chris's ferrets_____

258

P. **Noun Identification:**

    Directions: Underline any nouns in each sentence.

Remember: You may wish to circle determiners to help you find most nouns.

1. Charlie's father became a pilot in the Navy.

2. That can of sweet potatoes is behind two bags of beans.

3. Those pictures of your trip to Oregon are beautiful.

Q. **Singular and Plural Nouns:**

    Directions: Write the plural.

1. key - _____

2. glass - _____

3. wife - _____

4. tomato - _____

5. ox - _____

6. bubble - _____

7. bank - _____

8. father-in-law - _____

R. **Possessive Nouns:**

    Directions: Write the possessive form.

1. a boat belonging to Melissa

_____

2. a bus shared by many tourists

_____

3. a company owned by more than one man

_____

4. ferrets belonging to Chris

_____

S. **Sentence Types:**

Directions: Write the sentence type in the space provided.

Remember: The four sentence types are declarative, interrogative, imperative, and exclamatory.

1. _____imperative_____ Tie your shoe.

2. _____declarative_____ You need an extra zero in that number.

3. _____interrogative_____ What is your phone number?

4. _____declarative_____ The judge asked the witness to step down.

5. _____exclamatory_____ We're here!

6. _____imperative_____ Please wait your turn.

🍓🍓🍓🍓🍓🍓🍓🍓🍓🍓🍓🍓🍓🍓🍓🍓🍓🍓🍓🍓🍓🍓🍓🍓🍓🍓🍓🍓🍓

T. **Conjunctions:**

Directions: Circle any conjunctions.

1. I'll order a hamburger **or** hot dog.

2. A nurse **and** doctor entered the patient's room.

3. Mary **and** Sam's family is large, **but** everyone is always home for dinner.

🍓🍓🍓🍓🍓🍓🍓🍓🍓🍓🍓🍓🍓🍓🍓🍓🍓🍓🍓🍓🍓🍓🍓🍓🍓🍓🍓🍓🍓

U. **Interjections:**

Directions: Circle any interjections.

1. **No!** The car won't start!

2. **Whew!** We made it!

3. This meat smells rotten! **Yuck!**

260

S. **Sentence Types:**

Directions: Write the sentence type in the space provided.

Remember: The four sentence types are declarative, interrogative, imperative, and exclamatory.

1. _____ Tie your shoe.

2. _____ You need an extra zero in that number.

3. _____ What is your phone number?

4. _____ The judge asked the witness to step down.

5. _____ We're here!

6. _____ Please wait your turn.

T. **Conjunctions:**

Directions: Circle any conjunctions.

1. I'll order a hamburger or hot dog.

2. A nurse and doctor entered the patient's room.

3. Mary and Sam's family is large, but everyone is always home for dinner.

U. **Interjections:**

Directions: Circle any interjections.

1. No! The car won't start!

2. Whew! We made it!

3. This meat smells rotten! Yuck!

Name_____   **Cumulative Test**
                                        Adjective Unit
Date_____

This test contains four pages. However, it shouldn't take long for students to complete it.

A. **Prepositional Phrases:**

   Directions: Cross out any prepositional phrases. Underline the subject once and the verb/verb phrase twice. Label any direct object - <u>D.O.</u>

   1. A <u>surfer</u> <u>dashed</u> ~~across the sand~~.

                              D.O.
   2. (<u>You</u>) <u>Put</u> these old coins ~~into a drawer~~.

   3. Two <u>bicyclists</u> <u>pedaled</u> ~~along a path~~.

                              D.O.
   4. <u>Jarred</u> <u>placed</u> a house key ~~under a rock~~ ~~by the front door~~.

B. **Compounds:**

   Directions: Cross out any prepositional phrases. Underline the subject once and the verb/verb phrase twice.

   1. A <u>card</u> ~~for Mom and Dad~~ <u>arrived</u> ~~in the mail~~.

   2. The <u>toddler</u> <u>took</u> his first step and <u>fell</u>.

   3. A <u>cashier</u> and <u>customer</u> <u>talked</u> ~~about the new science museum~~.

   4. <u>Rob</u> <u>sneezed</u> lightly and <u>coughed</u>.

C. **Contractions:**

   Directions: Write the contraction.

   1. are not - _____aren't_____   5. where is - _____where's_____

   2. I am- _____I'm_____   6. had not - _____hadn't_____

   3. might not - _____mightn't_____   7. they have - _____they've_____

   4. we are - _____we're_____   8. I would - _____I'd_____

D. **Action?:**

   Directions: Write <u>Yes</u> if the boldfaced verb shows action; write <u>No</u> if the boldfaced verb does not show action.

      1. __Yes__   We **shivered** from the cold.

262 2. __No__   She **remained** calm during the earthquake.

A. **Prepositional Phrases:**

Directions: Cross out any prepositional phrases. Underline the subject once and the verb/verb phrase twice. Label any direct object - <u>D.O.</u>

1.   A surfer dashed across the sand.

2.   Put these old coins into a drawer.

3.   Two bicyclists pedaled along a path.

4.   Jarred placed a house key under a rock by the front door.

B. **Compounds:**

Directions: Cross out any prepositional phrases. Underline the subject once and the verb/verb phrase twice.

1.   A card for Mom and Dad arrived in the mail.

2.   The toddler took his first step and fell.

3.   A cashier and customer talked about the new science museum.

4.   Rob sneezed lightly and coughed.

C. **Contractions:**

Directions: Write the contraction.

1.   are not - _____   5.   where is - _____

2.   I am- _____   6.   had not - _____

3.   might not - _____   7.   they have - _____

4.   we are - _____   8.   I would - _____

D. **Action?:**

Directions: Write <u>Yes</u> if the boldfaced verb shows action; write <u>No</u> if the boldfaced verb does not show action.

1.   _____   We **shivered** from the cold.

2.   _____   She **remained** calm during the earthquake.   263

E. Regular or Irregular:

Directions: Write RV if the verb is regular. Write IV if the verb is irregular.

1. __IV__ to write   2. __RV__ to wash   3. __IV__ to fly   4. __RV__ to work

F. Subject-Verb Agreement:

Directions: Circle the verb that agrees with the subject.

Answers are in boldfaced print. Additional information has been provided.

1. That <u>puppy</u> (whimper, **whimpers**) so much.

2. <u>Opals</u> (is, **are**) very soft stones.

3. <u>One</u> ~~of the boys~~ (skate, **skates**) often.

G. Tenses:

Directions: Write the tense (present, past, or future) on the line provided.

Additional information has been provided.

Note: You may want to cross out prepositional phrases, underline subject once, and underline the verb/verb phrase twice to help determine the tense.

1. _____past_____   He <u>lost</u> his wedding ring.
2. _____future_____   A <u>pianist</u> <u>will play</u> ~~for us~~.
3. _____present_____   <u>I</u> <u>am</u> happy.
4. _____present_____   The <u>merchant</u> <u>gives</u> coupons ~~to his customers~~.

H. Irregular Verbs:

Directions: Circle the correct verb.

Answers are in boldfaced print. Additional information has been provided.

1. <u>He</u> <u>has</u> (began, **begun**) a new job.

2. <u>You</u> <u>should have</u> (took, **taken**) a different route.

3. <u>She</u> <u>has</u> (**swum**, swam) ~~on the team for three years~~.

4. The <u>actress</u> <u>must have</u> (**flown**, flew) ~~on an earlier flight~~.

5. That <u>fork</u> <u>has been</u> (**lying**, laying) ~~in the sink for two days~~.

264

E. **Regular or Irregular:**

Directions: Write <u>RV</u> if the verb is regular. Write <u>IV</u> if the verb is irregular.

1. ____ to write   2. ____ to wash   3. ____ to fly   4. ____ to work

F. **Subject-Verb Agreement:**

Directions: Circle the verb that agrees with the subject.

1. That puppy (whimper, whimpers) so much.

2. Opals (is, are) very soft stones.

3. One of the boys (skate, skates) often.

G. **Tenses:**

Directions: Write the tense (present, past, or future) on the line provided.

Note: You may want to cross out prepositional phrases, underline subject once, and underline the verb/verb phrase twice to help determine the tense.

1. _____ He lost his wedding ring.

2. _____ A pianist will play for us.

3. _____ I am happy.

4. _____ The merchant gives coupons to his customers.

H. **Irregular Verbs:**

Directions: Circle the correct verb.

1. He has (began, begun) a new job.

2. You should have (took, taken) a different route.

3. She has (swum, swam) on the team for three years.

4. The actress must have (flown, flew) on an earlier flight.

5. That fork has been (lying, laying) in the sink for two days.

265

6. The <u>patient had</u> (brung, **brought**) X-rays ~~with her~~.

7. <u>Have you</u> ever (went, **gone**) ~~to Canada~~?

8. The <u>curtain has been</u> (tore, **torn**) ~~from the rod~~.

9. <u>We could</u> not <u>have</u> (ran, **run**) further.

10. <u>They must have</u> (drank, **drunk**) our juice.

I. **Abstract and Concrete Nouns:**

   Directions: Write <u>A</u> if the noun is abstract; write <u>C</u> if the noun is concrete.

1. <u>C</u>   hammer   2. <u>A</u>   feelings   3. <u>C</u>   shampoo   4. <u>A</u>   love

J. **Common and Proper Nouns:**

   Directions: Write <u>CN</u> if the noun is common; write <u>PN</u> if the noun is proper.

1. <u>CN</u>   city   2. <u>CN</u>   wheel   3. <u>CN</u>   street   4. <u>PN</u>   Lund Avenue

K. **Noun Plurals:**

   Directions: Write the plural form.

1. delay - <u>delays</u>   6. zero - <u>zeros (zeroes-2nd choice)</u>

2. prize - <u>prizes</u>   7. catch - <u>catches</u>

3. deer - <u>deer</u>   8. dress - <u>dresses</u>

4. fireman - <u>firemen</u>   9. dairy - <u>dairies</u>

5. scarf - <u>scarves</u>   10. mother-in-law <u>mothers-in-law</u>

L. **Noun Possessives:**

   Directions: Write the possessive form.

1. a bottle belonging to a baby - <u>baby's bottle</u>

2. toys shared by several babies - <u>babies' toys</u>

3. a playground shared by more than one child - <u>children's playground</u>

6. The patient had (brung, brought) X-rays with her.

7. Have you ever (went, gone) to Canada?

8. The curtain has been (tore, torn) from the rod.

9. We could not have (ran, run) further.

10. They must have (drank, drunk) our juice.

I. **Abstract and Concrete Nouns:**

Directions: Write <u>A</u> if the noun is abstract; write <u>C</u> if the noun is concrete.

1. ____ hammer   2. ____ feelings   3. ____ shampoo   4. ____ love

J. **Common and Proper Nouns:**

Directions: Write <u>CN</u> if the noun is common; write <u>PN</u> if the noun is proper.

1. ____ city   2. ____ wheel   3. ____ street   4. ____ Lund Avenue

K. **Noun Plurals:**

Directions: Write the plural form.

1. delay - _____   6. zero - _____

2. prize - _____   7. catch - _____

3. deer - _____   8. dress - _____

4. fireman - _____   9. dairy - _____

5. scarf - _____   10. mother-in-law _____

L. **Noun Possessives:**

Directions: Write the possessive form.

1. a bottle belonging to a baby - _____

2. toys shared by several babies - _____

3. a playground shared by more than one child - _____

M. **Noun or Adjective?:**

   Directions: If the boldfaced word serves as a noun, write <u>N</u> in the space. If the boldfaced word serves as an adjective, write <u>A</u> in the space.

1. <u> N </u>   Please return this book to the **library**.

2. <u> A </u>   What did I do with my **library** card?

3. <u> A </u>   A **balloon** cluster was sent as a birthday gift.

4. <u> N </u>   A **balloon** was tied to their mailbox.

N. **Noun Identification:**

   Directions: Circle any nouns.
Nouns are in boldfaced print; determiners are underlined.
Suggestion: You may want to underline determiners to help you locate nouns.

1. <u>A</u> **pole** was decorated with <u>eight</u> red **hearts** and <u>several</u> **streamers** for <u>the</u> **party**.

2. <u>His</u> small **car** was parked next to <u>your</u> **uncle's** recreational **vehicle**.

3. For <u>that</u> **party**, **Mom** set <u>our</u> **table** with fine **china** and fancy **glasses**.

O. **Sentence Types:**

   Directions: Write the sentence type (declarative, interrogative, imperative, or exclamatory) in the space.

1. <u>   declarative   </u>   A baker from Vienna made the first bagel.

2. <u>   interrogative   </u>   Will they shop for new shoes?

3. <u>   imperative   </u>   Stack those boxes here, please.

4. <u>   exclamatory   </u>   Finally! We've received the bonus!

P. **Conjunctions and Interjections:**

   Directions: Write <u>Conj.</u> above any conjunction; write <u>Intj.</u> above any interjection.

    Intj.   **Conj.**
1. **Yeah!** Marcy **and** Tom are coming with us!!
    Conj.   **Conj.**
2. Alice **or** Yvonne may decide, **but** they must make their decision quickly.

268

M. **Noun or Adjective?:**
   Directions: If the boldfaced word serves as a noun, write <u>N</u> in the space. If the boldfaced word serves as an adjective, write <u>A</u> in the space.

1. _____   Please return this book to the **library**.

2. _____   What did I do with my **library** card?

3. _____   A **balloon** cluster was sent as a birthday gift.

4. _____   A **balloon** was tied to their mailbox.

N. **Noun Identification:**

   Directions: Circle any nouns

Suggestion: You may want to underline determiners to help you locate nouns.

1. A pole was decorated with eight red hearts and several streamers for the party.

2. His small car was parked next to your uncle's recreational vehicle.

3. For that party, Mom set our table with fine china and fancy glasses.

O. **Sentence Types:**
   Directions: Write the sentence type (declarative, interrogative, imperative, or exclamatory) in the space.

1. _____   A baker from Vienna made the first bagel.

2. _____   Will they shop for new shoes?

3. _____   Stack those boxes here, please.

4. _____   Finally! We've received the bonus!

P. **Conjunctions and Interjections:**
   Directions: Write Conj. above any conjunction; write Intj. above any interjection.

1. Yeah! Marcy and Tom are coming with us!!

2. Alice or Yvonne may decide, but they must make their decision quickly.

TO THE TEACHER:

The full definition of adverbs may confuse your students.

Definition: **Adverbs tell how, when, where, and to what extent and may modify verbs, adjectives, or other adverbs.**

I recommend that you simply teach each component and its definition.

Adverbs that tell HOW modify a verb.

Adverbs that tell WHEN modify a verb.

Adverbs that tell WHERE modify a verb.

Adverbs that tell TO WHAT EXTENT may modify an adjective, an adverb, or a verb.

GAMES:

The explanation of the games appears on the next two pages. Although the game that is used with adverbs that tell *where* is included in this explanation, you should wait until you introduce that concept to play it.

Suggestion: I recommend that you ocassionally dismiss students by asking the past participle form of irregular verbs. You simply say, " We will review past participles. Who knows the past participle of *to sing*?" As students answer, excuse them. (Hint: I usually call on those who need the extra practice near the end. I think that they benefit from hearing the entire review.)

ADVERBS

TO THE TEACHER:

A Game That Teaches *How*

<u>Game 1</u>: "Teacher, May I?"

This game, designed for active learning, is based on the primary game, "Mother, May I?" and includes giant steps, baby steps, hops, etc. Although the entire game requires approximately ten minutes, the students benefit from it.

Before the game: On index cards, write the following commands. (As you think of other commands, add them. Some of the commands listed here were actually students' ideas.)

Take two baby steps quietly.
Carefully, take one giant step backwards.
Turn sideways and take one step gingerly to the right.
Hop excitedly three steps forward.
Take four steps energetically to the left.
Take two giant steps quickly.
Take five baby steps briskly.
Take one giant step breathlessly.
Do eight hops forward excitedly.
Take seven steps fast.
Slowly, take four baby steps.
Take three baby steps laughingly to the left.
Smilingly, take five steps forward.

(You may have to explain the meaning of *gingerly*.)

I recommend going outside for this game. I have my students form two lines and spread apart like we would be doing jumping jack exercises.

The procedure of the game is simple:

You give the command.
In unison, the students must ask, "Teacher, May I?"
Your response is, "Yes, you may."
The students, then, must ask, "HOW shall we take four baby steps?"
Your response is the adverb on the card. "Slowly take four baby steps."

Students who move before asking for permission or asking *how* step out of the game. They help to watch for other offenders.

272

A Game That Teaches *Where*

Game 2:   **Match Your Leader**

This is a simplistic learning game, but most students enjoy it.   The purpose of the game is for students to learn that some adverbs tell *where* and to learn specific adverbs that do so.   **Please do not let two pages of directions frighten you; this game is easy to set up, play, and score!**

Materials needed:

1. For optimum fun, each student needs a dry erase board and marker. (You can use regular writing paper and crayons, markers, etc. However, dry erase boards have been recommended for class reviews as well. I highly recommend that a classroom set be purchased. You will use them in many subject areas.)

2. A chalkboard or overhead/transparency where you will write the adverbs that tell *where*.

Before the game:

1. Write the adverbs that tell *where* on the chalkboard/overhead. (Notice that I have included more adverbs listed here than on the introduction page.)

here	in	up	along	past
forward	uptown	inside	there	out
down	everywhere	over	nowhere	downtown
outside	backward	home	upstream	around
anywhere	downstream	somewhere	where	

    You may place these in any order; also, you may add adverbs or delete any of the ones listed here. Be sure that students understand that they can give only **one word** answers. *To the store* is a prepositional phrase, not a single-word adverb.

2. Divide the class into three groups.   Choose a leader. This leader will come to the front of the class.

3. Explain the rules.   You will write a sentence on the board. Each student will immediately write an adverb that tells *where* on the dry erase board. Each team receives a point for correct matches with the leader's response. Leaders, if placed near the chalkboard, can easily keep score.

4. You will need to have a sentence list ready. (See next page.)

Write the sentence on the chalkboard. (Unfortunately, if you say it, your inflection may solicit certain answers. It's more fair and fun just to write the sentence on the board. Again, feel free to delete or add your own sentences.)

Sentences:

Come _____.   Swim _____.

Stay _____.   Run _____.

Look _____.   Plunge _____.

Go _____.   Jump _____.

Walk _____.   Drive _____.

John and Kathy went _____.

Do you want to go _____?

Stand _____.

A SIMILAR GAME:

This game can be adapted to adverbs that tell *when*. List the adverbs that tell when:

tonight	soon	ever	tomorrow
today	sooner	never	daily
now	when	forever	yesterday
late	always	whenever	early
later	yet	then	afterwards

Again, you may wish to add to this list or even delete some words.

Compose sentences: Example: We shall go _____.
Let's go camping _____.
They always arrive _____.

ANOTHER GAME:

You may wish to adapt this game to adverbs that tell *how*: Proceed in the same fashion.
274

Adverbs tell *how*.

Most adverbs that tell *how* **go over to (modify) a verb.**

Most adverbs end in <u>ly</u>.

    Example: <u>Do</u> that quickly!

                Quickly tells *how* you should **do** that.

Crossing out prepositional phrases will help simplify the sentence. It will help you to find an adverb easily.

        He stood quietly for ten minutes.

        <u>He</u> <u>stood</u> quietly ~~for ten minutes~~.

        Quietly tells *how* he stood.

Some adverbs that tell *how* are listed here. There are many more!

quickly	carefully	quietly
slowly	happily	angrily
sadly	sincerely	helpfully
fast	hard	well

Answers are in boldfaced print.
Directions: Fill in the blanks.

Example: She rocked the baby gently.

Gently tells ____**how**____ she ___**rocked the baby**___.

1.   The cook stirred the soup vigorously.

Vigorously tells ____**how**____ the cook __**stirred the soup**__.

2.   A child squirmed restlessly in his seat.

Restlessly tells ____**how**____ the child __**squirmed in his seat**__.

3.   Thunder boomed loudly around us.

Loudly tells ____**how**____ the thunder __**boomed around us**__.

4.   A witness explained the robbery carefully.

Carefully tells ____**how**____ the witness __**explained the robbery**__.

5.   Several cloggers danced well.

Well tells ____**how**____ the cloggers __**danced**__.

6.   All of the travelers arrived safely.

Safely tells ____**how**____ the travelers __**arrived**__.

7.   A boat sailed smoothly out to sea.

Smoothly tells ____**how**____ a boat __**sailed out to sea**__.

276

Name_____   **ADVERBS**
                                                        How?
Date_____

Directions: Fill in the blanks.

Example: She rocked the baby gently.

Gently tells ___**how**___ she ___**rocked the baby**___.

1. The cook stirred the soup vigorously.

   Vigorously tells _____ the cook _____.

2. A child squirmed restlessly in his seat.

   Restlessly tells _____ the child _____.

3. Thunder boomed loudly around us.

   Loudly tells _____ the thunder _____.

4. A witness explained the robbery carefully.

   Carefully tells _____ the witness _____.

5. Several cloggers danced well.

   Well tells _____ the cloggers _____.

6. All of the travelers arrived safely.

   Safely tells _____ the travelers _____.

7. A boat sailed smoothly out to sea.

   Smoothly tells _____ a boat _____.

Adverbs are in boldfaced print; the verb is in italics.

Directions: Circle the adverb that tells *when* in the following sentences. Draw an
arrow to the verb it goes over to (modifies).

Note: Crossing out prepositional phrases helps to find adverbs.

🍓To the Teacher: Be sure to read each sentence aloud and discuss that the adverb
modifies the verb.

1.   He *spoke* **loudly**.

2.   Jennipher *smiled* **brightly**.

3.   The batter *hit* the ball **hard**.

4.   We *work* **together**.

5.   The frog *jumped* **high**.

6.   Aunt Joy **carefully** *planted* a tree.

7.   The ice cream man *did* his job **cheerfully**.

8.   A rabbit *hopped* **quickly** ~~down the dusty path~~.

9.   That tennis player *chuckles* **softly** ~~during each game~~.

10.   The skier *slid* **dangerously** ~~across the finish line~~.

278

Directions: Circle the adverb that tells *when* in the following sentences. Draw an arrow to the verb it goes over to (modifies).

Note: Crossing out prepositional phrases helps to find adverbs.

1. He spoke loudly.

2. Jennipher smiled brightly.

3. The batter hit the ball hard.

4. We work together.

5. The frog jumped high.

6. Aunt Joy carefully planted a tree.

7. The ice cream man did his job cheerfully.

8. A rabbit hopped quickly down the dusty path.

9. That tennis player chuckles softly during each game.

10. The skier slid dangerously across the finish line.

PAGE 281 = WORKBOOK PAGE 116

Adverbs

Often a word has a noun form, an adjective form, and an adverb form.

	noun	adjective	adverb
Examples:	happiness	happy	happily
	creativity	creative	creatively
	laughter	laughing	laughingly
	intelligence	intelligent	intelligently

An adjective, as you have learned, describes a noun.

Mandy is a **soft** speaker.

Soft is an adjective that describes speaker.

The adverb form of *soft* is **softly**.

Incorrect: Mandy speaks soft.

Correct: Mandy speaks **softly**.

Softly is an adverb that tells HOW Mandy speaks.

There are two exceptions to this that you will frequently encounter: *fast* and *hard*.

Fast is the same in both the adjective form and adverb form:

Patty and Austin are *fast* runners.   (adjective describing runners)
Patty and Austin run *fast*.   (adverb telling how)

Hard is the same in both the adjective form and adverb form:

My mother is a *hard* hitter.   (adjective describing hitter)
My mother hits a baseball *hard*.   (adverb telling how)

Many adverb tell *how*.   Adverbs that tell *how* usually modify (go over to) a verb.

Most adverbs that tell *how* end in <u>ly</u>.

Frequently, the adverb form is similar to the adjective form.

Remember, adjectives modify nouns (or pronouns).

Example: That is a dangerous road.   *Dangerous* is an adjective describing road.

adjective - dangerous   adverb - dangerously

Example: Some people drive dangerously on that road.

Dangerously tells **how** some people drive.

🍓🍓🍓🍓🍓🍓🍓🍓🍓🍓🍓🍓🍓🍓🍓🍓🍓🍓🍓🍓🍓🍓🍓🍓🍓🍓🍓🍓🍓🍓🍓🍓🍓🍓🍓🍓

Directions: Write the adverb form of each adjective.

	ADJECTIVE	ADVERB
1.	sad	**sadly**
2.	loving	**lovingly**
3.	patient	**patiently**
4.	slow	**slowly**
5.	sincere	**sincerely**
6.	quick	**quickly**
7.	grump	**grumpily**
8.	cheerful	**cheerfully**
9.	fast	**fast**

282

Name_____   **ADVERBS**
                                          How?

Date_____

Many adverb tell *how*. Adverbs that tell *how* usually modify (go over to) a verb.

Most adverbs that tell *how* end in **ly**.

Frequently, the adverb form is similar to the adjective form.

    Remember, adjectives modify nouns (or pronouns).

  Example: That is a dangerous road. *Dangerous* is an adjective describing road.

      adjective - dangerous   adverb - dangerously

  Example: Some people drive dangerously on that road.

    Dangerously tells **how** some people drive.

Directions: Write the adverb form of each adjective.

ADJECTIVE	ADVERB
1. sad	_____
2. loving	_____
3. patient	_____
4. slow	_____
5. sincere	_____
6. quick	_____
7. grump	_____
8. cheerful	_____
9. fast	_____

Many adverb tell *how*.   Adverbs that tell *how* usually modify (go over to) a verb.

> Examples: Marilyn draws *carefully*.
>
> > *Carefully* tells how she <u>draws</u>.
>
> > A police officer motioned *vigorously* to the motorists.
>
> > *Vigorously* tells how the officer <u>motioned</u>.
>
> > They run *fast*.
>
> > *Fast* tells how they <u>run</u>.

Most adverbs that tell *how* end in <u>ly</u>.

🍓🍓🍓🍓🍓🍓🍓🍓🍓🍓🍓🍓🍓🍓🍓🍓🍓🍓🍓🍓🍓🍓🍓🍓🍓🍓🍓🍓🍓🍓🍓🍓🍓

Directions: Fill in the blanks.

> Example: They talked quietly.   *Quietly* tells ___**how**___ they ___**talked**___.

1. The cat purred softly. *Softly* tells ___**how**___ the cat ___**purred**___.

2. The soldiers ate hungrily. *Hungrily* tells ___**how**___ the soldiers ___**ate**___.

3. Grandma laughed happily as she opened her present. *Happily* tells ___**how**___

   Grandma ___**laughed**___.

4. The small boy looked tearfully at his father. *Tearfully* tells ___**how**___ the boy

   ___**looked at his father**___.

5. The man answered sternly. *Sternly* tells ___**how**___ the man ___**answered**___.

6. An electrician worked hard all afternoon. *Hard* tells ___**how**___ the electrician

   ___**worked**___.

Many adverb tell **how**.   Adverbs that tell **how** usually modify (go over to) a verb.

    Examples: Marilyn draws *carefully*.

                        Carefully tells how she <u>draws</u>.

                        A police officer motioned *vigorously* to the motorists.

                        Vigorously tells how the officer <u>motioned</u>.

                    They run *fast*.

                        Fast tells how they <u>run</u>.

Most adverbs that tell **how** end in <u>ly</u>.

🍓🍓🍓🍓🍓🍓🍓🍓🍓🍓🍓🍓🍓🍓🍓🍓🍓🍓🍓🍓🍓🍓🍓🍓🍓🍓🍓🍓🍓🍓🍓🍓🍓🍓🍓🍓

Directions: Fill in the blanks.

     Example: They talked quietly. *Quietly* tells ____**how**____ they ___**talked**___.

1. The cat purred softly. *Softly* tells _____ the cat _____.

2. The soldiers ate hungrily. *Hungrily* tells _____ the soldiers _____.

3. Grandma laughed happily as she opened her present. *Happily* tells _____

    Grandma _____.

4. The small boy looked tearfully at his father. *Tearfully* tells _____ the boy

    _____.

5. The man answered sternly. *Sternly* tells _____ the man _____.

6. An electrician worked hard all afternoon. *Hard* tells _____ the electrician

    _____.

It is important to use the correct form in our speaking and writing.

The following sentence is incorrect.   **Joel skates slow.**

Joel is a slow skater.   *Slow* is an adjective that modifies the noun, <u>skater</u>.

Since *slow* is an adjective, it cannot tell *how* Joel skates.

Correct: Joel skates slowly.

There are several words that are the same in both adjective and adverb forms.

Examples: hard   He is a hard hitter.   He hits the ball hard.

fast   I am a fast walker.   I walk fast.

However, **most words do change**. Use a **dictionary** to determine the adverb form. For <u>slow</u>, it will say *adv.* <u>slowly</u>. Often the adverb listing is in boldfaced print.

🍓🍓🍓🍓🍓🍓🍓🍓🍓🍓🍓🍓🍓🍓🍓🍓🍓🍓🍓🍓🍓🍓🍓🍓🍓🍓🍓🍓🍓🍓🍓🍓🍓🍓🍓🍓🍓

Directions: Fill in the blank with the adverb form of the word in parenthesis.

Example: (cheerful)   He always speaks __<u>cheerfully</u>__ to us.

1.   (proper)   Sit _____**properly**_____, please.

2.   (frequent)   That lady flies _____**frequently**_____.

3.   (rude)   Please don't speak _____**rudely**_____to me.

4.   (timid)   The speaker replied _____**timidly**_____.

5.   (forceful)   A falling skater hit the pavement _____**forcefully**_____.

6.   (tight)   The child hugged his teddy bear _____**tightly**_____.

7.   (firm)   The senator responded _____**firmly**_____.

8.   (skillful)   A craftsman _____**skillfully**_____ carved a statue.

286

It is important to use the correct form in our speaking and writing.

The following sentence is incorrect.   **Joel skates slow.**

    Joel is a slow skater.   *Slow* is an adjective that modifies the noun, <u>skater</u>.

    Since *slow* is an adjective, it cannot tell *how* Joel skates.

    Correct: Joel skates slowly.

There are several words that are the same in both adjective and adverb forms.

    Examples: hard   He is a hard hitter.   He hits the ball hard.

                  fast   I am a fast walker.   I walk fast.

However, **most words do change**. Use a **dictionary** to determine the adverb form.
For <u>slow</u>, it will say *adv.* <u>slowly</u>. Often the adverb listing is in boldfaced print.
🍓🍓🍓🍓🍓🍓🍓🍓🍓🍓🍓🍓🍓🍓🍓🍓🍓🍓🍓🍓🍓🍓🍓🍓🍓🍓🍓🍓🍓🍓🍓🍓🍓🍓🍓🍓🍓

Directions: Fill in the blank with the adverb form of the word in parenthesis.

    Example: (cheerful) He always speaks __cheerfully__ to us.

1.   (proper)   Sit _____, please.

2.   (frequent)   That lady flies _____.

3.   (rude)   Please don't speak _____ to me.

4.   (timid)   The speaker replied _____.

5.   (forceful)   A falling skater hit the pavement _____.

6.   (tight)   The child hugged his teddy bear _____.

7.   (firm)   The senator responded _____.

8.   (skillful)   A craftsman _____ carved a statue.

Adverbs tell *when*.

Most adverbs that tell *when* **usually go over to (modify) a verb.**

Example: They <u>left</u> **yesterday.**

Yesterday tells when they **left.**

Some adverbs that tell *when* are listed here:

now	**when**	**always**
then	**whenever**	**daily**
soon	**first**	**sometimes**
sooner	**afterwards**	**yesterday**
late	**never**	**today**
later	**forever**	**tomorrow**

Examples:

First, the telephone rang.	When? first
Then, the lady answered it.	When? then
She **never** turns on the answering machine.	When? never

Answers are in boldfaced print.

A. Directions: Unscramble these adverbs that tell *when*.

1. tela - __**late**_____   10. own - ___**now**_____

2. hewn - __**when**_____   11. roromotw - ___**tommorow**_____

3. noso - __**soon**_____   12. tirsf - __**first**_____

4. neth - __**then**_____   13. retal - __**later**_____

5. doyta - __**today**_____   14. vehnewre - __**whenever**_____

6. ernoos - __**sooner**_____   15. adyil - __**daily**_____

7. renev - __**never**_____   16. yawals - __**always**_____

8. stayderye - __**yesterday**____   17. netof - __**often**_____

9. mimessote - __**sometimes**____   18. drawsteafr - __**afterwards**____

B. Directions: Write the adverb that tells *when* in the space provided.

1. Antonym (opposite) for *late* - __**early**_____

2. by the hour - __**hourly**_____

3. synonym (same) for *tardy* -__**late**_____

4. every day - __**daily**_____

5. at all times - __**always**_____

Name_____   **ADVERBS**
                                            When?

Date_____

A.   Directions: Unscramble these adverbs that tell **when**.

1. tela - _____   10. own - _____

2. hewn - _____   11. roromotw - _____

3. noso - _____   12. tirsf - _____

4. neth - _____   13. retal - _____

5. doyta - _____   14. vehnewre - _____

6. ernoos - _____   15. adyil - _____

7. renev - _____   16. yawals - _____

8. stayderye - _____   17. netof - _____

9. mimessote - _____   18. drawsteafr - _____

B.   Directions: Write the adverb that tells *when* in the space provided.

1. antonym (opposite) for *late* - _____

2. by the hour - _____

3. synonym (same) for *tardy* -_____

4. every day - _____

5. at all times - _____

Directions: Circle the adverb that tells *when* in the following sentences. Draw an arrow to the verb it goes over to (modifies).

Note: Crossing out prepositional phrases helps to find adverbs.

<u>The adverb is in boldfaced print; the verb to which an arrow should be drawn is in italics.</u>

1. He *wants* an answer **now**.

2. That clerk **never** *leaves* ~~before dinner~~.

3. A barbecue *will be held* **tonight**.

4. The guide *arrived* **early** ~~in the morning~~.

5. His leader **seldom** *arrives* ~~on time~~.

6.   She **immediately** *looked* ~~around the room~~.

7. The student **sometimes** *walks* ~~to school~~.

8.   Some fishermen **always** *take* a net.

9. That golfer **frequently** *uses* pink golf balls.

10. Her grandfather *will visit* **today**.

Directions: Circle the adverb that tells *when* in the following sentences. Draw an
              arrow to the verb it goes over to (modifies).

Note: Crossing out prepositional phrases helps to find adverbs.

1.   He wants an answer now.

2.   That clerk never leaves before dinner.

3.   A barbecue will be held tonight.

4.   The guide arrived early in the morning.

5.   His leader seldom arrives on time.

6.   She immediately looked around the room.

7.   The student sometimes walks to school.

8.   Some fishermen always take a net.

9.   That golfer frequently uses pink golf balls.

10.   Her grandfather will visit today.

Adverbs tell *where*.

Adverbs that tell *where* **usually go over to (modify) a verb.**

      Example: I looked everywhere for our dog.

                Everywhere tells *where* I looked.

Some adverbs that tell *where* are listed here:

here	**anywhere**	**in**	**up**
there	**somewhere**	**out**	**down**
where	**everywhere**	**inside**	**near**
nowhere	**home**	**outside**	**far**

    Examples:

      Let's go **inside**.   Where? inside

      Sam went **home** ~~for lunch~~.   Where? home

🍓 Did you notice that some words that you learned as prepositions are on the list? They serve as adverbs only when they aren't in a prepositional phrase.

    Examples: Kelly went **inside**.   (adverb)

               Gregg hid **~~inside the front door~~**.   (preposition)

               She ran **~~up the hill~~**.   (preposition)

               She looked **up**.   (adverb)

A. Directions: Unscramble these adverbs that tell *where*.

1. pu - _____**up**_____   6. ownd - _____**down**_____

2. eerh - _____**here**_____   7. veywehreer - _____**everywhere**

3. emoh - _____**home**_____   8. raf - _____**far**_____

4. hrtee - _____**there**_____   9. setudoi - _____**outside**_____

5. tou- _____**out**_____   10. hewre - _____**where**_____

B. Directions: Write the adverb that tells *where* in the space provided.

1. antonym (opposite) for *far* - _____**near**_____

2. antonym (opposite) for *outside* - _____**inside**_____

3. where you live -_____**home**_____

C. Directions: Write any adverb that ends with *ere.*

1. _____**here**_____   5. _____**everywhere**_____

2. _____**there**_____   6. _____**somewhere**_____

3. _____**where**_____   7. _____**nowhere**_____

4. _____**anywhere**_____

A. Directions: Unscramble these adverbs that tell **where**.

1. pu - _____   6. ownd - _____

2. eerh - _____   7. veywehreer - _____

3. emoh - _____   8. raf - _____

4. hrtee - _____   9. setudoi - _____

5. tou- _____   10. hewre - _____

B. Directions: Write the adverb that tells *where* in the space provided.

1. antonym (opposite) for *far* - _____

2. antonym (opposite) for *outside* - _____

3. where you live -_____

C. Directions: Write any adverb that ends with *ere.*

1. _____   5. _____

2. _____   6. _____

3. _____   7. _____

4. _____

WORKBOOK PAGE 125   **Where?**

Date_____

Teacher: *Stress that the adverb tells where the child fell(#1),* *where Mark visited(#2), etc.*

Adverbs are in boldfaced print. The verb to which the arrow should be drawn is in italics.

Directions: Circle the adverb that tells *where* in the following sentences. Draw an arrow to the verb it goes over to (modifies).

Note: **Crossing out prepositional phrases helps to find adverbs.**

1. The child *fell* **down**.

2. Mark *visited* **there** last winter.

3. **Where** *may* I *sit*?

4. He *walked* **far**.

5. I *searched* **everywhere** ~~for my wallet.~~

6. They *played* **outside**.

7. Their sister *lives* **nearby**.

8. You *may come* **in**.

9. Chad *went* **somewhere** ~~with his mother.~~

10. Mary *stays* **here** ~~during the summer.~~

298

Directions: Circle the adverb that tells *where* in the following sentences. Draw an arrow to the verb it goes over to (modifies).

Note: Crossing out prepositional phrases helps to find adverbs.

1.   The child fell down.

2.   Mark visited there last winter.

3.   Where may I sit?

4.   He walked far.

5.   I searched everywhere for my wallet.

6.   They played outside.

7.   Their sister lives nearby.

8.   You may come in.

9.   Chad went somewhere with his mother.

10.   Mary stays here during the summer.

The ensuing page discusses a word functioning as a preposition or as an adverb. This is introduced quite simplistically. The worksheet for this concept, however, could present a challenge.

The following information is more difficult. It is for your knowledge and, if you choose, your teaching. I have not included any practice worksheets. Students will be introduced to this concept at a higher level.

Preposition or Adverb?

Sometimes a preposition and an adverb will stand side by side.

> He came **over**?   *Over* is an adverb telling *where*.

> He came **over** in the morning.

Continue to delete prepositional phrases.

> He came **over** ~~in the morning~~.

> *Over* is an adverb because it has no object.

To serve as a preposition, the word must have an object.

300

Adverbs

Adverbs are one-word modifiers. In other words, *down the road* tells **where**, but it is not an adverb.

> Examples: Stay **here**, please.
>
> Do you live **nearby**?

🍓🍓🍓🍓🍓🍓🍓🍓🍓🍓🍓🍓🍓🍓🍓🍓🍓🍓🍓🍓🍓🍓🍓🍓🍓🍓🍓🍓🍓🍓🍓🍓🍓🍓🍓🍓🍓

You have learned the following words as prepositions:

across	inside	over
along	near	past
around	on	through
down	out	under
in	outside	up

These words are prepositions when they are followed by a noun (or pronoun).

> The team went ~~inside the dugout~~.   (inside = preposition)
>
> *Inside the dugout* is a prepositional phrase.

These same words serve as adverbs when they are not followed by a noun (or pronoun).

> After lunch, the class went **inside**.   (inside = adverb)
>
> ***Inside*** tells *where* the class went.

Name_____   **ADVERBS**

Where?

Date_____

Note: This is a difficult page. You may want to do it orally. Mastery is not required.

A. Directions: Write <u>Prep</u>. if the boldfaced word serves as a preposition.
      Write <u>Adv</u>. if the boldfaced word serves as an adverb that tells *where*.

       Examples: <u> Adv. </u>   Come **along**.

                         <u> Prep. </u>   A horse trotted **along** a wooded trail.

1. <u> Prep. </u>   Chet fell **over** a chair.

2. <u> Adv. </u>   A broom fell **over**.

3. <u> Adv. </u>   The skater looked **down**.

4. <u> Prep. </u>   Mr. Ripple walks **down** the lane daily.

5. <u> Prep. </u>   She searched **through** the drawer for a sock.

6. <u> Adv. </u>   Do you need to come **through** here?

7. <u> Adv. </u>   The dog looked **around** and trotted off.

8. <u> Prep. </u>   That lady and her daughter walk **around** the block each evening.

B. Directions: Write a sentence, using the boldfaced word as an adverb.
      Then, write a sentence, using the boldfaced word as a preposition.

ANSWERS WILL VARY/REPRESENTATIVE ANSWERS:

1. **up**

       (adverb) <u> Come up. </u>

       (preposition) <u> I fell up the stairs yesterday. </u>

2. **outside**

       (adverb) <u> They went outside. </u>

       (preposition) <u> Do not step outside this line. </u>

302

Name_____   **ADVERBS**
                                              Where?
Date_____

A. Directions: Write <u>Prep.</u> if the boldfaced word serves as a preposition.
                 Write <u>Adv.</u> if the boldfaced word serves as an adverb that tells *where*.

               Examples: <u> Adv. </u>   Come **along**.

                             <u> Prep. </u>   A horse trotted **along** a wooded trail.

1. _____   Chet fell **over** a chair.

2. _____   A broom fell **over**.

3. _____   The skater looked **down**.

4. _____   Mr. Ripple walks **down** the lane daily.

5. _____   She searched **through** the drawer for a sock.

6. _____   Do you need to come **through** here?

7. _____   The dog looked **around** and trotted off.

8. _____   That lady and her daughter walk **around** the block each evening.

B. Directions: Write a sentence, using the boldfaced word as an adverb.
                 Then, write a sentence, using the boldfaced word as a preposition.

1. **up**

      (adverb) _____

      (preposition) _____

2. **outside**

      (adverb) _____

      (preposition) _____

303

PAGE 307 = WORKBOOK PAGE 128
PAGE 310 = WORKBOOK PAGE 130
PAGE 311 = WORKBOOK PAGE 131

TO THE TEACHER:

I am including additional information on this page. This is for your own knowledge and teaching. You may decide that this explanation is too difficult and that students aren't ready to determine if an adverb telling *to what extent* modifies an adjective, another adverb, or a verb. Hence, I have included the information only on this page. Worksheets included in this text do not ask students to determine what part of speech the modified word is.

Adverbs tell how, when, where, and to what extent.

> Adverbs that tell **how** usually modify (go over to) a verb.

> Adverbs that tell **when** usually modify a verb.

> Adverbs that tell **where** usually modify a verb.

However: Adverbs that tell *to what extent* may modify an adjective, an adverb, or a verb.

> Examples: His piano teacher is **very** talented.

> *Very* modifies the adjective, talented.

> I skip rather slowly.

> *Rather* modifies another adverb, slowly.

> We are **not** going.

> *Not* modifies the verb phrase, are going.

I have listed the seven adverbs that are commonly used to express *to what extent*. **I recommend that you require students to memorize those seven adverbs.**
Be sure that students comprehend that there are other adverbs that tell *to what extent*.

TO THE TEACHER:

When teaching the concept of *to what extent*, I use the seven examples given on the next page. I ask one of my "dramatic" students to act out each sentence:

I am not sick.   (The person just stands there and smiles.)

He is so sick.   (The person acts so-o-o-o-o ill!)

The student does this for each of the seven sentences. If the student truly does a great job, the others will promptly understand that these seven adverbs relate varying degrees of something (in this case, illness).

After I have one person act out all seven "sicks," I ask for volunteers. This time I hand each volunteer a large card with one of the seven adverbs that tells *to what extent* printed on it. Each volunteer shows the card, uses it in a sentence (such as, "I am very sick."), and then becomes an actor or actress.

You may choose to pass out the imprinted cards to other students. Students then volunteer to act out emotions such as sad, happy, etc. It's interesting how students choose to depict "not sad, so sad, somewhat sad, etc." I have found that students actively engaged in this manner often master concepts more readily!

Adverbs

To What Extent?

Seven adverbs are used frequently in our language to tell *to what extent*. They are **not**, **so**, **very**, **too**, **quite**, **rather**, and **somewhat**. When you see these in a sentence, they will be adverbs.

Examples: He is *not* sick.

He is *so* sick.

He is *very* sick.

He is *too* sick to go anywhere.

He is *quite* sick.

He is *rather* sick.

He is *somewhat* sick.

These adverbs tell to what extent the person is sick. As you know, there is a great difference between being somewhat sick and so sick. Adverbs such as *somewhat* and *so* tell *to what extent*.

🍓🍓🍓🍓🍓🍓🍓🍓🍓🍓🍓🍓🍓🍓🍓🍓🍓🍓🍓🍓🍓🍓🍓🍓🍓🍓🍓🍓🍓🍓🍓

There are other adverbs that tell *to what extent*.

Examples: That weight lifter has an **unusually** large appetite.

(To what extent large?   unusually large)

Her sister is **extremely** funny.

(To what extent funny?   extremely funny)

307

Answers are in boldfaced print.

Directions: Circle any adverb that tells *to what extent* in the following sentences.

1.   Beef was **not** served for lunch.

2.   The dog groomer is **so** busy today.

3.   An elephant is a **very** heavy animal.

4.   This chocolate pudding is **too** watery.

5.   That child was **quite** sick last week.

6.   An oarfish has a **rather** long body.

7.   His **somewhat** silly answer made us laugh.

8.   Their minister is **extremely** kind.

9.   Toby's finger swelled to an **unusually** large size.

10.   My best friend is **too** stubborn.

11.   I would **rather not** disturb my sleeping cat.

12.   Bruce is **somewhat** shy, but his brother is **so** talkative.

13.   The dentist examined her teeth **extremely** well.

14.   He's **quite** tall and **very** strong.

15.   Isn**'t** a paca a tropical rodent?

308

Directions: Circle any adverb that tells *to what extent* in the following sentences.

1.   Beef was not served for lunch.

2.   The dog groomer is so busy today.

3.   An elephant is a very heavy animal.

4.   This chocolate pudding is too watery.

5.   That child was quite sick last week.

6.   An oarfish has a rather long body.

7.   His somewhat silly answer made us laugh.

8.   Their minister is extremely kind.

9.   Toby's finger swelled to an unusually large size.

10.   My best friend is too stubborn.

11.   I would rather not disturb my sleeping cat.

12.   Bruce is somewhat shy, but his brother is so talkative.

13.   The dentist examined her teeth extremely well.

14.   He's quite tall and very strong.

15.   Isn't a paca a tropical rodent?

Degrees of Adverbs

Adverbs can be used to compare:

A.   Sometimes, two *things* are compared.

   Example: This car goes faster than that truck.

   Here we are comparing two items, a car and a truck. *Faster* is a form of *fast* which tells <u>HOW</u> they run.

When two items are compared, the **comparative** form is used. **There are three ways to form the comparative:**

1.   Add **<u>er</u>** to most one-syllable adverbs.

   soon - sooner

2.   Place **<u>more</u>** before most two or more syllable adverbs.

   recently - more recently

Some two syllable adverbs add **<u>er</u>**.

   early - earlier

Use a dictionary to help you decide the adverb form.

Here is the entry for the adverb, <u>early</u>:

   early, *adv.* **-lier**, liest

If <u>more</u> should be used, no <u>er</u> form will be given in the dictionary.

3.   Some adverbs totally change form.

well - better

B.   Sometimes, three or more *things* are compared.

Example: She runs fastest of the entire team.

There are three ways to form the superlative:

1.   Add **est** to most one-syllable adverbs.

hard/hardest

2.   Place **most** before many two or more syllable adverbs.

slowly/most slowly

Use a dictionary to help you decide the adverb form.

Here is the entry for the adverb, <u>early</u>:

early, *adv.* -lier, **liest**

If <u>most</u> should be used, no <u>est</u> form will be given in the dictionary.

3.   Some adverbs totally change form.

well/best

🍓🍓🍓🍓🍓🍓🍓🍓🍓🍓🍓🍓🍓🍓🍓🍓🍓🍓🍓🍓🍓🍓🍓🍓🍓🍓🍓🍓🍓🍓🍓

<u>Adverb</u>	<u>Comparative</u>	<u>Superlative</u>
happily	more happily	most happily
late	later	latest
well	better	best

Name_____

Date_____

ADVERBS
Degrees of Adverbs

A. Directions: Finish the sentence with the correct word.

1. a. Jeremy hits the ball far.

   b. However, his sister hits the ball _____farther_____.

2. a. Mrs. Bream talks softly.

   b. However, her friend talks ___more softly_____.

3. a. Our neighbor cuts her lawn early in the morning.

   b. Her husband cuts it _____earlier_____than she does.

4. a. Ginger drives very carefully.

   b. Her grandmother, however, drives even _____more carefully_____
      than Ginger.

B. Directions: Circle the correct answer.

1. The white top spins (**faster**, fastest) than the yellow one.

2. Mrs. King spoke (**more pleasantly**, most pleasantly) to the teacher than to her
   misbehaving son.

3. The wind blew (more violently, **most violently**) the third day of the hurricane.

4. Justin sanded the wooden toy (more rapidly, **most rapidly**) during the fourth
   sanding.

5. She fell (**harder,** hardest) the second time she tried to mount the horse.

6. He hit the golf ball (more powerfully, **most powerfully**) on his fifth try.

312

A. Directions: Finish the sentence with the correct word.

1. a: Jeremy hits the ball far.

    b.   However, his sister hits the ball _____.

2. a.   Mrs. Bream talks softly.

    b.   However, her friend talks _____.

3. a.   Our neighbor cuts her lawn early in the morning.

    b.   Her husband cuts it _____than she does.

4. a. Ginger drives very carefully.

    b.   Her grandmother, however, drives even _____
         than Ginger.

B. Directions: Circle the correct answer.

1. The white top spins (faster, fastest) than the yellow one.

2. Mrs. King spoke (more pleasantly, most pleasantly) to the teacher than to her
    misbehaving son.

3. The wind blew (more violently, most violently) the third day of the hurricane.

4. Justin sanded the wooden toy (more rapidly, most rapidly) during the fourth
    sanding.

5. She fell (harder, hardest) the second time she tried to mount the horse.

6. He hit the golf ball (more powerfully, most powerfully) on his fifth try.

A. Directions: Finish the sentence with the correct word.

1. a. Mika climbed high into the tree.

   b. However, her sister climbed _____higher_____.

2. a. Alvah arrived late.

   b. However, Marcos arrived _____later_____.

3. a. Amber skates smoothly.

   b. Her best friend skates _____more smoothly_____ than Amber.

B. Directions: Circle the correct answer.
Answers are in boldfaced print.

1. The red ball was hit (**harder**, hardest) than the blue one.

2. Of the two, Carlo whistles (**more softly**, most softly).

3. William asks (more politely, **most politely**) of all the boys.

4. My brother runs (faster, **fastest**) of his entire soccer team.

5. She signed her name (**more carefully**, most carefully) on the second paper.

6. Lulu's dad swims (more slowly, **most slowly**) on his tenth lap.

7. The fourth batch of cookies turned out (better, **best**).

8. Ken holds a bat (**more tightly**, most tightly) than his friend.

Name_____

Date_____

A. Directions: Finish the sentence with the correct word.

1. a. Mika climbed high into the tree.

    b. However, her sister climbed _____.

2. a. Alvah arrived late.

    b. However, Marcos arrived _____.

3. a. Amber skates smoothly.

    b. Her best friend skates _____than Amber.

B. Directions: Circle the correct answer.

1. The red ball was hit (harder, hardest) than the blue one.

2. Of the two, Carlo whistles (more softly, most softly).

3. William asks (more politely, most politely) of all the boys.

4. My brother runs (faster, fastest) of his entire soccer team.

5. She signed her name (more carefully, most carefully) on the second paper.

6. Lulu's dad swims (more slowly, most slowly) on his tenth lap.

7. The fourth batch of cookies turned out (better, best).

8. Ken holds a bat (more tightly, most tightly) than his friend.

PAGE 317 = WORKBOOK PAGE 134

Double Negatives

No, **not**, **never**, **none**, **no one**, **nobody**, **nothing**, **scarcely**, and **hardly**

are called *negative words*. Do not use more than one negative word in the same

sentence.

Example: Wrong: I am **not** doing **nothing**.

Right: I am **not** doing anything.

OR

I am doing **nothing**.

Wrong: Erma **never** goes **nowhere**.

Right: Erma **never** goes anywhere.

OR

Erma goes **nowhere**.

However, if *no* is used to answer a question, another negative word may be used in the sentence.

Are you allowed to go?

No, I am **not** allowed to go.

If you have been around anyone who uses double negatives, the incorrect usage may "sound" right. Always check to see if two of the words on your double negative list are in the same sentence.

Answers are in boldfaced print.

No, *not*, *never*, *none*, *no one*, *nobody*, *nothing*, *scarcely*, and *hardly* are negative words.

A. Directions: Circle the negative word in each sentence.

1. She **never** bites her nails.

2. The tile has **no** wax on it.

3. **Nothing** happened.

4. He could **scarcely** talk.

5. I want **none**, thanks.

6. They **hardly** had time to finish.

7. We saw **nobody** that we knew.

B. Directions: Write the sentence correctly.

1. This bottle doesn't have no lid.

     This bottle doesn't have any lid.   **or**   This bottle has no lid.

2. They would not carry nothing to the car.

     They wouldn't carry anything to the car.   **or**   They would carry nothing to the car.

3. He hardly has no clean socks.

     He hardly has any clean socks.

4. You never talk to nobody.

     You never talk to anybody.

318

Name_____

Date_____

No, *not*, *never*, *none*, *no one*, *nobody*, *nothing*, *scarcely*, and *hardly* are negative words.

A. Directions: Circle the negative word in each sentence.

1. She never bites her nails.

2. The tile has no wax on it.

3. Nothing happened.

4. He could scarcely talk.

5. I want none, thanks.

6. They hardly had time to finish.

7. We saw nobody that we knew.

B. Directions: Write the sentence correctly.

1. This bottle doesn't have no lid.

_____

2. They would not carry nothing to the car.

_____

3. He hardly has no clean socks.

_____

4. You never talk to nobody.

_____

ADVERBS
Double Negatives

No, *not*, *never*, *none*, *no one*, *nobody*, *nothing*, *scarcely*, and *hardly*
are negative words.

A.   Directions: Write each sentence correctly.

1.   The fisherman hadn't caught nothing.

   <u>The fisherman hadn't caught anything. or The fisherman had caught nothing.</u>

2.   I don't have none.

   <u>I have none.   or   I don't have any.</u>

3.   We never get no popsicles for lunch.

   <u>We never get any popsicles.   or   We get no popsicles.</u>

B.   Directions: Circle the correct word.
Answers are in boldfaced print.

1.   He won't take (nobody, **anybody**) with him.

2.   Our dog never has (**any**, no) bones.

3.   No one wants (**anything**, nothing) to eat yet.

4.   She hardly (never, **ever**) sits by the fire.

5.   Mom doesn't have (no, **any**) dimes or quarters.

6.   Harvey scarcely has (**anything**, nothing) to do.

7.   Lois has not written to (**any**, none) of her relatives.

8.   Joe doesn't want (nobody, **anybody**) to help him.

320

Name_____   **ADVERBS**
Double Negatives

Date_____

No, *not*, *never*, *none*, *no one*, *nobody*, *nothing*, *scarcely*, and *hardly*
are negative words.

A. Directions: Write the sentence correctly.

1. The fisherman hadn't caught nothing.

   _____

2. I don't have none.

   _____

3. We never get no popsicles for lunch.

   _____

B. Directions: Circle the correct word.

1. He won't take (nobody, anybody) with him.

2. Our dog never has (any, no) bones.

3. No one wants (anything, nothing) to eat yet.

4. She hardly (never, ever) sits by the fire.

5. Mom doesn't have (no, any) dimes or quarters.

6. Harvey scarcely has (anything, nothing) to do.

7. Lois has not written to (any, none) of her relatives.

8. Joe doesn't want (nobody, anybody) to help him.

A. **Adverbs:**

   Directions: Write the adverb form of the word.

1. brave - _____**bravely**_____   4. exact - _____**exactly**_____

2. excited - _____**excitedly**_____   5. stupid - _____**stupidly**_____

3. happy - _____**happily**_____   6. furious - _____**furiously**_____

B. **How?:**

   Directions: Circle any adverbs that tell *how*.

1. Please look **carefully** before crossing the street.

2. Sue talks **constantly** about her new cat.

3.   A six-year-old hit the ball and ran **fast** to first base.

4. The teenager listened **silently** as his father spoke.

C. **How?:**

   Directions: Write the adverb form for the boldfaced word.

1. Brandy has a **loud** voice.   Brandy speaks _____**loudly**_____.

2. That stewardess is a **polite** woman.   She treats all of the passengers

   _____**politely**_____.

3. Their friend has a **strange** laugh.   She laughs _____**strangely**_____.

4. Ned is a **fast** typist.   He types _____**fast**_____.

322

Name_____   **Adverb Review**

Date_____

A. **Adverbs:**

Directions: Write the adverb form of the word.

1. brave - _____   4. exact - _____

2. excited - _____   5. stupid - _____

3. happy - _____   6. furious - _____

B. **How?:**

Directions: Circle any adverbs that tell *how*.

1. Please look carefully before crossing the street.

2. Sue talks constantly about her new cat.

3.   A six-year-old hit the ball and ran fast to first base.

4. The teenager listened silently as his father spoke.

C. **How?:**

Directions: Write the adverb form for the boldfaced word.

1. Brandy has a **loud** voice.   Brandy speaks _____.

2. That stewardess is a **polite** woman.   She treats all of the passengers

_____.

3. Their friend has a **strange** laugh.   She laughs _____.

4. Ned is a **fast** typist.   He types _____.

WORKBOOK PAGE 138
Date_____

D. **Where?:**

> Directions: Circle any adverbs that tell *where*.

1. **Where** are you going?

2. Let's go **somewhere** to talk.

3. He stooped **down** and looked **up**.

4. The salesmen went **downtown** for a meeting.

E. **Adverb or Preposition?:**

> Directions: Write <u>Prep</u>. if the boldfaced word serves as a preposition.
> Write <u>Adv</u>. if the boldfaced word serves as an adverb.

> Examples: ____<u>Adv.</u>____   Marco came **over** ~~to my house~~.

1. ____<u>Adv.</u>____   Do you live **near**?

2. ____<u>Prep.</u>____   Do you live **near** a store?

3. ____<u>Adv.</u>____   Our dog needs to go **out** for a walk.

4. ____<u>Prep.</u>____   The dog ran **out** the open door.

F. **To What Extent?:**

> Directions: Circle any adverbs that tell *to what extent*.

1. You seem **quite** tired today.

2. Mr. and Mrs. Smith are **very** happy about their new twins.

3. She did **not** bowl **so** rapidly during her second game.

D. **Where?:**

    Directions: Circle any adverbs that tell *where*.

1. Where are you going?

2. Let's go somewhere to talk.

3. He stooped down and looked up.

4. The salesmen went downtown for a meeting.

E. **Adverb or Preposition?:**

    Directions: Write <u>Prep</u>. if the boldfaced word serves as a preposition.
                       Write <u>Adv</u>. if the boldfaced word serves as an adverb.

    Examples: ___Adv.___   Marco came **over** ~~to my house~~.

1. _____   Do you live **near**?

2. _____   Do you live **near** a store?

3. _____   Our dog needs to go **out** for a walk.

4. _____   The dog ran **out** the open door.

F. **To What Extent?:**

    Directions: Circle any adverbs that tell *to what extent*.

1. You seem quite tired today.

2. Mr. and Mrs. Smith are very happy about their new twins.

3. She did not bowl so rapidly during her second game.

G.   **Degrees of Adverbs:**

   Directions: Circle the correct adverb form.

1.   Janell throws the ball (**higher**, highest) than Lisa.

2.   Of the three race cars, the red one runs (faster, **fastest**).

3.   The shortstop plays (**more often**, oftener) than the first base person.

4.   That assistant performs (**better**, best) than her boss.

5.   Cindy danced (**more calmly**, most calmly) during the second performance.

6.   Of the three machines, the first one runs (more smoothly, **most smoothly**).

7.   Do you ride your bike (**more rapidly**, most rapidly) than your brother?

8.   Brett cleaned his room (more completely, **most completely**) the fourth time.

H.   **Double Negatives:**

   Directions: Circle the correct answer.

1.   Don't take (no, **any**) candy from a stranger.

2.   Kim never has (nothing, **anything**) to do.

3.   I don't want (**any**, none).

4.   She doesn't want (**anybody**, nobody) to see her.

5.   We shouldn't (never, **ever**) go swimming alone.

6.   Kent hardly has (no, **any**) time for hobbies.

Date_____

G. **Degrees of Adverbs:**

   Directions: Circle the correct adverb form.

1. Janell throws the ball (higher, highest) than Lisa.

2. Of the three race cars, the red one runs (faster, fastest).

3. The shortstop plays (more often, oftener) than the first base person.

4. That assistant performs (better, best) than her boss.

5. Cindy danced (more calmly, most calmly) during the second performance.

6. Of the three machines, the first one runs (more smoothly, most smoothly).

7. Do you ride your bike (more rapidly, most rapidly) than your brother?

8. Brett cleaned his room (more completely, most completely) the fourth time.

H. **Double Negatives:**

   Directions: Circle the correct answer.

1. Don't take (no, any) candy from a stranger.

2. Kim never has (nothing, anything) to do.

3. I don't want (any, none).

4. She doesn't want (anybody, nobody) to see her.

5. We shouldn't (never, ever) go swimming alone.

6. Kent hardly has (no, any) time for hobbies.

Name_____   **ADVERBS**
                                              Test

Date_____

A. Circle any adverbs that tell *how*:

1. He answered **calmly**.

2. They play **well together**.

3. A baby smiled **sweetly** at us.

B. Circle any adverbs that tell *when*:

1. Must you leave **soon**?

2. The children eat popcorn **nightly**.

3. **Yesterday**, Anne and I arrived **late** for work.

C. Circle any adverbs that tell *where*

1. Have you seen Sue's magazine **anywhere**?

2. **Here** is Aunt Faye's high school yearbook.

3. You may come **in**, but leave your boots **outside**.

D. Circle any adverbs that tell *to what extent*:

1. This food is **too** salty and **very** dry.

2. We're **so** happy about your news.

3. You are **not quite** as stubborn as your brother.

E. Circle the correct adverb form:

1. When the four girls competed, Shana won (more easily, **most easily**).

2. She finished (earlier, **earliest**) of all the contestants in the race.

3. This gray kitten laps milk (**more steadily**, most steadily) than the white one.

4. The older girl stood (**more quietly**, most quietly) than her little sister.

5. I worked the math problem (**more carefully**, most carefully) the second time.

328

Name_____ **ADVERBS**
                                        Test

Date_____

A. Circle any adverbs that tell *how*:

1. He answered calmly.

2. They play well together.

3. A baby smiled sweetly at us.

B. Circle any adverbs that tell *when*:

1. Must you leave soon?

2. The children eat popcorn nightly.

3. Yesterday, Anne and I arrived late for work.

C. Circle any adverbs that tell *where*

1. Have you seen Sue's magazine anywhere?

2. Here is Aunt Faye's high school yearbook.

3. You may come in, but leave your boots outside.

D. Circle any adverbs that tell *to what extent*:

1. This food is too salty and very dry.

2. We're so happy about your news.

3. You are not quite as stubborn as your brother.

E. Circle the correct adverb form:

1. When the four girls competed, Shana won (more easily, most easily).

2. She finished (earlier, earliest) of all the contestants in the race.

3. This gray kitten laps milk (more steadily, most steadily) than the gray one.

4. The older girl stood (more quietly, most quietly) than her little sister.

5. I worked the math problem (more carefully, most carefully) the second time.

TO THE TEACHER:

The cumulative review for the adverb section is quite lengthy. I recommend that you do the review over a period of several days.

On the last page, I have added the listing of forty prepositions. You may want to do some overall review of those forty before arriving at that page.

I have also included the listing of the twenty-three helping verbs. You may wish to practice these with students, also.

I realize that students have been using prepositions and helping verbs throughout the text. However, I have found in my own teaching that students benefit from listing them occasionally.

A. **Object of the Preposition:**

   Directions: Cross out any prepositional phrases. Label the object of the preposition - O.P.

                          O.P.
1. We sat ~~in the first row~~.

           O.P.   O.P.
2. ~~Before church~~, the family eats ~~at a small diner~~.

🍓🍓🍓🍓🍓🍓🍓🍓🍓🍓🍓🍓🍓🍓🍓🍓🍓🍓🍓🍓🍓🍓🍓🍓🍓🍓🍓🍓🍓🍓

B. **Compound Object of the Preposition:**

   Directions: Cross out any prepositional phrases. Label the object of the preposition - O.P.

   Remember: Compound means more than one.

              O.P.   O.P.
1. We hiked ~~with Toni and Andy~~.

                      O.P.   O.P.
2. A postal card ~~from Grandma and Grandpa~~ came today.

🍓🍓🍓🍓🍓🍓🍓🍓🍓🍓🍓🍓🍓🍓🍓🍓🍓🍓🍓🍓🍓🍓🍓🍓🍓🍓🍓🍓🍓🍓

C. **Compound Subject:**

   Directions: Cross out any prepositional phrases. Underline the subject once and the verb/verb phrase twice.

   Remember: Compound means more than one.

1. Their <u>dog</u> and <u>cat</u> <u>run</u> ~~through the house~~.

2. ~~Before school~~, <u>Cynthia</u> and her <u>mom</u> <u>went</u> ~~for a walk~~.

🍓🍓🍓🍓🍓🍓🍓🍓🍓🍓🍓🍓🍓🍓🍓🍓🍓🍓🍓🍓🍓🍓🍓🍓🍓🍓🍓🍓🍓🍓

D. **Imperative Sentences:**

   Directions: Cross out any prepositional phrases. Underline the subject once and the verb/verb phrase twice.

   <u>(You)</u>
1. <u>Put</u> this ~~into the cupboard~~.

   <u>(You)</u>
2. <u>Toss</u> the water balloon ~~to me~~.

332

A. **Object of the Preposition:**

> Directions: Cross out any prepositional phrases. Label the object of the preposition - O.P.

1. We sat in the first row.

2. Before church, the family eats at a small diner.

🍓🍓🍓🍓🍓🍓🍓🍓🍓🍓🍓🍓🍓🍓🍓🍓🍓🍓🍓🍓🍓🍓🍓🍓🍓🍓🍓🍓🍓🍓🍓🍓🍓🍓🍓

B. **Compound Object of the Preposition:**

> Directions: Cross out any prepositional phrases. Label the object of the preposition - O.P.

> **Remember: Compound means more than one.**

1. We hiked with Toni and Andy.

2. A postal card from Grandma and Grandpa came today.

🍓🍓🍓🍓🍓🍓🍓🍓🍓🍓🍓🍓🍓🍓🍓🍓🍓🍓🍓🍓🍓🍓🍓🍓🍓🍓🍓🍓🍓🍓🍓🍓🍓🍓🍓

C. **Compound Subject:**

> Directions: Cross out any prepositional phrases. Underline the subject once and the verb/verb phrase twice.

> **Remember: Compound means more than one.**

1. Their dog and cat run through the house.

2. Before school, Cynthia and her mom went for a walk.

🍓🍓🍓🍓🍓🍓🍓🍓🍓🍓🍓🍓🍓🍓🍓🍓🍓🍓🍓🍓🍓🍓🍓🍓🍓🍓🍓🍓🍓🍓🍓🍓🍓🍓🍓

D. **Imperative Sentences:**

> Directions: Cross out any prepositional phrases. Underline the subject once and the verb/verb phrase twice.

1. Put this into the cupboard.

2. Toss the water balloon to me.

E. **Compound Verbs:**

   Directions: Cross out any prepositional phrases. Underline the subject once and the verb/verb phrase twice.

1. I always <u>wash</u> and <u>wax</u> floors ~~in the morning~~.

2. <u>Judd</u> <u>called</u> my name and <u>motioned</u> ~~toward me~~.

🍓🍓🍓🍓🍓🍓🍓🍓🍓🍓🍓🍓🍓🍓🍓🍓🍓🍓🍓🍓🍓🍓🍓🍓🍓🍓🍓🍓🍓🍓🍓

F. **Infinitives:**

   Directions: Cross out any prepositional phrases. Underline the subject once and the verb twice. Place an infinitive in parenthesis ( ).

1. That <u>lady</u> <u>likes</u> (to work) ~~at her computer~~.

2. ~~After the flood~~, <u>people</u> <u>came</u> (to help).

🍓🍓🍓🍓🍓🍓🍓🍓🍓🍓🍓🍓🍓🍓🍓🍓🍓🍓🍓🍓🍓🍓🍓🍓🍓🍓🍓🍓🍓🍓🍓

G. **Contractions:**

   Directions: Write the contraction in the space provided.

1. do not - _____don't_____

2. you will - _____you'll_____

3. you are - _____you're_____

4. will not - _____won't_____

5. had not - _____hadn't_____

6. I shall - _____I'll_____

7. they are - _____they're_____

8. where is - _____where's_____

9. have not - _____haven't_____

10. we were - _____we're_____

11. cannot - _____can't_____

12. she is - _____she's_____

🍓🍓🍓🍓🍓🍓🍓🍓🍓🍓🍓🍓🍓🍓🍓🍓🍓🍓🍓🍓🍓🍓🍓🍓🍓🍓🍓🍓🍓🍓🍓

H. **Action Verb?:**

   Directions: Write <u>Yes</u> if the boldfaced verb shows action; write <u>No</u> if the boldfaced verb does not show action.

   1. __Yes__   He **climbed** a hill.

   2. __Yes__   I **eat** many bananas.

   3. __No__   You **seem** sad.

   4. __No__   The gong **sounds** loud

334

E. Compound Verbs:

 Directions: Cross out any prepositional phrases. Underline the subject once and the verb/verb phrase twice.

1. I always wash and wax floors in the morning.

2. Judd called my name and motioned toward me.

F. Infinitives:

 Directions: Cross out any prepositional phrases. Underline the subject once and the verb twice. Place an infinitive in parenthesis ( ).

1. That lady likes to work at her computer.

2. After the flood, people came to help.

G. Contractions:

 Directions: Write the contraction in the space provided.

1. do not - _____

2. you will - _____

3. you are - _____

4. will not - _____

5. had not - _____

6. I shall - _____

7. they are - _____

8. where is - _____

9. have not - _____

10. we were - _____

11. cannot - _____

12. she is - _____

H. Action Verb?:

 Directions: Write <u>Yes</u> if the boldfaced verb shows action; write <u>No</u> if the boldfaced verb does not show action.

1. _____ He **climbed** a hill.

2. _____ I **eat** many bananas.

3. _____ You **seem** sad.

4. _____ The gong **sounds** loud.

335

I. **Regular or Irregular:**

Directions: Write <u>RV</u> if the verb is regular. Write <u>IV</u> if the verb is irregular.

Remember: Regular verbs add <u>ed</u> to the past and past participle.

1. __RV__ to love   3. __IV__ to bleed   5. __RV__ to change

2. __IV__ to give   4. __IV__ to break   6. __IV__ to steal

J. **Tenses:**

Directions: Cross out any prepositional phrases. Underline the subject once and the verb/verb phrase twice. Write the tense on the line.

Remember: The tenses that we have learned are **present**, **past**, and **future**.

1. ____future____   <u>Mark</u> <u>will go</u> ~~to the beach in June~~.

2. ____present____   That scuba <u>diver</u> <u>enjoys</u> his hobby.

3. ____past____   <u>They</u> <u>surfed</u> ~~for several hours~~.

K. **Subject-Verb Agreement:**

Directions: Circle the verb that agrees with the subject.

1. Nina and Troy (**sing**, sings) in a choir.

2. Mrs. Dobbs (want, **wants**) to be an actress.

3. Those children (plays, **play**) well together.

L. **Irregular Verbs:**

Directions: Write the past participle form.

1. to run - ____(had)____ run   3. to go - ____(had)____ gone

2. to drink - __(had)__ drunk   4. to ride - ____(had)____ ridden

336

I. **Regular or Irregular:**

Directions: Write <u>RV</u> if the verb is regular. Write <u>IV</u> if the verb is irregular.

Remember: Regular verbs add <u>ed</u> to the past and past participle.

1. _____ to love   3. _____ to bleed   5. _____ to change

2. _____ to give   4. _____ to break   6. _____ to steal

J. **Tenses:**

Directions: Cross out any prepositional phrases. Underline the subject once and the verb/verb phrase twice. Write the tense on the line.

Remember: The tenses that we have learned are *present*, *past*, and *future*.

1. _____   Mark will go to the beach in June.

2. _____   That scuba diver enjoys his hobby.

3. _____   They surfed for several hours.

K. **Subject-Verb Agreement:**

Directions: Circle the verb that agrees with the subject.

1. Nina and Troy (sing, sings) in a choir.

2. Mrs. Dobbs (want, wants) to be an actress.

3. Those children (plays, play) well together.

L. **Irregular Verbs:**

Directions: Write the past participle form.

1. to run - ____(had)_____   3. to go - ____(had)_____

2. to drink - ____(had)_____   4. to ride - ____(had)_____

M. **Irregular Verbs:**

   Directions: Cross out prepositional phrases. Underline the subject once and the verb phrase twice. **(Be sure to underline the helping verbs + the main verb in parenthesis.)**

1. We have not (ate, **eaten**) lunch.

2. Several funnel clouds were (see, **seen**).

3. Where has Steve (went, **gone**)?

4. The driver may have (**come**, came) ~~for the packages~~.

5. Ted and Ike have (flew, **flown**) ~~in a large jet~~.

6. Hannah had (laid, **lain**) ~~by the pool before noon~~.

7. Marcia should have (gave, **given**) her dog a bath.

🍓🍓🍓🍓🍓🍓🍓🍓🍓🍓🍓🍓🍓🍓🍓🍓🍓🍓🍓🍓🍓🍓🍓🍓🍓🍓🍓🍓

N. **Concrete and Abstract Nouns:**

   Directions: Write C if the noun is concrete; write A if the noun is abstract.

1. __A__ friendship   2. __C__ honey   3. __C__ mop

🍓🍓🍓🍓🍓🍓🍓🍓🍓🍓🍓🍓🍓🍓🍓🍓🍓🍓🍓🍓🍓🍓🍓🍓🍓🍓🍓🍓

O. **Common and Proper Nouns:**

   Directions: Write CN if the noun is common; write PN is the noun is proper.

1. __CN__ APPLE   2. __PN__ ALASKA   3. __CN__ RUG

🍓🍓🍓🍓🍓🍓🍓🍓🍓🍓🍓🍓🍓🍓🍓🍓🍓🍓🍓🍓🍓🍓🍓🍓🍓🍓🍓🍓

P. **Noun Identification:**   **Nouns are in boldfaced print; determiners are underlined.**

   Directions: Underline any nouns in each sentence.

   Remember: You may wish to circle determiners to help you find most nouns.

1. Many **cows** grazed in a **meadow** near the large **barn**.

2. Two red **roses** in a glass **vase** had been placed on our dining **table**.
338

M. **Irregular Verbs:**

    Directions: Cross out prepositional phrases. Underline the subject once and the verb phrase twice. **(Be sure to underline the helping verbs + the main verb in parenthesis.)**

1. We have not (ate, eaten) lunch.

2. Several funnel clouds were (see, seen).

3. Where has Steve (went, gone)?

4. The driver may have (come, came) for the packages.

5. Ted and Ike have (flew, flown) in a large jet.

6. Hannah had (laid, lain) by the pool before noon.

7. Marcia should have (gave, given) her dog a bath.

N. **Concrete and Abstract Nouns:**

    Directions: Write C if the noun is concrete; write A if the noun is abstract.

1. _____   friendship   2. _____   honey   3. _____   mop

O. **Common and Proper Nouns:**

    Directions: Write CN if the noun is common; write PN is the noun is proper.

1. _____   APPLE   2. _____   ALASKA   3. _____   RUG

P. **Noun Identification:**

    Directions: Underline any nouns in each sentence.

    Remember: You may wish to circle determiners to help you find most nouns.

1. Many cows grazed in a meadow near the large barn.

2. Two red roses in a glass vase had been placed on our dining table.

Q. **Singular and Plural Nouns:**

Directions: Write the plural.

1. ray - _____rays_____   5. child - _____children_____

2. tomato - ___tomatoes___   6. sheep - _____sheep_____

3. mix - _____mixes_____   7. name - _____names_____

4. train - _____trains_____   8. dictionary - __dictionaries__

🍓🍓🍓🍓🍓🍓🍓🍓🍓🍓🍓🍓🍓🍓🍓🍓🍓🍓🍓🍓🍓🍓🍓🍓🍓🍓🍓🍓

R. **Possessive Nouns:**

Directions: Write the possessive form.

1. a horse belonging to Heidi

_____Heidi's horse_____

2. marbles owned by several boys

_____boys' marbles_____

3. a barn used for cows

_____cows' barn_____

🍓🍓🍓🍓🍓🍓🍓🍓🍓🍓🍓🍓🍓🍓🍓🍓🍓🍓🍓🍓🍓🍓🍓🍓🍓🍓🍓🍓

S. **Sentence Types:**

Directions: Write the sentence type in the space provided.
Remember: The four sentence types are declarative, interrogative, imperative, and exclamatory.

1. _____declarative_____   My friend's mother is waxing her car.

2. _____interrogative_____   Do you like to play games?

3. _____imperative_____   Wash your face.

4. _____exclamatory_____   I've been selected for the all-star team!

340

Q. **Singular and Plural Nouns:**

Directions: Write the plural.

1. ray - _____

2. tomato - _____

3. mix - _____

4. train - _____

5. child - _____

6. sheep - _____

7. name - _____

8. dictionary - _____

🍓🍓🍓🍓🍓🍓🍓🍓🍓🍓🍓🍓🍓🍓🍓🍓🍓🍓🍓🍓🍓🍓🍓🍓🍓🍓🍓🍓🍓🍓🍓🍓🍓🍓

R. **Possessive Nouns:**

Directions: Write the possessive form.

1. a horse belonging to Heidi

_____

2. marbles owned by several boys

_____

3. a barn used for cows

_____

🍓🍓🍓🍓🍓🍓🍓🍓🍓🍓🍓🍓🍓🍓🍓🍓🍓🍓🍓🍓🍓🍓🍓🍓🍓🍓🍓🍓🍓🍓🍓🍓🍓🍓

S. **Sentence Types**

Directions: Write the sentence type in the space provided.
Remember: The four sentence types are declarative, interrogative, imperative, and exclamatory.

1. _____ My friend's mother is waxing her car.

2. _____ Do you like to play games?

3. _____ Wash your face.

4. _____ I've been selected for the all-star team! 341

T. **Conjunctions and Interjections:**

Directions: Label any conjunction - CONJ.; label any interjection - INTJ.

    INTJ.   **CONJ.**

1. Yikes! John **and** Mary forgot their luggage!

                   CONJ.

2. We want Chinese **or** Mexican food tonight.

U. **Adjective?:**

Directions: Write <u>Yes</u> if the boldfaced word serves as an adjective. Write <u>No</u> if the boldfaced word does not serve as an adjective.

1. ___Yes___   Their **street** light is burned out.

2. ___No___   Several small trees were planted in a **field**.

3. ___Yes___   Have you ever seen a **field** mouse?

V. **Degrees of Adjectives:**

Directions: Circle the correct answer.

1. This Cajun chicken is (**spicier,** spiciest) than the barbecued chicken.

2. Of the three referees, she is the (fairer, **fairest**).

3. Lori is the (**more creative**, most creative) twin.

W. **Adjective Identification:**

Directions: Circle any adjectives.

Suggestion: First, look for limiting adjectives. Then, reread the sentence searching for descriptive adjectives.

1. **A few** bees have landed on **the yellow** flower.

2. **Two new** cars skidded on **an icy** street.

342

T. **Conjunctions and Interjections:**

   Directions: Label any conjunction - CONJ.; label any interjection - INTJ.

1. Yikes!   John and Mary forgot their luggage!

2. We want Chinese or Mexican food tonight.

🍓🍓🍓🍓🍓🍓🍓🍓🍓🍓🍓🍓🍓🍓🍓🍓🍓🍓🍓🍓🍓🍓🍓🍓🍓🍓🍓🍓🍓🍓🍓🍓🍓

U. **Adjective?:**

   Directions: Write <u>Yes</u> if the boldfaced word serves as an adjective. Write <u>No</u> if
   the boldfaced word does not serve as an adjective.

1. _____   Their **street** light is burned out.

2. _____   Several small trees were planted in a **field**.

3. _____   Have you ever seen a **field** mouse?

🍓🍓🍓🍓🍓🍓🍓🍓🍓🍓🍓🍓🍓🍓🍓🍓🍓🍓🍓🍓🍓🍓🍓🍓🍓🍓🍓🍓🍓🍓🍓🍓🍓

V. **Degrees of Adjectives:**

   Directions: Circle the correct answer.

1. This Cajun chicken is (spicier, spiciest) than the barbecued chicken.

2. Of the three referees, she is the (fairer, fairest).

3. Lori is the (more creative, most creative) twin.

🍓🍓🍓🍓🍓🍓🍓🍓🍓🍓🍓🍓🍓🍓🍓🍓🍓🍓🍓🍓🍓🍓🍓🍓🍓🍓🍓🍓🍓🍓🍓🍓🍓

W. **Adjective Identification:**

   Directions: Circle any adjectives.

Suggestion: First, look for limiting adjectives. Then, reread the sentence searching
   for descriptive adjectives.

1. A few bees have landed on the yellow flower.

2. Two new cars skidded on an icy street.

X. **Prepositions:**

Directions: List forty prepositions.

1.	about	21.	in
2.	above	22.	inside
3.	across	23.	into
4.	after	24.	near
5.	against	25.	of
6.	along	26.	off
7.	around	27.	on
8.	at	28.	out
9.	before	29.	outside
10.	behind	30.	over
11.	below	31.	past
12.	beneath	32.	through
13.	beside	33.	throughout
14.	between	34.	to
15.	by	35.	toward
16.	down	36.	under
17.	during	37.	until
18.	except	38.	up
19.	for	39.	with
20.	from	40.	without

Y. **Helping Verbs:**

Directions: List the twenty-three helping verbs.

do, does, did   has, have, had,   may, must, might

should, would, could   shall, will, can

is, am, are, was, were, be, being, been

X. **Prepositions:**

Directions: List forty prepositions.

1. _____
2. _____
3. _____
4. _____
5. _____
6. _____
7. _____
8. _____
9. _____
10. _____
11. _____
12. _____
13. _____
14. _____
15. _____
16. _____
17. _____
18. _____
19. _____
20. _____

21. _____
22. _____
23. _____
24. _____
25. _____
26. _____
27. _____
28. _____
29. _____
30. _____
31. _____
32. _____
33. _____
34. _____
35. _____
36. _____
37. _____
38. _____
39. _____
40. _____

Y. **Helping Verbs:**

Directions: List the twenty-three helping verbs.

_____

_____

_____

A. **Prepositional Phrases:**
   Directions: Cross out any prepositional phrases. Underline the subject once
   and the verb/verb phrase twice. Label any direct object - D.O.

   1. The <u>child</u> <u>hid</u> ~~under the table~~.

                              D.O.
   2. <u>Brad</u> <u>pushed</u> a pen ~~between the cushions of the sofa~~.

B. **Compounds:**
   Directions: Cross out any prepositional phrases. Underline the subject once
   and the verb/verb phrase twice.

   1. A <u>robin</u> and <u>swallow</u> <u>flew</u> ~~across the lawn~~.

   2. <u>We</u> <u>tied</u> the gift ~~with ribbon and a silk flower~~.

   3. A <u>shopper</u> <u>looked</u> ~~at jewelry~~ and <u>bought</u> a necklace.

C. **Contractions:**
   Directions: Write the contraction.

   1. I shall - _____I'll_____   6. is not - _____isn't_____

   2. could not- _____couldn't_____   7. they are - _____they're_____

   3. you are - _____you're_____   8. did not - _____didn't_____

   4. here is - _____here's_____   9. are not - _____aren't_____

   5. what is - _____what's_____   10. I have - _____I've_____

D. **Common and Proper Noun:**
   Directions: Find a proper noun for the boldfaced common noun.
   Write the letter of the proper noun in the space.

   1. __B__ *STATE*   (A) COUNTY   (B) TEXAS   (C) REGION
   2. __C__ *PERSON*   (A) BANKER   (B) GOLFER   (C) LAURA

Name_____

Date_____

A. **Prepositional Phrases:**

    Directions: Cross out any prepositional phrases. Underline the subject once and the verb/verb phrase twice. Label any direct object - <u>D.O.</u>

1. The child hid under the table.

2. Brad pushed a pen between the cushions of the sofa.

B. **Compounds:**

    Directions: Cross out any prepositional phrases. Underline the subject once and the verb/verb phrase twice.

1. A robin and swallow flew across the lawn.

2. We tied the gift with ribbon and a silk flower.

3. A shopper looked at jewelry and bought a necklace.

C. **Contractions:**

    Directions: Write the contraction.

1. I shall - _____

2. could not- _____

3. you are - _____

4. here is - _____

5. what is - _____

6. is not - _____

7. they are - _____

8. did not - _____

9. are not - _____

10. I have - _____

D. **Common and Proper Noun:**

    Directions: Find a proper noun for the boldfaced common noun.
    Write the letter of the proper noun in the space.

1. _____ *STATE*   (A) COUNTY   (B) TEXAS   (C) REGION

2. _____ *PERSON* (A) BANKER   (B) GOLFER   (C) LAURA

347

E. **Subject-Verb Agreement:**

   Directions: Circle the verb that agrees with the subject.

1. They often (has, **have**) hot chocolate for breakfast.

2. His ferrets (eats, **eat**) cereal.

3. Dad seldom (buy, **buys**) new shoes.

4. One of the women (bring, **brings**) an umbrella every day.

F. **Tenses:**

   Directions: Write the tense (present, past, or future) on the line provided.

Note: You may want to cross out prepositional phrases, underline the subject once, and underline the verb/verb phrase twice to help determine the tense.

1. _____past_____ A <u>bull</u> <u>stood</u> <s>inside a fence</s>.

2. _____present_____ <u>Many</u> <u>want</u> (to blow) bubbles.

3. _____future_____ <u>They</u> <u>will drive</u> <s>to Idaho</s>.

4. _____future_____ <u>I</u> <u>shall stay</u> here.

G. **Irregular Verbs:**

   Directions: Circle the correct verb.

1. The child had (grew, **grown**) four inches.

2. Have you (brung, **brought**) your lunch?

3. The show must have (began, **begun**).

4. These rugs have not been (shook, **shaken**).

5. Sandals were (**worn**, wore) on the hot sand.

6. She should have (ran, **run**) faster.

7. Hot dogs were (took, **taken**) on the picnic.

E. **Subject-Verb Agreement:**

Directions: Circle the verb that agrees with the subject.

1. They often (has, have) hot chocolate for breakfast.

2. His ferrets (eats, eat) cereal.

3. Dad seldom (buy, buys) new shoes.

4. One of the women (bring, brings) an umbrella every day.

F. **Tenses:**

Directions: Write the tense (present, past, or future) on the line provided.

Note: You may want to cross out prepositional phrases, underline the subject once, and underline the verb/verb phrase twice to help determine the tense.

1. _____ A bull stood inside a fence.

2. _____ Many want to blow bubbles.

3. _____ They will drive to Idaho.

4. _____ I shall stay here.

G. **Irregular Verbs:**

Directions: Circle the correct verb.

1. The child had (grew, grown) four inches.

2. Have you (brung, brought) your lunch?

3. The show must have (began, begun).

4. These rugs have not been (shook, shaken).

5. Sandals were (worn, wore) on the hot sand.

6. She should have (ran, run) faster.

7. Hot dogs were (took, taken) on the picnic.

349

8. Shannon might have (rode, **ridden**) her horse to the park.

9. Their team should not have (beat, **beaten**) us.

10. Many ice cubes were (froze, **frozen**) in plastic trays.

H. **Noun Plurals:**

    Directions: Write the plural form.

1. bunch - <u>   bunches   </u>

2. cactus - <u>   cacti (cactuses) </u>

3. roof - <u>   roofs   </u>

4. life - <u>   lives   </u>

5. gate - <u>   gates   </u>

6. toy - <u>   toys   </u>

7. woman - <u>   women   </u>

8. potato - <u>   potatoes   </u>

9. bush - <u>   bushes   </u>

10. story - <u>   stories   </u>

I. **Noun Possessives:**

    Directions: Write the possessive form.

1. a football belonging to a boy - <u>   a boy's football   </u>

2. a football shared by three boys - <u> (three) boys' football </u>

3. a jersey belonging to a player - <u> a player's jersey </u>

J. **Noun or Adjective?:**

    Directions: If the boldfaced word serves as a noun, write <u>N</u> in the space. If the boldfaced word serves as an adjective, write <u>A</u> in the space.

1. <u> A </u>   Our **door** knob is jammed.

2. <u> N </u>   Please open the **door**.

3. <u> N </u>   Your **television** is large.

4. <u> A </u>   That **television** screen seems small.

8. Shannon might have (rode, ridden) her horse to the park.

9. Their team should not have (beat, beaten) us.

10. Many ice cubes were (froze, frozen) in plastic trays.

H. **Noun Plurals:**

Directions: Write the plural form.

1. bunch - _____   6. toy - _____

2. cactus - _____   7. woman - _____

3. roof - _____   8. potato - _____

4. life - _____   9. bush - _____

5. gate - _____   10. story - _____

I. **Noun Possessives:**

Directions: Write the possessive form.

1. a football belonging to a boy - _____

2. a football shared by three boys - _____

3. a jersey belonging to a player - _____

J. **Noun or Adjective?:**

Directions: If the boldfaced word serves as a noun, write <u>N</u> in the space. If the boldfaced word serves as an adjective, write <u>A</u> in the space.

1. _____ Our **door** knob is jammed.

2. _____ Please open the **door**.

3. _____ Your **television** is large.

4. _____ That **television** screen seems small.

K. **Noun Identification:**

Directions: Circle any nouns.

Suggestion: You may want to underline determiners to help you locate nouns.

1. Your **shoes** with green **laces** are in the **closet**.

2. He ate two **pancakes**, an **egg**, and a **muffin** for **breakfast**.

L. **Sentence types:**

Directions: Write the sentence type (declarative, interrogative, imperative, or exclamatory) in the space.

1. _____exclamatory_____ No! Our dinner is burned!

2. _____imperative_____ Please tell me the truth.

3. _____declarative_____ The tile is cracked.

4. _____interrogative_____ May I read this book?

M. **Adjective Identification:**

Directions: Circle any adjectives.

1. **A tall, thin** model smiled at **the** audience.

2. **Few ice** storms occur in **this** area.

3. **Her long black** hair is **pretty**.

N. **Degrees of Adjectives:**

Directions: Circle the correct adjective form.

1. Of all the bird eggs, this is (tinier, **tiniest**).

2. The cake is (**more delicious**, most delicious) than the pie.

3. She is (short, **shortest**) in her family.

4. Division was my (more difficult, **most difficult**) part of math.

5. He is the (taller, **tallest**) one on his team.

352

K. **Noun Identification:**

Directions: Circle any nouns.

Suggestion: You may want to underline determiners to help you locate nouns.

1. Your shoes with green laces are in the closet.

2. He ate two pancakes, an egg, and a muffin for breakfast.

L. **Sentence types:**

Directions: Write the sentence type (declarative, interrogative, imperative, or exclamatory) in the space.

1. _____ No! Our dinner is burned!

2. _____ Please tell me the truth.

3. _____ The tile is cracked.

4. _____ May I read this book?

M. **Adjective Identification:**

Directions: Circle any adjectives.

1. A tall, thin model smiled at the audience.

2. Few ice storms occur in this area.

3. Her long black hair is pretty.

N. **Degrees of Adjectives:**

Directions: Circle the correct adjective form.

1. Of all the bird eggs, this is (tinier, tiniest).

2. The cake is (more delicious, most delicious) than the pie.

3. She is (short, shortest) in her family.

4. Division was my (more difficult, most difficult) part of math.

5. He is the (taller, tallest) one on his team.

353

TO THE TEACHER:

Pronouns are very difficult. This section has been set up very differently. Some of the concepts may seem too easy, but I want students to continue to enjoy their language. Do NOT be frustrated if your students do not have total mastery of concepts presented here.

To use pronouns properly, one needs to determine how the pronoun is used in the sentence, i.e. subject, predicate nominative, direct object, etc. This book does not contain all of the information needed to make decisions for correct usage. For example, predicate nominatives and indirect objects are not introduced in this text. Also, no worksheets for determining specific use have been included. (These are introduced at higher levels.) In this text, students are given a variety of techniques to help determine correct usage.

I have not included reflexive pronouns, demonstrative pronouns, or indefinite pronouns in this text. Under interrogative pronouns, I have not introduced *who* used as a predicate nominative or *whom* used as an indirect object. (These will be introduced at higher levels.) Although I discussed *whom* used as a direct object, I did not place any examples on worksheets.

Although the review sections cover all of the concepts, the test includes only selection of the correct pronoun.

PRONOUNS

PAGE 357 = WORKBOOK PAGE 147

PRONOUNS

Personal Pronouns

Pronouns take the place of nouns.

Nominative pronouns usually serve as the **subject** of a sentence. Nominative pronouns include **I**, **he**, **she**, **we**, **they**, **you**, **who**, and **it**.

Examples: **Mary** makes birdhouses.

She makes birdhouses.

Brett and Joe are selling popsicles.

They are selling popsicles.

Is **Mr. Dobbs** your friend?

Is **he** your friend?

Important: If you are talking about yourself, use the pronoun, **I,** at or near the beginning of a sentence.

Example: After lunch, **I** played with my friend.

When referring to yourself and another person, say the other person's name first.

Example: **Matt** and **I** bought ice cream.

🍓 🍓 🍓 **Do not say** Matt and me or me and Matt. 🍓 🍓 🍓

357

Directions: In part <u>A</u>, insert a person's name in the blank. In part <u>B</u>, use a pronoun to replace the person's name; in the double underlined part, finish the sentence.

Example: A. _____Josh_____ is my brother.

B. _____He_____ is<u> very nice to our dog.</u>

ANSWERS WILL VARY: REPRESENTATIVE ANSWERS

1. A. _____Ken_____ is my friend.

B. _____He_____ <u>is funny.</u>

2. A. ___Mrs. Lake_____ is my teacher.

B. ___She_____ is<u> very patient with us.</u>

3. A. ___Sandy_____ is a member of my family.

B. _____She_____ is<u> fifteen years old.</u>

4. A. ___Randall_____ is an older person who is important to me.

B. ___He_____ is<u> my uncle who lives in Kentucky.</u>

5. A. ___Corky_____ is an animal.

B. _____He_____ is<u> our neighbor's dog.</u>

358

Name_____

Date_____

PRONOUNS
As Subject

Directions: In part <u>A</u>, insert a person's name in the blank. In part <u>B</u>, use a pronoun to replace the person's name; in the double underlined part, finish the sentence.

Example: A.   _____Josh_____ is my brother.

B.   _____He_____ is__ very nice to our dog. __

1. A. _____ is my friend.

B. _____ is_____

2. A. _____ is my teacher.

B. _____ is_____

3. A. _____ is a member of my family.

B. _____ is_____

4. A. _____ is an older person who is important to me.

B. _____ is_____

5. A. _____ is an animal.

B. _____ is_____

359

A. Directions: On the line provided, write each sentence correctly.

1. I and my friend want to stay.

   _____My friend and I want to stay._____

2. My dad and me are going.

   _____My dad and I are going._____

3. Me and Terry played at the park.

   _____Terry and I played at the park._____

4. Me and my friends aren't doing that.

   _____My friends and I aren't doing that._____

B. Directions: Write the correct pronoun on the line.

___I___ 1. (Me, I) want to go, too.

_She__ 2. (Her, She) is the winner!

they 3. All afternoon (they, them) played in their yard.

_We___ 4. (We, Us) enjoy scary stories.

_he___ 5. Today, (he, him) is going to the zoo.

___I___ 6. May Mike and (me, I) help you?

360

Name_____

Date_____

A. Directions: On the line provided, write each sentence correctly.

1. I and my friend want to stay.

   _____

2. My dad and me are going.

   _____

3. Me and Terry played at the park.

   _____

4. Me and my friends aren't doing that.

   _____

B. Directions: Write the correct pronoun on the line.

_____ 1. (Me, I) want to go, too.

_____ 2. (Her, She) is the winner!

_____ 3. All afternoon (they, them) played in their yard.

_____ 4. (We, Us) enjoy scary stories.

_____ 5. Today, (he, him) is going to the zoo.

_____ 6. May Mike and (me, I) help you?

PAGE 363 = WORKBOOK PAGE 150

PRONOUNS

Pronouns take the place of nouns.

Objective pronouns are usually used after a preposition or as a direct object. Objective pronouns include **me**, **him**, **her**, **us**, **them**, **you**, **whom**, and **it**.

Examples: The coach is talking to the **girl.**

The coach is talking to **her**.   (object of the preposition)

The ball hit **Jack** on the leg.

The ball hit **him** on the leg.   (direct object)

A. Directions: Place an X above the preposition. Then, circle the correct pronoun.

> **Remember:**   **After a preposition, you will use an objective pronoun. Objective pronouns include *me*, *him*, *her*, *us*, *them*, *you*, and *it*.**

PREPOSITIONS ARE IN BOLDFACED ITALICS.

1. Are you going *with* (we, **us**)?

2. I have given the bag *to* (**him**, he).

3. This is *from* (they, **them**).

4. The story is *about* (**her**, she).

5. Sit *between* John and (I, **me**).

B. Directions: In sentence A, underline the subject once and the verb twice. Label the direct object - D.O. In part B, insert a pronoun for the word(s) labeled as a direct object.

                          D.O.
1. A. The <u>team</u> <u>chose</u> Jan.

    B. The team chose ___**her**___.

                          D.O.
2. A. A rubber <u>ball</u> <u>hit</u> John.

    B. A rubber ball hit ___**him**___.

                          D.O.
3. A. The <u>lady</u> <u>dropped</u> her wallet.

    B. The lady dropped ___**it**___.

                  D.O.   D.O.
4. A. <u>Dad</u> <u>hugged</u> Susie and Ryan.

    B. Dad hugged ___**them**___.

364

Name_____   **PRONOUNS**
                                  As Objects
Date_____

A. Directions: Place an X above the preposition. Then, circle the correct pronoun.

   Remember: After a preposition, you will use an objective pronoun. Objective pronouns include *me, him, her, us, them, you,* and *it.*

1. Are you going with (we, us)?

2. I have given the bag to (him, he).

3. This is from (they, them).

4. The story is about (her, she).

5. Sit between John and (I, me).

B. Directions: In sentence A, underline the subject once and the verb twice. Label the direct object - D.O. In part B, insert a pronoun for the word(s) labeled as a direct object.

1. A. The team chose Jan.

   B. The team chose _____.

2. A. A rubber ball hit John.

   B. A rubber ball hit _____.

3. A. The lady dropped her wallet.

   B. The lady dropped _____.

4. A. Dad hugged Susie and Ryan.

   B. Dad hugged _____.

Directions: Write a pronoun for the boldfaced noun(s).

ANSWERS FOR 1A WILL VARY.
1. A.   The puppy followed _____**Shirley**_____.
                                (your name)

    B.   The puppy followed ___**me**_____.

2. A.   A calendar was given to **Anne**.

    B.   A calendar was given to ___**her**_____.

3. A.   The singer sang to **Brad and Carol**.

    B.   The singer sang to ___**them**_____.

4. A.   A dog licked **Miss Post** for several seconds.

    B.   A dog licked ___**her**_____for several seconds.

5. A.   Their uncle went with **Shari and our family** to a baseball game.

    B.   Their uncle went with ___**us**_____ to a baseball game.

6. A.   Mother handed the **bird** to her friend.

    B.   Mother handed ___**it**_____ to her friend.

Directions: Write a pronoun for the boldfaced noun(s).

1. A.   The puppy followed _____.
             (your name)

    B.   The puppy followed _____.

2. A.   A calendar was given to **Anne**.

    B.   A calendar was given to _____.

3. A.   The singer sang to **Brad and Carol**.

    B.   The singer sang to _____.

4. A.   A dog licked **Miss Post** for several seconds.

    B.   A dog licked _____ for several seconds.

5. A.   Their uncle went with **Shari and our family** to a baseball game.

    B.   Their uncle went with _____ to a baseball game.

6. A.   Mother handed the **bird** to her friend.

    B.   Mother handed _____ to her friend.

Directions: On the line provided, write each sentence correctly.

1. Do you want to eat lunch with I?

   _____Do you want to eat lunch with **me**?_____

2. Marsha lives near he.

   _____Marsha lives near **him**._____

3. The artist talked to they about his painting.

   _____The artist talked to **them** about his painting._____

4. My friend gave I two pencils.

   _____My friend gave **me** two pencils._____

5. Please give we your answer!

   _____Please give **us** your answer!_____

6. This letter is from she.

   _____This letter is from **her**._____

7. Their moms met they at a park.

   _____Their moms met **them** at a park._____

Name_____   **PRONOUNS**
                                          As Objects

Date_____

Directions: On the line provided, write each sentence correctly.

1. Do you want to eat lunch with I?

    _____

2. Marsha lives near he.

    _____

3. The artist talked to they about his painting.

    _____

4. My friend gave I two pencils.

    _____

5. Please give we your answer!

    _____

6. This letter is from she.

    _____

7. Their moms met they at a park.

    _____

Compound Pronouns

The next section explains compound pronouns. You may have noted that little emphasis has been placed on knowing what function the pronoun serves in the sentence. In fact, pronouns used as predicate nominatives and indirect objects have not been introduced. (They will be taught at higher levels.)

Thus far, we have been trying to achieve two goals:

1. We want students to recognize the pronouns that function as subject of the sentence. (We have not introduced terms such as nominative or subjective pronouns. We are teaching very simplistically.)

2. We want students to recognize pronouns that function as objects. We have taught direct objects and objects of the preposition. Our goal is for students to recognize, for example, that *with* is a preposition and to use an objective pronoun after *with*.

It would be terrific if all students, at this point, understood the function of each pronoun in every sentence. Candidly, not all will be able to do this. However, the pronouns covered are used correctly so frequently that most students have assimilated the correct pronoun usage. (This is not true, however, of predicate nominatives or antecedent usage which will be taught in *Level 1*.) Hence, when teaching compound pronouns, it is perfectly acceptable to use the "pronoun finger trick" and determine correct pronoun usage somewhat by "sound" as outlined on the next page.

IMPORTANT NOTE:

There are three worksheets provided for practice with compounds. Please teach the lesson and do the first worksheet orally with students. Practice the finger trick with each sentence. On the ensuing day, do a "mini" teaching lessons, reviewing the use of the finger trick. Then, do the second worksheet orally with students. I recommend saving the third worksheet for the third day. You may want to review the concept by orally doing the first three or four together. I strongly recommend that you allow time in class for students (individually, not cooperatively) to finish the rest of that page. You may want to exchange papers for correcting. Of course, as in all good teaching, those who miss two or more need to become part of a small, reteaching group.

370

Compound Pronouns

Compound means more than one.

Sometimes, there is more than one subject of a sentence. This is called a **compound subject.**

Example: <u>**Lela**</u> and <u>**Kissa**</u> chose several guppies.

<u>**Lela**</u> and <u>**she**</u> chose several guppies.

Sometimes, there is more than one object in a sentence.

Examples: An older girl sat beside **Kami** and **Kyle**.

An older girl sat beside **Kami** and **him**.

Pronoun Finger Trick:

If you are unsure which pronoun to use, place your finger or fingers over the first part of the compound.

Example: Lela and (her, she) chose several guppies.

Her chose several guppies.   Incorrect!

She chose several guppies.   Correct!

Lela and (her, **she**) chose several guppies.

Example: An older girl sat beside Kami and (he, him).

An older girl sat beside   **he**.   Incorrect!

An older girl sat beside   **him**.   Correct!

An older girl sat beside Kami and (he, **him**).   371

Directions: Circle the correct pronoun.

Remember: Place your finger or fingers over the first part of the compound.   Then, reread the sentence and choose the correct pronoun.

1.   Pat and (me, **I**) decided to sell cookies during the summer.

2.   Come with Jarred and (**me**, I).

3.   The policeman and (**they**, them) talked for an hour.

4.   Glenn didn't ask Sally or (I, **me**) to his party.

5.   Dad and (him, **he**) often fish in that lake.

6.   The coach sat near Bob and (she, **her**) on the bleachers.

7.   Mrs. Winters and (her, **she**) often put puzzles together.

8.   A box of colored chalk was given to Jody and (**us**, we).

9.   Last week, his mother and (**he**, him) shopped for shoes.

10.   The librarian and (us, **we**) searched for a good fiction book.

11.   During the storm in the afternoon, the children and (**they**, them) rushed inside.

12.   The gift from Spencer's brother and (we, **us**) needs to be wrapped.

Directions: Circle the correct pronoun.

Remember: Place your finger or fingers over the first part of the compound. Then, reread the sentence and choose the correct pronoun.

1. Pat and (me, I) decided to sell cookies during the summer.

2. Come with Jarred and (me, I).

3. The policeman and (they, them) talked for an hour.

4. Glenn didn't ask Sally or (I, me) to his party.

5. Dad and (him, he) often fish in that lake.

6. The coach sat near Bob and (she, her) on the bleachers.

7. Mrs. Winters and (her, she) often put puzzles together.

8. A box of colored chalk was given to Jody and (us, we).

9. Last week, his mother and (he, him) shopped for shoes.

10. The librarian and (us, we) searched for a good fiction book.

11. During the storm in the afternoon, the children and (they, them) rushed inside.

12. The gift from Spencer's brother and (we, us) needs to be wrapped.

Directions: Circle the correct pronoun.

Remember: **Place your finger or fingers over the first part of the compound. Then, reread the sentence and choose the correct pronoun.**

1.   An invitation for Mandy and (she, **her**) came in the mail.

2.   Zek and (me, **I**) want to watch television.

3.   Have you asked your mother and (she, **her**) to help you?

4.   His pet turtle stayed by Ronnie and (**him**, he).

5.   Tomorrow, the principal and (**they**, them) will meet.

6.   Water from the puddle splashed Grandma and (**us**, we).

7.   Some of the girls and (him, **he**) are doing a skit.

8.   At the end of the day, several adults and (**we**, us) gathered to play baseball.

9.   Either Donna or (**she**, her) must have taken the letter to mail.

10.   May Justin and (me, **I**) put the chairs away?

11.   Please don't leave without Bo and (I, **me**).

12.   Uncle Stan saw Jeff and (she, **her**) at the hardware store.

Name_____ **PRONOUNS**
                                       Compounds
Date_____

Directions: Circle the correct pronoun.

**Remember: Place your finger or fingers over the first part of the
             compound. Then, reread the sentence and choose the
             correct pronoun.**

1. An invitation for Mandy and (she, her) came in the mail.

2. Zek and (me, I) want to watch television.

3. Have you asked your mother and (she, her) to help you?

4. His pet turtle stayed by Ronnie and (him, he).

5. Tomorrow, the principal and (they, them) will meet.

6. Water from the puddle splashed Grandma and (us, we).

7. Some of the girls and (him, he) are doing a skit.

8. At the end of the day, several adults and (we, us) gathered to play baseball.

9. Either Donna or (she, her) must have taken the letter to mail.

10. May Justin and (me, I) put the chairs away?

11. Please don't leave without Bo and (I, me).

12. Uncle Stan saw Jeff and (she, her) at the hardware store.

➪ <u>Before having students do this page,</u> instruct them to use the "finger trick."

➪ <u>When students read the answers,</u> instruct them to read the sentence twice. First, read it without the compound part. Then, read the sentence as it appears.

Directions: Circle the correct pronoun.

Remember: **Place your finger or fingers over the first part of the compound. Then, reread the sentence and choose the correct pronoun.**

1. You may go with Jenny and (I, **me**).

2. In the summer, his brother and (him, **he**) fished nearly every day.

3. Would you like to go with Rocky and (we, **us**)?

4. Miss Tarn and (them, **they**) walked to an art museum.

5. Did you see Pastor Kern and (they, **them**) at the picnic?

6. Allison and (us, **we**) make model airplanes.

7. The artist painted a portrait of her grandmother and (she, **her**).

8. A small child tapped Jerry and (**him**, he) on the legs with a tiny twig.

9. You and (**I**, me) must bring cola to the party.

10. During the camping trip, Amy and (**she**, her) waded in a stream.

11. Did Mary and (**he**, him) leave for the fair?

12. His jokes make Jalyn and (**me**, I) laugh.

13. Ben, Ralph, and (me, **I**) played basketball after school.

14. The card for his brother and (he, **him**) was from their aunt.

Directions: Circle the correct pronoun.

Remember: Place your finger or fingers over the first part of the compound.   Then, reread the sentence and choose the correct pronoun.

1.   You may go with Jenny and (I, me).

2.   In the summer, his brother and (him, he) fished nearly every day.

3.   Would you like to go with Rocky and (we, us)?

4.   Miss Tarn and (them, they) walked to an art museum.

5.   Did you see Pastor Kern and (they, them) at the picnic?

6.   Allison and (us, we) make model airplanes.

7.   The artist painted a portrait of her grandmother and (she, her).

8.   A small child tapped Jerry and (him, he) on the legs with a tiny twig.

9.   You and (I, me) must bring cola to the party.

10.   During the camping trip, Amy and (she, her) waded in a stream.

11.   Did Mary and (he, him) leave for the fair?

12.   His jokes make Jalyn and (me, I) laugh.

13.   Ben, Ralph, and (me, I) played basketball after school.

14.   The card for his brother and (he, him) was from their aunt.

Possessive Pronouns

Possessive pronouns include:

my	mine
his	
her	hers
your	yours
its	
our	ours
their	theirs

<u>*My*, *his*, *her*, *your*, *its*, *our*, and *their* will come before a noun (or pronoun).</u>

Your *dog* is cute.

<u>*Mine*, *hers*, *yours*, *ours*, and *theirs* will occur after a noun.</u>

These *books* are **mine**.

A possessive pronoun does two things:

A. **A possessive pronoun takes the place of a noun.**

B. **A possessive pronoun shows ownership.**

Examples: a watch belonging to Kathy

Kathy's watch

her watch

toys belonging to the children

children's toys

their toys

🍓🍓🍓🍓🍓A possessive pronoun does **not** have an apostrophe (').🍓🍓🍓🍓🍓

A.   Directions: Write a possessive pronoun on the line.

Example: A bird landed by me; _____its_____ head was blue.

1.   The little boy is three years old; ____**his**____ hair is blonde.

2.   Some children are playing tag; __**their/my**__ mother is watching them.

3.   I like to watch television; _____**my**_____ favorite shows are basketball games.

4.   My friends and I like to read; _____**our**_____ town library is just down the street.

5.   Patricia is flying to Utah; this is ____**her**____ first trip by airplane.

B.   Directions: Write the possessive pronoun and the word it modifies (goes over to)
               on the line.

Example: Where is our photo album?   _____our album_____

1.   Their dad is a waiter.   ____**Their   dad**_____

2.   Your shoe is untied.   ____**Your   shoe**_____

3.   Does her sister sew?   ____**her   sister**_____

4.   We like our neighbors.   ____**our   neighbors**_____

5.   My uncle lives near a lake.   ____**My   uncle**_____

6.   The cub went with its mother. ____**its   mother**_____

7.   Dee has a cut on her arm.   ____**her   arm**_____

Name_____   **PRONOUNS**
                                          Possessives
Date_____

A.   Directions: Write a possessive pronoun on the line.

        Example: A bird landed by me; _____its_____ head was blue.

1.   The little boy is three years old; _____ hair is blonde.

2.   Some children are playing tag; _____ mother is watching them.

3.   I like to watch television; _____ favorite shows are basketball games.

4.   My friends and I like to read; _____ town library is just down the street.

5.   Patricia is flying to Utah; this is _____ first trip by airplane.

B.   Directions: Write the possessive pronoun and the word it modifies (goes over to)
                    on the line.

        Example: Where is our photo album?   _____our album_____

1.   Their dad is a waiter.   _____

2.   Your shoe is untied.   _____

3.   Does her sister sew?   _____

4.   We like our neighbors.   _____

5.   My uncle lives near a lake.   _____

6.   The cub went with its mother. _____

7.   Dee has a cut on her arm.   _____

381

PAGE 383 = WORKBOOK PAGE 160
PAGE 388 = WORKBOOK PAGE 163
PAGE 389 = WORKBOOK PAGE 164

Possessive Pronouns

Antecedents:

To have an antecedent, you must have a possessive pronoun.

Jill washed **her** car.

If you chose not to use a possessive pronoun, you would have to use the noun again:

Jill washed **Jill's** new car.

The possessive pronoun *her* refers back to Jill. **Jill is called the antecedent**.

Definition: An antecedent is the noun or pronoun to which the possessive pronoun refers.

Example: The men talked about their new job.

a. *Their* is a possessive pronoun.
b. *Men* is the noun to which *their* refers back in the sentence.

The *men* talked about the *men's* new job.

c. *Men* is the antecedent of *their*.

Note: **An antecedent will not be a word in a prepositional phrase.**
The lamb with black ears followed its mother.
The lamb ~~with black ears~~ followed its mother.
antecedent for *its* = lamb

Antecedents agree in gender.   If you use *her* in a sentence, the antecedent will be female.
Incorrect: Joan wants a doll for *his* daughter.
Correct: Joan wants a doll for *her* daughter.

Antecedents agree in number.   If you use *her* in a sentence, the antecedent will be singular.
Incorrect: Joan wants a doll for *their* daughter.
Correct: Joan wants a doll for *her* daughter.

383

A. Directions: Write a possessive pronoun that agrees in number and gender with the boldfaced antecedent.

Example: **Julie** must take ___her___ film to be developed.

1. **Mark** asked to bring ___his___ dog along on the picnic.

2. The **girls** watched ___their___ brother swim a relay.

3. **You** must wait ___your___ turn.

4. My **family** and **I** are excited about ___our___ grandparents' visit.

B. Directions: Write the antecedent for the boldfaced possessive pronoun.

Example: _____Carl_____ Carl wants **his** change.

1. ___balloon___ A balloon has lost **its** string.

2. ___Mrs. Parker___ Mrs. Parker sits on **her** porch every evening.

3. ___robins___ Those robins built **their** nest early in the spring.

4. ___passenger___ A passenger picked up **her** purse and left the bus.

5. ___Dad/I___ Dad and I cleaned **our** entire house.

6. ___You___ You may bring **your** own towels to camp.

7. ___Peter___ Peter must drive **his** car to work.

8. ___Paul/Barry/Christy___ Paul, Barry, and Christy sailed on **their** boat.

384

A.   Directions: Write a possessive pronoun that agrees in number and gender with
the boldfaced antecedent.

Example: **Julie** must take ____her____ film to be developed.

1.   **Mark** asked to bring _____ dog along on the picnic.

2.   The **girls** watched _____ brother swim a relay.

3.   **You** must wait _____ turn.

4.   My **family** and **I** are excited about _____ grandparents' visit.

B.   Directions: Write the antecedent for the boldfaced possessive pronoun.

Example: _____Carl_____   Carl wants **his** change.

1.   _____   A balloon has lost **its** string.

2.   _____   Mrs. Parker sits on **her** porch every evening.

3.   _____   Those robins built **their** nest early in the spring.

4.   _____   A passenger picked up **her** purse and left the bus.

5.   _____   Dad and I cleaned **our** entire house.

6.   _____   You may bring **your** own towels to camp.

7.   _____   Peter must drive **his** car to work.

8.   _____   Paul, Barry, and Christy sailed on **their** boat.

Name_____

Date_____

PRONOUNS
Its, It's
Your, You're
Their, There, They're

Directions: Circle the correct word.

1. The cat swished (**its**, it's) tail.

2. (**They're**, Their) making cookies.

3. Tell me if (its, **it's**) true.

4. (They're, **Their**) brother is in college.

5. (**Its**, It's) foot was caught in a trap.

6. (You're, **Your**) cap is covered with dirt.

7. I wonder if (they're, **their**) roof is leaking.

8. Are you sure that (its, **it's**) raining?

9. We hope (**they're**, their) feeling better.

10. (You're, **Your**) dinner is ready.

11. I know that (**you're**, your) upset.

12. One of the pigeons hurt (**its**, it's) wing.

13. I hope that (**you're**, your) chosen for the play.

14. Was (they're, **their**) luggage lost?

386

PRONOUNS
Its, It's
Your, You're
Their, There, They're

Directions: Circle the correct word.

1. The cat swished (its, it's) tail.

2. (They're, Their) making cookies.

3. Tell me if (its, it's) true.

4. (They're, Their) brother is in college.

5. (Its, It's) foot was caught in a trap.

6. (You're, Your) cap is covered with dirt.

7. I wonder if (they're, their) roof is leaking.

8. Are you sure that (its, it's) raining?

9. We hope (they're, their) feeling better.

10. (You're, Your) dinner is ready.

11. I know that (you're, your) upset.

12. One of the pigeons hurt (its, it's) wing.

13. I hope that (you're, your) chosen for the play.

14. Was (they're, their) luggage lost?

Interrogative Pronouns

An Interrogative pronoun asks a question.

Interrogative pronouns include **who**, **whom**, **whose**, **which**, **and what**.

Examples:　**Who** is coming with me?
For **whom** did you buy that?
Whose is that?
Which is right?
What did you do last night?

LEARNING WHEN TO USE WHO AND WHOM:

1. *Who* is a nominative pronoun. *Who* will serve as subject of a sentence.

    Who is your teacher?   (subject)

2. *Whom* is an objective pronoun. *Whom* will serve as an object of a sentence.

    a. Object of a preposition:

        Incorrect:　Who did you give that **to**?

Do not end a sentence with *to, for, with* or *at*!

        Correct:　**To** whom did you give that?

Use <u>whom</u> after *to, for, with* or *at*!

        Correct:　<u>For whom</u> is that gift?
        <u>From whom</u> is that note?
        <u>With whom</u> will you stay?
        <u>At whom</u> was the dodge ball thrown?

b. Direct object:

A direct object receives the action of a verb. Use *whom* as a direct object in a sentence that asks a question.

The ball hit **whom** on the foot?

🍓🍓🍓🍓🍓🍓🍓🍓🍓🍓🍓🍓🍓🍓🍓🍓🍓🍓🍓🍓🍓🍓🍓🍓🍓🍓🍓🍓🍓

What, **which**, and **whose** are pronouns when they stand alone. However, they serve as adjectives when they modify (go over to) a noun (or pronoun) in a sentence.

Examples:

What are you reading?	(pronoun)
What book are you reading? __what book__	(adjective)
Which do you like best?	(pronoun)
Which cake do you like best? __which cake__	(adjective)
Whose is this?	(pronoun)
Whose pencil is this? __whose pencil__	(adjective)

🍓When you see <u>what</u>, <u>which</u>, or <u>whose</u>, always check to see if it modifies or goes over to another word in the sentence.

Example: **Which *answer*** was correct?   (adjective)

If <u>what</u>, <u>which</u>, or <u>whose</u> stands alone, it serves as a pronoun.

Example: **Which** was chosen?   (pronoun)

We do not know to what the word ***which*** refers.

A. Directions: Write *who* or *whom* in the space provided.

Remember: **Who** is used as the subject of the sentence.
Whom is used after prepositions (such as <u>to</u>, <u>for</u>, <u>with</u>, and <u>from</u>).

1. To ___**whom**_____ did you send that package?

2. ____**Who**_____ is your favorite singer?

3. You received a letter from ___**whom**_____?

4. After the game, ____**who**_____ wants to walk home with me?

5. With ___**whom**_____ are you going to the zoo?

B. Directions: Write an appropriate interrogative pronoun.

Remember: Interrogative pronouns include **what**, **which**, **who**, **whose**, and **whom**.

1. ____**What**_____ do you want to do?

2. For ____**whom**_____ did he ask?

3. ____**Whose/What**___ are these?

4. During the summer, ____**who**_____ is his babysitter?

5. ____**Which**_____ pair of pants did Charlie buy?

6. ____**Who**_____ is your best friend?

390

Name_____

Date_____

A. Directions: Write *who* or *whom* in the space provided.

Remember: **Who** is used as the subject of the sentence.
Whom is used after prepositions (such as <u>to</u>, <u>for</u>, <u>with</u>, and <u>from</u>).

1. To _____ did you send that package?

2. _____ is your favorite singer?

3. You received a letter from _____?

4. After the game, _____ wants to walk home with me?

5. With _____ are you going to the zoo?

B. Directions: Write an appropriate interrogative pronoun.

Remember: Interrogative pronouns include **what**, **which**, **who**, **whose**, and **whom**.

1. _____ do you want to do?

2. For _____ did he ask?

3. _____ are these?

4. During the summer, _____ is his babysitter?

5. _____ pair of pants did Charlie buy?

6. _____ is your best friend?

391

A. Directions: Write *who* or *whom* in the space provided.

Remember: **Who** is used as the subject of the sentence.
Whom is used after prepositions (such as <u>to</u>, <u>for</u>, <u>with</u>, and <u>from</u>).

1. To _____**whom**_____ are you talking?

2. From _____**whom**_____ have you received a gift?

3. With _____**whom**_____ are you leaving?

4. Today, _____**who**_____ would like to be first?

B. Directions: Write <u>P</u> if the boldfaced word serves as a pronoun.
Write <u>A</u> if the boldfaced word serves as an adjective. Then, write the
noun the boldfaced word modifies (goes over to).

   Example: __P__ **Which** do you want?   _____

              __A__ **Which** cereal do you want?   ____Which cereal____

1. __P__   **What** did he give you?   _____

2. __A__   **What** answer did he give you?   ____What answer_____

3. __P__   **Which** do you want?   _____

4. __A__   **Which** piece of toast do you want?   ____Which piece_____

5. __P__   **Whose** is this?   _____

6. __A__   **Whose** car is in the driveway?   ____Whose car_____

392

Name_____   **PRONOUNS**
                                                Interrogative
Date_____

A. Directions: Write *who* or *whom* in the space provided.

Remember: **Who** is used as the subject of the sentence.
                Whom is used after prepositions (such as <u>to</u>, <u>for</u>, <u>with</u>, and <u>from</u>).

1. To _____ are you talking?

2. From _____ have you received a gift?

3. With _____ are you leaving?

4. Today, _____ would like to be first?

B. Directions: Write <u>P</u> if the boldfaced word serves as a pronoun.
                Write <u>A</u> if the boldfaced word serves as an adjective. Then, write the
                noun the boldfaced word modifies (goes over to).

    Example: __P__ **Which** do you want? _____

              __A__ **Which** cereal do you want? ____which cereal_____

1. _____ **What** did he give you? _____

2. _____ **What** answer did he give you? _____

3. _____ **Which** do you want? _____

4. _____ **Which** piece of toast do you want? _____

5. _____ **Whose** is this? _____

6. _____ **Whose** car is in the driveway? _____

A. **Nominative Pronouns (used as subject of a sentence):**

Directions: Replace the boldfaced noun or nouns with a nominative pronoun.

1. My **dad** laughs often. _____**He**_____ is very funny.

2. Jacob's **sister** is ten years old. _____**She**_____ attends my church.

3. Our **family** loves winter. _____**We**_____ like to ski.

4. For their vacation, **Misty** and **Sam** went to Kentucky. _____**They**_____ went to

Mammoth Cave.

5. **Answers will vary.** likes to ___**Answers will vary**_____.
      (your name)   (something you like to do)

_____**I**_____ like it because ____**Answers will vary.**_____.

6. A **bird** flew onto a branch of a maple tree. _____**It**_____ had a twig in its beak.

B. **Objective Pronouns:**

Directions: Replace the boldfaced noun with an objective pronoun.

1. Ask **Mary** to help you. Ask ____**her**____ to help you.

2. The mayor talked to the **people**. The mayor talked to ____**them**____.

3. Please take **Answers will vary.** with you. Please take ____**me**____ with
    you.   (your name)

4. A clown pointed at a huge yellow **balloon** and laughed. A clown pointed at
    _____**it**_____ and laughed.

5. The aunt handed the baby **boy** to his mother. The aunt handed ____**him**____
    to his mother.

Name_____   **Pronoun Review**

Date_____

A. **Nominative Pronouns (used as subject of a sentence):**

    Directions: Replace the boldfaced noun or nouns with a nominative pronoun.

1. My **dad** laughs often. _____ is very funny.

2. Jacob's **sister** is ten years old. _____ attends my church.

3. Our **family** loves winter. _____ like to ski.

4. For their vacation, **Misty** and **Sam** went to Kentucky. _____ went to

   Mammoth Cave.

5. _____ likes to _____.
      (your name)   **(something you like to do)**

   _____ like it because _____.

6. A **bird** flew onto a branch of a maple tree. _____ had a twig in its beak.

B. **Objective Pronouns:**

    Directions: Replace the boldfaced noun with an objective pronoun.

1. Ask **Mary** to help you. Ask _____ to help you.

2. The mayor talked to the **people**. The mayor talked to _____.

3. Please take _____ with you. Please take _____ with
   you.   **(your name)**

4. A clown pointed at a huge yellow **balloon** and laughed. A clown pointed at
   _____ and laughed.

5. The aunt handed the baby **boy** to his mother. The aunt handed _____
   to his mother.   395

WORKBOOK PAGE 168
Date_____

C. **Nominative and Objective Pronouns:**

Directions: Circle the correct pronoun.

1. A child helped (**us**, we) in the garden.

2. Yesterday, (**I**, Me) fixed my bicycle.

3. On Tuesdays, (**he**, him) helps at a hospital.

4. A nurse spoke with (**them**, they) about the patient.

5. That dog follows (he, **him**) everywhere.

6. (Us, **We**) might be going on a hike.

7. Mary grabbed her papers and scattered (they, **them**) on the table.

8. A small boy kicked (she, **her**) under the table.

9. Our mother scolded (**us**, we) for standing on a ladder.

D. **Compound Pronouns:**

Directions: Circle the correct pronoun.

1. Please take Bonnie and (we, **us**) with you.

2. May Mike and (**I**, me) use your ball?

3. The cat just sat and stared at Jean and (**him**, he).

4. Autumn leaves fell on their teacher and (they, **them**).

5. Mr. King called my father and (I, **me**) yesterday.

396

C. **Nominative and Objective Pronouns:**

   Directions: Circle the correct pronoun.

1. A child helped (us, we) in the garden.

2. Yesterday, (I, Me) fixed my bicycle.

3. On Tuesdays, (he, him) helps at a hospital.

4. A nurse spoke with (them, they) about the patient.

5. That dog follows (he, him) everywhere.

6. (Us, We) might be going on a hike.

7. Mary grabbed her papers and scattered (they, them) on the table.

8. A small boy kicked (she, her) under the table.

9. Our mother scolded (us, we) for standing on a ladder.

D. **Compound Pronouns:**

   Directions: Circle the correct pronoun.

1. Please take Bonnie and (we, us) with you.

2. May Mike and (I, me) use your ball?

3. The cat just sat and stared at Jean and (him, he).

4. Autumn leaves fell on their teacher and (they, them).

5. Mr. King called my father and (I, me) yesterday.

E. Possessive Pronouns

Directions: Write the possessive pronoun and the word it modifies (goes over to) on the line.

1. Her hair is red.   _____**Her hair**_____

2. Is your brother fifteen?   _____**your brother**_____

3. Some boys left their snacks on the floor.   _____**their snacks**_____

4. Where is my red striped shirt?   _____**my shirt**_____

5. Our relatives live in Maryland.   _____**Our relatives**_____

6. Mindy and Mort went with their friends to a zoo.   _____**their friends**____

F. Antecedents:

Directions: Write the antecedent for the boldfaced pronoun on the line.

1. _____**Jamie**_____   Jamie showed **her** bandage to the class.

2. _____**boy**_____   The boy chose **his** own bedspread.

3. _____**dogs**_____   Several dogs jump on **their** hind legs.

4. _____**coyote**_____   A coyote hunted **its** food.

5. _____**One**_____   One ~~of their girls~~ shows **her** pigs at the fair.

6. _____**Meg/she**_____   Meg and she want **their** posters on the wall.

E. **Possessive Pronouns**

  Directions: Write the possessive pronoun and the word it modifies (goes over
              to) on the line.

1. Her hair is red. _____

2. Is your brother fifteen? _____

3. Some boys left their snacks on the floor. _____

4. Where is my red striped shirt? _____

5. Our relatives live in Maryland. _____

6. Mindy and Mort went with their friends to a zoo. _____

F. **Antecedents:**

  Directions: Write the antecedent for the boldfaced pronoun on the line.

1. _____ Jamie showed **her** bandage to the class.

2. _____ The boy chose **his** own bedspread.

3. _____ Several dogs jump on **their** hind legs.

4. _____ A coyote hunted **its** food.

5. _____ One of their girls shows **her** pigs at the fair.

6. _____ Meg and she want **their** posters on the wall.

G.   **Interrogative Pronouns:**

Directions: Circle the correct pronoun.

1.   (**Who**, Whom) is the author of <u>Heidi</u>?

2.   With (who, **whom**) did you go to the baseball game?

3.   After your trip to Canada, to (who, **whom**) did you show your slides?

H.   **Objective Pronouns:**

Directions: Write <u>P</u> if the boldfaced word serves as a pronoun.
Write <u>A</u> if the boldfaced word serves as an adjective. Then, write
the noun the boldfaced word modifies (goes over to).

Example: __A__   **What** reward was offered?   _____what reward_____

__P__   **What** is your name?   _____

1.   __A__   **Which** door was open?   _____**Which door**_____

2.   __P__   **What** did you decide?   _____

3.   __A__   **Whose** key is on the floor?   _____**Whose key**_____

4.   __A__   In **what** events did he enter?   _____**what events**_____

5.   __P__   **Whose** is this?   _____

6.   __P__   "**Which** do you prefer?" asked the clerk.   _____

G. **Interrogative Pronouns:**

Directions: Circle the correct pronoun.

1. (Who, Whom) is the author of <u>Heidi</u>?

2. With (who, whom) did you go to the baseball game?

3. After your trip to Canada, to (who, whom) did you show your slides?

H. **Objective Pronouns:**

Directions: Write <u>P</u> if the boldfaced word serves as a pronoun.
Write <u>A</u> if the boldfaced word serves as an adjective. Then, write
the noun the boldfaced word modifies (goes over to).

Example: __A__ **What** reward was offered?   _____what reward_____

__P__   **What** is your name? _____

1. _____   **Which** door was open? _____

2. _____   **What** did you decide? _____

3. _____   **Whose** key is on the floor? _____

4. _____   In **what** events did he enter? _____

5. _____   **Whose** is this? _____

6. _____   "**Which** do you prefer?" asked the clerk. _____

Name_____

Date_____

Directions: Circle the correct pronoun.

1. My friend and (me, **I**) like to roller skate.

2. The shirt purchased for (he, **him**) was too small.

3. Are Joy and (**I**, me) allowed to come, too?

4. The leader and (**they**, them) attended a meeting.

5. Yesterday, Scott and (us, **we**) read three short stories.

6. From (**whom**, who) did you receive birthday cards?

7. Ashley saw (they, **them**) at the beach.

8. Several waitresses counted (her, **their**) tips.

9. Each of the ladies drove (**her**, their) own car.

10. The report about frogs was written by (she, **her**).

11. (**Who**, Whom) won that race?

12. Please stand between Jim and (I, **me**).

13. Help (**us**, we) to do this job, please.

14. The pebble hit (he, **him**) on the leg.

15. Herb, Janice, and (**she**, her) entered the contest.

PRONOUNS
Test

Directions: Circle the correct pronoun.

1.   My friend and (me, I) like to roller skate.

2.   The shirt purchased for (he, him) was too small.

3.   Are Joy and (I, me) allowed to come, too?

4.   The leader and (they, them) attended a meeting.

5.   Yesterday, Scott and (us, we) read three short stories.

6.   From (whom, who) did you receive birthday cards?

7.   Ashley saw (they, them) at the beach.

8.   Several waitresses counted (her, their) tips.

9.   Each of the ladies drove (her, their) own car.

10.   The report about frogs was written by (she, her).

11.   (Who, Whom) won that race?

12.   Please stand between Jim and (I, me).

13.   Help (us, we) to do this job, please.

14.   The pebble hit (he, him) on the leg.

15.   Herb, Janice, and (she, her) entered the contest.

TO THE TEACHER:

The cumulative review for the pronoun unit is located on the following pages. This section is **very long** and should be spaced over many days. If you find lack of understanding in some concepts, you will want to review that concept before giving the cumulative exam.

The cumulative exam at the end of the pronoun unit is also lengthy. You will probably want to space the testing over several days.

Use the cumulative test to determine concepts that need to be retaught. Reteaching for understanding is a good idea.

Don't forget that the assessment test is located at the beginning of this text. You will want to copy it and use it as a posttest at some point after all concepts have been taught. See the note on page *IV* for suggestions in comparing the pretest and the postest.

A. **Object of the Preposition:**

Directions: Cross out any prepositional phrases. Label the object of the preposition - <u>O.P.</u> *Object of the preposition is boldfaced.*

1. A man waited ~~on the street~~ **corner**.

2. The sandwich ~~for~~ **lunch** is ~~in this~~ **bag**.

🍓🍓🍓🍓🍓🍓🍓🍓🍓🍓🍓🍓🍓🍓🍓🍓🍓🍓🍓🍓🍓🍓🍓🍓🍓🍓🍓🍓

B. **Prepositions:**

Directions: Cross out any prepositional phrases. Underline the subject once and the verb/verb phrase twice. Label any direct object - <u>D.O.</u>

                            D.O.
1. ~~After dinner~~, <u>Grandpa</u> <u>takes</u> a short walk.

                    D.O.
2. The <u>librarian</u> <u>read</u> a poem ~~about a knight~~.

                 D.O.
3. <u>Gail</u> <u>brushes</u> her teeth ~~at bedtime~~.

🍓🍓🍓🍓🍓🍓🍓🍓🍓🍓🍓🍓🍓🍓🍓🍓🍓🍓🍓🍓🍓🍓🍓🍓🍓🍓🍓🍓

C. **Compound Subject:**

Directions: Cross out any prepositional phrases. Underline the subject once and the verb/verb phrase twice.

Remember: Compound means more than one.

1. His <u>sister</u> and <u>brother</u> <u>belong</u> ~~to a basketball team~~.

2. Three <u>letters</u> and a <u>magazine</u> <u>were thrown</u> ~~into the trash~~.

🍓🍓🍓🍓🍓🍓🍓🍓🍓🍓🍓🍓🍓🍓🍓🍓🍓🍓🍓🍓🍓🍓🍓🍓🍓🍓🍓🍓

D. **Imperative Sentences:**

Directions: Cross out any prepositional phrases. Underline the subject once and the verb/verb phrase twice.

<u>(You)</u>
1. Please <u>stand</u> ~~for the pledge~~.

<u>(You)</u>
2. <u>Sit</u> ~~by the fire~~.

<u>(You)</u>
3. <u>Print</u> your name here.

A. **Object of the Preposition:**

Directions: Cross out any prepositional phrases. Label the object of the preposition - O.P.

1. A man waited on the street corner.

2. The sandwich for lunch is in this bag.

🍓🍓🍓🍓🍓🍓🍓🍓🍓🍓🍓🍓🍓🍓🍓🍓🍓🍓🍓🍓🍓🍓🍓🍓🍓🍓🍓🍓🍓🍓🍓🍓🍓🍓

B. **Prepositions:**

Directions: Cross out any prepositional phrases. Underline the subject once and the verb/verb phrase twice. Label any direct object - D.O.

1. After dinner, Grandpa takes a short walk.

2. The librarian read a poem about a knight.

3. Gail brushes her teeth at bedtime.

🍓🍓🍓🍓🍓🍓🍓🍓🍓🍓🍓🍓🍓🍓🍓🍓🍓🍓🍓🍓🍓🍓🍓🍓🍓🍓🍓🍓🍓🍓🍓🍓🍓🍓

C. **Compound Subject:**

Directions: Cross out any prepositional phrases. Underline the subject once and the verb/verb phrase twice.

Remember: **Compound means more than one.**

1. His sister and brother belong to a basketball team.

2. Three letters and a magazine were thrown into the trash.

🍓🍓🍓🍓🍓🍓🍓🍓🍓🍓🍓🍓🍓🍓🍓🍓🍓🍓🍓🍓🍓🍓🍓🍓🍓🍓🍓🍓🍓🍓🍓🍓🍓🍓

D. **Imperative Sentences:**

Directions: Cross out any prepositional phrases. Underline the subject once and the verb/verb phrase twice.

1. Please stand for the pledge.

2. Sit by the fire.

3. Print your name here.

E. **Compound Objects of the Preposition:**

Directions: Cross out any prepositional phrases. Underline the subject once and the verb/verb phrase twice.

1. I went ~~to Texas with my cousins and uncle~~.

2. Snow often falls ~~in October or November~~.

F. **Compound Verbs:**

Directions: Cross out any prepositional phrases. Underline the subject once and the verb/verb phrase twice.

1. A toddler lifted her toy and threw it.

2. George rides his bike and delivers newspapers.

G. **Infinitives:**

Directions: Cross out any prepositional phrases. Underline the subject once and the verb twice. Place an infinitive in parenthesis ( ).

1. The gerbil likes (to run) ~~in his cage~~.

2. Mr. Harper needs (to go) ~~to the bank~~.

H. **Contractions:**

Directions: Write the contraction in the space provided.

1. we are - _____we're_____

2. who is - _____who's_____

3. are not - _____aren't_____

4. will not - _____won't_____

5. you are - _____you're_____

6. I am - _____I'm_____

7. cannot - _____can't_____

8. he is - _____he's_____

408

E. **Compound Objects of the Preposition:**

> Directions: Cross out any prepositional phrases. Underline the subject once and the verb/verb phrase twice.

1. I went to Texas with my cousins and uncle.

2. Snow often falls in October or November.

F. **Compound Verbs:**

> Directions: Cross out any prepositional phrases. Underline the subject once and the verb/verb phrase twice.

1. A toddler lifted her toy and threw it.

2. George rides his bike and delivers newspapers.

G. **Infinitives:**

> Directions: Cross out any prepositional phrases. Underline the subject once and the verb twice. Place an infinitive in parenthesis (   ).

1. The gerbil likes to run in his cage.

2. Mr. Harper needs to go to the bank.

H. **Contractions:**

> Directions: Write the contraction in the space provided.

1. we are - _____

2. who is - _____

3. are not - _____

4. will not - _____

5. you are - _____

6. I am - _____

7. cannot - _____

8. he is - _____

I. **Action Verb?:**

Directions: Write <u>Yes</u> if the boldfaced verb shows action; write <u>No</u> if the boldfaced verb does not show action.

1. __Yes__ His cat **drank** milk.   3. __No__ The bell **sounds** loud.

2. __No__ The child **grew** tired.   4. __Yes__ A lady **planted** roses.

🍓🍓🍓🍓🍓🍓🍓🍓🍓🍓🍓🍓🍓🍓🍓🍓🍓🍓🍓🍓🍓🍓🍓🍓🍓🍓

J. **Regular or Irregular:**

Directions: Write <u>RV</u> if the verb is regular. Write <u>IV</u> if the verb is irregular.

Remember: Regular verbs add <u>ed</u> to the past and past participle.

1. __RV__ to count   3. __IV__ to teach   5. __IV__ to sit

2. __IV__ to fall   4. __RV__ to stir   6. __IV__ to rise

🍓🍓🍓🍓🍓🍓🍓🍓🍓🍓🍓🍓🍓🍓🍓🍓🍓🍓🍓🍓🍓🍓🍓🍓🍓🍓

K. **Tenses:**

Directions: Cross out any prepositional phrases. Underline the subject once and the verb/verb phrase twice. Write the tense on the line.

Remember: The tenses that we have learned are **present**, **past**, and **future**.

1. _____present_____   <u>Donna</u> <u>writes</u> letters daily.

2. _____past_____   <u>Donna</u> <u>wrote</u> a letter ~~to her aunt~~.

3. _____future_____   <u>Donna</u> <u>will write</u> a letter ~~to Bo~~ tomorrow.

🍓🍓🍓🍓🍓🍓🍓🍓🍓🍓🍓🍓🍓🍓🍓🍓🍓🍓🍓🍓🍓🍓🍓🍓🍓🍓

L. **Subject-Verb Agreement:**

Directions: Circle the verb that agrees with the subject.

1. He (spend, **spends**) most of his time alone.

2. Each ~~of the men~~ (eat, **eats**) his lunch at noon.

3. <u>Diane</u> and <u>Dirk</u> (**jog**, jogs) three miles every day.

410

I. Action Verb?:

Directions: Write <u>Yes</u> if the boldfaced verb shows action; write <u>No</u> if the boldfaced verb does not show action.

1. _____ His cat **drank** milk.   3. _____ The bell **sounds** loud.

2. _____ The child **grew** tired.   4. _____ A lady **planted** roses.

J. Regular or Irregular:

Directions: Write <u>RV</u> if the verb is regular. Write <u>IV</u> if the verb is irregular.

Remember: Regular verbs add <u>ed</u> to the past and past participle.

1. _____ to count   3. _____ to teach   5. _____ to sit

2. _____ to fall   4. _____ to stir   6. _____ to rise

K. Tenses:

Directions: Cross out any prepositional phrases. Underline the subject once and the verb/verb phrase twice. Write the tense on the line.

Remember: The tenses that we have learned are **present**, **past**, and **future**.

1. _____   Donna writes letters daily.

2. _____   Donna wrote a letter to her aunt.

3. _____   Donna will write a letter to Bo tomorrow.

L. Subject-Verb Agreement:

Directions: Circle the verb that agrees with the subject.

1. He (spend, spends) most of his time alone.

2. Each of the men (eat, eats) his lunch at noon.

3. Diane and Dirk (jog, jogs) three miles every day.

411

M. **Irregular Verbs:**

Directions: Circle the correct verb.

1. Has Mr. Lind (came, **come**) yet?

2. Janice must have (flew, **flown**) to Denver early today.

3. Their coach should have (gave, **given**) the pitcher a new ball.

4. We have (lain, **laid**) two clean towels in the bathroom.

N. **Concrete and Abstract Nouns:**

Directions: Write C if the noun is concrete; write A if the noun is abstract.

1.	_C_	lemon	3.	_A_	honesty	5.	_C_	fog
2.	_C_	coin	4.	_C_	flag	6.	_A_	laughter

O. **Common and Proper Nouns:**

Directions: Write CN if the noun is common; write PN if the noun is proper.

1.	_PN_	AMERICA	3.	_CN_	FRIEND	5.	_CN_	LAKE
2.	_CN_	HORSE	4.	_PN_	FRANCE	6.	_PN_	DAVE

P. **Noun Identification:** *Nouns are boldfaced; determiners are underlined.*

Directions: Underline any nouns in each sentence.

Remember: You may wish to circle determiners to help you find most nouns.

1. Two **pies** and a jello **dessert** were served at our **picnic**.

2. That **bicycle** with small **wheels** and an enormous **seat** is unusual.

3. Many **deer** stood in the **meadow** by their **home**.

412

Name_____

Date_____

M. **Irregular Verbs:**

  Directions: Circle the correct verb.

1. Has Mr. Lind (came, come) yet?

2. Janice must have (flew, flown) to Denver early today.

3. Their coach should have (gave, given) the pitcher a new ball.

4. We have (lain, laid) two clean towels in the bathroom.

🍓🍓🍓🍓🍓🍓🍓🍓🍓🍓🍓🍓🍓🍓🍓🍓🍓🍓🍓🍓🍓🍓🍓🍓🍓🍓🍓🍓🍓

N. **Concrete and Abstract Nouns:**

  Directions: Write <u>C</u> if the noun is concrete; write <u>A</u> if the noun is abstract.

1. _____ lemon   3. _____ honesty   5. _____ fog

2. _____ coin   4. _____ flag   6. _____ laughter

🍓🍓🍓🍓🍓🍓🍓🍓🍓🍓🍓🍓🍓🍓🍓🍓🍓🍓🍓🍓🍓🍓🍓🍓🍓🍓🍓🍓🍓

O. **Common and Proper Nouns:**

  Directions: Write <u>CN</u> if the noun is common; write <u>PN</u> if the noun is proper.

1. _____ AMERICA   3. _____ FRIEND   5. _____ LAKE

2. _____ HORSE   4. _____ FRANCE   6. _____ DAVE

🍓🍓🍓🍓🍓🍓🍓🍓🍓🍓🍓🍓🍓🍓🍓🍓🍓🍓🍓🍓🍓🍓🍓🍓🍓🍓🍓🍓🍓

P. **Noun Identification:**

  Directions: Underline any nouns in each sentence.

  Remember: You may wish to circle determiners to help you find most nouns.

1. Two pies and a jello dessert were served at our picnic.

2. That bicycle with small wheels and an enormous seat is unusual.

3. Many deer stood in the meadow by their home.

413

Q. **Singular and Plural Nouns:**

   Directions: Write the plural.

1. latch - _____latches_____   5. moose - _____moose_____

2. potato - _____potatoes_____   6. goose - _____geese_____

3. mouse - _____mice_____   7. guess - _____guesses_____

4. tissue - _____tissues_____   8. calf - _____calves_____

🍓🍓🍓🍓🍓🍓🍓🍓🍓🍓🍓🍓🍓🍓🍓🍓🍓🍓🍓🍓🍓🍓🍓🍓🍓🍓

R. **Possessive Nouns:**

   Directions: Write the possessive form.

1. a brush belonging to Nancy

   _____Nancy's brush_____

2. a hospital room shared by two patients

   _____patients' hospital room_____

3. friends of my uncle

   _____my uncle's friends_____

🍓🍓🍓🍓🍓🍓🍓🍓🍓🍓🍓🍓🍓🍓🍓🍓🍓🍓🍓🍓🍓🍓🍓🍓🍓🍓

S. **Sentence Types:**

   Directions: Write the sentence type in the space provided.
   Remember: The four sentence types are declarative, interrogative, imperative,
   and exclamatory.

1. _____interrogative_____   Why did you do that?

2. _____declarative_____   Peter asked his dad for the car.

3. _____imperative_____   Give this to Ronnie.

4. _____exclamatory_____   Yeah! We are allowed to go!

414

Q. **Singular and Plural Nouns:**
   Directions: Write the plural.

1. latch - _____   5. moose - _____

2. potato - _____   6. goose - _____

3. mouse - _____   7. guess - _____

4. tissue - _____   8. calf - _____

R. **Possessive Nouns:**
   Directions: Write the possessive form.

1. a brush belonging to Nancy

   _____

2. a hospital room shared by two patients

   _____

3. friends of my uncle

   _____

S. **Sentence Types:**
   Directions: Write the sentence type in the space provided.
   Remember: The four sentence types are declarative, interrogative, imperative, and exclamatory.

1. _____   Why did you do that?

2. _____   Peter asked his dad for the car.

3. _____   Give this to Ronnie.

4. _____   Yeah! We are allowed to go!

415

T. **Conjunctions and Interjections:**

   Directions: Label any conjunction - CONJ.; label any interjection - INTJ.

                   CONJ.   **CONJ.**
1. A security guard **and** policeman spoke, **but** no decision was made.
   INTJ.   CONJ.
2. **Wow!** Dad **or** Mom will drive us to an amusement park!

🍓🍓🍓🍓🍓🍓🍓🍓🍓🍓🍓🍓🍓🍓🍓🍓🍓🍓🍓🍓🍓🍓🍓🍓🍓🍓🍓🍓🍓🍓🍓🍓🍓

U. **Adjective?:**

   Directions: Write <u>Yes</u> if the boldfaced word serves as an adjective. Write <u>No</u> if
                the boldfaced word does not serve as an adjective.

1. _____Yes_____   His **flower** garden is blooming.

2. _____No_____   A single **flower** was placed in a crystal vase.

3. _____Yes_____   I liked **that** movie.

4. _____No_____   I love **that**!

🍓🍓🍓🍓🍓🍓🍓🍓🍓🍓🍓🍓🍓🍓🍓🍓🍓🍓🍓🍓🍓🍓🍓🍓🍓🍓🍓🍓🍓🍓🍓🍓🍓

V. **Proper Adjectives:**

   Directions: Capitalize any proper adjectives.

1. An **Arizona** sunset is colorful.

2. He drives his **Ford** truck on the **German** roads.

🍓🍓🍓🍓🍓🍓🍓🍓🍓🍓🍓🍓🍓🍓🍓🍓🍓🍓🍓🍓🍓🍓🍓🍓🍓🍓🍓🍓🍓🍓🍓🍓🍓

W. **Degrees of Adjectives:**

   Directions: Circle the correct answer.

1. This picture of you is (more pretty, **prettier**) than that one.

2. Sandra is the (shorter, **shortest**) triplet.

3. Of the two job offers, I think the first one is (**better**, best).

416

T. **Conjunctions and Interjections:**

Directions: Label any conjunction - CONJ.; label any interjection - INTJ.

1. A security guard and policeman spoke, but no decision was made.

2. Wow! Dad or Mom will drive us to an amusement park!

U. **Adjective?:**

Directions: Write <u>Yes</u> if the boldfaced word serves as an adjective. Write <u>No</u> if the boldfaced word does not serve as an adjective.

1. _____ His **flower** garden is blooming.

2. _____ A single **flower** was placed in a crystal vase.

3. _____ I liked **that** movie.

4. _____ I love **that**!

V. **Proper Adjectives:**

Directions: Capitalize any proper adjective.

1. An arizona sunset is colorful.

2. He drives his ford truck on the german roads.

W. **Degrees of Adjectives:**

Directions: Circle the correct answer.

1. This picture of you is (more pretty, prettier) than that one.

2. Sandra is the (shorter, shortest) triplet.

3. Of the two job offers, I think the first one is (better, best).

417

X. **Adjective Identification:**

   Directions: Circle any adjectives.

Suggestion: First, look for limiting adjectives. Then, reread the sentence searching
              for descriptive adjectives.

1. **His** mother made **three large banana** splits with **whipped** cream.

2. **That red** tricycle with **many colorful** balloons is **a birthday** gift.

3. **An oblong** loaf of **raisin** bread was placed on **our** table.

🍓🍓🍓🍓🍓🍓🍓🍓🍓🍓🍓🍓🍓🍓🍓🍓🍓🍓🍓🍓🍓🍓🍓🍓🍓🍓🍓🍓🍓🍓🍓🍓

Y. **Adverbs:**

   Directions: Write the adverb form of the word.

1. crazy - _____**crazily**_____   3. joyous - _____**joyously**_____

2. sudden - _____**suddenly**_____   4. timid - _____**timidly**_____

🍓🍓🍓🍓🍓🍓🍓🍓🍓🍓🍓🍓🍓🍓🍓🍓🍓🍓🍓🍓🍓🍓🍓🍓🍓🍓🍓🍓🍓🍓🍓🍓

Z. **Adverbs - How?:**

   Directions: Circle any adverbs that tell *how*.

1. He walks **quickly** in cold weather.

2. Several hikers walked **noisily** through the forest.

🍓🍓🍓🍓🍓🍓🍓🍓🍓🍓🍓🍓🍓🍓🍓🍓🍓🍓🍓🍓🍓🍓🍓🍓🍓🍓🍓🍓🍓🍓🍓🍓

AA. **Adverbs - How?:**

   Directions: Write the adverb form for the boldfaced word.

1. Stan is a **slow** driver.   He drives _____**slowly**_____.

2. The lady is a **soft** whistler.   She whistles _____**softly**_____.

3. Mom and Dad are **hard** workers.   They work _____**hard**_____.

418

X. **Adjective Identification:**

Directions: Circle any adjectives.

Suggestion: First, look for limiting adjectives. Then, reread the sentence searching for descriptive adjectives.

1. His mother made three large banana splits with whipped cream.

2. That red tricycle with many colorful balloons is a birthday gift.

3. An oblong loaf of raisin bread was placed on our table.

Y. **Adverbs:**

Directions: Write the adverb form of the word.

1. crazy - _____

2. sudden - _____

3. joyous - _____

4. timid - _____

Z. **Adverbs - How?:**

Directions: Circle any adverbs that tell *how*.

1. He walks quickly in cold weather.

2. Several hikers walked noisily through the forest.

AA. **Adverbs - How?:**

Directions: Write the adverb form for the boldfaced word.

1. Stan is a **slow** driver.   He drives _____.

2. The lady is a **soft** whistler.   She whistles _____.

4. Mom and Dad are **hard** workers.   They work _____.

BB. **Adverbs - Where?:**

   Directions: Circle any adverbs that tell *where*.

1. You may go **anywhere** you like.

2. Our friends invited us **over** for dinner.

🍓🍓🍓🍓🍓🍓🍓🍓🍓🍓🍓🍓🍓🍓🍓🍓🍓🍓🍓🍓🍓🍓🍓🍓🍓🍓🍓🍓🍓🍓🍓🍓🍓🍓

CC. **Adverbs - To What Extent?:**

   Directions: Circle any adverbs that tell *to what extent*.

1. Your project is **very** good.

2. This pancake syrup is **not too** sticky.

🍓🍓🍓🍓🍓🍓🍓🍓🍓🍓🍓🍓🍓🍓🍓🍓🍓🍓🍓🍓🍓🍓🍓🍓🍓🍓🍓🍓🍓🍓🍓🍓🍓🍓

DD. **Degrees of Adverbs:**

   Directions: Circle the correct adverb form.

1. The artist drew this sketch (**more carefully**, most carefully) than that one.

2. Jamie's handwriting is (**clearer**, more clear) than his friend's.

3. Our new puppy is the (more energetic, **most energetic**) one of the four.

4. That jockey rode (harder, **hardest**) during his third race.

🍓🍓🍓🍓🍓🍓🍓🍓🍓🍓🍓🍓🍓🍓🍓🍓🍓🍓🍓🍓🍓🍓🍓🍓🍓🍓🍓🍓🍓🍓🍓🍓🍓🍓

EE. **Double Negatives:**

   Directions: Circle the correct answer.

1. He wouldn't give (**anyone**, no one) a dollar.

2. They aren't inviting (no, **any**) children to their Christmas party.

3. He doesn't want (nothing, **anything**).

420

BB. **Adverbs - Where?:**

Directions: Circle any adverbs that tell **where**.

1. You may go anywhere you like.

2. Our friends invited us over for dinner.

CC. **Adverbs - To What Extent?:**

Directions: Circle any adverbs that tell **to what extent**.

1. Your project is very good.

2. This pancake syrup is not too sticky.

DD. **Degrees of Adverbs:**

Directions: Circle the correct adverb form.

1. The artist drew this sketch (more carefully, most carefully) than that one.

2. Jamie's handwriting is (clearer, more clear) than his friend's.

3. Our new puppy is the (more energetic, most energetic) one of the four.

4. That jockey rode (harder, hardest) during his third race.

EE. **Double Negatives:**

Directions: Circle the correct answer.

1. He wouldn't give (anyone, no one) a dollar.

2. They aren't inviting (no, any) children to their Christmas party.

3. He doesn't want (nothing, anything).

421

A. **Prepositional Phrases:**

   Directions: Cross out any prepositional phrases. Underline the subject once and the verb/verb phrase twice. Label any direct object - D.O.

                                              D.O.

1. His <u>mom</u> and <u>dad</u> <u>like</u> salads ~~with cheese~~.

2. One <u>boy</u> <u>slid</u> ~~down the slide~~ and <u>fell</u> ~~on the sand~~.

3. <u>Do</u> <u>you</u> <u>want</u> (to go) ~~with Gregg and me~~?

4. (<u>You</u>) <u>Sit</u> ~~by the fire for a few minutes~~.

B. **Contractions:**

   Directions: Write the contraction.

1. will not - _____won't_____

2. cannot- _____can't_____

3. where is - _____where's_____

4. were not - _____weren't_____

5. I am - _____I'm_____

6. does not - _____doesn't_____

7. they will - _____they'll_____

8. I would - _____I'd_____

9. should not - _____shouldn't_____

10. we are - _____we're_____

C. **Common and Proper Nouns:**

   Directions: Write <u>CN</u> if the word is a common noun; write <u>PN</u> if the word is a proper noun.

1. _CN_ MUSIC

2. _PN_ FLORIDA

3. _CN_ NAIL

4. _PN_ MEXICO

D. **Concrete and Abstract Nouns:**

   Directions: Write <u>A</u> if the noun is abstract; write <u>C</u> if the noun is concrete.

1. _C_ hair

2. _A_ sadness

3. _A_ friendship

4. _C_ napkin

422

A. **Prepositional Phrases:**

Directions: Cross out any prepositional phrases. Underline the subject once and the verb/verb phrase twice. Label any direct object - <u>D.O.</u>

1. His mom and dad like salads with cheese.

2. One boy slid down the slide and fell on the sand.

3. Do you want to go with Gregg and me?

4. Sit by the fire for a few minutes.

B. **Contractions:**

Directions: Write the contraction.

1. will not - _____

2. cannot- _____

3. where is - _____

4. were not - _____

5. I am - _____

6. does not - _____

7. they will - _____

8. I would - _____

9. should not - _____

10. we are - _____

C. **Common and Proper Nouns:**

Directions: Write <u>CN</u> if the word is a common noun; write <u>PN</u> if the word is a proper noun.

1. _____ MUSIC

2. _____ FLORIDA

3. _____ NAIL

4. _____ MEXICO

D. **Concrete and Abstract Nouns:**

Directions: Write <u>A</u> if the noun is abstract; write <u>C</u> if the noun is concrete.

1. _____ hair

2. _____ sadness

3. _____ friendship

4. _____ napkin

E. Subject-Verb Agreement:

Directions: Circle the verb that agrees with the subject.

1.   Many children (plays, **play**) at the beach.

2.   Each person (**has**, have) to bring his own lunch.

3.   One ~~of the golfers~~ (hit, **hits**) the ball very hard.

4.   Penny and Katie (**shop**, shops) together.

F. Tenses:

Directions: Write the tense (present, past, or future) on the line provided.

1.   _____present_____   This car needs new tires.

2.   _____past_____   Her hat blew into the street.

3.   _____future_____   Nancy will bring her new dog along.

4.   _____present_____   Jackie and Craig live near us.

G. Verb Phrases:

Directions: Underline the entire verb phrase.

1.   David <u>must have realized</u> his mistake.

2.   <u>May</u> I <u>help</u> you?

3.   Janet <u>had been given</u> five dollars.

4.   The pastor <u>should</u> **not** <u>have talked</u> so long.

H. Irregular Verbs:

Directions: Circle the correct verb.

1.   Joy has (came, **come**) to see you.

2.   A truck driver had (took, **taken**) the package.

3.   Jeremy must have (ate, **eaten**) the last piece of pie.

4.   Your book is (**lying**, laying) on the table.

424

E. **Subject-Verb Agreement:**

Directions: Circle the verb that agrees with the subject.

1. Many children (plays, play) at the beach.

2. Each person (has, have) to bring his own lunch.

3. One of the golfers (hit, hits) the ball very hard.

4. Penny and Katie (shop, shops) together.

F. **Tenses:**

Directions: Write the tense (present, past, or future) on the line provided.

1. _____ This car needs new tires.

2. _____ Her hat blew into the street.

3. _____ Nancy will bring her new dog along.

4. _____ Jackie and Craig live near us.

G. **Verb Phrases:**

Directions: Underline the entire verb phrase.

1. David must have realized his mistake.

2. May I help you?

3. Janet had been given five dollars.

4. The pastor should not have talked so long.

H. **Irregular Verbs:**

Directions: Circle the correct verb.

1. Joy has (came, come) to see you.

2. A truck driver had (took, taken) the package.

3. Jeremy must have (ate, eaten) the last piece of pie.

4. Your book is (lying, laying) on the table.

5. Their neighbor has (went, **gone**) to England.

6. He had not (spoke, **spoken**) for several minutes.

7. The children had (swam, **swum**) all afternoon.

8. Susan's baby has (drank, **drunk**) his entire bottle of milk.

9. They must have (rode, **ridden**) their bikes to school.

10. The sun has (rose, **risen**).

11. Their team has (**flown**, flew) to Michigan.

12. The judge was (**sworn**, swore) into office.

13. (**Set**, Sit) the groceries here on the counter.

14. Have you (did, **done**) your homework?

15. Chad must have (took, **taken**) his roller skates with him.

I. **Noun Plurals:**

Directions: Write the plural form.

1. gulf - _____gulfs_____

2. radish - _____radishes_____

3. lane - _____lanes_____

4. worry - _____worries_____

5. tooth - _____teeth_____

6. man - _____men_____

7. window - _____windows_____

8. tomato - _____tomatoes_____

9. bus - _____buses_____

10. monkey - _____monkeys_____

J. **Noun Possessives:**

Directions: Write the possessive form.

1. a wallet belonging to Kathy - _____Kathy's wallet_____

2. birthday cards given to a girl - _____a girl's birthday cards_____

3. a basketball shared by two boys - _____(two) boys' basketball_____

426

5. Their neighbor has (went, gone) to England.

6. He had not (spoke, spoken) for several minutes.

7. The children had (swam, swum) all afternoon.

8. Susan's baby has (drank, drunk) his entire bottle of milk.

9. They must have (rode, ridden) their bikes to school.

10. The sun has (rose, risen).

11. Their team has (flown, flew) to Michigan.

12. The judge was (sworn, swore) into office.

13. (Set, Sit) the groceries here on the counter.

14. Have you (did, done) your homework?

15. Chad must have (took, taken) his roller skates with him.

I. **Noun Plurals:**

   Directions: Write the plural form.

1. gulf - _____

2. radish - _____

3. lane - _____

4. worry - _____

5. tooth - _____

6. man - _____

7. window - _____

8. tomato - _____

9. bus - _____

10. monkey - _____

J. **Noun Possessives:**

   Directions: Write the possessive form.

1. a wallet belonging to Kathy - _____

2. birthday cards given to a girl - _____

3. a basketball shared by two boys - _____

427

K. **Noun Identification:**

   Directions: Circle any nouns.

   Suggestion: *You may want to underline determiners to help you locate nouns.*

1. <u>The</u> lovely **bride** danced <u>several</u> slow **dances** with <u>her</u> smiling **father**.

2. <u>Two</u> brown **rabbits** sat beneath <u>a</u> rose **bush** in <u>Tony's</u> front **yard**.

L. **Sentence types:**

   Directions: Write the sentence type (declarative, interrogative, imperative, or exclamatory) in the space.

1. _____exclamatory_____   Let's eat!

2. _____interrogative_____   Is dinner ready?

3. _____declarative_____   Dinner is ready.

4. _____imperative_____   Wash your hands before dinner.

M. **Adjective Identification:**

   Directions: Circle any adjectives.

   Remember: Find both limiting and descriptive adjectives.

1. **That young** man met **three** friends for **a birthday** lunch.

2. **Many large palm** trees grow by **their old** house near **the** ocean.

N. **Degrees of Adjectives:**

   Directions: Circle the correct adjective form.

1. Jane's sister is (**taller**, tallest) than she.

2. The peach ice cream was (**more delicious**, most delicious) than the vanilla.

3. Of the five houses on our block, ours is (smaller, **smallest**).

4. Mr. Jackson's fifth son is (more athletic, **most athletic**).

O. **Adverb Usage:**

   Directions: Circle the correct word

1. Her friend runs (**slowly**, slow).

428

K. **Noun Identification:**

Directions: Circle any nouns.

Suggestion: *You may want to underline determiners to help you locate nouns.*

1. The lovely bride danced several slow dances with her smiling father.

2. Two brown rabbits sat beneath a rose bush in Tony's front yard.

L. **Sentence types:**

Directions: Write the sentence type (declarative, interrogative, imperative, or exclamatory) in the space.

1. _____ Let's eat!

2. _____ Is dinner ready?

3. _____ Dinner is ready.

4. _____ Wash your hands before dinner.

M. **Adjective Identification:**

Directions: Circle any adjectives.

Remember: Find both limiting and descriptive adjectives.

1. That young man met three friends for a birthday lunch.

2. Many large palm trees grow by their old house near the ocean.

N. **Degrees of Adjectives:**

Directions: Circle the correct adjective form.

1. Jane's sister is (taller, tallest) than she.

2. The peach ice cream was (more delicious, most delicious) than the vanilla.

3. Of the five houses on our block, ours is (smaller, smallest).

4. Mr. Jackson's fifth son is (more athletic, most athletic).

O. **Adverb Usage:**

Directions: Circle the correct word

1. Her friend runs (slowly, slow).

429

2. He didn't get (none, **any**).

3. That man is acting (strange, **strangely**).

4. They don't want (**anything**, nothing).

P. **Degrees of Adverbs:**

Directions: Circle the correct adverb.

1. Henry runs (**faster**, fastest) than Jerry.

2. My grandmother sews (**more neatly**, most neatly) than her sister.

3. She works (harder, **hardest**) of all the employees.

4. The printer did his third job (more quickly, **most quickly**).

Q **Pronoun Usage:**

Directions: Circle the correct pronoun.

1. Chris and (me, **I**) need to sweep.

2. Does (**he**, him) need an answer today?

3. (**We**, Us) would like to speak with you.

4. Can you help (they, **them**)?

5. Put your books beside Terry and (I, **me**).

6. The scout leader and (them, **they**) went camping.

7. A dog followed (we, **us**) around the playground.

8. Carey went with Lance and (**her**, she) on vacation.

R. **Conjunctions and Interjections:**

Directions: Label any conjunction - CONJ.; label any interjection - INTJ.

       CONJ.
1. A doe **and** a fawn walked in the open meadow.

  INTJ.
2. Hurrah! Our team tied for first!

            CONJ.   **CONJ.**
3. You may take a small bag **or** backpack, **but** pack two heavy sweaters.

430

2. He didn't get (none, any).

3. That man is acting (strange, strangely).

4. They don't want (anything, nothing).

P. **Degrees of Adverbs:**

Directions: Circle the correct adverb.

1. Henry runs (faster, fastest) than Jerry.

2. My grandmother sews (more neatly, most neatly) than her sister.

3. She works (harder, hardest) of all the employees.

4. The printer did his third job (more quickly, most quickly).

Q **Pronoun Usage:**

Directions: Circle the correct pronoun.

1. Chris and (me, I) need to sweep.

2. Does (he, him) need an answer today?

3. (We, Us) would like to speak with you.

4. Can you help (they, them)?

5. Put your books beside Terry and (I, me).

6. The scout leader and (them, they) went camping.

7. A dog followed (we, us) around the playground.

8. Carey went with Lance and (her, she) on vacation.

R. **Conjunctions and Interjections:**

Directions: Label any conjunction - CONJ.; label any interjection - INTJ.

1. A doe and a fawn walked in the open meadow.

2. Hurrah! Our team tied for first!

3. You may take a small bag or backpack, but pack two heavy sweaters.

431

TO THE TEACHER:

When you introduce the friendly letter, **model** it on the chalkboard or transparency. Students need to **see** your letter. Then, hand out paper and follow this procedure:

1. If you are using paper with red margin lines, explain the margins. Have students hold the paper to the light so that they can see the red line on the right side. Either have students place a fold on the right hand side or mark it lightly with small dots. I tell my students that this is the "danger zone." We do not flow out into the "danger zone" when we are writing.

2. Explain every component of the heading, line by line. The first time is crucial in that you will need to check each student's first line to ascertain that they do not use abbreviations and that they do not flow over into the "danger zone." Also, check the second line to determine that it is absolutely aligned with the first.

3. Explain that the number of lines skipped between the heading and greeting depends on the length of the letter. We don't want the letter bunched at the top of the page. (For this short letter, I suggest that they skip approximately six lines.)

4. Do the greeting with the students. Be sure that they line the "Dear" right up to the margin. (I'm amazed at the number of students who want to indent it.) Be sure that they understand that the comma goes at the end. (This may sound silly, but I have had a few pupils who want to place the comma after the first word of the greeting.) Be sure to stress proper capitalization and punctuation.

5. Skip a line for the body. To start the topic sentence of their paragraph, I instruct students to count in five spaces. This falls neatly at the space after "dear" which makes a good point of reference. (You may wish to have them indent more letters.) For this paragraph, we briefly discuss the purpose of the letter. (Our purpose is to write a class paragraph that they can keep as a sample in their notebooks.) As I compose and write the paragraph, students copy it.

6. Instruct students to skip one or two lines after the body. (I like two!) Model that the first letter of the closing must be aligned with the heading. Be sure to discuss that only the first word is capitalized and that a comma is used at the end.

7. In teaching the signature, have students align the first letter of their name with the first letter of the closing.

8. Using a ruler, have students draw a perforated colored pencil line in front of the heading down through the body, closing, and signature. This reinforces that the heading, closing, and signature are aligned.

9. With colored pencil, have students write "SAMPLE" diagonally across the letter. Be sure to check each letter. Then, have students place the letter in a notebook.

432 This model serves as a great reference throughout the year.

FRIENDLY LETTERS

Be sure that students are given many opportunities to write friendly letters throughout the school year. *PAGE 435 = WORKBOOK PAGE 179*
PAGE 436 = WORKBOOK PAGE 180
PAGE 437 = WORKBOOK PAGE 181

Students need to follow the writing process:
A. **Discuss the purpose and share ideas** (Brainstorm)
B. **Write a rough draft**
C. **Edit and revise** (I suggest that you do the final editing and revision.)
D. **Write the published (final) copy**

IDEAS FOR FRIENDLY LETTERS

🍓 Write you a letter about ideas from the previous year's class. (This also helps you to obtain new ideas.)

🍓 Write to you a letter about themselves.

🍓 Write a letter to a friend in the class.

🍓 Write a letter to the principal telling about themselves.

🍓 For Thanksgiving, write a letter to someone to thank him. (I usually have my students write to their parents and we actually mail the letter. Parents are delighted!)

🍓 On Valentine's Day, write a letter of appreciation to someone. (I usually have students write to a former teacher who has influenced them greatly. Yes, these are sent!

🍓 In connection with history, students research an inventor. Using our information, we write a two paragraph letter from the inventor to someone he may have known. In paragraph one, we write about the inventor's personal life. In paragraph two, we write about his invention. Students then make the letter appear "antique" so that one may believe they found the letter in someone's attic. (Be careful with the antiquing process. As a safety factor, I advise students **not** to burn edges of letters in order to make them appear old. This particular assignment can be expanded to many historical figures.

🍓 Write a letter to the librarian. Share about an exciting book the student has read.

🍓 Write a letter that the main character of a reading selection may have written to someone.

🍓 When parents send food for class parties, etc., friendly letters can be used to thank them. (I have students who brought food write their parents' names on the board. Then, we divide the class so that only a few students write to one person. The published copy is actually sent to the parents.)

🍓 Obtain pen pals and find other ideas that are applicable to your students.

434

FRIENDLY LETTER

The **heading**, the **greeting**, the **body**, the **closing**, and the **signature** are the parts of a friendly letter. The greeting is also called the salutation.

A three-lined **formal** heading will be used. In **informal** letters, the date is frequently the only item included. However, the formal heading is important to know.

In a formal letter, as in all formal writing, abbreviations are not used. The **exception** to this is the postal code for states. A postal code is capitalized, and no punctuation is used.

Examples: New York = NY   Texas = TX
                 Arizona = AZ   Virginia = VA

FRIENDLY LETTER PARTS:

POST OFFICE BOX
or
HOUSE NUMBER AND STREET NAME

heading   CITY, STATE   ZIP CODE

COMPLETE DATE (not abbreviated)

greeting Dear (Person)   **,**

     The body is also called the message. It is written here. You indent at least five letters. You may skip a line between the greeting and the body.

body   Note that you have margins on each side of the paper.

     Remember that every time you change topics, you begin a new paragraph.

closing   Your friend,
signature   Writer's Name

435

Commas:

1. Be sure to put a **comma** between the city and state in the second line of the heading.

2. Be sure to put a **comma** after the name in the greeting.

3. Be sure to put a **comma after the closing.** However, **no comma** is placed between the state and the zip code.

Capitalization:

1. Capitalize the first word and a name in a greeting. If you can insert a person's name, capitalize it.

   Examples:

   > **D**ear **B**etty,
   > **D**ear **S**on,   (Son is capitalized because you can insert the son's name.)

   > **M**y dear friend,

2. Capitalize only the first word of a closing.

   Examples:

   > **T**ruly yours,
   > **Y**our friend,

3. The first word of each line of the heading begins at the same place. The same is true of the closing and signature. Also, the heading, closing, and signature are lined up. **You should be able to place a ruler in front of the heading, the closing, and the signature and draw a straight line.**

4. A letter should not be crowded at the top of a page. The number of lines skipped between the heading and body will depend on the length of the message. The letter should be spaced down the page.

Envelope:

1. Place a return address in the upper left hand corner. The purpose of the return address is so that the post office can return the letter to you if, for some reason, the letter cannot be delivered.

Look at the sample return address on the envelope below.
- On the first line, write your name.

- On the second line, write your house number and street name. Be sure to capitalize your entire street name. In formal letters, do not use abbreviations.

- On the third line, write your city, state, and zip code. Be sure that you place a comma between the city and state. Do not place a comma between state and zip code. You may use a postal code for the state.

- **Do not include the date.** The post office doesn't need this information.

2. The main address is important. It contains the name and address of the person who will be receiving your letter.

Look at the sample main address on the envelope below.

- On the first line, write the name of the person to whom you are sending the letter.

- On the second line, write that person's house number and street name. Be sure to capitalize the entire street name. Do not use abbreviations.

- On the third line, write the city, state, and zip code of the person who will be receiving your letter. Be sure that you place a comma between the city and state. Do not place a comma between state and zip code. You may use a postal code for the state.

Your First and Last Name
House Number and Street Name   **return address**
City, State   Zip Code

main address   Person to Whom You Are Sending the Letter
                         Person's House Number and Street Name
                         City, State   Zip Code

TO THE TEACHER:

Capitalization is not easy. To help students, I have placed the rules at the top of each page. These are the same on both pages where students practice using the rules given. You will note that I have placed sentences that incorporate **only** the rules on that page. The exception to this is capitalizing the first word of a sentence. After all rules are taught, worksheets incorporating all rules have been provided for practice.

If you are teaching capitalization before the noun unit, it is helpful to explain common and proper nouns. Students need to understand that proper nouns are capitalized.

Be sure to read and discuss each rule in this unit.

I suggest that you write other examples **familiar** to your students. In fact, solicit examples for each rule from your students when possible. I think that it's important for you to **write** these examples on a chalkboard or a transparency. Students gain by seeing the capitalization.

I usually review the previous rules. For example, if I am preparing to teach the page with rules 11-14, I review rules 1-10 and ask for examples. Review is important.

Ten review lessons from *Daily Grams: Guided Review Aiding Mastery Skills - Grade 4* have been provided on pages **562-573**. Number 1 is always a capitalization review. I recommend that you try these; they are an outstanding resource for helping children to understand capitalization.

CAPITALIZATION

WORKBOOK PAGE 182
Date_____

Rule 1: Capitalize a person's name.

Examples: **T**ama

Yuri **T**odman

Rule 2: Capitalize initials.

Examples: **K**oko **A. K**irk

L. B. Shane

Rule 3: Capitalize a title with a name.

Examples: **A**unt **K**esi   **M**rs. **A**nne **W**ing

Governor **C**ontos   **D**r. **L**iston

However, do not capitalize a title if it is a career choice.

Abel wants to become a doctor.
Mrs. Keokuk is running for governor of her state.

Rule 4: Capitalize the pronoun I.

Rule 5: Capitalize the first word of a sentence.

Directions: Write your answer on the line.
Answers will vary.   Representative Answers:
1.   Write the first and last name of your best friend. ____Ben Jones____

2.   Write your name. Include your middle initial. ____Susan A. Jones____

3.   Write the name of a relative such as your aunt, uncle, grandmother, or grandfather

with a name. Example: Aunt Hetty ____Grandma Brown____

4.   Write a complete sentence using the pronoun I. ____Meredith and I like to eat____
____brownies.____

5.   If you would become a senator, what would your name be with the title added?
Write it. ____Senator Williams____

6.   Write your teacher's name. Use Miss, Mrs., or Mr. with it. ____Mr. Woods____
440

Name_____

Date_____

Rule 1: Capitalize a person's name.

        Examples: **Tama**
                        Yuri Todman

Rule 2: Capitalize initials.

        Examples: **Koko A. Kirk**
                        L. B. Shane

Rule 3: Capitalize a title with a name.

        Examples: **Aunt Kesi**   **Mrs. Anne Wing**
                        Governor Contos   **Dr. Liston**

        However, do not capitalize a title if it is a career choice.

             Abel wants to become a doctor.
             Mrs. Keokuk is running for governor of her state.

Rule 4: Capitalize the pronoun I.

Rule 5: Capitalize the first word of a sentence.

Directions: Write your answer on the line.

1. Write the first and last name of your best friend. _____

2. Write your name. Include your middle initial. _____

3. Write the name of a relative such as your aunt, uncle, grandmother, or grandfather

    with a name. Example: Aunt Hetty _____

4. Write a complete sentence using the pronoun I. _____

_____

5. If you would become a senator, what would your name be with the title added?

    Write it. _____

6. Write your teacher's name. Use Miss, Mrs., or Mr. with it. _____

Rule 1: Capitalize a person's name.

Examples: **T**ama
Yuri **T**odman

Rule 2: Capitalize initials.

Examples: **K**oko **A. K**irk
L. B. Shane

Rule 3: Capitalize a title with a name.

Examples: **A**unt **K**esi   **M**rs. **A**nne **W**ing
Governor **C**ontos   **D**r. **L**iston

However, do not capitalize a title if it is a career choice.

Abel wants to become a doctor.
Mrs. **K**eokuk is running for governor of her state.

Rule 4: Capitalize the pronoun I.

Rule 5: Capitalize the first word of a sentence.

Directions: Write the capital letter above any word that needs to be capitalized.
Answers are in boldfaced print.
1. **M**rs. **I**si **P. B**loom is their neighbor.

2. **M**ay **A**ren and **I** have milk?

3. **Y**esterday, **G**overnor **Y**assie visited us.

4. **H**e is **M**ayor **R**oy **H. R**igas.

5. **M**r. and **M**rs. **S. T. H**ull won a trip.

6. **T**ara and **M**iss **B**rock met with **D**r. **H**arden.

7. **R**alph, **T**homas, and **M**osi went to church together.

8. **B**arton **E. P**reston is their state's new governor.
442

Name_____

Date_____

Rule 1: Capitalize a person's name.

Examples: **T**ama
Yuri **T**odman

Rule 2: Capitalize initials.

Examples: **K**oko **A. K**irk
L. B. Shane

Rule 3: Capitalize a title with a name.

Examples: **A**unt **K**esi   **M**rs. **A**nne **W**ing
Governor **C**ontos   **D**r. **L**iston

However, do not capitalize a title if it is a career choice.

Abel wants to become a doctor.
Mrs. Keokuk is running for governor of her state.

Rule 4: Capitalize the pronoun I.

Rule 5: Capitalize the first word of a sentence.

Directions: Write the capital letter above any word that needs to be capitalized.

1. mrs. isi p. bloom is their neighbor.

2. may aren and i have milk?

3. yesterday, governor yassie visited us.

4. he is mayor roy h. rigas.

5. mr. and mrs. s. t. hull won a trip.

6. tara and miss brock met with dr. harden.

7. ralph, thomas, and mosi went to church together.

8. barton e. preston is their state's new governor.

Name_____   CAPITALIZATION

Date_____

Rule 6: Capitalize the name of a school, college, hospital, or library.

Examples: Liberty School   Boswell Hospital

Shippensburg University   Mesquite Library

Do not capitalize a school, college, hospital, or library unless a specific name is given.

We like to go to the library.
He attends a junior high school.

Rule 7: Capitalize the name of a business.

Examples: London Company   Market Cable, Inc.

Kodiac Express   My Favorite Florist

Clover Jewelers   Computers Plus

Lighthouse Bakery   Parrot Food Club

Magic Fashions   Princess Travel

Triumph Hotel   Aster Medical Equipment

Ribbons Drugstore   Palm Department Store

Bell Shopping Center Westwood Mall

Directions: Write your answer on the line. **Answers will vary.**   **Representative Answers:**

1.   _____Sunrise Middle School_____ is near my house.
          (name of school)

2.   I sometimes eat at _____Bluegrass Restaurant_____.
                            (name of restaurant)

3.   A hospital near my home is _____Franklin Hospital_____.

4.   My ___grandmother___ works at ___Frosty Yogurt Shoppe_____.
          (person)   (name of business)

5.   I buy ___baseball cards___ at _____Wallace's Sport Center_____.
          (item)   (name of business)

444

Rule 6: Capitalize the name of a school, college, hospital, or library.

Examples: Liberty School   Boswell Hospital

Shippensburg University   Mesquite Library

Do not capitalize a school, college, hospital, or library unless a specific name is given.

We like to go to the library.
He attends a junior high school.

Rule 7: Capitalize the name of a business.

Examples: London Company   Market Cable, Inc.

Kodiac Express   My Favorite Florist

Clover Jewelers   Computers Plus

Lighthouse Bakery   Parrot Food Club

Magic Fashions   Princess Travel

Triumph Hotel   Aster Medical Equipment

Ribbons Drugstore   Palm Department Store

Bell Shopping Center   Westwood Mall

Directions: Write your answer on the line.

1. _____ is near my house.
(name of school)

2. I sometimes eat at _____.
(name of restaurant)

3. A hospital near my home is _____.

4. My _____ works at _____.
(person)   (name of business)

5. I buy _____ at _____.
(item)   (name of business)

Date_____

Rule 6: Capitalize the name of a school, college, hospital, or library.

    Examples: Liberty School   Boswell Hospital

                       Shippensburg University   Mesquite Library

    Do not capitalize a school, college, hospital, or library unless a specific name is given.

               We like to go to the library.

               He attends a junior high school.

Rule 7: Capitalize the name of a business.

    Examples: London Company   Market Cable, Inc.

                      Kodiac Express   My Favorite Florist

                      Clover Jewelers   Computers Plus

                      Lighthouse Bakery   Parrot Food Club

                      Magic Fashions   Princess Travel

                      Triumph Hotel   Aster Medical Equipment

                      Ribbons Drugstore   Palm Department Store

                      Bell Shopping Center   Westwood Mall

Directions: Write the capital letter above any word that needs to be capitalized.

1. Seth attends Latham College.

2. She lives near a middle school by Dover Library.

3. His brother works at Garret Tile Company.

4. They ate lunch at Royce's Texas Cafe.

5. Grandmother entered York Hospital for tests.

6. Sparkle Cleaning Service just opened for business.

7. Their neighbor owns Cameo Bakery near Baltimore Art School.

Rule 6: Capitalize the name of a school, college, hospital, or library.

Examples: Liberty School   Boswell Hospital

Shippensburg University   Mesquite Library

Do not capitalize a school, college, hospital, or library unless a specific name is given.

We like to go to the library.
He attends a junior high school.

Rule 7: Capitalize the name of a business.

Examples:	London Company	Market Cable, Inc.
	Kodiac Express	My Favorite Florist
	Clover Jewelers	Computers Plus
	Lighthouse Bakery	Parrot Food Club
	Magic Fashions	Princess Travel
	Triumph Hotel	Aster Medical Equipment
	Ribbons Drugstore	Palm Department Store
	Bell Shopping Center	Westwood Mall

Directions: Write the capital letter above any word that needs to be capitalized.

1. seth attends latham college.

2. she lives near a middle school by dover library.

3. his brother works at garret tile company.

4. they ate lunch at royce's texas cafe.

5. grandmother entered york hospital for tests.

6. sparkle cleaning service just opened for business.

7. their neighbor owns cameo bakery near baltimore art school.

Rule 8: Capitalize days and months.

      Examples: Tuesday   January

Rule 9: Capitalize holidays and special days.

      Examples: Thanksgiving   Independence Day

Rule 10: Capitalize the name of special events.

Examples:	Tampa Arts Festival	Arizona Senior Olympics
	Kingsdale Carnival	Phoenix Open Golf Tournament
	Four Seasons Rodeo	Orange Bowl Parade.
	All State Horse Show	Barrett Jackson Auto Auction

Do not capitalize the event unless a specific name is given.

Jan played in a golf tournament.

Directions: Write your answer on the line.

Answers will vary.   Representative answers:

1. My favorite day of the week is _____Sunday_____.

2. Do you like Thanksgiving or Christmas better? ____Christmas____

3. My favorite holiday is ___Memorial Day___.

4. My favorite special day is ____Valentine's Day____.

5. My birthday is in the month of ____April____.

6. Another month that I like is ____July____ because ___our family goes on vacation.___

7. A special event I attended this year was ___Kingsdale Carnival___.

8. A special event I would like to attend is ____Daytona 500____.

448

Name_____

Date_____

Rule 8: Capitalize days and months.

      Examples: Tuesday   January

Rule 9: Capitalize holidays and special days.

      Examples: Thanksgiving   Independence Day

Rule 10: Capitalize the name of special events.

Examples:	Tampa Arts Festival	Arizona Senior Olympics
	Kingsdale Carnival	Phoenix Open Golf Tournament
	Four Seasons Rodeo	Orange Bowl Parade.
	All State Horse Show	Barrett Jackson Auto Auction

Do not capitalize the event unless a specific name is given.

Jan played in a golf tournament.

Directions: Write your answer on the line.

1. My favorite day of the week is _____.

2. Do you like Thanksgiving or Christmas better? _____

3. My favorite holiday is _____.

4. My favorite special day is _____.

5. My birthday is in the month of _____.

6. Another month that I like is _____ because _____

_____

7. A special event I attended this year was _____.

8. A special event I would like to attend is _____.

449

Rule 8: Capitalize days and months.

      Examples: Tuesday   January

Rule 9: Capitalize holidays and special days.

      Examples: Thanksgiving   Independence Day

Rule 10: Capitalize the name of special events.

Examples:	Tampa Arts Festival	Arizona Senior Olympics
	Bonneauville Carnival	Phoenix Open Golf Tournament
	Four Seasons Rodeo	Orange Bowl Parade.
	All State Horse Show	Barrett Jackson Auto Auction

Do not capitalize the event unless a specific name is given.

Jan played in a golf tournament.

🍓🍓🍓🍓🍓🍓🍓🍓🍓🍓🍓🍓🍓🍓🍓🍓🍓🍓🍓🍓🍓🍓🍓🍓🍓🍓🍓🍓🍓🍓🍓🍓🍓🍓

Directions: Write the capital letter above any word that needs to be capitalized.

1. **O**n **A**rbor **D**ay, their class planted trees.

2. **W**e will go to the **S**outh **M**ountain **F**air on **M**onday.

3. **P**ennsylvania **S**ampler **C**rafts **S**how was held last year.

4. **O**n **S**aturday, **O**ctober 18, we attended an art show.

5. **T**he **R**ose **B**owl **P**arade will be held again this year.

6. **L**ast **V**alentine's **D**ay, their parents went to the **L**incoln **S**weethearts' **B**all.

7. **T**he girls met in **M**arch to celebrate **S**t. **P**atrick's **D**ay.

8. **I**s the **F**iesta **B**owl **P**arade held on **N**ew **Y**ear's **D**ay?

9. **E**ach **J**uly, our family enjoys watching cowboys compete at the **P**rescott **R**odeo.

450

Rule 8: Capitalize days and months.

       Examples: Tuesday   January

Rule 9: Capitalize holidays and special days.

       Examples: Thanksgiving   Independence Day

Rule 10: Capitalize the name of special events.

       Examples: **Tampa Arts Festival**   **Arizona Senior Olympics**

                      Bonneauville Carnival   **Phoenix Open Golf Tournament**

                      Four Seasons Rodeo   **Orange Bowl Parade.**

                      All State Horse Show   **Barrett Jackson Auto Auction**

Do not capitalize the event unless a specific name is given.

Jan played in a golf tournament.

Directions: Write the capital letter above any word that needs to be capitalized.

1. on arbor day, their class planted trees.

2. we will go to the south mountain fair on monday.

3. pennsylvania sampler crafts show was held last year.

4. on saturday, october 18, we attended an art show.

5. the rose bowl parade will be held again this year.

6. last valentine's day, their parents went to the lincoln sweethearts' ball.

7. the girls met in march to celebrate st. patrick's day.

8. is the fiesta bowl parade held on new year's day?

9. each july, our family enjoys watching cowboys compete at the prescott rodeo.

Rule 11: Capitalize the name of a language.

        Examples: **E**nglish   **G**erman

Rule 12: Capitalize the first word in a line of poetry.

        Examples: **T**hough I travel to the song of a fife,
                      And you to the sound of the distant drum,
                      We sing the music of friendship.

Rule 13: Capitalize the first word of a greeting and a closing of a letter.

        Examples: **D**ear Tara,   **T**ruly yours,

Rule 14: Capitalize brand names but not the products.

        Examples: **A**ppleland juice   **L**ittle **A**ngel baby shoes

Directions: Write your answer on the line.

Answers will vary.   Representative answers:
You may need to help students with sentences 6 and 7.

1.   The language I speak is _____**English**_____.

2.   I would also like to speak ____**French**____.

3.   If I were to write a letter, the greeting would say: ____**Dear Lela,**____.

4.   The closing of my letter would say: ____**Y**our aunt,____.

5.   My favorite cereal is ____**Lampton**____   ____shredded wheat____.
                      (brand name)   (product)

6.   I have bought _____**Redman shoes**_____ at a ____department____ store.
                (brand name + product)   (type)

7.   Write a line of poetry that rhymes with the one given:

     Through the woods came a big brown bear,

     Looking for food. Campers, beware!

Name_____

Date_____

Rule 11: **Capitalize the name of a language.**
   Examples: **E**nglish **G**erman

Rule 12: **Capitalize the first word in a line of poetry.**
   Examples: **T**hough I travel to the song of a fife,
        And you to the sound of the distant drum,
        We sing the music of friendship.

Rule 13: **Capitalize the first word of a greeting and a closing of a letter.**
   Examples: **D**ear Tara,   **T**ruly yours,

Rule 14: **Capitalize brand names but not the products.**
   Examples: **A**ppleland juice   **L**ittle **A**ngel baby shoes

Directions: Write your answer on the line.

1. The language I speak is _____.

2. I would also like to speak _____.

3. If I were to write a letter, the greeting would say: _____.

4. The closing of my letter would say: _____.

5. My favorite cereal is _____ _____.
          (brand name)   (product)

6. I have bought _____ at a _____ store.
      (brand name + product)   (type)

7. Write a line of poetry that rhymes with the one given:

   Through the woods came a big brown bear,

   _____

Date_____

Rule 11: Capitalize the name of a language.

      Examples: English   German

Rule 12: Capitalize the first word in a line of poetry.

      Examples: Though I travel to the song of a fife,
                And you to the sound of the distant drum,
                We sing the music of friendship.

Rule 13: Capitalize the first word of a greeting and a closing of a letter.

      Examples: Dear Lyndsey,   Truly yours,

Rule 14: Capitalize brand names but not the products.

      Examples: Dole juice   Nike shoes

Directions: Write the capital letter above any word that needs to be capitalized.

1. Is Spanish spoken here?

2. GREETING: Dear Nikko,

3. His dad teaches German at a high school.

4. CLOSING: Your friend,

5. Lisa likes Harbor iced tea.

6. poetry: In the days of olden year,
            Lived Mary Anna Doone,
            So sweet, so pretty, and so fair,
            That all the men did swoon.

7. My dear cousin,
      I'll be visiting you in August.   Let's roast Peppy Time hot dogs over a fire!
                            Love,
                            Toya

Rule 11: Capitalize the name of a language.

      Examples: **E**nglish   **G**erman

Rule 12: Capitalize the first word in a line of poetry.

      Examples: **T**hough I travel to the song of a fife,
                  And you to the sound of the distant drum,
                  We sing the music of friendship.

Rule 13: Capitalize the first word of a greeting and a closing of a letter.

      Examples: **D**ear Lyndsey,   **T**ruly yours,

Rule 14: Capitalize brand names but not the products.

      Examples: **D**ole juice   **N**ike shoes

Directions: Write the capital letter above any word that needs to be capitalized.

1. is spanish spoken here?

2. GREETING: dear nikko,

3. his dad teaches german at a high school.

4. CLOSING: your friend,

5. lisa likes harbor iced tea.

6. poetry: in the days of olden year,
               lived Mary Anna Doone,
               so sweet, so pretty, and so fair,
               that all the men did swoon.

7. my dear cousin,
      I'll be visiting you in August. Let's roast peppy time hot dogs over a fire!
                                    love,
                                    Toya

Rule 15: Capitalize Mother, Dad, and other words if you can insert a person's name.

> Example: **D**id **M**om buy cookies?

> (If *Joan* is the mom's name, you can insert it. Did *Joan* buy cookies? You can replace *Mom* with *Joan*; therefore, *Mom* is capitalized.

> **Do not capitalize Mother, Dad, and other words if <u>my</u>, <u>his</u>, <u>her</u>, <u>your</u>, <u>its</u>, <u>our</u>, or <u>their</u> comes before it.**

> > Example: My mom is very funny.

Rule 16: Capitalize historical events.

> > Example: **A**merican **R**evolution
> >
> > **B**attle of **G**ettysburg

Rule 17: Capitalize the first word of a direct quotation.

> > Example: Bonnie said, "**T**hanks for the gift."

> **Do not capitalize the word following a quotation unless it is a proper noun.**

> > Example: "**Y**ou're welcome," said Megan.

🍓🍓🍓🍓🍓🍓🍓🍓🍓🍓🍓🍓🍓🍓🍓🍓🍓🍓🍓🍓🍓🍓🍓🍓🍓🍓🍓🍓🍓🍓

Directions: Write the capital letter above any word that needs to be capitalized.

1. **H**e asked, "**A**re you coming along?"

2. "**Y**es," replied his friend.

3.   **D**id **G**randma buy chocolate chip cookies?

4. **H**is father watched a show about the **B**attle of **C**oncord.

5. **D**oes **A**unt **T**rina like to read about the **C**ivil **W**ar?

6. **T**he police officer said, "**W**e will help you."

Rule 15: Capitalize Mother, Dad, and other words if you can insert a person's name.

        Example: **D**id **M**om buy cookies?

        (If *Joan* is the mom's name, you can insert it. Did *Joan* buy cookies?
You can replace *Mom* with *Joan*; therefore, *Mom* is capitalized.

        Do not capitalize Mother, Dad, and other words if <u>my</u>, <u>his</u>, <u>her</u>, <u>your</u>, <u>its</u>, <u>our</u>, or <u>their</u> comes before it.

        Example: My mom is very funny.

Rule 16: Capitalize historical events.

        Example: **A**merican **R**evolution

                    Battle of **G**ettysburg

Rule 17: Capitalize the first word of a direct quotation.

        Example: Bonnie said, "Thanks for the gift."

        Do not capitalize the word following a quotation unless it is a proper noun.

        Example: "You're welcome," said Megan.

Directions: Write the capital letter above any word that needs to be capitalized.

1. he asked, "are you coming along?"

2. "yes," replied his friend.

3. did grandma buy chocolate chip cookies?

4. his father watched a show about the battle of concord.

5. does aunt trina like to read about the civil war?

6. the police officer said, "we will help you."

Rule 15: Capitalize Mother, Dad, and other titles if you can insert a person's name.

Example: **D**id **M**om buy cookies?

(If *Jamilla* is the mom's name, you can insert it. Did *Jamilla* buy cookies? You can replace *Mom* with *Jamilla*; therefore, *Mom* is capitalized.

Do not capitalize Mother, Dad, and other titles if <u>my</u>, <u>his</u>, <u>her</u>, <u>your</u>, <u>its</u>, <u>our</u>, or <u>their</u> comes before it.

Example: My mom is very funny.

Rule 16: Capitalize historical events.

Example: **A**merican **R**evolution

Battle of **G**ettysburg

Rule 17: Capitalize the first word of a direct quotation.

Example: Alona said, "**T**hanks for the gift."

Do not capitalize the word following a quotation unless it is a proper noun.

Example: "**Y**ou're welcome," said Tansy.

Directions: Write the capital letter above any word that needs to be capitalized.

1. **H**e enjoys **B**riar **P**atch fruit cocktail.

2. "**W**ill you open the door for me?" asked his mother.

3. **Y**esterday, **D**ad mowed the lawn.

4. **D**oes **U**ncle **L**azlo like **L**ady **F**riday's apple sauce?

5. **W**e studied about the **F**rench and **I**ndian **W**ar.

6. "**L**et's eat soon," said the boy.

Rule 15: **Capitalize Mother, Dad, and other titles if you can insert a person's name.**

Example: **D**id **M**om buy cookies?

(If *Jamilla* is the mom's name, you can insert it. Did *Jamilla* buy cookies? You can replace *Mom* with *Jamilla*; therefore, *Mom* is capitalized.

Do not capitalize Mother, Dad, and other titles if my, his, her, your, its, our, or their comes before it.

Example: My mom is very funny.

Rule 16: **Capitalize historical events.**

Example: **A**merican **R**evolution

Battle of **G**ettysburg

Rule 17: **Capitalize the first word of a direct quotation.**

Example: Alona said, "**T**hanks for the gift."

Do not capitalize the word following a quotation unless it is a proper noun.

Example: "**Y**ou're welcome," said Tansy.

Directions: Write the capital letter above any word that needs to be capitalized.

1. he enjoys briar patch fruit cocktail.

2. "will you open the door for me?" asked his mother.

3. yesterday, dad mowed the lawn.

4. does uncle lazlo like lady friday's apple sauce?

5. we studied about the french and indian war.

6. "let's eat soon," said the boy.

459

Rule 18: **Capitalize the first word, the last word, and all important words of any title. Do not capitalize** *a, an, the, and, but, or, nor,* **or** <u>**prepositions of four or less letters**</u> **unless they are the first or last word of a title. Capitalize all other words.**

Examples: "Jack and Jill"

<u>The Indian in the Cupboard</u>

Capitalize any verb in a title.

"What <u>I</u>s Music?"

Rule 19: **Capitalize the Roman numerals and the letters of the first major topics in an outline. Capitalize the first word in an outline.**

Examples: I.   Summer activities

A. Swimming

B. Arts and crafts

II.   Winter activities

🍓🍓🍓🍓🍓🍓🍓🍓🍓🍓🍓🍓🍓🍓🍓🍓🍓🍓🍓🍓🍓🍓🍓🍓🍓🍓🍓🍓🍓🍓🍓

Directions: Write the capital letter above any word that needs to be capitalized.

1.   CAPITALIZE THESE TITLES:

a.   "Internet"

b.   <u>The Fire Cat</u>

c.   <u>Sheep in a Shed</u>

d.   <u>The Legs of the Moon</u>

e.   <u>The Sky Is Falling</u>

2.   I. Types of flowers

A.   Flowers with bulbs

B.   Flowers with roots

II.   Types of ferns

460

Rule 18: **Capitalize the first word, the last word, and all important words of any title. Do not capitalize** *a, an, the, and, but, or, nor,* **or** <u>**prepositions of four or less letters**</u> **unless they are the first or last word of a title. Capitalize all other words.**

Examples: "Jack and Jill"

<u>The Indian in the Cupboard</u>

Capitalize any verb in a title.

"What <u>I</u>s Music?"

Rule 19: **Capitalize the Roman numerals and the letters of the first major topics in an outline. Capitalize the first word in an outline.**

Examples: I. Summer activities

A. Swimming

B. Arts and crafts

II. Winter activities

🍓🍓🍓🍓🍓🍓🍓🍓🍓🍓🍓🍓🍓🍓🍓🍓🍓🍓🍓🍓🍓🍓🍓🍓🍓🍓🍓🍓🍓🍓🍓🍓

Directions: Write the capital letter above any word that needs to be capitalized.

1. CAPITALIZE THESE TITLES:

    a. "internet"

    b. <u>the fire cat</u>

    c. <u>sheep in a shed</u>

    d. <u>the legs of the moon</u>

    e. <u>the sky is falling</u>

2. i. types of flowers

    a. flowers with bulbs

    b. flowers with roots

  ii. types of ferns

461

Rule 18: **Capitalize the first word, the last word, and all important words of any title. Do not capitalize** *a,* *an,* *the,* *and,* *but,* *or,* *nor,* **or** <u>**prepositions of four or less letters**</u> **unless they are the first or last word of a title. Capitalize all other words.**

   Examples: "Jack and Jill"

   <u>The Indian in the Cupboard</u>

Capitalize any verb in a title.

   "What <u>Is</u> Music?"

Rule 19: **Capitalize the Roman numerals and the letters of the first major topics in an outline. Capitalize the first word in an outline.**

   Examples: I.   Summer activities

   A.   Swimming

   B.   Arts and crafts

   II.   Winter activities

🍓🍓🍓🍓🍓🍓🍓🍓🍓🍓🍓🍓🍓🍓🍓🍓🍓🍓🍓🍓🍓🍓🍓🍓🍓🍓🍓🍓🍓🍓🍓🍓

Directions: Write the capital letter above any word that needs to be capitalized.

1. **I.** Reference books

   A. Atlases

   B. Dictionaries and gazetteers

   II. Fiction books

2. CAPITALIZE THESE TITLES:

   a. <u>Children in History</u>

   b. "Spring Thaw"

   c. <u>The Cabin Faced West</u>

   d. <u>Rosie's Fishing Trip</u>

   e. <u>The Girl Who Could Fly</u>

462

Rule 18: **Capitalize the first word, the last word, and all important words of any title. Do not capitalize** *a,* *an,* *the,* *and,* *but,* *or,* *nor,* **or** <u>**prepositions of four or less letters**</u> **unless they are the first or last word of a title. Capitalize all other words.**

        Examples: "Jack and Jill"

                <u>The Indian in the Cupboard</u>

Capitalize any verb in a title.

        "What <u>I</u>s Music?"

Rule 19: **Capitalize the Roman numerals and the letters of the first major topics in an outline. Capitalize the first word in an outline.**

        Examples: I. **S**ummer activities

                A. **S**wimming

                B. **A**rts and crafts

          II. **W**inter activities

Directions: Write the capital letter above any word that needs to be capitalized.

1. i.   reference books

    a.   atlases

    b.   dictionaries and gazetteers

  ii.   fiction books

2. CAPITALIZE THESE TITLES:

    a.   <u>children in history</u>

    b.   "spring thaw"

    c.   <u>the cabin faced west</u>

    d.   <u>rosie's fishing trip</u>

    e.   <u>the girl who could fly</u>

Rule 20: **Capitalize the name of buildings, canals, tunnels, roads, and bridges.**

Examples: Lincoln Memorial   Turner Turnpike

Erie Canal   Interstate 270

Blueridge Tunnel   London Bridge

Rule 21: **Capitalize the name of a geographic place:**

continent	-	North America	ocean	-	Pacific Ocean
country	-	United States	sea	-	Bering Sea
state	-	Nebraska	gulf	-	Gulf of Mexico
county	-	Franklin County	lake	-	Lake Superior
township	-	Mt. Joy Township	river	-	Missouri River
town or city	-	Dublin	streams	-	Miller Creek
regions	-	East	cave	-	Cove Cave
island	-	Hawaii	canyon	-	Bryce Canyon
mountain(s)	-	Mt. Rushmore	spring	-	Hot Springs
		Rocky Mountains	valley	-	Death Valley
forest	-	Tonto National Forest	dam	-	Hoover Dam
park	-	Sunset Park	desert	-	Gobi Desert

🍓🍓🍓🍓🍓🍓🍓🍓🍓🍓🍓🍓🍓🍓🍓🍓🍓🍓🍓🍓🍓🍓🍓🍓🍓🍓🍓🍓🍓🍓🍓🍓🍓🍓

Directions: Write the capital letter above any word that needs to be capitalized.

1. **S**anta **C**laus is the name of a town in **I**ndiana.

2. **I**s **R**ichardson **H**ighway in **A**laska?

3. **H**artwell **D**am is on the **S**avannah **R**iver.

4. **G**arden **W**all **M**ountain is in **G**lacier **N**ational **P**ark.

5. **T**he **F**iji **I**slands are in the **P**acific **O**cean.

6. **H**ave you been on the **A**rlington **M**emorial **B**ridge?

7. **O**tter **T**ail **C**ounty in **M**innesota has over a thousand lakes.

Name_____

Date_____

Rule 20: **Capitalize the name of buildings, canals, tunnels, roads, and bridges.**

Examples:	Lincoln Memorial	Turner Turnpike
	Erie Canal	Interstate 270
	Blueridge Tunnel	London Bridge

Rule 21: **Capitalize the name of a geographic place:**

continent	-	North America	ocean	-	Pacific Ocean
country	-	United States	sea	-	Bering Sea
state	-	Nebraska	gulf	-	Gulf of Mexico
county	-	Franklin County	lake	-	Lake Superior
township	-	Mt. Joy Township	river	-	Missouri River
town or city	-	Dublin	streams	-	Miller Creek
regions	-	East	cave	-	Cove Cave
island	-	Hawaii	canyon	-	Bryce Canyon
mountain(s)	-	Mt. Rushmore	spring	-	Hot Springs
		Rocky Mountains	valley	-	Death Valley
forest	-	Tonto National Forest	dam	-	Hoover Dam
park	-	Sunset Park	desert	-	Gobi Desert

Directions: Write the capital letter above any word that needs to be capitalized.

1. santa claus is the name of a town in indiana.

2. is richardson highway in alaska?

3. hartwell dam is on the savannah river.

4. garden wall mountain is in glacier national park.

5. the fiji islands are in the pacific ocean.

6. have you been on the arlington memorial bridge?

7. otter tail county in minnesota has over a thousand lakes.

465

Rule 20: Capitalize the name of buildings, canals, tunnels, roads, and bridges.

Examples:	Lincoln Memorial	Turner Turnpike
	Erie Canal	Interstate 270
	Blueridge Tunnel	London Bridge

Rule 21: Capitalize the name of a geographic place:

continent	-	North America	ocean	-	Pacific Ocean
country	-	United States	sea	-	Bering Sea
state	-	Nebraska	gulf	-	Gulf of Mexico
county	-	Franklin County	lake	-	Lake Superior
township	-	Mt. Joy Township	river	-	Missouri River
town or city	-	Dublin	streams	-	Miller Creek
regions	-	East	cave	-	Cove Cave
island	-	Hawaii	canyon	-	Bryce Canyon
mountain(s)	-	Mt. Rushmore	spring	-	Hot Springs
		Rocky Mountains	valley	-	Death Valley
forest	-	Tonto National Forest	dam	-	Hoover Dam
park	-	Sunset Park	desert	-	Gobi Desert

Directions: Write the capital letter above any word that needs to be capitalized.

1. The Colorado Desert is in southern California.

2. They always go to Lake Powell to fish.

3. Is Australia the smallest continent?

4. The Cascade Mountains are in Oregon.

5. Have you ever been in the Lincoln Tunnel?

6. We went to Gallagher Canyon in Cozad, Nebraska.

7. Jewel Cave is in the Black Hills of South Dakota.

466

Rule 20: Capitalize the name of buildings, canals, tunnels, roads, and bridges.

Examples: Lincoln Memorial   Turner Turnpike

Erie Canal   Interstate 270

Blueridge Tunnel   London Bridge

Rule 21: Capitalize the name of a geographic place:

continent	-	North America	ocean	-	Pacific Ocean
country	-	United States	sea	-	Bering Sea
state	-	Nebraska	gulf	-	Gulf of Mexico
county	-	Franklin County	lake	-	Lake Superior
township	-	Mt. Joy Township	river	-	Missouri River
town or city	-	Dublin	streams	-	Miller Creek
regions	-	East	cave	-	Cove Cave
island	-	Hawaii	canyon	-	Bryce Canyon
mountain(s)	-	Mt. Rushmore	spring	-	Hot Springs
		Rocky Mountains	valley	-	Death Valley
forest	-	Tonto National Forest	dam	-	Hoover Dam
park	-	Sunset Park	desert	-	Gobi Desert

Directions: Write the capital letter above any word that needs to be capitalized.

1.   the colorado desert is in southern california.

2.   they always go to lake powell to fish.

3.   is australia the smallest continent?

4.   the cascade mountains are in oregon.

5.   have you ever been in the lincoln tunnel?

6.   we went to gallagher canyon in cozad, nebraska.

7.   jewel cave is in the black hills of south dakota.

Rule 22: Capitalize the name of an organization.

        Examples: **4-H C**lub   International **P**latform **A**ssociation

        Do not capitalize prepositions of four or less letters in names.
        Girl **S**couts <u>of</u> **A**merica

Rule 23: Capitalize the name of a religion, religious documents, and for a supreme being.

        Examples: **G**od
                      Torah
                      Allah

Rule 24: Capitalize the name of a church, synagogue, temple, or other religious dwellings.

🍓🍓🍓🍓🍓🍓🍓🍓🍓🍓🍓🍓🍓🍓🍓🍓🍓🍓🍓🍓🍓🍓🍓🍓🍓🍓🍓🍓🍓🍓🍓🍓🍓

Directions: Write the capital letter above any word that needs to be capitalized.

1.   **I**s **M**icah's temple located in that village?

2.   **J**ina and **B**ianca read a book about the **C**hristian faith.

3.   **P**atterson **L**ion's **C**lub meets in a local church.

4.   **T**he **B**oy **S**couts of **A**merica held a jamboree.

5.   **A** **J**ewish rabbi read from the **T**anak.

6.   **T**he **D**iamond **R**iding **C**lub has just formed.

7.   **S**t. **F**rancis **X**avier **C**hurch is beautiful.

Rule 22: Capitalize the name of an organization.

Examples: **4-H C**lub   **I**nternational **P**latform **A**ssociation

Do not capitalize prepositions of four or less letters in names.
Girl **S**couts <u>of</u> **A**merica

Rule 23: Capitalize the name of a religion, religious documents, and for a supreme being.

Examples: **G**od
Torah
Allah

Rule 24: Capitalize the name of a church, synagogue, temple, or other religious dwellings.

Directions: Write the capital letter above any word that needs to be capitalized.

1.   is micah's temple located in that village?

2.   jina and bianca read a book about the christian faith.

3.   patterson lion's club meets in a local church.

4.   the boy scouts of america held a jamboree.

5.   a jewish rabbi read from the tanak.

6.   the diamond riding club has just formed.

7.   st. francis xavier church is beautiful.

Rule 22: Capitalize the name of an organization.

> Examples: **4-H C**lub   **I**nternational **P**latform **A**ssociation

> **Do not capitalize prepositions of four or less letters in names.**
> **G**irl **S**couts <u>of</u> **A**merica

Rule 23: Capitalize the name of a religion, religious documents, and for a supreme being.

> Examples: **G**od
>
> **T**orah
>
> **A**llah

Rule 24: Capitalize the name of a church, synagogue, temple, or other religious dwellings.

Directions: Write the capital letter above any word that needs to be capitalized.

1.   **O**ur meeting is held at **C**hapel **H**ill **C**hurch.

2.   **M**others **A**gainst **D**runk **D**rivers is an active organization.

3.   **D**eka is doing a report about the **H**indu religion.

4.   **A**n organization called **V**alley **B**ig **B**rothers is popular.

5.   **I**van's brother attends **T**emple **B**eth **E**meth.

6.   **M**y cousin belongs to the **Y**ork **K**iwanis **C**lub.

7.   **T**he first five books of the **O**ld **T**estament are called the **P**entateuch.

Rule 22: Capitalize the name of an organization.

Examples: **4-H C**lub   International **P**latform **A**ssociation

Do not capitalize prepositions of four or less letters in names.
Girl **S**couts <u>of</u> **A**merica

Rule 23: Capitalize the name of a religion, religious documents, and for a supreme being.

Examples: **G**od
Torah
Allah

Rule 24: Capitalize the name of a church, synagogue, temple, or other religious dwellings.

Directions: Write the capital letter above any word that needs to be capitalized.

1. our meeting is held at chapel hill church.

2. mothers against drunk drivers is an active organization.

3. deka is doing a report about the hindu religion.

4. an organization called valley big brothers is popular.

5. ivan's brother attends temple beth emeth.

6. my cousin belongs to the york kiwanis club.

7. the first five books of the old testament are called the pentateuch.

Name_____   **DO NOT CAPITALIZE**

WORKBOOK PAGE 198

Date_____

Rule 1: **Do not capitalize north, south, east, or west when they are used as directions.**

> Example: I live north of the post office.
>
> **Capitalize the direction when it appears with a geographic place.**
>
> Sandy lives at 224 East Elm Street.

Rule 2: **Do not capitalize school subjects unless they state a language, or they are numbered.**

> Examples: I like **E**nglish.
> Is **A**rt I offered?
> My favorite subjects are science and math.

Rule 3: **Do not capitalize seasons of the year.**

> Examples: spring   winter

Rule 4: **Do not capitalize foods, games, musical instruments, animals, diseases, and plants.**

foods:	apple	hamburger
*games:**	checkers	basketball
musical instruments:	guitar	piano
diseases:	chicken pox	flu
plant:	daisy	pine tree
animals:	dog	ape

Capitalize trademarked games such as Monopoly.

🍓🍓🍓🍓🍓🍓🍓🍓🍓🍓🍓🍓🍓🍓🍓🍓🍓🍓🍓🍓🍓🍓🍓🍓🍓🍓🍓🍓🍓🍓

Directions: Write your answer on the line.   **Answers will vary.**   **Representative answers:**

1. My favorite season of the year is _____summer_____.

2. My favorite subject is _____math_____.

3. I live _____west_____ (direction) of the closest store.

4. I like to play ___basketball_____.

5. The animal I like best is the _____kangaroo_____.

6. My favorite food is ___pizza_____.

7. The musical instrument I play (or might like to play) is the _____clarinet_____.

472

Name_____   **DO NOT CAPITALIZE**

Date_____

Rule 1: **Do not capitalize north, south, east, or west when they are used as directions.**

>   Example: I live north of the post office.

>   **Capitalize the direction when it appears with a geographic place.**

>   Sandy lives at 224 East Elm Street.

Rule 2: **Do not capitalize school subjects unless they state a language, or they are numbered.**

>   Examples: I like **E**nglish.
>   Is **A**rt I offered?
>   My favorite subjects are science and math.

Rule 3: **Do not capitalize seasons of the year.**

>   Examples: spring   winter

Rule 4: **Do not capitalize foods, games, musical instruments, animals, diseases, and plants.**

foods:	apple	hamburger
*games:**	checkers	basketball
musical instruments:	guitar	piano
diseases:	chicken pox	flu
plant:	daisy	pine tree
animals:	dog	ape

*Capitalize trademarked games such as Monopoly.

Directions: Write your answer on the line.

1. My favorite season of the year is _____.

2. My favorite subject is _____.

3. I live _____ (direction) of the closest store.

4. I like to play _____.

5. The animal I like best is the _____.

6. My favorite food is _____.

7. The musical instrument I play (or might like to play) is the _____.

Rule 1: **Do not capitalize north, south, east, or west when they are used as directions.**

       Example: I live north of the post office.

       Capitalize the direction when it appears with a geographic place.

       Sandy lives at 224 East Elm Street.

Rule 2: **Do not capitalize school subjects unless they state a language, or they are numbered.**

       Examples: I like **E**nglish.
                       Is **A**rt I offered?
                       My favorite subjects are science and math.

Rule 3: **Do not capitalize seasons of the year.**

       Examples: spring   winter

Rule 4: **Do not capitalize foods, games, musical instruments, animals, diseases, and plants.**

foods:	apple	hamburger
*games:**	checkers	basketball
musical instruments:	guitar	piano
diseases:	chicken pox	flu
plant:	daisy	pine tree
animals:	dog	ape

*Capitalize trademarked games such as Monopoly.

Directions: Write a capital letter above any word that needs to be capitalized.

1. **H**as your father ever had the chicken pox?

2. **T**eresa planted pansies on the west side of her house.

3. **D**uring the winter, many deer roam those woods.

4. **H**er sister started playing the flute last year.

5. **T**heir football team met at the field located at 150 **S**outh Main Street.

6. **J**ordan likes science, spelling, **E**nglish, and history.

Rule 1: **Do not capitalize north, south, east, or west when they are used as directions.**

Example: I live north of the post office.

Capitalize the direction when it appears with a geographic place.

Sandy lives at 224 East Elm Street.

Rule 2: **Do not capitalize school subjects unless they state a language, or they are numbered.**

Examples: I like English.
Is Art I offered?
My favorite subjects are science and math.

Rule 3: **Do not capitalize seasons of the year.**

Examples: spring   winter

Rule 4: **Do not capitalize foods, games, musical instruments, animals, diseases, and plants.**

foods:	apple	hamburger
*games:**	checkers	basketball
musical instruments:	guitar	piano
diseases:	chicken pox	flu
plant:	daisy	pine tree
animals:	dog	ape

*Capitalize trademarked games such as Monopoly.

🍓🍓🍓🍓🍓🍓🍓🍓🍓🍓🍓🍓🍓🍓🍓🍓🍓🍓🍓🍓🍓🍓🍓🍓🍓🍓🍓🍓🍓🍓🍓🍓🍓🍓

Directions: Write a capital letter above any word that needs to be capitalized.

1.   has your father ever had the chicken pox?

2.   teresa planted pansies on the west side of her house.

3.   during the winter, many deer roam those woods.

4.   her sister started playing the flute last year.

5.   their football team met at the field located at 150 south Main Street.

6.   jordan likes science, spelling, english, and history.

Directions: Write the capital letter above any word that needs to be capitalized.

1. The waiter asked, "May I help you?"

2. Lynn attends Harvard University.

3. Have you seen Mother's wallet?

4. A Methodist church is on Park Street.

5. Kyle served Gorton's fish with apple fritters.

6. Is Colonial Motel near Williamsburg, Virginia?

7. Last Wednesday, Mayor Tornbee went sailing.

8. His dad works at Pretzel Plus Shop.

9. Is Banks Island in the Beaufort Sea?

10. The poet, Ralph Waldo Emerson, wrote the following lines about success:

    To appreciate beauty;

    To find the best in others;

11. The American Red Cross began during the Civil War.

12. Does Dr. Brine work at St. Joseph's Hospital?

13. Hannah R. Roger's new address in Chicago is 510 South Ash Lane.

14. He plays the saxophone on a riverboat on the Mississippi River.

15. Does Senator Stone belong to the Payson Women's Club?

Directions: Write the capital letter above any word that needs to be capitalized.

1. the waiter asked, "may i help you?"

2. lynn attends harvard university.

3. have you seen mother's wallet?

4. a methodist church is on park street.

5. kyle served gorton's fish with apple fritters.

6. is colonial motel near williamsburg, virginia?

7. last wednesday, mayor tornbee went sailing.

8. his dad works at pretzel plus shop.

9. is banks island in the beaufort sea?

10. the poet, ralph waldo emerson, wrote the following lines about success:

    to appreciate beauty;

    to find the best in others;

11. the american red cross began during the civil war.

12. does dr. brine work at st. joseph's hospital?

13. hannah r. roger's new address in chicago is 510 south ash lane.

14. he plays the saxophone on a riverboat on the mississippi river.

15. does senator stone belong to the payson women's club?

Name_____   CAPITALIZATION
WORKBOOK PAGE 201   REVIEW
Date_____

Directions: Write the capital letter above any word that needs to be capitalized.

1. Their grandmother owns Apple Tree Fashions.

2.   Dear Sammy,

         Let's go to Michaux State Forest next Saturday.

                    Your cousin,

                    Brad

3. A patient with the flu entered Dr. Fox's office.

4. Cheyenne Frontier Days are held in the state of Wyoming.

5. We crossed a bridge near the Thomas Jefferson Memorial.

6. Did they go to the Gulf of California last spring?

7. The country of Greece joined the North Atlantic Treaty Organization in 1952.

8. Capitalize these titles:

    a. <u>Simply Fun</u>

    b. <u>Wingman on Ice</u>

    c. <u>A Pair of Red Clogs</u>

    d. "Here's a Happy Song"

9. The Battle of Clearwater took place in Idaho.

10. A poem begins, "My candle burns at both ends."

11. Has Mother ever been to Barren Island off Canada?

478

Directions: Write the capital letter above any word that needs to be capitalized.

1. their grandmother owns apple tree fashions.

2. dear sammy,

   let's go to michaux state forest next saturday.

                    your cousin,

                    brad

3. a patient with the flu entered dr. fox's office.

4. cheyenne frontier days are held in the state of wyoming.

5. we crossed a bridge near the thomas jefferson memorial.

6. did they go to the gulf of california last spring?

7. the country of greece joined the north atlantic treaty organization in 1952.

8. Capitalize these titles:

   a. simply fun

   b. wingman on ice

   c. a pair of red clogs

   d. "here's a happy song"

9. the battle of clearwater took place in idaho.

10. a poem begins, "my candle burns at both ends."

11. has mother ever been to barren island off canada?

Directions: Write the capital letter above any word that needs to be capitalized.

1.   Their family attends United Christian Church.

2.   The guide said, "Welcome to our museum."

3.   Egg Harbor is a village on Green Bay.

4.   The Draft Horse and Mule Festival is held in Virginia.

5.   Their sister read <u>The Last Leaf</u> by O. Henry.

6.   My friend and I went to Varsity Barber Shop today.

7.   Kent likes history at Mesa High School.

8.   Dear Mr. Price,

     We will meet with you in Dallas next summer.

                Sincerely yours,
                Captain Briggs

9.   We took Interstate 495 last November.

10.   Several girls played chess at a school on Locust Avenue.

11.   A librarian read <u>Peggy's New Brother</u> at Denton Library.

12.   We celebrate Columbus Day on October 12.

13.   I.   Famous people in history

     A.   Women

     B.   Men

   II.   Famous animals in history

Name_____

Date_____

Directions: Write the capital letter above any word that needs to be capitalized.

1.   their family attends united christian church.

2.   the guide said, "welcome to our museum."

3.   egg harbor is a village on green bay.

4.   the draft horse and mule festival is held in virginia.

5.   their sister read <u>the last leaf</u> by o. henry.

6.   my friend and i went to varsity barber shop today.

7.   kent likes history at mesa high school.

8.   dear mr. price,

   we will meet with you in dallas next summer.

                              sincerely yours,
                              captain briggs

9.   we took interstate 495 last november.

10.   several girls played chess at a school on locust avenue.

11.   a librarian read <u>peggy's new brother</u> at denton library.

12.   we celebrate columbus day on october 12.

13.   i.   famous people in history

        a.   women

        b.   men

     ii.   famous animals in history

Name_____ CAPITALIZATION
                                         Test
Date_____

Directions: Write the capital letter above any word that needs to be capitalized.

1. The Bear Paw Mountains are forty miles from Canada.

2. Did the Westinghouse Company start the first radio station?

3. Our family celebrates Christmas at Grandpa Barton's house.

4. Their teacher read <u>Doll in the Garden.</u>

5. The man asked, "Do you like Kringle's corn flakes?"

6. He attends a Baptist church by Marsh Creek.

7. Dear Miss Rankin,

     Have a great trip to Mission Beach on Friday.

                              Truly yours,
                              Tom Hulse

8. I. Types of art

     A. Pop art

     B. Cowboy art

9. Will Micah attend Hillsdale College in Michigan?

10. Our family had a picnic on Independence Day in July.

11. A poem by J. Ciardi begins, "The morning that the world began."

12. In history, I learned about an organization called the Green Mountain Boys.

13. Did Mother learn French during the summer she learned to play the piano?
482

Name_____   **CAPITALIZATION**
                                          Test
Date_____

Directions: Write the capital letter above any word that needs to be capitalized.

1. the bear paw mountains are forty miles from canada.

2. did the westinghouse company start the first radio station?

3. our family celebrates christmas at grandpa barton's house.

4. their teacher read <u>doll in the garden</u>.

5. the man asked, "do you like kringle's corn flakes?"

6. he attends a baptist church by marsh creek.

7. dear miss rankin,

    have a great trip to mission beach on friday.

                              truly yours,
                              tom hulse

8. i. types of art

    a. pop art

    b. cowboy art

9. will micah attend hillsdale college in michigan?

10. our family had a picnic on independence day in july.

11. a poem by j. ciardi begins, "the morning that the world began."

12. in history, i learned about an organization called the green mountain boys.

13. did mother learn french during the summer she learned to play the piano?

TO THE TEACHER: Please read this page entirely before proceeding.

The punctuation unit can be challenging.   In all cases (except periods) the rules appear at the top of the page. Thus, students can reconfirm their answers by perusing the rules readily available to them. As in capitalization, each concept is taught individually. The final reviews, however, include all concepts.

When teaching a concept, always use examples with which your students are familiar. For example, when teaching the placement of a comma between parts of an address, use the school address. Then, have students practice writing their own address in sentence form. (Check this; many students place a comma after their house address!)

I recommend that you **teach concepts prior to having students read the rules and example(s) provided.**

I recommend that you do the **first lesson orally** with students, discussing why you are adding the particular punctuation. **I do not assign punctuation worksheets for homework.** In fact, I usually do an oral review of the rules on the second day. Then, I ask students to do the second worksheet individually and to **stand** when they have completed it. As other students who are finished stand, I pair them. Their task is to compare answers and discuss if they disagree. Their first point of reference in a disagreement is at the top of their worksheet, the rules. If they still disagree, they discuss it with me. After everyone has paired, we discuss answers orally.

I recommend that you **use a** <u>**Daily Grams: Guided Review Aiding Mastery Skills***</u> **text.** These are designed to **review capitalization, punctuation, and grammar usage throughout the year.** Students do one "ten minute" review per day for 180 days. Hence, rules are no longer being taught and possibly forgotten due to lack of reinforcement. Students tend to master concepts more readily when they use them on an on-going basis. The first ten lessons of *Grade 4* is placed at the end of this text for you to enjoy.

I recommend that you **review concepts occasionally.** This is another place where dry erase (white) boards will prove helpful. For example, if you are reviewing commas, you can say, "Austin, Texas." On their dry erase boards, students write the city and state, inserting the needed comma. This is active learning. Remember; English can be fun!

The following are available:
> *Daily Grams: Guided Review Aiding Mastery Skills* - *Grade 3*
> *Daily Grams: Guided Review Aiding Mastery Skills* - *Grade 4*
> *Daily Grams: Guided Review Aiding Mastery Skills* - *Grade 5*
> *Daily Grams: Guided Review Aiding Mastery Skills* - *Grade 6*
> *Daily Grams: Guided Review Aiding Mastery Skills* - *Grade 7*
> *Daily Grams: Guided Review Aiding Mastery Skills* - *Jr./Sr. High*

484

PUNCTUATION

PUNCTUATION

PERIOD (.):

Rule 1: **Place a period at the end of a declarative sentence.**

I purchased a box of tissues.

Rule 2: **Place a period at the end of an imperative sentence.**

Press this button.

Rule 3: **Place a period after initials.**

Charity K. Pope

Rule 4: **Place a period after an abbreviation for days.**

Sunday - Sun.	Thursday - Thurs., Thur.*
Monday - Mon.	Friday - Fri.
Tuesday - Tues., Tue.*	Saturday - Sat.
Wednesday - Wed.	

*The first abbreviation is preferred.

Rule 5: **Place a period after the abbreviation for months.**

January - Jan.	September - Sept.
February - Feb.	October - Oct.
March - Mar.	November - Nov.
April - Apr.	December - Dec.
August - Aug.	

Note: May, June, and July have no abbreviations.

Rule 6: **Place a period after the abbreviation of titles.**

Mr. - Mister
Mrs. - title used before a married woman's name
Ms. - title that does not show if a woman is married or unmarried
Dr. - Doctor
Sen. - Senator
Gen. - General
Pres. - President

Do not place a period after Miss used as a title: Miss Barnett

Rule 7: **Place a period after the name of places.**

St. - Street	Holly St.
Ave. - Avenue	Victory Ave.
Ln. - Lane	Marker Ln.
Dr. - Drive	Jefferson Dr.
Mt. - Mountain	Mt. Everest
Mts. - Mountains	Rocky Mts.
U.S. - United States	
S. Am. - South America	

Always use a dictionary to check for correct abbreviations.

Use the two letter **postal code** without a period for an abbreviation of states.

MO - Missouri	OH - Ohio
NM - New Mexico	WA - Washington

A postal code list can be found in the back of many dictionaries.

Rule 8: **Place a period after many abbreviations.**

Co. - Company
A. D. - in the year of our Lord
P. M. or p. m. - from noon until midnight

Always use a dictionary to check for correct abbreviations.

If a sentence ends with an abbreviation, do not place an additional period.

Henry VIII of England was born in 1491 A.D.

Do not place a period after metric units: m = meter

Rule 9: **Place a period after the letter(s) and number(s) in an outline.**

I. Foods
   A. Vegetables
   B. Fruits
      1. Cherries
      2. Oranges

II. Drinks

487

Directions: Place a period where needed.

1.   Write the correct abbreviation for each day of the week.

   a.   Monday - _____Mon._____   e.   Thursday - _____Thurs._____

   b.   Wednesday - ___Wed._____   f.   Saturday - _____Sat._____

   c.   Friday - _____Fri._____   g.   Sunday - _____Sun._____

   d.   Tuesday - _____Tues._____

2.   Write the correct abbreviation for each month of the year.

   a.   September - __Sept._____   f.   November - _____Nov._____

   b.   October - ____Oct._____   g.   December - _____Dec._____

   c.   March - _____Mar._____   h.   January - _____Jan._____

   d.   April - _____Apr._____   i.   February - _____Feb._____

   e.   August - _____Aug._____

3.   Write the correct abbreviation for the following:

   a.   Maple Street - _____Maple St._____

   b.   Doctor Prance - _____Dr. Prance_____

   c.   North America - _____N. Am._____

   d.   Captain Troy - _____Capt. Troy_____

   e.   Governor Hamel - _____Gov. Hamel_____

   f.   South Dakota - _____SD or S.D._____

   g.   Ural Mountains - _____Ural Mts._____

Name_____

Date_____

Directions: Place a period where needed.

1.   Write the correct abbreviation for each day of the week.

    a.   Monday - _____   e.   Thursday - _____

    b.   Wednesday - _____   f.   Saturday - _____

    c.   Friday - _____   g.   Sunday - _____

    d.   Tuesday - _____

2.   Write the correct abbreviation for each month of the year.

    a.   September - _____   f.   November - _____

    b.   October - _____   g.   December - _____

    c.   March - _____   h.   January - _____

    d.   April - _____   i.   February - _____

    e.   August - _____

3.   Write the correct abbreviation for the following:

    a.   Maple Street - _____

    b.   Doctor Prance - _____

    c.   North America - _____

    d.   Captain Troy - _____

    e.   Governor Hamel - _____

    f.   South Dakota - _____

    g.   Ural Mountains - _____

A. Directions: Place a period where needed.

1. Dr. Cathy P. Banks is our friend.

2. Her address is 20 N. Stratton St.

3. Give this to Mrs. Pyne, please.

4. She was born Wed., Dec. 27.

5. I. Types of cats

       A. Siamese

       B. Persian

    II. Types of dogs

6. They went to Eur. in Sept.

7. Is Mt. Baldy in Arizona?

B. Directions: Write the abbreviation.

      1. Tuesday - ____Tues._____

      2. Thursday - ____Thurs._____

      3. November - ____Nov._____

      4. January - _____Jan._____

      5. February - _____Feb._____

      6. Company - _____Co._____

      7. Wednesday - __Wed._____

490

Name_____

Date_____

A. Directions: Place a period where needed.

1. Dr Cathy P Banks is our friend

2. Her address is 20 N Stratton St

3. Give this to Mrs Pyne, please

4. She was born Wed , Dec 27

5. I Types of cats

    A Siamese

    B Persian

  II Types of dogs

6. They went to Eur in Sept

7. Is Mt Baldy in Arizona?

B. Directions: Write the abbreviation.

    1. Tuesday - _____

    2. Thursday - _____

    3. November - _____

    4. January - _____

    5. February - _____

    6. Company - _____

    7. Wednesday - _____

Name_____

WORKBOOK PAGE 207

Date_____

Rule 1:   Use an apostrophe in a contraction to show where a letter or letters have been omitted.

wasn't = was not   she's = she is

Rule 2:   Use an apostrophe to show possession (ownership):
   A.   If the word is singular (one), add apostrophe + s.

a man's watch   one girl's tent

Even if the singular noun ends in s, add 's.

Dennis's sister

   B.   If the word is plural (more than one) and ends in s, add an apostrophe after the s.

dogs' owner   girls' coach

   C.   If the word is plural (more than one) and does not end in s, add apostrophe + s.

singular:	child	woman
plural:	children	women
plural possessive:	children's camp	women's team

Directions: Write the possessive.

1. a car belonging to Ernie: _____ Ernie's car _____

2. a dish belonging to three cats: _____ (three) cats' dish _____

3. fields belonging to a farmer: _____ (a) farmer's fields _____

4. the sleeve of a shirt: _____ (a) shirt's sleeve _____

5. the father of several boys: _____ (several) boys' father _____

6. dogs owned by Chris: _____ Chris's dogs _____

7. magazines belonging to her sister: _____ (her) sister's magazines _____

492

Rule 1: **Use an apostrophe in a contraction to show where a letter or letters have been omitted.**

wasn't = was not   she's = she is

Rule 2: **Use an apostrophe to show possession (ownership):**
   A. **If the word is singular (one), add apostrophe + s.**

   a man's watch   one girl's tent

   Even if the singular noun ends in s, add 's.

   Dennis's sister

   B. **If the word is plural (more than one) and ends in s, add an apostrophe after the s.**

   dogs' owner   girls' coach

   C. **If the word is plural (more than one) and does not end in s, add apostrophe + s.**

singular:	child	woman
plural:	children	women
plural possessive:	children's camp	women's team

Directions: Write the possessive.

1. a car belonging to Ernie: _____

2. a dish belonging to three cats: _____

3. fields belonging to a farmer: _____

4. the sleeve of a shirt: _____

5. the father of several boys: _____

6. dogs owned by Chris: _____

7. magazines belonging to her sister: _____

493

Rule 1: **Use an apostrophe in a contraction to show where a letter or letters have been omitted.**

wasn't = was not   she's = she is

Rule 2: **Use an apostrophe to show possession (ownership):**
A.   **If the word is singular (one), add apostrophe + <u>s</u>.**

a man's watch   one girl's tent

Even if the singular noun ends in <u>s</u>, add '<u>s</u>.

Dennis's sister

B.   **If the word is plural (more than one) and ends in <u>s</u>, add an apostrophe after the <u>s</u>.**

dogs' owner   girls' coach

C.   **If the word is plural (more than one) and does not end in <u>s</u>, add apostrophe + <u>s</u>.**

singular:	child	woman
plural:	children	women
plural possessive:	children's camp	women's team

A.   Directions: Write the possessive.

1.   buttons on a remote: _____ (a) remote's buttons _____

2.   a restroom belonging to all men: _____ men's restroom _____

3.   a trail for runners: _____ runners' trail _____

B.   Directions: Insert needed apostrophes.

1.   "Don't forget your umbrella," said Benny's mother.

2.   Her brother's best friend can't go with us.

3.   Where's Cynthia's new coat?

4.   Mary's sister likes to swing at a children's playground.

494

Rule 1: **Use an apostrophe in a contraction to show where a letter or letters have been omitted.**

wasn't = was not   she's = she is

Rule 2: **Use an apostrophe to show possession (ownership):**
   A.   If the word is singular (one), add apostrophe + s.

a man's watch   one girl's tent

   Even if the singular noun ends in s, add 's.

Dennis's sister

   B.   If the word is plural (more than one) and ends in s, add an apostrophe after the s.

dogs' owner   girls' coach

   C.   If the word is plural (more than one) and does not end in s, add apostrophe + s.

singular:	child	woman
plural:	children	women
plural possessive:	children's camp	women's team

A.   Directions: Write the possessive.

1.   buttons on a remote: _____

2.   a restroom belonging to all men: _____

3.   a trail for runners: _____

B.   Directions: Insert needed apostrophes.

1.   "Dont forget your umbrella," said Bennys mother.

2.   Her brothers best friend cant go with us.

3.   Wheres Cynthias new coat?

4.   Marys sister likes to swing at a childrens playground.

Rule 1: **Use a comma to invert a name. Place the last name, a comma, and the first name.**

Lincoln, Abe
⬆

If the middle name or initial is given, place the middle name or initial after the first name.

Swanson, Susan Lee   or   Swanson, Susan L.

Rule 2: **Place a comma after the greeting of a friendly letter.**

Dear Christine,
⬆

Rule 3: **Place a comma after the closing of any letter.**

Love,
Jo ⬆

Rule 4: **Place a comma after three or more items in a series.**
Do not place a comma after the last item in a series.

He handed a dime, two nickels, and a quarter to me.
⬆   ⬆

🍓🍓🍓🍓🍓🍓🍓🍓🍓🍓🍓🍓🍓🍓🍓🍓🍓🍓🍓🍓🍓🍓🍓🍓🍓🍓🍓🍓🍓🍓🍓🍓🍓🍓🍓🍓🍓

A.   Directions: Write answers on the line.
Answers will vary.   Representative answers:
1.   Write your last name and then your first name. _____ Dodds, Jim _____

2.   Write a friend's last name and then the first name. ____ Davis, Karen _____

B.   Directions: Insert needed commas.

1.   Wendy, Brian, and I had fun at the beach.

2.   Dear Mike,

    I'll see you soon!

        Your friend,
        Corrine

3.   We ate chicken, potatoes, and pasta at the picnic.

Rule 1: **Use a comma to invert a name. Place the last name, a comma, and the first name.**

Lincoln, Abe
⬆

If the middle name or initial is given, place the middle name or initial after the first name.

Swanson, Susan Lee   or   Swanson, Susan L.

Rule 2: **Place a comma after the greeting of a friendly letter.**

Dear Christine,
⬆

Rule 3: **Place a comma after the closing of any letter.**

Love,
Jo ⬆

Rule 4: **Place a comma after three or more items in a series.**
Do not place a comma after the last item in a series.

He handed a dime, two nickels, and a quarter to me.
⬆   ⬆

A. Directions: Write answers on the line.

1. Write your last name and then your first name. _____

2. Write a friend's last name and then the first name. _____

B. Directions: Insert needed commas.

1. Wendy Brian and I had fun at the beach.

2. Dear Mike

   I'll see you soon!
      Your friend
      Corrine

3. We ate chicken potatoes and pasta at the picnic.

Rule 5: **Use a comma to separate introductory words.**
Frequently used introductory words are *yes*, *no*, and *well*.

Yes, you are right.

⬆

Rule 6: **Use a comma with a noun of direct address.**

A. If the person is addressed (spoken to) at the beginning of a sentence, place a comma **after** the person's name.

Ron, do you want a banana?

⬆

B. If the person is addressed (spoken to) at the end of a sentence, place a comma **before** the person's name.

Do you want a banana, Ron?

⬆

C. If the person is addressed (spoken to) in the middle of a sentence, place a comma **before** and **after** the person's name.

Do you, Ron, want a banana?

⬆   ⬆

Directions: Insert a comma where needed.

1. Mrs. Ross, have you voted?

2. No, I don't want any more pizza.

3. Would you like a brownie, Jenny?

4. Yes, an ambulance has been called.

5. I know, Gloria, that you're usually on time.

6. Well, I'm finally finished.

7. Yes, Patty, you may begin.

Rule 5: **Use a comma to separate introductory words.**
Frequently used introductory words are *yes*, *no*, and *well*.

Yes, you are right.

⬆

Rule 6: **Use a comma with a noun of direct address.**

A. If the person is addressed (spoken to) at the beginning of a sentence, place a comma **after** the person's name.

Ron, do you want a banana?

⬆

B. If the person is addressed (spoken to) at the end of a sentence, place a comma **before** the person's name.

Do you want a banana, Ron?

⬆

C. If the person is addressed (spoken to) in the middle of a sentence, place a comma **before** and **after** the person's name.

Do you, Ron, want a banana?

⬆ ⬆

Directions: Insert a comma where needed.

1. Mrs. Ross have you voted?

2. No I don't want any more pizza.

3. Would you like a brownie Jenny?

4. Yes an ambulance has been called.

5. I know Gloria that you're usually on time.

6. Well I'm finally finished.

7. Yes Patty you may begin.

Rule 7: **Use a comma to make a sentence clear.**

During the day, games were played.

⬆

Rule 8: **Use a comma to set off interrupters.**
Words and phrases often used as interrupters are: *by the way, therefore, however, in fact,* and *I believe.* Of course, there are others.

This covered bridge, in fact, was built in 1875.

⬆   ⬆

Rule 9: **Use a comma at the end of most direct quotations.**
A direct quotation states exactly what the person says.

"I'll help you," said Lenny.

⬆

If the person who is making the statement is given first, place a comma after the person's name.

Sally said, "My lunch box is missing."

⬆

🍓🍓🍓🍓🍓🍓🍓🍓🍓🍓🍓🍓🍓🍓🍓🍓🍓🍓🍓🍓🍓🍓🍓🍓🍓🍓🍓🍓🍓🍓🍓🍓🍓

Directions: Insert a comma where needed.

1. Your dad, I believe, just left for work.

2. "I'll trade you baseball cards," said Anthony.

3. This ring, in fact, was my grandmother's wedding band.

4. Holly said, "I'm going to the library."

5. That water, however, may not be safe to drink.

6. By the way, has anyone asked you to go tubing?

7. Loni whispered, "Excuse me, please."

Rule 7:   **Use a comma to make a sentence clear.**

During the day, games were played.

⬆

Rule 8:   **Use a comma to set off interrupters.**
Words and phrases often used as interrupters are: *by the way, therefore, however, in fact,* and *I believe.* Of course, there are others.

This covered bridge, in fact, was built in 1875.

⬆   ⬆

Rule 9:   **Use a comma at the end of most direct quotations.**
A direct quotation states exactly what the person says.

"I'll help you," said Lenny.

⬆

If the person who is making the statement is given first, place a comma after the person's name.

Sally said, "My lunch box is missing."

⬆

🍓🍓🍓🍓🍓🍓🍓🍓🍓🍓🍓🍓🍓🍓🍓🍓🍓🍓🍓🍓🍓🍓🍓🍓🍓🍓🍓🍓🍓🍓🍓🍓🍓🍓

Directions: Insert a comma where needed.

1. Your dad I believe just left for work.

2. "I'll trade you baseball cards " said Anthony.

3. This ring in fact was my grandmother's wedding band.

4. Holly said   "I'm going to the library."

5. That water however may not be safe to drink.

6. By the way has anyone asked you to go tubing?

7. Loni whispered   "Excuse me, please."

501

Rule 10: **Place a comma between the day and year in a date.**

> July 4, 1776
> ↑

Place a comma between the name of a day and date.

> Saturday, June 29, 1996

Rule 11: **Place a comma between a town (village, city) and a state.**

> Columbus, Ohio
> ↑

Place a comma between a city and a country.

> London, England
> ↑

In a street address, place a comma after the street and after the city. Do not place a comma between the state and zip code. Do not place a comma between the house number and the street address.

> They live at 2 Ridge Lane, Waynesville, NC 28786.

Do not place a comma after the street when addressing an envelope.

Rule 12: **Use a comma between two or more descriptive adjectives (describing words) *unless one is a color or number*.**

> A tiny, playful kitten romped through the house.
> ↑

> A tiny white kitten romped through the house.   (no comma)

Directions: Insert a comma where needed.

1. She was born on August 3, 1985.

2. Does Joan live in Anaheim, California?

3. That reporter travels to Paris, France.

4. Smooth, round balls were used for a game.

5. His address is 1249 Cedar Drive, Warrenton, Missouri 63383.

6. Beautiful, unusual orchids were delivered on Friday, November 20, 1996.

Rule 10: **Place a comma between the day and year in a date.**

July 4, 1776

↑

Place a comma between the name of a day and date.

Saturday, June 29, 1996

Rule 11: **Place a comma between a town (village, city) and a state.**

Columbus, Ohio

↑

Place a comma between a city and a country.

London, England

↑

In a street address, place a comma after the street and after the city. Do not place a comma between the state and zip code. Do not place a comma between the house number and the street address.

They live at 2 Ridge Lane, Waynesville, NC 28786.

Do not place a comma after the street when addressing an envelope.

Rule 12: **Use a comma between two or more descriptive adjectives (describing words) *unless one is a color or number*.**

A tiny, playful kitten romped through the house.

↑

A tiny white kitten romped through the house.   (no comma)

Directions: Insert a comma where needed.

1. She was born on August 3 1985.

2. Does Joan live in Anaheim California?

3. That reporter travels to Paris France.

4. Smooth round balls were used for a game.

5. His address is 1249 Cedar Drive Warrenton Missouri 63383.

6. Beautiful unusual orchids were delivered on Friday November 20 1996.

503

Rule 1: **Use a colon in writing the time.**

5:30 P. M.

Rule 2: **Use a colon to set off lists.**

Food for picnic:
- hot dogs
- rolls
- marshmallows

The following are needed for first aid class: bandages, gauze, and tape.

Rule 3: **Use a colon after divisions of topics.**

Class Rules:
At Your Seat: Keep your desk cleared.

Push in your chair when leaving.

Directions: Insert a colon where needed.

1.   Items needed for our camping trip:
- tent
- lantern
- ice chests

2.   I have asked the following people to help: Tate, Val, and Pedro.

3.   Playground Rules:

Rules for Slide: Do not go down on your stomach.
Wait until the person in front of you is out of the area.

4.   Lala ordered the following: napkins, a tablecloth, and place mats.

5.   Please bring the following items to the 7:00 art class: brushes, paints, and pads.

Rule 1: Use a colon in writing the time.

5:30 P. M.

Rule 2: Use a colon to set off lists.

Food for picnic:
- hot dogs
- rolls
- marshmallows

The following are needed for first aid class: bandages, gauze, and tape.

Rule 3: Use a colon after divisions of topics.

Class Rules:
At Your Seat: Keep your desk cleared.
Push in your chair when leaving.

Directions: Insert a colon where needed.

1. Items needed for our camping trip
    - tent
    - lantern
    - ice chests

2. I have asked the following people to help Tate, Val, and Pedro.

3. Playground Rules

   Rules for Slide Do not go down on your stomach.
   Wait until the person in front of you is out of the area.

4. Lala ordered the following napkins, a tablecloth, and place mats.

5. Please bring the following items to the 7 00 art class brushes, paints, and pads.

Name_____

WORKBOOK PAGE 214

Date_____

PUNCTUATION
Question Mark
Exclamation Point

Question Mark (?):

    Rule: **Use a question mark at the end of an interrogative sentence.**
        An interrogative sentence asks a question.

                May I take your coat?

Exclamation Point (Mark) (!):

    Rule 1: **Use an exclamation point after an exclamatory sentence.**
           An exclamatory sentence shows strong feeling.

                We're just about finished!

    Rule 2: **Use an exclamation point after a word or phrase that shows strong feeling.** A phrase is a group of words that does not have a subject and verb.

                Yeah!   Hurrah! We're the champions!

A. Directions: Write on the line provided. **Answers will vary.** **Representative answers.**

1. Write a question you might ask someone in your family. _____

      _____Is dinner ready?_____

2. Write a question you might ask a friend. _____

      _____Do you want to play a game?_____

B. Directions: Insert question marks or exclamation points where needed.

1. " We won **!** " Jana exclaimed.

2. Do you know how to polish rocks**?**

3. Yippee**!** I'm going up in a hot air balloon soon!

4. How many grams are in an ounce**?**

Question Mark (?):

Rule: **Use a question mark at the end of an interrogative sentence.** An interrogative sentence asks a question.

May I take your coat**?**

Exclamation Point (Mark) (!):

Rule 1: **Use an exclamation point after an exclamatory sentence.** An exclamatory sentence shows strong feeling.

We're just about finished!

Rule 2: **Use an exclamation point after a word or phrase that shows strong feeling.** A phrase is a group of words that does not have a subject and verb.

Yeah!   Hurrah! We're the champions!

🍓🍓🍓🍓🍓🍓🍓🍓🍓🍓🍓🍓🍓🍓🍓🍓🍓🍓🍓🍓🍓🍓🍓🍓🍓🍓🍓🍓🍓🍓🍓🍓

A. Directions: Write on the line provided.

1. Write a question you might ask someone in your family. _____

_____

2. Write a question you might ask a friend. _____

_____

B. Directions: Insert question marks or exclamation points where needed.

1. " We won " Jana exclaimed.

2. Do you know how to polish rocks

3. Yippee   I'm going up in a hot air balloon soon

4. How many grams are in an ounce

Rule 1: **Use a hyphen between fractions.**

> one-half   two-thirds

Rule 2: **Use a hyphen between two digit word numbers between 21 and 99.**

> twenty-one   fifty-eight

Rule 3: **Use a hyphen between a series of page numbers.**

> I read pages 32-35 in my science book.

Rule 4: **Use a hyphen to combine some closely related words.**

> forget-me-nots (flowers)   five-speed

Rule 5: **Use a hyphen when dividing a word of two or more syllables at the end of a line.** <u>**You must have at least two letters on the first line and three on the following line.**</u>

> _____ bat-
> ter   re-
> maining _____

Directions: Insert hyphens where needed.

1. One-third of the doughnuts had been eaten.

2.   _____ During the summer, our fam-
        ily went to Washington, D. C., our
        nation's capitol. We toured the Jef-
        ferson Memorial which honors one
        of our nation's great men.

3. His uncle has a farm with thirty-five dairy cows.

4. John's happy-go-lucky attitude makes him fun.

5. Kerry read from pages 77-109 to finish her book.

Rule 1: **Use a hyphen between fractions.**

one-half   two-thirds

Rule 2: **Use a hyphen between two digit word numbers between 21 and 99.**

twenty-one   fifty-eight

Rule 3: **Use a hyphen between a series of page numbers.**

I read pages 32-35 in my science book.

Rule 4: **Use a hyphen to combine some closely related words.**

forget-me-nots (flowers)   five-speed

Rule 5: **Use a hyphen when dividing a word of two or more syllables at the end of a line. <u>You must have at least two letters on the first line and three on the following line</u>.**

_____ bat-
ter _____ re-
maining _____

Directions: Insert hyphens where needed.

1.   One third of the doughnuts had been eaten.

2.   _____ During the summer, our fam
ily went to Washington, D. C., our
nation's capitol. We toured the Jef
ferson Memorial which honors one
of our nation's great men.

3.   His uncle has a farm with thirty five dairy cows.

4.   John's happy go lucky attitude makes him fun.

5.   Kerry read from pages 77 109 to finish her book.

Rule 1: **Underline the name of ships, planes, and trains.**

The airplane, <u>Sky Queen</u>, is very fast.

Rule 2: **Underline the title of a book.**

My brother read the book <u>The Egg Tree</u>.

Rule 3: **Underline the title of a magazine.**

The woman was reading a copy of <u>Business Update</u>.

Rule 4: **Underline the title of a newspaper.**

His grandfather enjoys <u>The Western Journal</u>.

Rule 5: **Underline the title of a movie or television show.**

Have you seen the movie, <u>My Fair Lady</u>?
Their family usually watches <u>Kyla's Cooking Show</u> together.

NOTE: **If you are using a computer or a typewriter, a name or title that is usually underlined will be in italics.** *This sentence is in italic print.*

Their family watches *Kyla's Cooking Show* together.

🍓🍓🍓🍓🍓🍓🍓🍓🍓🍓🍓🍓🍓🍓🍓🍓🍓🍓🍓🍓🍓🍓🍓🍓🍓🍓🍓🍓🍓🍓🍓🍓

Directions: Underline where needed.

1.   Have you ever seen a picture of the ship, <u>Lusitania</u>?

2.   His dad read him a children's book entitled <u>Ali's School Bus</u>.

3.   <u>Gone with the Wind</u> is still her favorite movie.

4.   Mother's favorite television show is <u>Jeopardy</u>.

5.   Dad usually reads <u>The Evening Sun</u> (newspaper).

6.   <u>Tom Thumb</u> was the first locomotive (train) in America.

Rule 1: **Underline the name of ships, planes, and trains.**

The airplane, <u>Sky Queen</u>, is very fast.

Rule 2: **Underline the title of a book.**

My brother read the book <u>The Egg Tree</u>.

Rule 3: **Underline the title of a magazine.**

The woman was reading a copy of <u>Business Update</u>.

Rule 4: **Underline the title of a newspaper.**

His grandfather enjoys <u>The Western Journal</u>.

Rule 5: **Underline the title of a movie or television show.**

Have you seen the movie, <u>My Fair Lady</u>?
Their family usually watches <u>Kyla's Cooking Show</u> together.

NOTE: **If you are using a computer or a typewriter, a name or title that is usually underlined will be in italics.** *This sentence is in italic print.*

Their family watches *Kyla's Cooking Show* together.

🍓🍓🍓🍓🍓🍓🍓🍓🍓🍓🍓🍓🍓🍓🍓🍓🍓🍓🍓🍓🍓🍓🍓🍓🍓🍓🍓🍓🍓🍓🍓🍓

Directions: Underline where needed.

1.   Have you ever seen a picture of the ship, Lusitania?

2.   His dad read him a children's book entitled Ali's School Bus.

3.   Gone with the Wind is still her favorite movie.

4.   Mother's favorite television show is Jeopardy.

5.   Dad usually reads The Evening Sun (newspaper).

6.   Tom Thumb was the first locomotive (train) in America.

Rule 1:   Place quotation marks around exactly what a person says.

Mr. Brown said, "I bought a new camera today."
"Where did you buy it?" asked his wife.

A. **In a split quotation, place quotation marks around each part spoken.**

"Do you know," asked Sandra, "if the grocery store closes at ten o'clock?"

B. **In conversation, begin a new paragraph each time a different person speaks.**

Marty asked, "Why are party hats, horns, and streamers lying on the kitchen table?"
"We are having a surprise birthday party for Billy," said **Joyce** with a smile.
"Have you made a cake?" asked **Marty**.

Rule 2:   Place quotation marks around the titles of articles, short stories, short poems, songs, and chapters.

"Working at Home"   (article)
"Abe Lincoln Grows Up"   (short story)
"Do You Fear the Force of the Wind?"   (poem)
"Go Down, Moses"   (song)
"Plants"   (chapter)

Place commas and periods inside quotation marks.   I wrote a poem entitled "Me."

🍓🍓🍓🍓🍓🍓🍓🍓🍓🍓🍓🍓🍓🍓🍓🍓🍓🍓🍓🍓🍓🍓🍓🍓🍓🍓🍓🍓🍓🍓🍓🍓🍓

Directions: Insert needed quotation marks.

1.   Miss Fenton wrote an article entitled "Nuts and Bolts."

2.   "My science project is about magnets," said Krissy.

3.   "See the Trees" is a poem by Carl Sandburg.

4.   Robert asked, "Why is the floor wet?"

5.   Have you read the story, "Trademark," by Jessamyn West?

6.   "I think," said Ed, "that I'd like a snack."

512

Rule 1: **Place quotation marks around exactly what a person says.**

Mr. Brown said, "I bought a new camera today."
"Where did you buy it?" asked his wife.

A. **In a split quotation, place quotation marks around each part spoken.**

"Do you know," asked Sandra, "if the grocery store closes at ten o'clock?"

B. **In conversation, begin a new paragraph each time a different person speaks.**

Marty asked, "Why are party hats, horns, and streamers lying on the kitchen table?"
"We are having a surprise birthday party for Billy," said **Joyce** with a smile.
"Have you made a cake?" asked **Marty**.

Rule 2: **Place quotation marks around the titles of articles, short stories, short poems, songs, and chapters.**

"Working at Home"	(article)
"Abe Lincoln Grows Up"	(short story)
"Do You Fear the Force of the Wind?"	(poem)
"Go Down, Moses"	(song)
"Plants"	(chapter)

Place commas and periods inside quotation marks. I wrote a poem entitled "Me."

Directions: Insert needed quotation marks.

1. Miss Fenton wrote an article entitled Nuts and Bolts.

2. My science project is about magnets, said Krissy.

3. See the Trees is a poem by Carl Sandburg.

4. Robert asked, Why is the floor wet?

5. Have you read the story, Trademark, by Jessamyn West?

6. I think, said Ed, that I'd like a snack.

Directions: Insert needed punctuation.

period (.)　　　　　　　　　　**exclamation point (!)**

apostrophe (')　　　　　　　　**hyphen (-)**

comma (,)　　　　　　　　　　**underlining (_)**

colon (:)　　　　　　　　　　**quotation marks (" ")**

question mark (?)

1. Was Frank's arm broken**?**

2. They need the following drinks: lemonade, punch, and soda.

3. Wow! We're state champions!

4. Nate said,　"The line forms here."

5. He moved to Seattle on Saturday, July 5, 1996.

6. The ladies' bathroom had been closed at 9:00 P. M.

7. Gail**,** do you want a copy of <u>Rising Tide</u> magazine**?**

8. Twenty-eight students rode a bus to Orem, Utah.

9. She read a magazine article entitled "A Choice for Change."

10. Glenda's favorite book is <u>Indian Captive</u>.

11. No**,** you can't eat in the living room.

12. Mr. Freed said,　"I must leave now."

Date_____

Directions: Insert needed punctuation.

period (.)   **exclamation point (!)**
apostrophe (')   **hyphen (-)**
comma (,)   **underlining (_)**
colon (:)   **quotation marks (" ")**
question mark (?)

1.   Was Franks arm broken

2.   They need the following drinks   lemonade punch and soda

3.   Wow   Were state champions

4.   Nate said   The line forms here

5.   He moved to Seattle on Saturday July 5 1996

6.   The ladies bathroom had been closed at 9 00 P M

7.   Gail do you want a copy of Rising Tide magazine

8.   Twenty eight students rode a bus to Orem Utah

9.   She read a magazine article entitled A Choice for Change

10.   Glendas favorite book is Indian Captive

11.   No you cant eat in the living room

12.   Mr Freed said   I must leave now

Directions: Insert needed punctuation.

period (.)   **exclamation point (!)**
apostrophe (')   **hyphen (-)**
comma (,)   **underlining (_)**
colon (:)   **quotation marks (" ")**
question mark (?)

1. Dear Joanna,

    It hasn't rained for several months here in our desert val-

    ley.   However, we believe that you'll like life in Phoenix, Arizona.

                              See you soon,
                              Annette

2. Please give this envelope to Sen. R. Ross.

3. He didn't win the men's golf tournament.

4. Three-fourths of the entrants had won a ribbon.

5. Things for camp:
    - toothbrush
    - toothpaste

6. During the summer, rain fell.

7. Jill has read the poem entitled "The Last of the Books."

8. I. Water forms

    A. Oceans
    B. Gulfs and bays

9. Did Madeline's dad buy that huge, plastic barrel for trash?

PUNCTUATION
Review

Directions: Insert needed punctuation.

period (.)	**exclamation point (!)**
apostrophe (')	**hyphen (-)**
comma (,)	**underlining (_)**
colon (:)	**quotation marks (" ")**
question mark (?)	

1. Dear Joanna

      It hasnt rained for several months here in our desert val

ley   However we believe that youll like life in Phoenix Arizona

      See you soon
      Annette

2. Please give this envelope to Sen R Ross

3. He didnt win the mens golf tournament

4. Three fourths of the entrants had won a ribbon

5. Things for camp
   - toothbrush
   - toothpaste

6. During the summer rain fell

7. Jill has read the poem entitled The Last of the Books

8. I   Water forms
   A   Oceans
   B   Gulfs and bays

9. Did Madelines dad buy that huge plastic barrel for trash

Directions: Insert needed punctuation.

period (.)	**exclamation point (!)**
apostrophe (')	**hyphen (-)**
comma (,)	**underlining (_)**
colon (:)	**quotation marks (" ")**
question mark (?)	

1. Jacy's family reunion will be held on Sunday, Aug. 23.

2. Miss Bencze said, "We don't need the following: glue, paper, or crayons."

3. Yeah! Our team has won another championship!

4. My brother and sister have read the book entitled <u>What I Like About Toads</u>.

5. "We haven't been to Atlantic City," said Mrs. Lopez.

6. Forty-two gifts had been placed on the bride's table.

7. Adams, John Q.

8. Is their new address 9987 W. Cherry Drive, Elmira, OR 97404**?**

9. The three girls' dad has given them a magazine subscription.

10. Dear Jemima,
       We will meet you on Sat. by the old mill at 8:30 A. M.
                Love,
                Cousin Thang

11. No, those sweaters, slacks, and blouses aren't for sale.

PUNCTUATION
Review

Directions: Insert needed punctuation.

period (.)	**exclamation point (!)**
apostrophe (')	**hyphen (-)**
comma (,)	**underlining (_)**
colon (:)	**quotation marks (" ")**
question mark (?)	

1.   Jacys family reunion will be held on Sunday Aug 23

2.   Miss Bencze said We dont need the following glue paper or crayons

3.   Yeah   Our team has won another championship

4.   My brother and sister have read the book entitled What I Like About Toads

5.   We havent been to Atlantic City   said Mrs Lopez

6.   Forty two gifts had been placed on the brides table

7.   Adams John Q

8.   Is their new address 9987 W Cherry Drive Elmira OR   97404

9.   The three girls dad has given them a magazine subscription

10.   Dear Jemima
         We will meet you on Sat by the old mill at 8 30 A M
                                                    Love
                                                    Cousin Thang

11.   No those sweaters slacks and blouses arent for sale

519

Name_____   **PUNCTUATION**
                                                Test
Date_____

Directions: Insert needed punctuation.

period (.)   **exclamation point (!)**
apostrophe (')   **hyphen (-)**
comma (,)   **underlining (_)**
colon (:)   **quotation marks (" ")**
question mark (?)

1. Yes, she does live in Tustin, California.

2. Juan said, "Come in."

3. Yeah! Our dog won first prize!

4. This dungeon, by the way, was once used.

5. They sold their home on Friday, Sept. 6, 1996.

6. Sally, may we take your little sister's skates with us?

7. <u>Big Cowboy Western</u> is her favorite book.

8. Jim's uncle works at a children's playground.

9. We need the following for our games: two balls, a jump rope, and prizes.

10. Dear Hattie,
            We will arrive at 2:00 P. M.
                        Sincerely,
                        Victor

11. They live at 4663 E. Grove Street, Richmond, VA   23226.

12. The lady said, "I picked twenty-two buckets of cherries today."

520

Name_____

PUNCTUATION
Test

Date_____

Directions: Insert needed punctuation.

period (.)   **exclamation point (!)**
apostrophe (')   **hyphen (-)**
comma (,)   **underlining (_)**
colon (:)   **quotation marks (" ")**
question mark (?)

1. Yes she does live in Tustin California

2. Juan said   Come in

3. Yeah   Our dog won first prize

4. This dungeon by the way was once used

5. They sold their home on Friday Sept 6 1996

6. Sally may we take your little sisters skates with us

7. Big Cowboy Western is her favorite book

8. Jims uncle works at a childrens playground

9. We need the following for our games   two balls a jump rope and prizes

10. Dear Hattie
        We will arrive at 2 00 P M
                Sincerely
                Victor

11. They live at 4663 E Grove Street Richmond VA   23226

12. The lady said   I picked twenty two buckets of cherries today   521

MY OWN NOTES

WRITING SENTENCES

TO THE TEACHER:

This writing unit teaches students how to write items in a series and appositives. You may choose to do these lessons as a separate writing unit or to teach the unit over a period of weeks.

A *best practice* would be to teach the concepts in this lesson before reading and discussing the lesson with your students.

I have provided note sheets entitled "My Own Notes" for students. You may want to have students write your examples and/or their own examples on these pages. These can also be used to write examples as you review the preceding lesson.

MY OWN NOTES

A sentence expresses a complete thought. The subject of a sentence is **who** or **what** is being discussed in the sentence.

Example: My hermit crab wakes at night.

We are talking about a crab. *Crab* is the subject of the sentence.

Sometimes, the sentence is about more than one thing.

Example: His aunt and uncle camp.

We are talking about his aunt **and** uncle. *Aunt* and *uncle* are the subjects of the sentence. We call this a **compound subject**. Usually, we use **and** to join two words in a compound subject.

🐎🐎🐎🐎🐎🐎🐎🐎🐎🐎🐎

Directions: Use **and** to join the subject of these sentences.

Example: Lori washed a dog. Tate washed a dog.
        <u>**Lori and Tate washed a dog.**</u>

1. Tara made brownies. Her brother made brownies, too.

    <u>**Tara and her brother made brownies.**</u>

    _____

2. A hen ate grain. Little chicks ate grain, also.

    <u>**A hen and her little chicks ate grain.**</u>

    _____

3. An art fair will be held on Friday. A farmers' market will be held on Friday.

    <u>**An art fair and a farmers' market will be held on Friday.**</u>

    _____

A sentence expresses a complete thought. The subject of a sentence is **who** or **what** is being discussed in the sentence.

> **Example:** My hermit crab wakes at night.

We are talking about a crab. *Crab* is the subject of the sentence.

Sometimes, the sentence is about more than one thing.

> **Example:** His aunt and uncle camp.

We are talking about his aunt **and** uncle. *Aunt* and *uncle* are the subjects of the sentence. We call this a **compound subject**. Usually, we use **and** to join two words in a compound subject.

డ్రాడ్రాడ్రాడ్రాడ్రాడ్రాడ్రాడ్రాడ్రాడ్రా

Directions: Use **and** to join the subject of these sentences.

> **Example:** Lori washed a dog. Tate washed a dog.
> **Lori and Tate washed a dog.**

1. Tara made brownies. Her brother made brownies, too.

_____

_____

2. A hen ate grain. Little chicks ate grain, also.

_____

_____

3. An art fair will be held on Friday. A farmers' market will be held on Friday.

_____

_____

TO THE TEACHER:

The next lesson discusses that a verb may change when subjects are combined.

Examples: A rat **is** a rodent.
A beaver **is** a rodent.

_____ A rat and a beaver **are** rodents. _____

Marla **likes** pasta.
Kelly **likes** pasta.

_____ Marla and Kelly **like** pasta. _____

Be sure to teach this concept carefully!

MY OWN NOTES

The subject of a sentence is **who** or **what** the sentence is "about."

Sometimes, a verb may change.

> **Example:**   Lee **packs** a snack. Tessa **packs** a snack, too.

When we talk about one (singular), we use a singular verb. Each person ***packs*** a snack. However, when we join *Lee* and *Tessa*, we have two items (plural) in the subject. The verb must agree with the plural subject. A plural verb in present time does **not** end in *s*. Therefore, Lee and Tessa <u>**pack**</u> a snack.

ॐ ॐ ॐ

A verb may change form with a compound subject.

> **Example:**   His bike **was** stolen. His skateboard **was** also stolen.

When we talk about one (singular), we use a singular verb *(was)*. When we are talking about **two or more** joined by ***and***, we must use a verb that agrees.

    Wrong: His bike and skateboard <u>**was**</u> stolen.

    Right: His bike and skateboard <u>**were**</u> stolen.

ॐ ॐ ॐ ॐ ॐ ॐ ॐ ॐ ॐ ॐ ॐ

Directions: Use ***and*** to join the subjects of two sentences.

> **Example:**   My friend has ice skates. I have
> ice skates.
>
> <u>**My friend and I have ice**</u>
>
> <u>**skates.**</u>

1. Venus is a planet. Pluto is a planet.

     <u>**Venus and Pluto are planets.**</u>

     _____

The subject of a sentence is **who** or **what** the sentence is "about."

Sometimes, a verb may change.

> **Example:** Lee **packs** a snack. Tessa **packs** a snack, too.

When we talk about one (singular), we use a singular verb. Each person *packs* a snack. However, when we join *Lee* and *Tessa*, we have two items (plural) in the subject. The verb must agree with the plural subject. A plural verb in present time does **not** end in *s*. Therefore, Lee and Tessa **pack** a snack.

હ હ હ

A verb may change form with a compound subject.

> **Example:** His bike **was** stolen. His skateboard **was** also stolen.

When we talk about one (singular), we use a singular verb *(was)*. When we are talking about **two or more** joined by *and*, we must use a verb that agrees.

>   Wrong: His bike and skateboard **was** stolen.

>   Right: His bike and skateboard **were** stolen.

હ હ હ હ હ હ હ હ હ હ હ

Directions: Use *and* to join the subjects of two sentences.

> **Example:**   My friend has ice skates. I have ice skates.
>
>   **My friend and I have ice**
>
>   **skates.**

1.   Venus is a planet. Pluto is a planet.

_____

_____

2. His pug sleeps on his bed. His collie sleeps on his bed, too.

      His pug and collie sleep on his bed.

3. Miss Hill teaches at Jefferson Middle School. Mr. Lane teaches at Jefferson Middle School.

      Miss Hill and Mr. Lane teach at Jefferson Middle School.

4. Their mother sings to them. Their grandmother sings to them, too.

      Their mother and grandmother sing to them.

5. Her boss talks on the telephone often. She talks on the telephone often, also.

      Her boss and she talk on the telephone often.

6. Borax is a mineral. Jet is a mineral.

      Borax and jet are minerals.

7. Jo skis every winter. Gary skis every winter.

      Jo and Gary ski every winter.

2. His pug sleeps on his bed. His collie sleeps on his bed, too.

_____

_____

3. Miss Hill teaches at Jefferson Middle School. Mr. Lane teaches at Jefferson Middle School.

_____

_____

4. Their mother sings to them. Their grandmother sings to them, too.

_____

_____

5. Her boss talks on the telephone often. She talks on the telephone often, also.

_____

_____

6. Borax is a mineral. Jet is a mineral.

_____

_____

7. Jo skis every winter. Gary skis every winter.

_____

_____

The subject of a sentence is **who** or **what** the sentence is "about."

Sometimes, a verb may change.

> **Example:**   Their car **runs** well. Their truck **runs** well.

When we talk about one (singular), we use a singular verb. Each car **_runs_** well.

However, when we join *car* and *truck*, we have two items (plural) in the subject.

The verb must agree with the plural subject. A plural verb in present time does

not end in *s*. Therefore, their car and truck **run** well.

ৡ ৡ ৡ

A verb may change form with a compound subject.

> **Example:**   Ken **has** a job. Amy **has** a job.

When we talk about one (singular), we use a singular verb *(has)*. When we are

talking about **two or more** joined by **and**, we must use a verb that agrees.

> Wrong: Ken and Amy **has** a job.

> Right: Ken and Amy **have** a job.

ৡ ৡ ৡ ৡ ৡ ৡ ৡ ৡ ৡ ৡ

Directions: Use **and** to join the subjects of two sentences.

> **Example:**   His sister raises pigs.
>   His brother raises pigs.

> **His sister and brother raise pigs.**

1. Alvah likes to paint flowers on chairs.
    His mother likes to paint flowers on chairs.

> **Alvah and his mother like to paint flowers on chairs.**

_____

534

The subject of a sentence is **who** or **what** the sentence is "about."

Sometimes, a verb may change.

> **Example:**   Their car **runs** well. Their truck **runs** well.

When we talk about one (singular), we use a singular verb. Each car *runs* well. However, when we join *car* and *truck*, we have two items (plural) in the subject. The verb must agree with the plural subject. A plural verb in present time does **not** end in *s*. Therefore, their car and truck **run** well.

ฝ ฝ ฝ

A verb may change form with a compound subject.

> **Example:**   Ken **has** a job. Amy **has** a job.

When we talk about one (singular), we use a singular verb *(has)*. When we are talking about **two or more** joined by *and*, we must use a verb that agrees.

   Wrong: Ken and Amy **has** a job.

   Right: Ken and Amy **have** a job.

ฝ ฝ ฝ ฝ ฝ ฝ ฝ ฝ ฝ ฝ

Directions: Use *and* to join the subjects of two sentences.

> **Example:**   His sister raises pigs.
> His brother raises pigs.

His sister and brother raise pigs.

1.   Alvah likes to paint flowers on chairs.
     His mother likes to paint flowers on chairs.

_____

_____

2. Barbie hands out programs at baseball games.
Her father also hands out programs at baseball games.

_____**Barbie and her father hand out programs at baseball**_____

_____**games.**_____

3. My grandma is a greeter for a department store.
He is a greeter for a department store, also.

_____**My grandma and he are greeters for a department**_____

_____**store.**_____

4. Our friend buys Christmas gifts during the summer.
Her husband buys Christmas gifts during the summer, too.

_____**Our friend and her husband buy Christmas gifts during**_____

_____**the summer.**_____

5. Chessa talks loudly.
Randy talks loudly.
Their older brother also talks loudly.

_____**Chessa, Randy, and their teenaged brother talk loudly.**_____

_____

6. A striped pillow is lying on the wooden floor.
A bright throw is lying on the wooden floor.

_____**A striped pillow and a bright throw are lying on the**_____

_____**wooden floor.**_____

7. That electrician installs lights.
The electrician's son installs lights.

_____**That electrician and his son install lights.**_____

_____

2. Barbie hands out programs at baseball games.
   Her father also hands out programs at baseball games.

   _____

   _____

3. My grandma is a greeter for a department store.
   He is a greeter for a department store, also.

   _____

   _____

4. Our friend buys Christmas gifts during the summer.
   Her husband buys Christmas gifts during the summer, too.

   _____

   _____

5. Chessa talks loudly.
   Randy talks loudly.
   Their older brother also talks loudly.

   _____

   _____

6. A striped pillow is lying on the wooden floor.
   A bright throw is lying on the wooden floor.

   _____

   _____

7. That electrician installs lights.
   The electrician's son installs lights.

   _____

   _____

TO THE TEACHER:

If your students are not using individual white-boards, you may consider using them. They are terrific for students to write your examples or their own examples on as you teach the lesson. Students seem to find writing on these boards exciting. Consider using them in all subject areas.

MY OWN NOTES

Two items can be joined by a conjunction; the coordinating conjunctions are **and, or,** and **but**. Items joined do **not** have to be the subject of a sentence.

Examples: Please *read this paper* and *sign* at the bottom.

We do our homework *before* or *after* dinner.

The ushers for the play were *she and I*.

Nicky's bedspread is *bright pink* and *lacy*.

I'll take your *pennies* or *dimes*.

৵৵৵

Sometimes, <u>three or more items</u> are joined.

Example: A tractor, a plow, and a hay wagon are in that barn.

Place a comma after the items in a series that occur before *and*. Do not place a comma after **and/or** or after the *last item*.

Example: His mother bought a hammer, a saw, nails, and wood for the project.

৵৵৵৵৵৵৵৵৵৵৵

Directions: Join sentences.

Example: I like fresh fruit.
I like fruit cocktail.
I like dried fruit.

<u>**I like fresh fruit, fruit cocktail, and dried fruit.**</u>

1.   Her uncle is tall.
Her uncle is tan.
Her uncle is muscular.

<u>**Her uncle is tall, tan, and muscular.**</u>

_____

Two items can be joined by a conjunction; the coordinating conjunctions are *and, or,* and *but*. Items joined do **not** have to be the subject of a sentence.

Examples: Please *read this paper* and *sign* at the bottom.

We do our homework *before* or *after* dinner.

The ushers for the play were *she and I*.

Nicky's bedspread is *bright pink* and *lacy*.

I'll take your *pennies* or *dimes*.

ఌ ఌ ఌ

Sometimes, three or more items are joined.

Example: A tractor, a plow, and a hay wagon are in that barn.

Place a comma after the items in a series that occur before *and*. Do not place a comma after **and/or** or after the *last item*.

Example: His mother bought a hammer, a saw, nails, and wood for the project.

ఌ ఌ ఌ ఌ ఌ ఌ ఌ ఌ ఌ ఌ ఌ

Directions: Join sentences.

Example: I like fresh fruit.
I like fruit cocktail.
I like dried fruit.

I like fresh fruit, fruit cocktail, and dried fruit.

1. Her uncle is tall.
   Her uncle is tan.
   Her uncle is muscular.

   _____

   _____

2. Linda will be a bridesmaid in their wedding.
   Mika will be a bridesmaid in their wedding.
   Lea will be a bridesmaid in their wedding.

   Linda, Mika, and Lea will be bridesmaids in their

   wedding.

3. That toddler scribbles on walls.
   That toddler scribbles on floors.
   That toddler also scribbles on furniture.

   That toddler scribbles on walls, floors, and furniture.

4. Peter works slowly.
   Peter works carefully.
   Peter works tirelessly.

   Peter works slowly, carefully, and tirelessly.

5. The clerk smiled.
   The clerk handed the customer change.
   The clerk thanked him.

   The clerk smiled, handed the customer change, and

   thanked him.

6. Visitors from Japan come to Hoover Dam.
   Visitors from India come to Hoover Dam.
   Visitors from Peru come to Hoover Dam.

   Visitors from Japan, India, and Peru come to Hoover Dam.

542

2. Linda will be a bridesmaid in their wedding.
   Mika will be a bridesmaid in their wedding.
   Lea will be a bridesmaid in their wedding.

   _____

   _____

3. That toddler scribbles on walls.
   That toddler scribbles on floors.
   That toddler also scribbles on furniture.

   _____

   _____

4. Peter works slowly.
   Peter works carefully.
   Peter works tirelessly.

   _____

   _____

5. The clerk smiled.
   The clerk handed the customer change.
   The clerk thanked him.

   _____

   _____

6. Visitors from Japan come to Hoover Dam.
   Visitors from India come to Hoover Dam.
   Visitors from Peru come to Hoover Dam.

   _____

   _____

Two items can be joined by a conjunction; the coordinating conjunctions are **and, or,** and **but**. Items joined do **not** have to be the subject of a sentence.

Examples: A *tartan* **and** a *skiff* are boats.

The champion was *Kari* **or** her *sister*.

Carlo collects *shells* **and** *marbles*.

The four-year-old <u>frowned</u> **but** <u>did</u>n't <u>cry</u>.

She seemed *quiet* **and** *shy*.

ई॰ ई॰ ई॰

Sometimes, <u>three or more items</u> are joined.

Example: A tractor**,** a plow**,** and a hay wagon are in that barn.

Place a comma after the items in a series that occur before *and*. Do not place a comma after **and/or** or after the *last item*.

Example: Gail bought sheets**,** pillowcases**,** and a blanket.

ई॰ई॰ई॰ई॰ई॰ई॰ई॰ई॰ई॰ई॰ई॰

Directions: Join sentences.

Example: Her tart is covered with strawberries.
Her tart is covered with blueberries.
Her tart is covered with raspberries.

 <u>**Her tart is covered with strawberries, blueberries,**</u>

 <u>**and raspberries.**</u>

1. The children are decorating birthday cupcakes with frosting.
The children are decorating birthday cupcakes with coconut.
The children are decorating birthday cupcakes with sprinkles.

 <u>**The children are decorating birthday cupcakes with**</u>

 <u>**frosting, coconut, and sprinkles.**</u>

Two items can be joined by a conjunction; the coordinating conjunctions are
and, or, and **but**. Items joined do **not** have to be the subject of a sentence.

> **Examples:**   A *tartan* **and** a *skiff* are boats.
>
> The champion was *Kari* **or** her *sister*.
>
> Carlo collects *shells* **and** *marbles*.
>
> The four-year-old <u>frowned</u> **but** <u>did</u>n't <u>cry</u>.
>
> She seemed *quiet* **and** *shy*.

ཚ ཚ ཚ

Sometimes, <u>three or more items</u> are joined.

> **Example:**   A tractor, a plow, and a hay wagon are in that barn.

Place a comma after the items in a series that occur before *and*. Do not place a

comma after **and/or** or after the *last item*.

> **Example:**   Gail bought sheets, pillowcases, and a blanket.

ཚ ཚ ཚ ཚ ཚ ཚ ཚ ཚ ཚ ཚ ཚ

Directions: Join sentences.

> **Example:**   Her tart is covered with strawberries.
>   Her tart is covered with blueberries.
>   Her tart is covered with raspberries.
>
> **_Her tart is covered with strawberries, blueberries,_**
>
> **_and raspberries._**

1. The children are decorating birthday cupcakes with frosting.
    The children are decorating birthday cupcakes with coconut.
    The children are decorating birthday cupcakes with sprinkles.

_____

_____

2. Plastic shelves have been added to their closet.
   Plastic bins have been added to their closet.
   Plastic hooks have been added to their closet.

   Plastic shelves, bins, and hooks have been added

   to their closet.

3. The baby waved his hands excitedly.
   The baby laughed.
   The baby jumped up and down.

   The baby waved his hands excitedly, laughed, and

   jumped up and down.

4. A skater should use knee pads.
   A skater should use a mouth guard.
   A skater should use a helmet.

   A skater should use knee pads, a mouth guard, and

   a helmet.

5. This gadget peels lemons.
   This gadget peels limes.
   This gadget peels oranges.

   This gadget peels lemons, limes, and oranges.

6. His apple pie turned out flaky.
   His apple pie turned out delicious.

   His apple pie turned out flaky and delicious.

2. Plastic shelves have been added to their closet.
   Plastic bins have been added to their closet.
   Plastic hooks have been added to their closet.

   _____

   _____

3. The baby waved his hands excitedly.
   The baby laughed.
   The baby jumped up and down.

   _____

   _____

4. A skater should use knee pads.
   A skater should use a mouth guard.
   A skater should use a helmet.

   _____

   _____

5. This gadget peels lemons.
   This gadget peels limes.
   This gadget peels oranges.

   _____

   _____

6. His apple pie turned out flaky.
   His apple pie turned out delicious.

   _____

   _____

TO THE TEACHER:

Students will learn to write appositives in this section. The lessons are introduced at a simplistic level. Again, I recommend that you teach and complete these lessons with your students.

MY OWN NOTES

An appositive is a word or phrase (group of words) that explains something in a sentence.

> **Example:**   Franco, ***my barber***, is from Italy.
>
> **Appositive**

An appositive is placed next to the word it explains.

> **Example:**   I like Fendi, ***her dog***.
>
> **appositive**

An appositive is set off by commas.

> **Examples:**   Do you want to visit Newberg, a city in Oregon?
>
> Their doctor, Dr. Hand, won a 5K race.

๖ะ๖ะ๖ะ๖ะ๖ะ๖ะ๖ะ๖ะ๖ะ๖ะ

Directions: Place the appositive by the word it explains. Be sure to insert a comma or commas where needed.

> **Example:**   A puffin has a brightly colored bill.
> A puffin is a bird.

__**A puffin**_____**has a brightly colored bill.**__
__**A puffin,** *a bird*__, **has a brightly colored bill.**____

1.   Cassie is my older sister. Cassie loves to talk on the telephone.

____**Cassie,** *my older sister*__, **loves to talk on the telephone.**___

_____

An appositive is a word or phrase (group of words) that explains something in a sentence.

> **Example:**   Franco, ***my barber***, is from Italy.
>
>   **appositive**

An appositive is placed next to the word it explains.

> **Example:**   I like Fendi, ***her dog***.
>
>   **appositive**

An appositive is set off by commas.

> **Examples:**   Do you want to visit Newberg, a city in Oregon?
>
>   Their doctor, Dr. Hand, won a 5K race.

ન્ઠ ન્ઠ ન્ઠ ન્ઠ ન્ઠ ન્ઠ ન્ઠ ન્ઠ ન્ઠ ન્ઠ ન્ઠ

Directions: Place the appositive by the word it explains. Be sure to insert a comma or commas where needed.

> **Example:**   A puffin has a brightly colored bill.
>   A puffin is a bird.

A puffin **has a brightly colored bill.**

A puffin, *a bird***, has a brightly colored bill.**

1.   Cassie is my older sister. Cassie loves to talk on the telephone.

Cassie **loves to talk on**

the telephone.

2. Kari is my cousin's new baby. Kari weighs six pounds, nine ounces.

   Kari, *my cousin's new baby,* **weighs six**

   pounds, nine ounces.

3. Hannah and Devi like to ride Chester. Chester is their horse.

   Hannah and Devi like to ride Chester, *their horse.*

4. Teiglach is good. Teiglach is a mixture of dough and honey.

   Teiglach, *a mixture of dough and honey,*

   is good.

5. His best friend visited a castle. His best friend's name is Robert Lee.

   His best friend, *Robert Lee,* **visited a castle.**

6. A three-year-old is crying. Her name is Katie.

   Katie, *a three-year-old,* **is crying.**

7. They spied a spatangoid. A spatangoid is a heart-shaped sea urchin.

   They spied a spatangoid, *a heart-shaped sea urchin.*

8. My grandparents visited Zermatt. Zermatt is a town in Switzerland.

   My grandparents visited Zermatt, *a town in Switzerland.*

552

2. Kari is my cousin's new baby. Kari weighs six pounds, nine ounces.

   Kari **weighs six pounds, nine ounces.**

3. Hannah and Devi like to ride Chester. Chester is their horse.

   Hannah and Devi like to ride Chester

4. Teiglach is good. Teiglach is a mixture of dough and honey.

   Teiglach **is good.**

5. His best friend visited a castle. His best friend's name is Robert Lee.

   His best friend **visited a castle.**

6. A three-year-old is crying. Her name is Katie.

   Katie **is crying.**

7. They spied a spatangoid. A spatangoid is a heart-shaped sea urchin.

   They spied a spatangoid

8. My grandparents visited Zermatt. Zermatt is a town in Switzerland.

   My grandparents visited Zermatt

An appositive is a word or phrase (group of words) that explains something in a sentence.

Example: Coco, **my canary**, is yellow.

appositive

An appositive is placed next to the word it explains.

Example: Have you read this book, **a mystery**?

appositive

An appositive is set off by commas.

Examples: Hand me the ladle, that spoon with a long handle.

Abraham Lincoln, the 16th president, was tall.

ଈଈଈଈଈଈଈଈଈଈ

Directions: Place the appositive by the word it explains. Be sure to insert a comma or commas where needed.

Example: We went to Sitka.
Sitka is a seaport in Alaska.

_____**We went to Sitka**_____

_____**We went to Sitka,** *a seaport in Alaska.*_____

1.   His father loves to hike on weekends. His father is a manager.

_____**His father,** *a manager,* **loves to hike on weekends.**_____

_____

An appositive is a word or phrase (group of words) that explains something in a sentence.

> **Example:** Coco, *my canary*, is yellow.
>
> appositive

An appositive is placed next to the word it explains.

> **Example:** Have you read this book, *a mystery*?
>
> appositive

An appositive is set off by commas.

> **Examples:** Hand me the ladle, that spoon with a long handle.
>
> Abraham Lincoln, the 16th president, was tall.

$\approx$ $\approx$ $\approx$ $\approx$ $\approx$ $\approx$ $\approx$ $\approx$ $\approx$ $\approx$ $\approx$ $\approx$

Directions: Place the appositive by the word it explains. Be sure to insert a comma or commas where needed.

> **Example:** We went to Sitka.
> Sitka is a seaport in Alaska.

_____**We went to Sitka**_____

_____**We went to Sitka,** *a seaport in Alaska.*_____

1. His father loves to hike on weekends. His father is a manager.

_____**His father**_____**loves to hike on**_____

_____**weekends.**_____

2. Aegina is known for its beauty and clean air. Aegina is an island in Greece.

       Aegina, *an island in Greece,* is known for its

       beauty and clean air.

3. Do you want to see Poppy? Poppy is my pet pig.

       Do you want to see Poppy, *my pet pig?*

4. The leaves of puha are used as vegetables in some lands. Puha is a plant.

       The leaves of puha, *a plant,* are used as

       vegetables in some lands.

5. Miss Lipos sold our home for us. Miss Lipos is our neighbor.

       Miss Lipos, *our neighbor,* sold our home for us.

6. Bo is a kitten. Bo is Parker's favorite pet.

       Bo, *a kitten,* is Parker's favorite pet.

7. I like honey. It is the only food that doesn't spoil.

       I like honey, *the only food that doesn't spoil.*

8. A dentist removed plaque from Andy's teeth. Plaque is a hard substance.

       A dentist removed plaque, *a hard substance,*

       from Andy's teeth.

2. Aegina is known for its beauty and clean air. Aegina is an island in Greece.

   _____**Aegina**_____**is known for its**_____

   _____**beauty and clean air.**_____

3. Do you want to see Poppy? Poppy is my pet pig.

   _____**Do you want to see Poppy**_____

   _____

4. The leaves of puha are used as vegetables in some lands. Puha is a plant.

   _____**The leaves of puha**_____**are used as**_____

   _____**vegetables in some lands.**_____

5. Miss Lipos sold our home for us. Miss Lipos is our neighbor.

   _____**Miss Lipos**_____**sold our home for us.**_____

6. Bo is a kitten. Bo is Parker's favorite pet.

   _____**Bo**_____**is Parker's favorite pet.**_____

7. I like honey. It is the only food that doesn't spoil.

   _____**I like honey**_____

   _____

8. A dentist removed plaque from Andy's teeth. Plaque is a hard substance.

   _____**A dentist removed plaque**_____

   _____**from Andy's teeth.**_____

An appositive is a word or phrase (group of words) that explains something in a sentence.

Example: Bruno, **my dog**, is playful.

appositive

My dog explains who Bruno is. Look at the sentence without *my dog*.

Bruno is playful.

We have no idea who Bruno is. Perhaps he is a cat, a ferret, or even a person. *My dog* explains who Bruno is.

An appositive is placed next to the word it explains.

Example: Do you know Miss Logan, *my teacher*?

appositive

An appositive is set off by commas.

Example: Brad, my best friend, is moving to New York.

ॐ ॐ ॐ ॐ ॐ ॐ ॐ ॐ ॐ ॐ ॐ ॐ ॐ ॐ

Directions: Using an appositive, combine these sentences. Be sure to use commas where needed.

Example: Peter is a police officer.
Peter is our son.

Peter, our son, is a police officer.

1. Mr. Sine is nice.
Mr. Sine is the manager of a hardware store.

Mr. Sine, the manager of a hardware store, is nice.

_____

558

An appositive is a word or phrase (group of words) that explains something in a sentence.

> **Example:**   Bruno, ***my dog***, is playful.
>
> **appositive**

My dog explains who Bruno is. Look at the sentence without *my dog*.

> Bruno is playful.

We have no idea who Bruno is. Perhaps he is a cat, a ferret, or even a person. *My dog* explains who Bruno is.

An appositive is placed next to the word it explains.

> **Example:**   Do you know Miss Logan, *my teacher*?
>
> **appositive**

An appositive is set off by commas.

> **Example:**   Brad**,** my best friend**,** is moving to New York.

ತ್ತ್ತ್ತ್ತ್ತ್ತ್ತ್ತ್ತ್ತ್

Directions: Using an appositive, combine these sentences. Be sure to use commas where needed.

> **Example:**   Peter is a police officer.
> Peter is our son.

> **Peter, our son, is a police officer.**

1. Mr. Sine is nice.
    Mr. Sine is the manager of a hardware store.

_____

_____

2. Newgate was a famous London prison.
    It was torn down in 1902.

    Newgate, a famous London prison, was torn down

    in 1902.

3. Moody draws colorful cartoons.
    Moody is a high school art student.

    Moody, a high school art student, draws colorful

    cartoons.

4. My aunt and uncle live in Tampa.
    Tampa is a city in Florida.

    My aunt and uncle live in Tampa, a city in Florida.

5. They visited the Louvre.
    The Louvre is an art museum in Paris.

    They visited the Louvre, an art museum in Paris.

6. Their children are Pablo, Maria, and Anita.
    Their children will be visiting during the holidays.

    Their children, Pablo, Maria, and Anita, will be visiting

    during the holidays.

7. They picked blackberries.
    Blackberries are fruit that grows on a bramble bush.

    They picked blackberries, fruit that grows on a bramble

    bush.

560

2. Newgate was a famous London prison.
   It was torn down in 1902.

   _____

   _____

3. Moody draws colorful cartoons.
   Moody is a high school art student.

   _____

   _____

4. My aunt and uncle live in Tampa.
   Tampa is a city in Florida.

   _____

   _____

5. They visited the Louvre.
   The Louvre is an art museum in Paris.

   _____

   _____

6. Their children are Pablo, Maria, and Anita.
   Their children will be visiting during the holidays.

   _____

   _____

7. They picked blackberries.
   Blackberries are fruit that grows on a bramble bush.

   _____

   _____

TO THE TEACHER:

The first 10 lessons (days) of **DAILY GRAMS: Grade 4** appear on the ensuing pages.

This will provide you an opportunity to see how students react to and benefit from a daily review.

Suggestions:

1. Make a copy for each student. Have students complete a *Daily Gram* at the beginning of English class. (This should take only a few minutes.) If you ask for volunteers to write the sentence combining on the board, it may take longer. Although this does take more time, it is beneficial because students can learn much by reading what others have written. It is also a time for group editing and an opportunity for you to praise good writing and academic growth.

2. Ask students to read or write in journals until everyone is finished.

3. Using a transparency that you have made before class, go over the lesson. Be sure to solicit answers from students and discuss them. (The *Answer Key* is located after Day 10.)

4. Upon completion, move on to whatever you are doing in your regular lesson.

www.easygrammar.com

CAPITALIZATION:

> **Capitalize a name.**
>> Example: Patty

> **Capitalize initials.**
>> Example: P. T. Lutz

> **Capitalize a title with a name.**
>> Examples: Mr. Scott   Mayor Hill   Uncle Peter

1.   have dr. and mrs. c. winston visited lately?

PUNCTUATION:

> **Place a period after an abbreviation.**

> **Write the abbreviation.**

2.   A.   Avenue - _____   C. Mister - _____   E. inch - _____

   B.   gallon - _____   D. foot - _____   F. Street - _____

ALPHABETIZING

> **Write these words in alphabetical order:**

3.   dream   dart   cream   egg   breath

   (a) _____   (d) _____

   (b) _____   (e) _____

   (c) _____

SUBJECT/VERB:
The subject of a sentence tells <u>who</u> or <u>what</u> the sentence is about.
The verb tells what <u>is</u> (<u>was</u>) or <u>what happens</u> (<u>happened</u>).

4.   Suddenly Janet sneezed.

SENTENCE COMBINING:

5.   Her brother is making cookies.
   They are for a bake sale.

   _____

   _____ 563

DAY 2

CAPITALIZATION:

Capitalize a title if it appears with a name.   Example: Grandma Rich

Do not capitalize a title if it appears alone.   Example: I like my grandma.

1.   has uncle mike met miss diaz?

PUNCTUATION:

Place a period at the end of a declarative sentence (statement).
Place a period at the end of an imperative sentence (command).

2.   Dont go

PARTS OF SPEECH: VERBS

A contraction combines two words and omits a letter or letters.
An apostrophe (') is placed where the letter or letters have been left out.

Example: we are - we're

Write the contraction:

3.   A.   is not - _____

B.   they are - _____

C.   cannot - _____

PARTS OF SPEECH: NOUNS

A noun names a person, place, or thing.

4.   Write a noun that names a person: _____

SENTENCE COMBINING:

5.   A book is on a table.
     It is a library book.

_____

_____

564

CAPITALIZATION:

> **Capitalize the days of the week.**
>
> > Example: Sunday
>
> **Capitalize the months of the year.**
>
> > Example: January

1.   their party is on the last saturday in july.

PUNCTUATION:

> **Place an exclamation point (!) after an interjection (word that shows emotion).**
> **Place an exclamation point at the end of an exclamatory sentence (one that shows emotion).**

2.   Wow I won

SUBJECT/VERB:

> **The subject of a sentence tells <u>who</u> or <u>what</u> the sentence is about.**
> **The verb tells what <u>is</u> (<u>was</u>) or what <u>happens</u> (<u>happened</u>).**
>
> **Underline the subject once and the verb twice.**

3.   A band marches every morning.

PARTS OF SPEECH: NOUNS

> **A noun names a person, place or thing.**

4.   Write a noun that names a thing: _____

SENTENCE COMBINING:

5.   Mark is sick today.
     Mark had to stay home.

     _____

     _____

DAY 4

CAPITALIZATION:

Capitalize the name of a geographic place.

Examples:

town or city - Abilene

state - Utah

1. my aunt lives in san diego, california.

PUNCTUATION:

Place a question mark (?) at the end of an interrogative sentence.

2. Arent we leaving soon

PARTS OF SPEECH: ADJECTIVES

Some adjectives describe; they are called descriptive adjectives.

Write a descriptive adjective in each blank:

3. Two _____ cars were parked by the _____house.

PARTS OF SPEECH: VERBS

Underline the subject once and the verb twice:

4. Our dog licks us.

SENTENCE COMBINING:

5. The basket is broken.
   The basket is green and pink.

   _____

   _____

566

CAPITALIZATION:

Capitalize the name of a geographic place.

Examples: **country** - Canada

continent - North America

1.   the country of finland is in Europe*.

*name of a continent

PUNCTUATION:

**Place a comma after three or more items in a series.
Do not place a comma after the last item.**

Example: I saw goats, cows, and chicks at a farm.

2.   Mira Frank and Chan were first

SYNONYMS:

Synonyms are words with similar meanings.

Circle a synonym for the boldfaced word:

3.   **respect:**   a) dislike   b) admire   c) despise

PARTS OF SPEECH: ADVERBS

**Adverbs often tell how.
Underline any adverbs that tell <u>how</u>:**

4.   She did her work carefully.

SENTENCE COMBINING:

5.   The telephone rang.
     Ted answered it.

_____

_____

DAY 6

CAPITALIZATION:

1.   carissa drove to austin, texas, last tuesday.

PUNCTUATION:

> **Place a comma after a noun of direct address. This is a person to whom someone is speaking.**

> Example: Lori, sit here.

2. Tom can you play

PARTS OF SPEECH: ADVERBS

> **Adverbs often tell when.**

> **Circle any adverbs that tell <u>when</u>:**

3.   Our picnic is today.

PARTS OF SPEECH: PRONOUNS

> **Pronouns take the place of nouns.**
> ***I, he, she, we, they, you, it*, and *who* are pronouns that can serve as subjects.**

> **Circle the correct pronoun:**

4. Jasper and _____ (me, I) are right.

SENTENCE COMBINING:

5.   Tama's bike had a flat tire.
     Tama fixed her flat tire.

_____

_____

CAPITALIZATION:

Capitalize the name of a holiday or special day.

Examples:

holiday - Labor Day
special day - St. Patrick's Day

1.   susan's family went to hawaii last christmas.

PUNCTUATION:

Place a comma between a town or city and a state.

Example: Gunder, Iowa

2.   Mary have you been to Denver Colorado

PARTS OF SPEECH: ADVERBS

Adverbs often tell where.

Circle any adverbs that tell <u>where</u>:

3.   A child fell down.

SENTENCE TYPES:
A declarative sentence makes a statement.
An interrogative sentence asks a question.

Write the sentence type:

4.   Are you leaving?   _____

SENTENCE COMBINING:

5.   The dish was dropped.
      The dish broke into many pieces.

_____

_____

DAY 8

CAPITALIZATION:

Capitalize the name of a geographic place:

Examples:

ocean - Pacific Ocean		**island** - Egg Island	
river - Snake River		**mountain** - Brock Mountain	
lake - Soda Lake		**canyon** - Grand Canyon	
bay - Bua Bay		**beach** - Stone Beach	

1. they visited the ozark mountains in missouri in august.

PUNCTUATION:

Place a comma between the number for a day and the year in a date.
Place a comma between a day and a date.

Example: Tuesday, October 23, 2001

2. He was born on Oct 20 1980

PARTS OF SPEECH: CONJUNCTIONS

Write the coordinating conjunction that rhymes with each word.

3. A. sand - _____   B. more - _____   C. mutt - _____

PARTS OF SPEECH: ADJECTIVES

Some adjectives describe; they are called descriptive adjectives.

Circle any descriptive adjectives:

4. White fluffy clouds were painted above the iron bed.

SENTENCE COMBINING:

5. Joe's mom is a dentist.
    Joe's dad is a dentist.

_____

_____

570

CAPITALIZATION:

Capitalize the first word of a greeting (salutation) of a friendly letter.

Example: Dear Susie,

1.   dear marco,

terry and i will visit fish lake next thursday.

Brian

PUNCTUATION:

2.   Tara and I visited Anaheim California

SENTENCE TYPES:

A declarative sentence makes a statement.

An interrogative sentence asks a question.

Write the type of sentence:

3.   A. Will you go?   _____

B. The sun is bright.   _____

SUBJECT/VERB:

Underline the subject once and the verb twice:

4.   That horse chews hay.

SENTENCE COMBINING:

5.   The roses were blooming.
The daisies were not blooming.

_____

_____

DAY 10

CAPITALIZATION:

Capitalize the name of a geographic place.

Examples:

valley - Round Valley		**cape** - Cape Horn	
springs - Holly Springs		**dam** - Beaver Dam	
creek - Clear Creek		**point** - Fairbanks Point	
gulf - Gulf of Biscayne		**waterfalls** - Miners Fall	

1. is bighorn falls near marsh peak?

PUNCTUATION:

2. Maria Frank and Laylah left early

DIFFICULT WORDS:

<u>**They're**</u> **is a contraction for** *they are*.   Example: They're finished.

<u>**There**</u> **is an adverb telling** *where*.   Example: Stand there.

<u>**Their**</u> **is a possessive pronoun .**   Example: I'm their cousin.

Circle the correct word:

3. (They're, There, Their) dad is a carpenter.

PARTS OF SPEECH: PREPOSITIONS

Prepositions are words that appear with other words to form prepositional phrases. These phrases add details or more information. Common prepositions are *at, by, for, from, in, on, to*, **and** *with*.

Examples: The teenager stood **by** his father.

The message **on** the card was scribbled.

Finish this sentence:

4. We laughed **at** _____.

SENTENCE COMBINING:

5. Jason mailed a letter.
    He did it for his dad.

_____

_____

572

Sentence combining: Although only one or two possibilities are presented, other answers are acceptable.

AMV/RA: ANSWERS MAY VARY/REPRESENTATIVE ANSWERS

Day 1:   **1.** Have, Dr., Mrs., C., Winston   **2.** A. Ave. B. gal. C. Mr. D. ft. E. in.
F. St.   **3.** (a) breath (b) cream (c) dart (d) dream (e) egg   **4.** <u>Janet</u> <u>sneezed</u>
5. AMV/RA: Her brother is making cookies for a bake sale.

Day 2:   **1.** Has, Uncle, Mike, Miss, Diaz   **2.** Don't go.   **3.** A. isn't B. they're
C. can't   **4.** AMV/RA: boy, Paul, policeman   **5.** AMV/RA: A library book is on the table.
The book that is on the table is from the library.

Day 3:   **1.** Their, Saturday, July   **2.** Wow! I won!   **3.** <u>band</u> <u>marches</u>   **4.** AMV/RA:
spoon, bib   **5.** AMV/RA: Mark is sick today, and he had to stay home. Mark stayed
home today because he is sick.

Day 4:   **1.** My, San, Diego, California   **2.** Aren't we leaving soon?   **3.** AMV/RA:
blue (cars), old (house)   **4.** <u>dog</u> <u>licks</u>   **5.** AMV/RA: The green and pink basket is
broken. The broken basket is green and pink.

Day 5:   **1.** The, Finland, Europe   **2.** Mira, Frank, and Chan were first.   **3.** b) admire
4. carefully   **5.** AMV/RA: The telephone rang, and Ted answered it. When the
telephone rang, Ted answered it.

Day 6:   **1.** Carissa, Austin, Texas, Tuesday   **2.** Tom, can you play?   **3.** today
4. I (subject)   **5.** AMV/RA: Tama fixed her bike's flat tire. When Tama's bike had a
flat tire, she fixed it.

Day 7:   **1.** Susan's, Hawaii, Christmas   **2.** Mary, have you been to Denver, Colorado?
3. down   **4.** interrogative   **5.** AMV/RA: The dish dropped and broke into many
pieces. When the dish was dropped, it broke into many pieces.

Day 8:   **1.** They, Ozark, Mountains, Missouri, August   **2.** He was born on Oct. 20, 1980.
3. A. and B. or C. but   **4.** White (clouds), fluffy (clouds), iron (bed)   **5.** AMV/RA:
Joe's mom and dad are dentists. Both Joe's mom and dad are dentists.

Day 9:   **1. D**ear **M**arco,
           Terry and **I** will visit **F**ish **L**ake next **T**hursday.
                                Brian
2. Tara and I visited Anaheim, California.   **3.** A. interrogative B. declarative
4. <u>horse</u> <u>chews</u>   **5.** AMV/RA: The roses were blooming, but the daisies were not.
Although the roses were blooming, the daisies were not.

Day 10:   **1.** Is, Bighorn, Falls, Marsh, Peak   **2.** Maria, Frank, and Laylah left early.
3. Their (dad)   **4.** AMV/RA: at his funny remark   **5.** AMV/RA: Jason mailed a letter
for his dad. Jason mailed his dad's letter.

ASSESSMENT ANSWERS: (200 points)

You may use your own point system.

A.   Sentence Types: (4 points)

1. __**Imperative**__   Go slowly.
2. __**Interrogative**__   Is that your cat?
3. __**Exclamatory**__   My balloon popped!
4. __**Declarative**__   She makes dolls.

B. Capitalization: (19 points – ½ point for each)
NOTE: If students capitalize any words that should not be capitalized, deduct a point.

1. **D**id **G**overnor **R**uiz read <u>**I**ndian in the **C**upboard</u> to your class at **A**ztec **S**chool?

2. **T**he visitor from **S**pain spoke to the **R**otary **C**lub about the **M**exican **W**ar.

3. **H**as **M**om bought **B**erryland* iced tea and **A**frican daisies at **C**aremart **C**ompany on **C**ole **A**venue in **T**aneytown?

4. **O**ne student asked, "**I**s the **E**rie **C**anal in **N**ew **Y**ork?"

5. **D**ear **P**am,

    My dad and **I** will attend **P**rescott **P**ioneers **D**ay in **J**une.

                              Your friend,
                              Paco

C. Common and Proper Nouns: (6 points)

1. ✓ TURTLE   3. ✓ BEAGLE   5. ___ SUPERMAN
2. ___ ATLANTA   4. ___ CANADA   6. ✓ BRICKLAYER

D. Concrete and Abstract Nouns: (4 points)

1. ☒ fear   2. ☒ faith   3. ___ fig   4. ___ forest

E. Singular and Plural Nouns: (16 points)

1. berry - __**berries**__
2. tax - __**taxes**__
3. mouse - __**mice**__
4. deer - __**deer**__
5. replay - __**replays**__
6. sofa - __**sofas**__
7. gas - __**gases**__
8. patch - __**patches**__

574

F. Possessive Nouns: (6 points)

1. room belonging to his sister - _____ **(his) sister's room**

2. an office used by more than one woman - **women's office**

3. wading pool shared by two toddlers - **toddlers' (wading) pool**

G. Identifying Nouns: (4 points)
NOTE: If students circle any words that are not nouns, deduct a point.

1. Three **movies** about **birds** of the **desert** were shown at our **library** yesterday.

H. Punctuation:
NOTE: If students insert additional punctuation, deduct a point.

1. No, we won't be moving to Purdy, Washington. (*or* **!**)

2. Kama asked, "Was Emma born on Thursday, May 20, 1982**?**"

3. They hope to sell forty-two tickets for our team's carnival by 4:30 today.

4. By the way, wash your ears, face, and neck with this suds-free soap.

5. His new address is 22 Brook Avenue, Nyles, MI   49102.

I. Subjects and Verbs: (16 points)
NOTE: Deleting prepositional phrases helps students to identify subject and verb.
        However, this was not part of the instructions.
        Count 2 points for each correct subject and 2 for each correct verb.
        Both parts of a compound must be identified!

1. A **package** ~~from Emily~~ **arrived** ~~before dinner~~ ~~on Friday~~.

2. A **nurse** and an **aide** **helped** the patient ~~into bed~~.

3. **Four** ~~of the girls~~ **looked** ~~at the stars~~ ~~during the outdoor party~~.

4. (**You**) **Come** ~~inside the house~~ ~~through the front door~~.

J. Contractions: (6 points)

1. were not - **weren't**   3. I have - **I've**   5. would not - **wouldn't**
2. they will - **they'll**   4. will not - **won't**   6. what is - **what's**

K. You're/Your, It's/Its, and They're/Their/There:

1. Take (there, **their**, they're) picture.
2. I think that (**you're**, your) upset.
3. Let me know when (**it's**, its) time to leave.

L. Subject-Verb Agreement: (12 points)
<u>NOTE: Deleting prepositional phrases helps students to make subject and verb agree.</u>
<u>However, this was not part of the instructions.</u>
<u>Count 2 points for each correct subject and 2 for each correct verb.</u>
<u>DO NOT GIVE SEPARATE POINTS FOR THE COMPOUND IN #3! (2 points or 0)</u>

1. Your **idea** (sound, **sounds**) interesting.

2. The **woman** ~~with the huge green glasses~~ (take, **takes**) orders.

3. His **brother** and **she** (hikes, **hike**) everywhere.

M. Irregular Verbs: (20 points)
<u>NOTE: Deleting prepositional phrases helps students to determine that there is no direct</u>
<u>object in # 1. It also helps to determine the direct object in #8; therefore, *set*</u>
<u>must be used. However, this was not part of the instructions.</u>
<u>Count 1 point for the correct helping verb(s), and 1 point for each correct past</u>
<u>participle. (The subject was only required to help students determine verb phrase.)</u>

1. The <u>dog</u> **was** (**lying**, laying) ~~on the porch~~.

2. <u>Parker</u> **had** (rode, <u>ridden</u>) her horse fast.

3. <u>She</u> **has** (ate, **eaten**) lunch.

4. <u>I</u> **could have** (**run**, ran) more than fifty yards.

5. <u>We</u> **were** (**given**, gave) large red markers.

6. My <u>pencil</u> **is** (broke, **broken**).

7. **Have** <u>you</u> (did, **done**) your homework?

8. <u>We</u> **should have** (**set**, sat) our lunches ~~in the ice chest~~.

9. The <u>bell</u> **may have** already (rang, **rung**).

10. Kama's <u>balloon</u> **had** (busted, **burst**).

576

N. Tenses:
NOTE: Deleting prepositional phrases helps students to determine subject and verb.
         However, this was not part of the instructions.
         Count 1 point for a correct subject *and* verb, and 1 point for correct tense.
1. _____**PAST**_____   The **child colored** a picture.

2. _____**FUTURE**_____   You **will turn** left ~~at the next street~~.

3. _____**PRESENT**_____   Their **dad is** a beekeeper.

O. Usage and Knowledge: (18 points)

1. Circle any infinitive that is a regular verb: **to flash**   to fly   **to flip**

2. Circle the interjection: **Wow!** This soup is hot and spicy.

3. Circle the possessive pronoun: The girls are enjoying **their** new puppy.

4. Write the antecedent of the possessive pronoun in sentence 3:   _____**girls**_____

5. Circle the conjunction: Yikes! Mo **or** Bo has fallen in the stream.

6. Circle the correct answer: We haven't received (no, **any**) money.

7. Circle the correct answer: My brother acts (strange, **strangely**) sometimes.

8. Circle the correct answer: I didn't play very (good, **well**) in the first game.

9. Circle the correct answer: Are you feeling (good, **well**)?

P. Identifying Adjectives: (6 points)
NOTE: If students circle any words that are not adjectives, deduct a point.

1. **One elderly** lady wore **silver** sandals with **many** stones and **a low** heel.

Q. Degrees of Adjectives: (6 points)

1. The fifth storm was (more violent, **most violent**).

2. This is the (**uglier**, ugliest) mask of the two.

3. You are (**more creative**, most creative) than I.

R. Adverbs: (6 points)
NOTE: If students circle any words that are not adverbs, deduct a point.

1. My friend talks **too loudly sometimes**.   577

2. They **never** go **anywhere early**.

S. Degrees of Adverbs: (6 points)

1. Paco runs (faster, **fastest**) in his high school.

2. Kit answers the phone (**more politely** , mostly politely) than his brother.

3. When we travel, Aunt Jo stops (**more often**, most often) than Uncle Bo.

T. Pronouns: (14 points)

1. (Me and Lana, **Lana and I**, Lana and me) made a clay pot.

2. Don't hit Jacob and (I, **me**)!

3. The scouts must take (his, **their**) canteens.

4. (**They**, Them) attend a rodeo every year.

5. Our grandparents and (**we**, us) are going to Idaho.

6. The baker fried the doughnuts (hisself, **himself**).

7. Matt left with Sarah and (she, **her**).

U. Nouns Used as Subjects, Direct Objects, and Objects of the Preposition: (6 points)

1. **O.P.**   During the **winter**, Tara skis.

2. **D.O.**   Give the **rattle** to the baby.

3. **S.**   After the parade, our **family** went to a café for lunch.

INDEX

579

CORRELATION of

Easy Grammar Workbook 4 with

Easy Grammar: Grade 4 teacher edition